3-D COMPUTER ANIMATION

3-D COMPUTER ANIMATION

JOHN VINCE
Rediffusion Simulation Ltd

WOKINGHAM, ENGLAND • READING, MASSACHUSETTS • MENLO PARK, CALIFORNIA • NEW YORK
DON MILLS, ONTARIO • AMSTERDAM • BONN • SYDNEY • SINGAPORE
TOKYO • MADRID • SAN JUAN • MILAN • PARIS • MEXICO CITY • SEOUL • TAIPEI

The programs in this book have been included for their instructional value. They have been tested with care but are not guaranteed for any particular purpose. The publisher does not offer any warranties or representations, nor does it accept any liabilities with respect to the programs.

Many of the designations used by manufacturers and sellers to distinguish their products are claimed as trademarks. Addison-Wesley has made every attempt to supply trademark information about manufacturers and their products mentioned in this book. A list of the trademark designations and their owners appears on p. xiv.

Cover designed by Designers & Partners of Oxford and
printed by The Riverside Printing Co. (Reading) Ltd.
The picture on the front cover is taken from the 'Locomotion' sequence and is reproduced courtesy of Pacific Data Images Inc. The back cover sequences showing raindrops hitting a pool of water and CAL's fish logo rising out of a pool of water are based on work by Michael Kass and Gavin Miller.

Typeset by CRB (Drayton) Typesetting Services, Norwich, Norfolk.
Printed in Great Britain by William Clowes, Beccles, Suffolk.

First printed 1992. Reprinted 1993.

ISBN: 0 201 62756 6

British Library Cataloguing in Publication Data
A catalogue record for this book is available from the British Library.

Library of Congress Cataloging in Publication Data
Vince, John
3-D computer animation / John Vince.
p. cm.
Includes bibliographical references and index.
ISBN 0-201-62756-6
1. Computer animation. 2. Computer graphics. I. Title.
TR897.5.V56 1992
006.6--dc20 92-26697
CIP

This book is affectionately dedicated to Annie, Samantha, Anthony and Ben

Preface

When I first put pen to paper (or should I say, put finger to keyboard) to map out this book, I was very clear in my own mind the audience for whom it was written, the scope of the subject area, and the technical level to which each topic would be covered. Having now completed the text it is difficult to say whether these objectives have been met: only you, the reader, can be the judge of this.

The book is intended for anyone who needs to acquire a rapid understanding of how computer graphics is used in creating 3-D animation sequences, but without having to wade through all of the mathematical and algorithmic underpinning that holds the subject together. As I wanted to include subjects such as free-form curves and surfaces and quaternions, I was faced with the dilemma as to whether they should be explained in a matter of a few paragraphs, or whether I should be brave, and attempt to describe them using some elementary mathematics. In the end, I opted for the latter approach, and decided that if the mathematics were kept simple and consistent, by only using basic matrices and parametric expressions, I could maintain the reader's attention and succeed in communicating an idea. However, the book is not dominated by mathematics: it can be ignored if so wished, and the descriptive explanations followed.

For those readers who have never used matrices, or have forgotten their usage, I have deliberately included their explanation at the point in the text where they first appear. In this way, hopefully, it will be seen that they are just a convenient way of organizing numbers, and highly relevant to the subject of computer graphics. The same goes for polynomials – they are introduced quite naturally when interpolation techniques are studied. The only two topics that have been treated as an appendix are trigonometric functions and vectors. The trigonometric function section revises the measurement of angles and the relationship between certain functions, while the section on vectors explains vectors from a geometric standpoint to maintain their relevance to computer graphics.

Another problem I faced while writing the manuscript concerned the prior knowledge of computer graphics a typical reader would possess. This, I assumed, would vary wildly. Some would be total newcomers to pixels and polygons, while others might already be competent programmers, mathematically literate, and wanting a quick insight into the nature of synthetic image generation. To cater for the needs of the newcomer, Chapter 2 reviews the principles of computer graphics and perhaps can be ignored by those readers already familiar with these topics. More experienced readers will have to choose a convenient point at which they should rendezvous with the text.

The chapters appear in what I hope to be a logical fashion: Chapter 1 is a quick introduction to computer animation, followed by a review of computer graphics principles. Chapter 3 introduces the major modelling strategies employed in computer graphics, from polygons to voxel spaces, but I have placed most emphasis upon those techniques that are important to computer animation.

Chapters 5 and 6 examine the subjects of rendering and realism, and introduce topics such as illumination models, reflection models, hidden-surface techniques, anti-aliasing, motion blur and procedural texture. This is a point in the book where some very important topics begin to surface, many of them resulting from papers published in SIGGRAPH proceedings. If the reader wishes to pursue any of these to a greater depth, the reference section includes the relevant sources for acquiring these technical papers and specialist books.

Chapter 6 summarizes the landmarks in cinematography and animation from Plateau inventing the phenakistoscope in 1831, to Ken Knowlton's work at Bell Laboratories in the early 1960s, where computer animation began to blossom.

Chapter 7 investigates some of the useful mathematical techniques that support animation systems and provide the tools by which the 3-D animation environment can be manipulated. This last area is the subject for Chapter 8, where I review the techniques for positioning objects, cameras and lights. I have placed particular emphasis on interpolating methods as this is important in computer animation, and one special subject deserves explaining – that of quaternions. In recent years these have found their way into computer animation, having been neglected, even by mathematicians, for over a century. Do not imagine that they are something mysterious; try following the examples and hopefully their benefits will be appreciated.

Chapter 9 returns to modelling once more, but addresses the conflicts caused by animation requirements influencing model constructing. Some of these issues are carried forward to Chapter 10 which looks at special animation techniques; this is an exciting area as some of the topics could require an entire book to address all of the issues.

In Chapter 11, the origins of computer animation systems are traced from Knowlton's BELFIX system to the very latest commercial products. In fact, I have summarized the major features of five well-known systems used by the computer animation community, not with the intent to identify the 'best' system, but to demonstrate the different approaches taken to provide animators with a user-friendly environment.

Chapters 12 and 13 deal with hardware and applications for computer animation respectively. I have deliberately avoided identifying specific makes and models as the technology is advancing so rapidly, and any advice would become quickly out-of-date. Finally, Chapter 14 looks towards the future, and here I admit that technologists do not possess any special skills in predicting the future. History has shown that our technological society has taken some strange turns recently and confounded the experts.

At the end of each chapter I have included a variety of exercises which the reader may wish to attempt. Many of the problems are of a descriptive nature and will establish whether an idea or concept has been understood or not. Some of them require a program to be written, and those readers who really intend to begin writing computer animation software may find these problems useful in developing their software skills. I have also made suggestions for further reading, consisting of some well-known books, articles and papers.

I have deliberately avoided including too many references in the text to important papers and articles, as I felt that this would have destroyed the continuity I was attempting to achieve. Instead, I have prepared a References Appendix so that the reader can gain immediate access to the relevant references.

Just one last word – remember that computer graphics is still evolving and computer animation software is moving in several directions: some will fall by the wayside and others will have major influences on future research and applications. Hopefully, this book provides a snapshot at where the subject is today.

Acknowledgements

During the final weeks of writing my last book *The Language of Computer Graphics*, I vowed that I would never write another; however, within a few days of it being published, I began mapping out the contents of this book. And as I write this last page I am already beginning to forget the hours spent in front of my Apple computer typing the manuscript and preparing the illustrations. So my first acknowledgement is to Professor Bruce Brown of Brighton Polytechnic for lending me this hardware and making it all possible. I would also like to thank Colin Jackson for the *ad hoc* tutorials he gave me on the use of Microsoft WORD.

Thanks also go to Professor Peter Comninos at the National Centre for Computer Animation at Bournemouth Polytechnic, for reading an early draft of the manuscript and making some very useful suggestions. I must still take full responsibility for any errors, mathematical, or otherwise, as many changes have since been made to the text.

Like many other authors one is always faced with the problem of finding recent and exciting colour illustrations, and therefore I would like to thank the following people for their kind assistance in supplying the illustrations for the book. Thank you: Debbie Gaeta at Pacific Data Images, Dr Keith Waters, Dr Gordon Selley, John Speirs and Chris Fynnes at Infynity Computer Animation, Jeremy Schwartz and Mark Schafer at Symbolics (who also provided the flick images), Stewart McEwan at Electric Image, Maggi Allison at The Moving Picture Company, Geoff and Brian Wyvill, Semania Luk Cheung at Design Vision Inc., Susan Amkraut and Michael Girard.

Finally, a special thank you to the many friends who have helped in various ways from answering technical questions over the telephone, to conversations over dinner clarifying specific concepts of computer animation.

John Vince
June 1992

Contents

1 Introduction

Computer graphics is a fascinating subject as it provides a mechanism to build and view three-dimensional objects without any physical materials. The objects may be teapots, logos, cars, buildings, human bodies, molecules, bridges, clouds, mountains or worms – in fact there are no limits to what can be simulated within a computer's memory. Computer animation introduces the dimension of time into this virtual world and allows us to manipulate these objects and create the illusion of animated movement.

Television programme logos can be made to fly in from nowhere, perform perfect acrobatics and fly off to infinity. Human skeletons can be trained to walk and explode into a myriad of gold balls and reform into equally bizarre objects. Even table lamps can be brought to life with such realism that one is finally tempted to enquire as to how these effects are achieved.

Although computer animation has found an excellent niche in advertising, film special effects and television credits, it is also being used for visualizing a wide variety of 3-D databases and numerical data sets. For instance, computer aided design (CAD) techniques are central to the activities of a modern architectural practice, which employs computer animation to visualize an architectural project. This might be an animated sequence shown as an aerial fly-over, or an interior walk-through. Research systems already exist where virtual reality (VR) techniques enable stereoscopic views of an environment to be displayed in real-time. Similar VR technology is also being used to evaluate the design of lighting fittings for building interiors.

Industrial applications of computer animation include product visualizations of cars, engineering components and construction projects such as bridges, tunnels and hydro-electric schemes. In flight simulators, real-time image generators create sophisticated 3-D coloured scenes of international airports, and within the safety of these virtual environments, pilots can be trained to develop flying skills and practise emergency procedures.

Computer animation is also being used in educational graphics to describe two- and three-dimensional problems in mathematics, physics, astronomy, science, biology and chemistry. And where data is collected from experiments, or from computer simulations, the techniques of scientific visualization become powerful tools for translating multi-dimensional data sets into animated images. Such sequences offer an extraordinary insight into phenomena that might have remained undetected without these visualizing tools.

No two animation projects are the same: but they will all involve modelling, scripting and rendering. In commercial projects it would be unthinkable to proceed with any of these phases before a detailed storyboard had been prepared. This describes the story in the form of a sequence of key images, and acts as a discussion document to clarify issues of timings, mood, backgrounds, colour schemes, lighting, characters, post-production requirements, motion control and costs.

Even though the storyboard only consists of one or two dozen sketches, it does provide the first glimpse of what the final animation will look like. When these static images are unable to convey a designer's ideas of dynamics and pace, an animatic is prepared which shows the storyboard as an animated sequence with the key images located at their correct place in time. The animatic may also introduce a soundtrack.

When the project is started, one of the first activities is to identify any physical objects that might be needed to form the basis of the virtual objects in the animation. These could include household objects such as cutlery, furniture, sinks, milk bottles and teapots; and consumer products such as cars, detergent packets, watches, soft drinks and sweets. The storyboard could also call for planes, bridges, planets, spacecraft, animals and entire cities!

Translating some of these objects into geometric data is relatively straightforward, as it only involves measuring a few vital dimensions. However, it is more than likely that detailed drawings describing their 3-D geometry in the form of elevations will be needed for most of them. Other objects might already be in a digital form, as they were initially designed using a CAD system. But there are many formats for holding such data, and it may be necessary to develop software to translate one format into another. Whatever the source of the data, whether it involves cutting the model into pieces, scanning it with a laser, measuring it with a ruler, reading from drawings, or copying a computer disk, it must be available before the modelling process can begin.

Commercial computer animation systems provide an interactive environment where the user can construct 3-D models using various software tools. A menu-driven interface provides the user with a wealth of features that include: a library of graphic primitives such as boxes, spheres, cylinders, pyramids and cones; facilities for sculpting, bending, twisting, joining, bevelling, extruding and sweeping; and some very powerful tools for forming smooth continuous surfaces. However, a shrewd modeller will always have access to models used on previous projects which, with a little modification, can be used over again.

The next stage depends upon the complexity of the project, which may only call for a logo to rotate, but could, on the other hand, call for a hundred milk bottles to dance behind a milkman as he delivers his milk! Therefore, on the assumption that something out of the ordinary will be required, the animator's next task is to solve these special animation problems. Once more, the animation system will provide a variety of tools for animating objects which may be sufficient to solve the problem, but it is also possible that special software will have to be written.

The animator may possess the programming skills to develop this software; if not, it is given to someone in the team who can write this original code. This can be a critical stage in any animation project: suddenly, some special movement that looked relatively easy on the storyboard, now gives cause for concern. The client's designer, assigned to monitor the progress of the project, may reject the animator's solutions. These situations, which are a daily event in any computer animation company, are eventually resolved either by finding a satisfactory solution or agreeing to some form of compromise.

Traditional animators have direct control over their medium of pencil and paper, and they have developed extraordinary skills in the ease with which they can make a collection of lines appear to possess some internal character. Computer animators share the same objective, but must channel their requirements through an interactive computer interface. This is normally in the form of a script which drives the computer animation system. The scripting language entails the description of an animation sequence in terms of how objects are to behave on a frame-by-frame basis. For example, the key-frame approach enables the positions of objects, light sources and the camera to be specified at particular frame numbers. The computer can then be used to compute the intermediate positions that should hold for all of the in-between frames. But as one can imagine, there must be an infinite range of solutions to this problem.

The motion of a bouncing ball is a familar occurrence in the real world, but in the virtual world of computer graphics such motion must be specified explicitly. This might be in the form of equations where the dynamics of the ball are expressed using our knowledge of ballistics, or perhaps using a graphical technique, where a curve controls the position of the ball at any point in time. With the latter approach, the animator must develop the curve until it creates the desired visual effect.

Animation, however, is not just concerned with the motion of objects; it involves the motion of an imaginary camera, the way lights move, the way colours change, and it must even address the rate at which a smile appears upon someone's face. Controlling such a wide range of attributes has resulted in a plethora of techniques that are examined in some detail in later chapters. Consequently, algorithms for generating curves play an important role in computer animation, and special techniques have been developed where short curve segments can be joined together to form one seamless curve.

At some stage the animator must address the issues of colour and realism, and the computer animation system once more provides the tools for assigning objects with a wide range of physical attributes in the form of colour and texture. The surface of an object can be adjusted to any colour, and made to appear matte, satin, gloss or even covered in chrome. The technique of texture mapping enables any real-world image to be input and mapped onto any arbitrary surface. Similar processes are available to simulate the effects of transparency, bumpiness and mirror reflections.

An animator must be prepared to spend considerable time in illuminating this imaginary world, for decisions must be made on where each light source is to be positioned, its intensity and colour. The background ambient intensity must be fixed, and rendering tests must be made to guarantee that the entire sequence retains an acceptable level of continuity.

The computer animation sequence may even become composited with live action or involve the use of motion control cameras, which is where digital post-production techniques are employed. The rendered images are transferred to a digital edit system where any number of images can be mixed without any degradation in quality. Nowadays, post-production techniques have become so sophisticated that one cannot ignore their potential. Their ability to composite many layers of images in hardware with delicate transparent effects, has educated the modern computer animator not to attempt such operations using software.

Although computer-animated images are magical in their own right, as we have just seen, there is nothing magical behind their creation – they are produced with a variety of techniques that have been developed over a period of years by people who have been captivated by the subject. What could be more exciting than to develop computer programs that describe how a tree grows and actually show it evolving from a sapling to a fully-grown specimen? Imagine the problems of building a synthetic human-like face and animating it to talk with natural human gestures. Some researchers do not think of such tasks as work – it is a creative activity that brings untold satisfaction even though incredible dedication is needed to pursue what appear impossible goals.

The majority of these techniques are based upon some very simple concepts, which to master, requires a knowledge of computers, although not to any real technical level. A logical approach to problem-solving is a distinct advantage and a basic understanding of simple mathematics is useful but, above all, one must be prepared to spend long sessions at workstations designing, testing, debugging and rewriting software.

A knowledge of mathematics is very often useful, and one must be prepared to employ more and more mathematical techniques as one moves towards the advanced topics such as dynamic simulation. Sometimes it is not possible to acquire a level of mathematical understanding demanded by some subjects, and there will be no other alternative but to introduce a mathematician to the project to advise on these matters. However, the majority of the techniques explained in the following chapters only resort to a few mathematical tools which are consistently used to solve different problems.

Computer animation, as you will discover, has not yet developed into a discipline where a universal language is used by animators to communicate with computers. It is a mixture of traditional animation terms such as fairing, inbetweening, walk-cycles, dope sheets and line tests, together with some jargon from computer graphics such as Phong shading, Bézier surface patches, NURBS and fractals, with a scattering of mathematical terms like rotation matrix, vector, quaternion and tensor.

Mastering these terms is incredibly easy, and once you have written a program that actually uses the concepts and get the program to work, you will realize that there is no better way of developing this understanding. Very soon, you will develop the confidence to mix relevant techniques together, and be able to research into other exciting areas of computer animation.

As you read this book remember that computer animation has only just begun: the techniques we are currently using are being used simply because a better or more cost-effective solution is unavailable. Today we use polygons, patches, particles and fractals to model our virtual world. We use Gouraud shading, ray tracing and radiosity to render coloured scenes, and we animate objects and cameras with NURBS, Bézier curves and matrices. Tomorrow, something else will be discovered and we could easily discard a familar technique for this new arrival. So bear in mind the fluidity of the subject. Do not treat computer animation as though the rules have been cast in iron and cannot be changed. The very fact that computer animation involves the use of a computer means that it can be changed, new ideas are waiting to be developed, and they will only be discovered by those people who manage to keep an open mind.

2 Review of Computer Graphics

Many of the algorithms in computer graphics use Cartesian coordinates for describing two-and three-dimensional space, and in this chapter the conventions for this space are covered, as are the operations derived for scaling, translating, rotating and shearing points. As objects are frequently subjected to two or more geometric operations, matrix notation is introduced and examples are used to show how one compound matrix can be concatenated from any sequence of individual matrices.

In computer animation, a virtual camera needs to be placed and oriented anywhere in the world space to obtain a perspective projection of the modelled objects. The technique of roll, pitch and yaw angles is explored using homogeneous coordinates, and matrix operations are derived to create a perspective projection from the camera's frame of reference. As the camera becomes mixed with the objects, the ideas behind clipping the camera's field of view are examined.

Eventually the cameras' viewpoint will be rendered into a frame store, and colour theory is revised to support the idea of creating an image from three primary colour separations. This includes the action of the human eye, RGB and HSV colour spaces.

Finally, the chapter examines some of the hardware used in computer graphics, including digitizers, graph plotters, frame stores, colour monitors, film recorders and workstations.

Introduction

Computer animation concerns the application of computer systems in the production of animated images. Both the technology of computers and the art of animation are well documented as independent topics and are relatively easy to comprehend, but a totally new world is created when the sensitive world of animation is transposed to the calculating silicon domain of computers.

To understand this strange marriage of techniques one must first appreciate how the numerical world of computers is used to process images – this subject area is known as 'computer graphics', which is also well documented. Readers who are not yet familiar with the principles of computer graphics should, perhaps, be prepared to read an introductory text on the subject and discover some of the concepts that transform a computer into a graphic design tool. However, for the sake of completeness, this chapter may be a sufficient introduction for the beginner and also serve as a useful reminder for those already familiar with the subject.

2.1 Principles of computer graphics

Computer graphics is not a totally original subject, for to define and resolve its problems it draws upon some well-established techniques from geometry, algebra, optics and human physiology. Geometry is exploited to provide a framework for describing two- and three-dimensional space, while algebraic techniques are used to define and evaluate equations associated with this space. The science of optics provides models for describing the behaviour of light, and human physiology offers models for human vision and colour perception.

Although this range of topics suggests an air of complexity, computer graphics is, in fact, relatively easy to understand – for the individual topics used to simulate a virtual world of shape, scale, colour and movement call only upon some very basic technical principles. As one might expect, when computer graphics is used to explore specialist subjects such as molecular modelling or medical diagnosis, these basic principles must be enhanced by extra techniques. There are even aspects of computer animation that require some unusual mathematical and scientific knowledge but, even then, this should not prevent the inquisitive person from using or experimenting with such systems, for the interface between the human operator and the computer is also developing, which helps isolate the user from any irrelevant internal complexity.

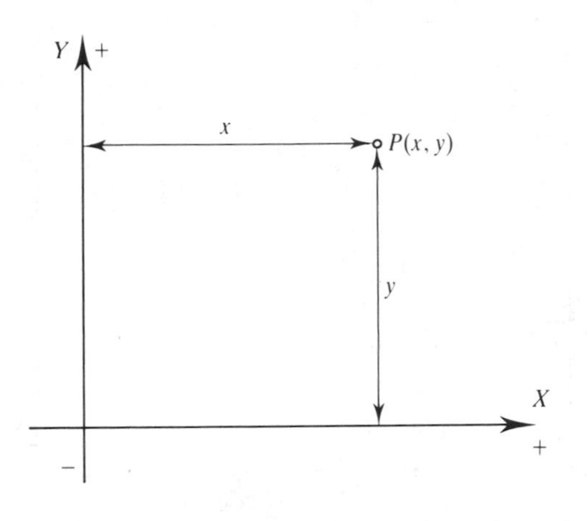

Figure 2.1
The *x*- and *y*-coordinates of point *P* are specified by the horizontal and vertical distances of *P* from the origin. Note the sign conventions for the coordinates.

2.1.1 2-D computer graphics

Central to all computer graphics is the concept of Cartesian coordinates. In the 2-D case, this enables a point on a flat surface to be addressed with the aid of a pair of horizontal and vertical axes. A point is located by measuring two distances parallel with the axes from their intersection point called the origin. The horizontal and vertical measurements for any point are unique and are called its *x*- and *y*-coordinates respectively. Figure 2.1 illustrates this scheme and also shows the convention for positive and negative directions.

Any 2-D shape can be represented by a sequence of points or vertices as shown in Figure 2.2 and, as each vertex consists of an ordered pair of numbers (i.e. the *x*-coordinate followed by a *y*-coordinate), they can easily be stored within a computer. However, our personal knowledge

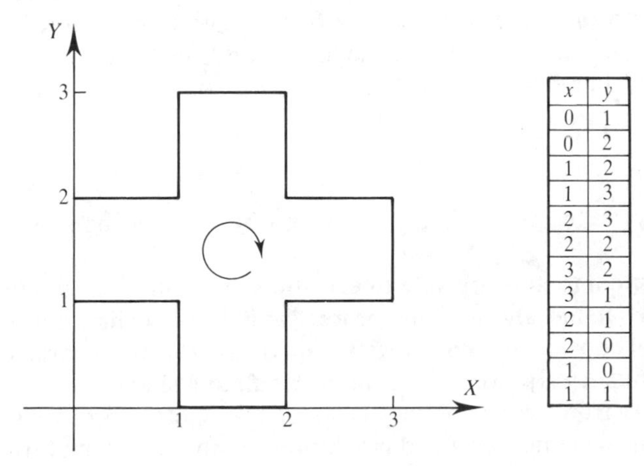

x	y
0	1
0	2
1	2
1	3
2	3
2	2
3	2
3	1
2	1
2	0
1	0
1	1

Figure 2.2
The illustrated shape consists of 12 vertices; their coordinates are listed in the table. Note that the vertices have been traversed in a clockwise sequence.

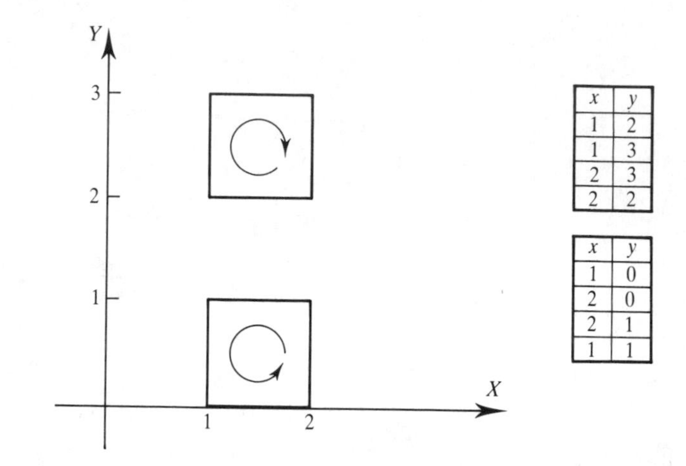

Figure 2.3
These two squares have been digitized in a clockwise and counter-clockwise sequence. Although both techniques are valid, some software may be sensitive to vertex direction.

of this boundary shape is visual and is established by traversing its border in a clockwise or anti-clockwise direction. This boundary direction must also be preserved in the computer by ordering the vertex coordinates in one of two sequences as shown in Figure 2.3.

Two-dimensional coordinates are grouped together in brackets as follows (2.5, 1.5), where 2.5 and 1.5 refer to the x- and y-coordinates respectively. There are several useful consequences of this coordinate notation: first, if the coordinate values are doubled in value they are equivalent to a shape twice the original size, therefore scaling can be performed as follows:

$$x' = rx$$
$$y' = ry$$

where (x, y) is the vertex being scaled by r to create (x', y'). Secondly, if the x-coordinates are increased by one unit, the new coordinates are equivalent to the same shape shifted or translated one unit to the right of the original shape. However, a shape can be translated in the x- and the y-direction, therefore the translation operation is summarized as:

$$x' = x + u$$
$$y' = y + v$$

where (x, y) is the vertex being translated by (u, v) to its new position of (x', y').

Most computers are able to execute several million arithmetic operations in a second and are, therefore, capable of scaling and translating large sets of coordinates almost instantaneously. It is this characteristic that makes them such a powerful tool in manipulating shapes.

Apart from scaling and translation, the operation of rotation about the origin is also important and is achieved by the following formulae:

$$x' = x\cos(\theta) - y\sin(\theta)$$
$$y' = x\sin(\theta) + y\cos(\theta)$$

where (x, y) is the point being rotated by the angle θ to its new position (x', y'). The rotation is anti-clockwise when θ is positive, and vice versa. To rotate a complete shape by θ, the cosine and sine functions are evaluated first to reduce the process to four multiplications, one addition and one subtraction for each vertex. For those readers not familiar with scientific programming techniques, the sine and cosine functions do take some time to evaluate, and one would waste unnecessary time if they were evaluated for each vertex in the shape. Therefore they are evaluated once before the entire shape's coordinates are processed.

Shearing is also a useful transformation and is computed as follows:

$$x' = x + y\tan(\theta)$$
$$y' = y$$

where (x, y) is the point being sheared by the angle θ to its new position (x', y').

These four operations – scale, translate, rotate and shear – form the fundamental shape manipulation operations in 2-D graphics and have a compact description using matrix notation. To understand this notation, consider the relationship:

$$x' = 3x + 5y$$

this can be rewritten using matrix notation as:

$$x' = [3 \ \ 5]\begin{bmatrix} x \\ y \end{bmatrix}$$

All that we have done is to isolate the constants from the variables. The constants 3 and 5 form a row vector while the variables x and y are called a column vector, as they are arranged in a column. To evaluate x' we must multiply the row vector by the column vector, which is achieved by multiplying corresponding terms together and summing them. In this case we multiply 3 by x and 5 by y, and add the results together.

In general, the relationship:

$$x' = ax + by$$

is written as:

$$x' = [a \ \ b]\begin{bmatrix} x \\ y \end{bmatrix}$$

However, the coordinate notation employed in computer graphics involves expressions for x- and y-coordinates, and eventually a z-coordinate is needed for three-dimensional work. This is when matrix notation starts to be useful; for example, consider these relationships:

$$x' = 3x + 2y$$
$$y' = 8x + 4y$$

they can be rewritten in matrix form as:

$$\begin{bmatrix} x' \\ y' \end{bmatrix} = \begin{bmatrix} 3 & 2 \\ 8 & 4 \end{bmatrix} \begin{bmatrix} x \\ y \end{bmatrix}$$

Thus to evaluate the value for x' we multiply the first row of the matrix by the column vector, and for y' we multiply the second row of the matrix by the column vector. Readers are warned that there are two ways of creating matrix operations: the above method is called postmultiplying by column vectors, which is a modern convention. However, there are still some books that reverse the operation by premultiplying matrices by row vectors. The above operation can be transposed into the alternative convention as follows:

$$[x' \ y'] = [x \ y] \begin{bmatrix} 3 & 8 \\ 2 & 4 \end{bmatrix}$$

Let us now consider an extension to this notation and see how the following relationships can be expressed using matrices:

$$x' = 2x + 3y + 8$$
$$y' = 4x + 2y + 6$$

Somehow we must find a mechanism to include the extra constants 8 and 6. These extra terms can be accommodated as follows:

$$\begin{bmatrix} x' \\ y' \\ 1 \end{bmatrix} = \begin{bmatrix} 2 & 3 & 8 \\ 4 & 2 & 6 \\ 0 & 0 & 1 \end{bmatrix} \begin{bmatrix} x \\ y \\ 1 \end{bmatrix}$$

This notation employs homogeneous coordinates which are used in projective geometry – and the extra term is treated as a scaling term. For example, the following homogeneous coordinates $(1, 2, 1)$, $(2, 4, 2)$, $(3, 6, 3)$, and $(5, 10, 5)$ represent the same point $(1, 2)$ if the third term in each vertex is divided into the first two terms. In general, a point (X, Y) is represented in its homogeneous form as (HX, HY, H), thus when $H = 1$ its action can be ignored.

One can easily visualize this process if the homogeneous space is treated as a 3-D space with X, Y, and H axes. For instance, one can draw a

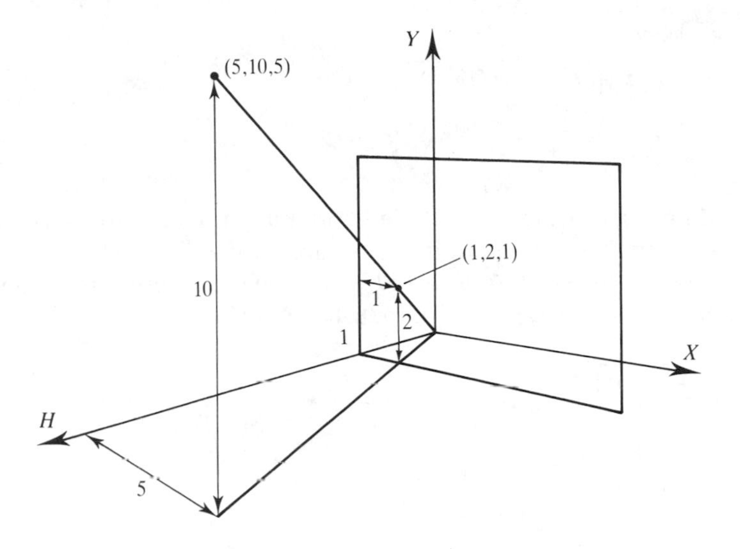

Figure 2.4
This 3-D set of axes shows how a point (5, 10, 5) can be projected back onto a plane where $H = 1$. This point has coordinates (1, 2, 1) and is a scaled version of the original. It forms the basis of homogeneous coordinates.

straight line through the points $(0,0,0)$, $(1,2,1)$, $(2,4,2)$, $(3,6,3)$, and $(4,8,4)$, as shown in Figure 2.4. Thus any collection of points having a homogeneous coordinate of 1 can be projected onto an x-y plane having a homogeneous value of 5, by scaling the x- and y-coordinates by 5. This suggests that we can imagine that the 2-D plane, where scaling, translation, rotation, and shearing operations are performed, can be anywhere along the H-axis (apart from $H = 0$). We must remember to divide the coordinates by H at the end of the operation. For convenience, H is set to 1.

Returning to the scaling, translation, rotation operations described above, these can now be rewritten as:

Scaling:

$$\begin{bmatrix} x' \\ y' \\ 1 \end{bmatrix} = \begin{bmatrix} r & 0 & 0 \\ 0 & r & 0 \\ 0 & 0 & 1 \end{bmatrix} \begin{bmatrix} x \\ y \\ 1 \end{bmatrix}$$

Translation:

$$\begin{bmatrix} x' \\ y' \\ 1 \end{bmatrix} = \begin{bmatrix} 1 & 0 & u \\ 0 & 1 & v \\ 0 & 0 & 1 \end{bmatrix} \begin{bmatrix} x \\ y \\ 1 \end{bmatrix}$$

Rotation:

$$\begin{bmatrix} x' \\ y' \\ 1 \end{bmatrix} = \begin{bmatrix} \cos(\theta) & -\sin(\theta) & 0 \\ \sin(\theta) & \cos(\theta) & 0 \\ 0 & 0 & 1 \end{bmatrix} \begin{bmatrix} x \\ y \\ 1 \end{bmatrix}$$

Shearing:

$$\begin{bmatrix} x' \\ y' \\ 1 \end{bmatrix} = \begin{bmatrix} 1 & \tan(\theta) & 0 \\ 0 & 1 & 0 \\ 0 & 0 & 1 \end{bmatrix} \begin{bmatrix} x \\ y \\ 1 \end{bmatrix}$$

Matrices provide a convenient notation for describing geometric operations, and they also permit two or more operations to be represented by a single matrix which is derived by multiplying together the individual matrices. For example, given two matrices A and B:

$$A = \begin{bmatrix} a & b \\ c & d \end{bmatrix} \qquad B = \begin{bmatrix} r & s \\ t & u \end{bmatrix}$$

then AB is defined as:

$$AB = \begin{bmatrix} ar + bt & as + bu \\ cr + dt & cs + du \end{bmatrix}$$

This multiplication process is called 'concatenating', and although it may not be immediately obvious, AB is not equivalent to BA. For the reverse matrix operation is:

$$BA = \begin{bmatrix} ra + sc & rb + sd \\ ta + uc & tb + ud \end{bmatrix}$$

which clearly shows that the matrix elements are not equivalent.

Let us illustrate this with an example. Consider the following operations where the first rotates a point anti-clockwise 90° and is represented by matrix A, while the second translates the point +1 unit in the x-direction and is represented by matrix B.

$$A = \begin{bmatrix} 0 & -1 & 0 \\ 1 & 0 & 0 \\ 0 & 0 & 1 \end{bmatrix} \qquad B = \begin{bmatrix} 1 & 0 & 1 \\ 0 & 1 & 0 \\ 0 & 0 & 1 \end{bmatrix}$$

When concatenating the two matrices we must remember to keep the first matrix operation on the right-hand side of the operation, which means that they must be evaluated as BA, which produces:

$$\begin{bmatrix} x' \\ y' \\ 1 \end{bmatrix} = \begin{bmatrix} 1 & 0 & 1 \\ 0 & 1 & 0 \\ 0 & 0 & 1 \end{bmatrix} \begin{bmatrix} 0 & -1 & 0 \\ 1 & 0 & 0 \\ 0 & 0 & 1 \end{bmatrix} \begin{bmatrix} x \\ y \\ 1 \end{bmatrix}$$

Therefore the combined rotation and translation can be represented as:

$$\begin{bmatrix} x' \\ y' \\ 1 \end{bmatrix} = \begin{bmatrix} 0 & -1 & 1 \\ 1 & 0 & 0 \\ 0 & 0 & 1 \end{bmatrix} \begin{bmatrix} x \\ y \\ 1 \end{bmatrix}$$

This can be tested by substituting an arbitrary point such as $(2, 0)$. A rotation of 90° moves it to $(0, 2)$, and the translation moves it to $(1, 2)$. Confirming this using the above matrix we have:

$$\begin{bmatrix} x' \\ y' \\ 1 \end{bmatrix} = \begin{bmatrix} 0 & -1 & 1 \\ 1 & 0 & 0 \\ 0 & 0 & 1 \end{bmatrix} \begin{bmatrix} 2 \\ 0 \\ 1 \end{bmatrix}$$

which produces the point $(1, 2)$ as predicted.

If the matrices are evaluated in reverse order we have:

$$\begin{bmatrix} x' \\ y' \\ 1 \end{bmatrix} = \begin{bmatrix} 0 & -1 & 0 \\ 1 & 0 & 0 \\ 0 & 0 & 1 \end{bmatrix} \begin{bmatrix} 1 & 0 & 1 \\ 0 & 1 & 0 \\ 0 & 0 & 1 \end{bmatrix} \begin{bmatrix} x \\ y \\ 1 \end{bmatrix}$$

which concatenates to:

$$\begin{bmatrix} x' \\ y' \\ 1 \end{bmatrix} = \begin{bmatrix} 0 & -1 & 0 \\ 1 & 0 & 1 \\ 0 & 0 & 1 \end{bmatrix} \begin{bmatrix} x \\ y \\ 1 \end{bmatrix}$$

thus the point $(2, 0)$ would first be translated by $(1, 0)$ and then rotated by 90° to produce the point $(0, 3)$:

$$\begin{bmatrix} x' \\ y' \\ 1 \end{bmatrix} = \begin{bmatrix} 0 & -1 & 0 \\ 1 & 0 & 1 \\ 0 & 0 & 1 \end{bmatrix} \begin{bmatrix} 2 \\ 0 \\ 1 \end{bmatrix}$$

which is not equivalent to the original operation.

2.1.2 3-D computer graphics

Extending Cartesian coordinates into three dimensions requires that every point in 3-D space is located using three coordinates. However, illustrating such a scheme with diagrams introduces a slight drawback in that it is convenient to employ a perspective image to convey a sense of spatial depth where, in reality, there is no perspective information stored within the coordinates. In fact, a geometric technique will be used to convert the 3-D coordinates into a 2-D perspective projection.

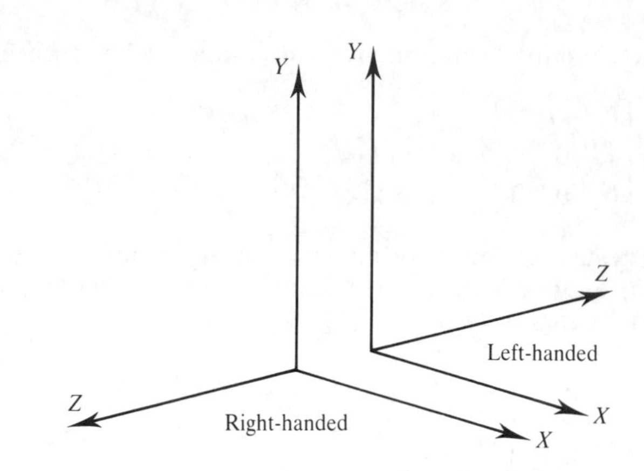

Figure 2.5

A set of 3-D axes can be described as 'left-handed' or 'right-handed'. Depending upon the hand, it is possible to align the thumb with the x-axis, the first finger with the y-axis and the middle finger with the z-axis. Although the systems are equally valid, a consistent convention must be used within a computer graphics system.

If a 3-D set of mutually orthogonal axes is defined, the point where they intersect at a common point is again called the origin. Figure 2.5 illustrates a set of right-handed 3-D axes, where one's right hand thumb aligns with the x-axis, the first finger aligns with the y-axis and the middle finger aligns with the z-axis. This configuration is a popular convention within computer graphics and is employed throughout this text. A left-handed system is created by reversing one of the axes. When it comes to choosing the vertical axis, there does not seem to be any universal convention. Some authors choose the y-axis and others the z-axis: in this text a vertical y-axis is used as this is the same convention for 2-D graphics.

Throughout this text a right-handed 3-D system of axes is used for describing the positions of objects, cameras and lights and is called the world coordinate system (WCS). Any point in 3-D space is located by three coordinates (x, y, z) representing the parallel distances along the three axes (Figure 2.6), and objects can be constructed from a collection of polygons

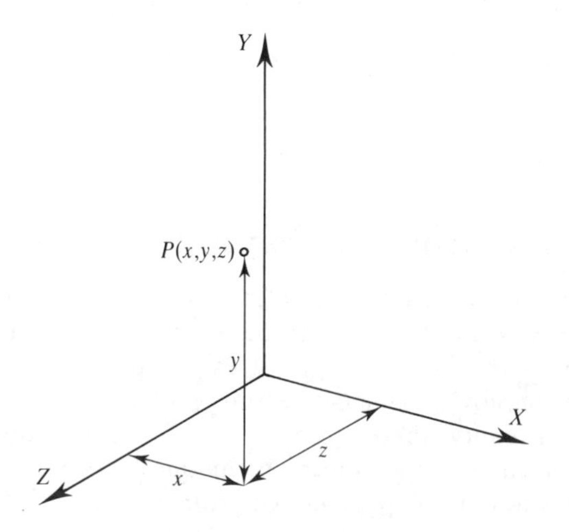

Figure 2.6

In 3-D the point P is located by the three Cartesian coordinates (x, y, z) representing the distances measured parallel with the three orthogonal axes.

whose vertices are defined using this coordinate notation. If a planar polygon is created from an arbitrary chain of straight edges, the directional sense of the boundary depends upon the side of the polygon from which one views the boundary. Therefore a convention is normally adopted so that the concept of sense can be applied, but this topic will be covered in detail in Chapter 3, which addresses modelling schemes. For the moment, let us assume that, using the basic building element of the 3-D vertex, it is possible to construct 3-D descriptions of familiar everyday artefacts and proceed with how these models can be manipulated.

Once again, the operations of scaling, translation, rotation and shearing can be defined using homogeneous coordinates. The scaling operation is:

$$\begin{bmatrix} x' \\ y' \\ z' \\ 1 \end{bmatrix} = \begin{bmatrix} r & 0 & 0 & 0 \\ 0 & r & 0 & 0 \\ 0 & 0 & r & 0 \\ 0 & 0 & 0 & 1 \end{bmatrix} \begin{bmatrix} x \\ y \\ z \\ 1 \end{bmatrix}$$

where (x, y, z) is scaled by r to (x', y', z').

The translation operation is:

$$\begin{bmatrix} x' \\ y' \\ z' \\ 1 \end{bmatrix} = \begin{bmatrix} 1 & 0 & 0 & u \\ 0 & 1 & 0 & v \\ 0 & 0 & 1 & w \\ 0 & 0 & 0 & 1 \end{bmatrix} \begin{bmatrix} x \\ y \\ z \\ 1 \end{bmatrix}$$

where (x, y, z) is translated by (u, v, w) to (x', y', z').

As a point can be rotated about any axis, three matrices are needed to describe the rotations. For the x- y- and z-axes respectively, they are:

$$\begin{bmatrix} x' \\ y' \\ z' \\ 1 \end{bmatrix} = \begin{bmatrix} 1 & 0 & 0 & 0 \\ 0 & \cos(pitch) & -\sin(pitch) & 0 \\ 0 & \sin(pitch) & \cos(pitch) & 0 \\ 0 & 0 & 0 & 1 \end{bmatrix} \begin{bmatrix} x \\ y \\ z \\ 1 \end{bmatrix}$$

$$\begin{bmatrix} x' \\ y' \\ z' \\ 1 \end{bmatrix} = \begin{bmatrix} \cos(yaw) & 0 & \sin(yaw) & 0 \\ 0 & 1 & 0 & 0 \\ -\sin(yaw) & 0 & \cos(yaw) & 0 \\ 0 & 0 & 0 & 1 \end{bmatrix} \begin{bmatrix} x \\ y \\ z \\ 1 \end{bmatrix}$$

$$\begin{bmatrix} x' \\ y' \\ z' \\ 1 \end{bmatrix} = \begin{bmatrix} \cos(roll) & -\sin(roll) & 0 & 0 \\ \sin(roll) & \cos(roll) & 0 & 0 \\ 0 & 0 & 1 & 0 \\ 0 & 0 & 0 & 1 \end{bmatrix} \begin{bmatrix} x \\ y \\ z \\ 1 \end{bmatrix}$$

where *pitch*, *yaw* and *roll* are the angles of rotation. Euler's theorem states that any (x, y, z)-coordinate system can be brought into coincidence with a second (x', y', z')-coordinate system with the same origin by rotation through three angles: pitch, yaw and roll.

The shearing operation, like rotation, is associated with an axis, and for the x-, y-, and z-axes respectively, they are:

$$\begin{bmatrix} x' \\ y' \\ z' \\ 1 \end{bmatrix} = \begin{bmatrix} 1 & \tan(\theta) & 0 & 0 \\ 0 & 1 & 0 & 0 \\ 0 & 0 & 1 & 0 \\ 0 & 0 & 0 & 1 \end{bmatrix} \begin{bmatrix} x \\ y \\ z \\ 1 \end{bmatrix}$$

$$\begin{bmatrix} x' \\ y' \\ z' \\ 1 \end{bmatrix} = \begin{bmatrix} 1 & 0 & 0 & 0 \\ \tan(\theta) & 1 & 0 & 0 \\ 0 & 0 & 1 & 0 \\ 0 & 0 & 0 & 1 \end{bmatrix} \begin{bmatrix} x \\ y \\ z \\ 1 \end{bmatrix}$$

$$\begin{bmatrix} x' \\ y' \\ z' \\ 1 \end{bmatrix} = \begin{bmatrix} 1 & 0 & 0 & 0 \\ 0 & 1 & 0 & 0 \\ 0 & \tan(\theta) & 1 & 0 \\ 0 & 0 & 0 & 1 \end{bmatrix} \begin{bmatrix} x \\ y \\ z \\ 1 \end{bmatrix}$$

where θ is the angle of shear.

The rotation matrices can be applied individually to sets of vertices to perform a rotation about an axis, but there is nothing to prevent one from rotating the vertices about the x-axis followed by another rotation about the y-axis, and even a third rotation about the z-axis. This would create some compound 3-D rotation which works perfectly well, but is difficult to imagine and control, especially when the angular rotations are different for each axis. This compound rotation can be represented by a single matrix by multiplying together (concatenating) the individual matrices.

Already the reader can begin to see some of the problems facing the 3-D animator when describing complex three-dimensional movements. Another consequence of creating a compound rotation from two or three axial rotations is that the rotations are not commutative – that is to say that a set of vertices rotated in turn about the x-, y- and z-axis, will not, in general, be equivalent to rotating them about the x-, z- and then the y-axis. The two sequences will generally give rise to two different final positions for the vertices, and the animator must be consistent in specifying the sequence of axes for such rotations.

Objects defined as a collection of vertices frequently need to be rotated about an arbitrary axis, and as one might expect there is a matrix describing this operation. However, it would serve no purpose to describe it as it is complex and is well documented elsewhere (Rogers, 1990). Furthermore, a good animation system will provide this facility without involving the animator with the background mathematics.

So far, we have discovered the mechanism for describing vertex positions in 3-D space: this will be employed for constructing a wealth of objects including tables, wine glasses, human faces, water, clouds and fireworks. This wide range of objects requires an equally wide range of software tools to build them and is a major feature of any animation system. Such techniques are examined in detail in later sections. We have also discovered that when an object has a coordinate definition, these coordinates can be processed by matrices, which effectively alters their position in space. Such techniques will be enhanced by other manipulative procedures which will bend, distort and transform objects to mimic the skills of the traditional animator.

The only remaining aspect of 3-D computer graphics relevant to this review concerns how a virtual camera can be positioned in front of our 3-D objects to capture a perspective view. The dynamics of this virtual camera also play a vital part in computer animation, and we will discover that whatever manipulative operations are used for objects can, in general, be applied to cameras.

2.2 The camera's coordinate system

The visual output from an animation system is what is effectively 'seen' by the camera, therefore one important task of the animator is to find creative methods for controlling its position and orientation. As the camera has no physical existence (it will be defined by a few numbers), it can be positioned anywhere in the 3-D space describing our virtual computer world, even inside objects! For the moment it will be convenient to position the camera at the origin of the world coordinate system (WCS) and directed along the positive z-axis as shown in Figure 2.7.

If one assumes that a collection of vertices are located in the WCS and are visible to the camera, a perspective projection of these vertices can be computed by assuming that the camera has a pinhole construction with its aperture located at the origin. An imaginary ground glass viewing screen is positioned a distance d behind this pinhole to capture an inverted perspective scene. This optical phenomenon of reversing the image will not cause us any problems, for within this imaginary world the reversal can be corrected by rotating the viewing screen axes as shown in Figure 2.8.

Using the geometry of similar triangles, Figure 2.9 shows a side and plan elevation of the WCS axial system and the camera's axial system. The

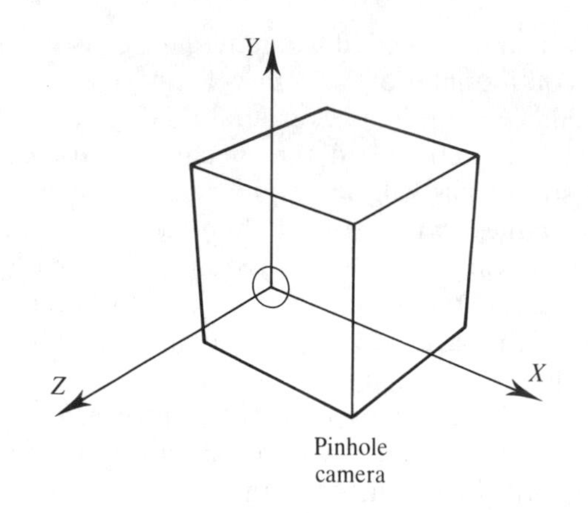

Figure 2.7

In computer graphics it is convenient to use a pinhole camera to explain the action of capturing a perspective image. Here the camera is oriented such that its hole is at the origin of the axes and directed along the positive z-axis.

position of a point (x, y, z) is located at (x_i, y_i) on the viewing screen using the following relationships:

$$\frac{y}{z} = \frac{y_i}{d}$$

and

$$\frac{x}{z} = \frac{-x_i}{d}$$

therefore:

$$x_i = \frac{-dx}{z} \qquad y_i = \frac{dy}{z}$$

these two calculations are all that is necessary for the perspective projection.

There are three observations worth making about these calculations: the first concerns the negative sign appearing in the calculation of x_i; this is due to the left-handed system of axes used for the camera's image space (IS). If this sign change was not included, the image would appear horizontally transposed. Secondly, the distance d is a multiplying term which we already know performs a scaling action. Therefore if d is varied, the final size of the image alters, acting like a zoom control for the camera. Thirdly, the x- and y-coordinates of the point in the WCS are both divided by their z-coordinate; this means that distant points will have a large z-value and a corresponding small x_i and y_i on the viewing screen. Thus, as an object recedes from the camera, its image becomes increasingly smaller, which is what happens when we see things in the real world.

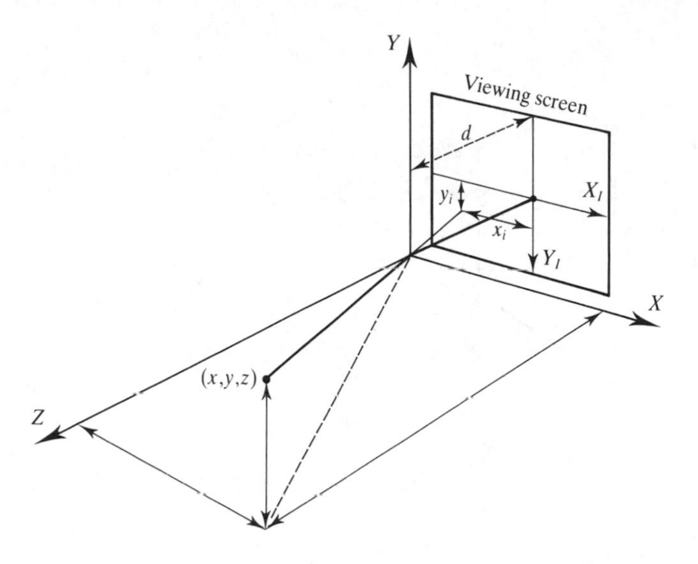

Figure 2.8
With the viewing screen positioned distance *d* behind the origin, the pinhole camera model inverts the image both horizontally and vertically. Assuming that the virtual camera is positioned upside-down, the image has to be corrected for a horizontal flip. This horizontal inversion occurs because the world coordinate space is right-handed while the image space is left-handed.

The above perspective calculations also have a matrix form which is derived as follows:

$$\begin{bmatrix} x_i \\ y_i \\ z_i \\ 1 \end{bmatrix} = \begin{bmatrix} \frac{-d}{z} & 0 & 0 & 0 \\ 0 & \frac{d}{z} & 0 & 0 \\ 0 & 0 & \frac{d}{z} & 0 \\ 0 & 0 & 0 & 1 \end{bmatrix} \begin{bmatrix} x \\ y \\ z \\ 1 \end{bmatrix}$$

where we observe that points in the camera's coordinate system (CCS) become transformed into the IS as:

$$x_i = \frac{-dx}{z}$$

$$y_i = \frac{dy}{z}$$

$$z_i = d$$

Note that the value of z_i equals the distance of the viewing plane.

Unfortunately, this matrix contains references to the z-coordinate of the vertex being projected, and this must be removed if the matrix is to have any independent value. In fact, if we multiply throughout by z/d, the entire relationship can be simplified. And as we are working in homogeneous coordinates, the left-hand side of the operation can be scaled by

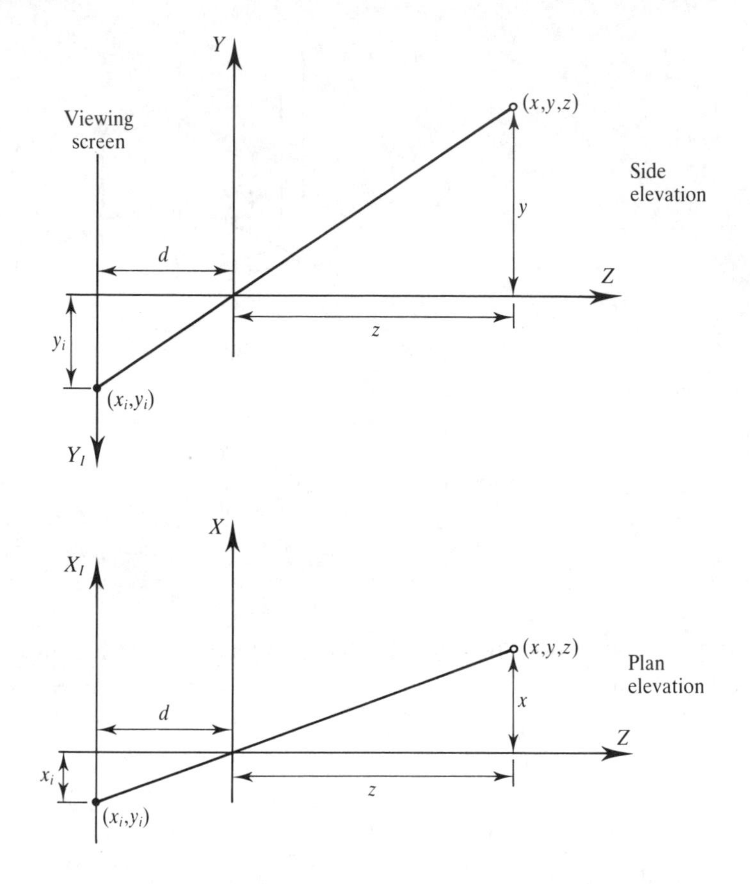

Figure 2.9
The side elevation of the viewing screen reveals the geometry of similar triangles relating y_i to d, and y to z. The plan elevation reveals similar geometry for relating x_i to d, and x to z.

modifying the homogeneous scaling term. The matrix is scaled by multiplying every term as follows:

$$\begin{bmatrix} x_i \\ y_i \\ z_i \\ \frac{z}{d} \end{bmatrix} = \begin{bmatrix} -1 & 0 & 0 & 0 \\ 0 & 1 & 0 & 0 \\ 0 & 0 & 1 & 0 \\ 0 & 0 & 0 & \frac{z}{d} \end{bmatrix} \begin{bmatrix} x \\ y \\ z \\ 1 \end{bmatrix}$$

But even this matrix still contains a reference to the z-coordinate; however, it can be removed completely by this subterfuge:

$$\begin{bmatrix} x_i \\ y_i \\ z_i \\ \frac{z}{d} \end{bmatrix} = \begin{bmatrix} -1 & 0 & 0 & 0 \\ 0 & 1 & 0 & 0 \\ 0 & 0 & 1 & 0 \\ 0 & 0 & \frac{1}{d} & 0 \end{bmatrix} \begin{bmatrix} x \\ y \\ z \\ 1 \end{bmatrix}$$

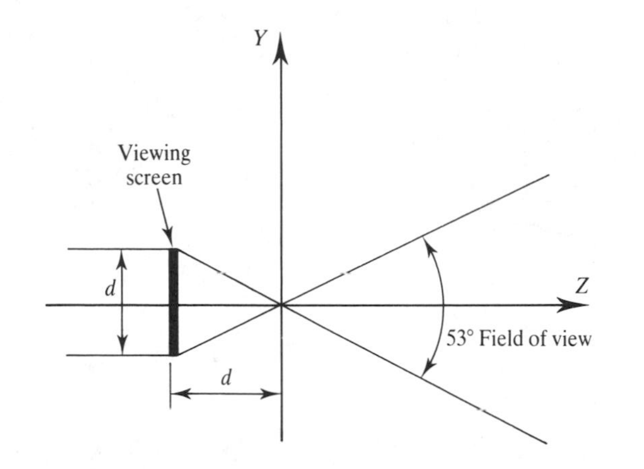

Figure 2.10

If the viewing screen is positioned d units from the origin and its image size is also d, then the effective field of view is approximately 53°. As the screen distance and image size can be changed independently, the camera's field of view can be changed dynamically during an animation sequence.

Now we have a simple matrix for producing a perspective projection that is only dependent upon the viewing plane distance.

Anyone familiar with cameras will know that the focal length of the lens controls its field of view, and consequently the degree of perspective captured in the final image. This too can be simulated within the computer. To understand this effect, consider the geometry of the camera's viewing screen with its image size, as shown in Figure 2.10. If the maximum image height is d (which is also the distance of the viewing screen from the pinhole) the viewing angle is approximately 53°. Now if the image size is preserved, but the screen distance is halved to $d/2$, the viewing angle increases to 90°, creating a wide-angle effect. A narrow field of view can be created by holding the image size constant and increasing the screen distance.

This adjustment, which is easily implemented within an animation system, means that the animator can dynamically adjust the focal length of the camera during an animation sequence. There is no need to change lenses, as it can be adjusted on the fly as if the camera were equipped with an infinitely adjustable lens.

The above description assumes that the camera is situated at the origin of the WCS, and directed along the z-axis. This is convenient for computing the perspective image, but is rather restrictive for achieving any animation! We must now extend this model so that the camera can be positioned anywhere in space and focused on any arbitrary point. However, the method one uses to achieve this influences the future animation of the camera, and such problems are examined in Section 8.2.2. Therefore, the following description employs a simple method of positioning the camera using roll, pitch and yaw angles, but it should be remembered that many other methods exist.

To begin with, imagine that the camera's axial system is aligned with that of the WCS (Figure 2.11a). The camera can be moved to another point

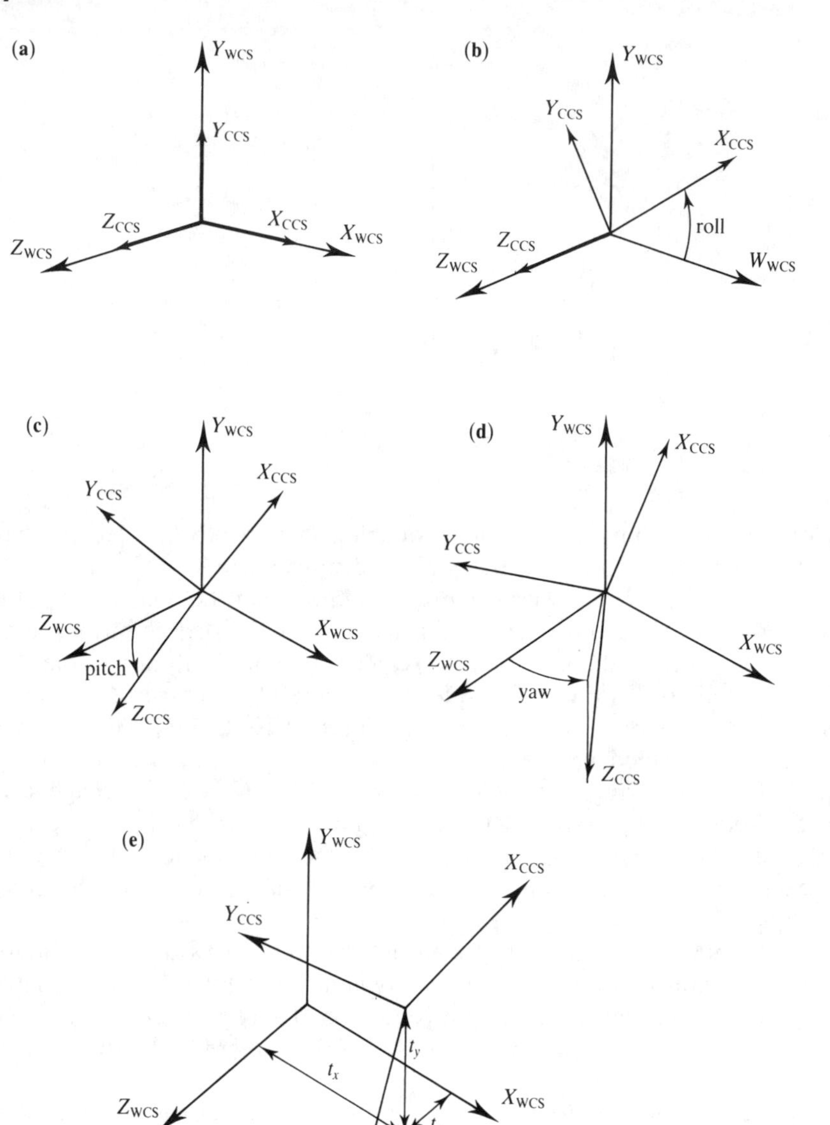

Figure 2.11

These five diagrams illustrate how the camera can be located in space with an arbitrary orientation: (a) shows the CCS aligned with the WCS; (b) shows the CCS after a roll rotation; (c) shows the position of the CCS after a further pitch rotation; (d) shows the CCS after a further roll rotation; (e) shows the CCS after a translation of (t_x, t_y, t_z).

in space with an arbitrary orientation by applying a roll rotation about the z-axis (Figure 2.11b), followed by a pitch rotation about the x-axis (Figure 2.11c), and a yaw rotation about the y-axis (Figure 2.11d). Finally, the camera is translated by (t_x, t_y, t_z) (Figure 2.11e). The camera's position is thus determined by the four operations: roll, pitch, yaw and translate.

Consider, then, a camera orientated somewhere in space using this method, and directed at some group of objects. If we reverse the sequence of roll, pitch, yaw and translate, the camera will move back to its original alignment with the WCS. Moreover, if the objects are moved in the same way, the relationship between the camera and objects will not change. But the important thing about moving the objects back to the CCS aligned with the WCS is that it is easy to perform the perspective projection. Therefore, as the camera is not really a physical entity, all that needs to be performed is to subject the coordinates of the objects to a reverse set of the operations that were initially applied to the camera. This entails a translate operation followed by a yaw, pitch, and roll rotation.

Given that the three angles and position of the camera are roll, pitch, yaw and (t_x, t_y, t_z), the following four matrices will perform the desired movements and return it to the origin:

Translate $(-t_x, -t_y, -t_z)$:

$$\begin{bmatrix} 1 & 0 & 0 & -t_x \\ 0 & 1 & 0 & -t_y \\ 0 & 0 & 1 & -t_z \\ 0 & 0 & 0 & 1 \end{bmatrix}$$

Rotate $-yaw$ about y-axis:

$$\begin{bmatrix} \cos(-yaw) & 0 & \sin(-yaw) & 0 \\ 0 & 1 & 0 & 0 \\ -\sin(-yaw) & 0 & \cos(-yaw) & 0 \\ 0 & 0 & 0 & 1 \end{bmatrix}$$

Rotate $-pitch$ about x-axis:

$$\begin{bmatrix} 1 & 0 & 0 & 0 \\ 0 & \cos(-pitch) & -\sin(-pitch) & 0 \\ 0 & \sin(-pitch) & \cos(-pitch) & 0 \\ 0 & 0 & 0 & 1 \end{bmatrix}$$

Rotate $-roll$ about z-axis:

$$\begin{bmatrix} \cos(-roll) & -\sin(-roll) & 0 & 0 \\ \sin(-roll) & \cos(-roll) & 0 & 0 \\ 0 & 0 & 1 & 0 \\ 0 & 0 & 0 & 1 \end{bmatrix}$$

These matrices can be simplified using the following trigonometric identities:

$$-\sin(\theta) = \sin(-\theta)$$
$$\cos(\theta) = \cos(-\theta)$$

Rotate $-yaw$ about y-axis:

$$\begin{bmatrix} \cos(yaw) & 0 & -\sin(yaw) & 0 \\ 0 & 1 & 0 & 0 \\ \sin(yaw) & 0 & \cos(yaw) & 0 \\ 0 & 0 & 0 & 1 \end{bmatrix}$$

Rotate $-pitch$ about x-axis:

$$\begin{bmatrix} 1 & 0 & 0 & 0 \\ 0 & \cos(pitch) & \sin(pitch) & 0 \\ 0 & -\sin(pitch) & \cos(pitch) & 0 \\ 0 & 0 & 0 & 1 \end{bmatrix}$$

Rotate $-roll$ about z-axis:

$$\begin{bmatrix} \cos(roll) & \sin(roll) & 0 & 0 \\ -\sin(roll) & \cos(roll) & 0 & 0 \\ 0 & 0 & 1 & 0 \\ 0 & 0 & 0 & 1 \end{bmatrix}$$

To obtain the single matrix for translating points in the WCS to the CCS the above rotation matrices are concatenated with the translation matrix in the sequence: translate, yaw, pitch, then roll. This produces the following matrix:

$$\begin{bmatrix} T_{11} & T_{12} & T_{13} & T_{14} \\ T_{21} & T_{22} & T_{23} & T_{24} \\ T_{31} & T_{32} & T_{33} & T_{34} \\ T_{41} & T_{42} & T_{43} & T_{44} \end{bmatrix}$$

where:

$$\begin{aligned}
T_{11} &= \cos(yaw)\cos(roll) + \sin(yaw)\sin(pitch)\sin(roll) \\
T_{12} &= \cos(pitch)\sin(roll) \\
T_{13} &= -\sin(yaw)\cos(roll) + \cos(yaw)\sin(pitch)\sin(roll) \\
T_{14} &= -(t_xT_{11} + t_yT_{12} + t_zT_{13}) \\
T_{21} &= -\cos(yaw)\sin(roll) + \sin(yaw)\sin(pitch)\cos(roll) \\
T_{22} &= \cos(pitch)\cos(roll) \\
T_{23} &= \sin(yaw)\sin(roll) + \cos(yaw)\sin(pitch)\cos(roll) \\
T_{24} &= -(t_xT_{21} + t_yT_{22} + t_zT_{23}) \\
T_{31} &= \sin(yaw)\cos(pitch) \\
T_{32} &= -\sin(pitch) \\
T_{33} &= \cos(yaw)\cos(pitch) \\
T_{34} &= -(t_xT_{31} + t_yT_{32} + t_zT_{33})
\end{aligned}$$

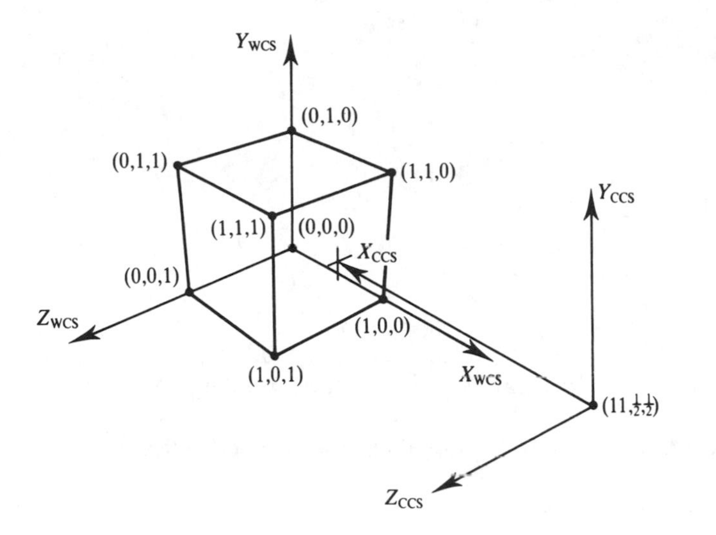

Figure 2.12
This diagram shows the CCS after it has been subjected to a yaw rotation of −90°, and a translation of (11, 1/2, 1/2). The point (1, 1, 1) in the WCS has coordinates (1/2, 1/2, 10) in the CCS, and the point (0, 0, 1) in the WCS has coordinates (1/2, −1/2, 11) in the CCS.

$$T_{41} = 0$$
$$T_{42} = 0$$
$$T_{43} = 0$$
$$T_{44} = 1$$

Therefore, any point (x, y, z) in the WCS can be converted to (X, Y, Z) in the CCS as follows:

$$\begin{bmatrix} X \\ Y \\ Z \\ 1 \end{bmatrix} = \begin{bmatrix} T_{11} & T_{12} & T_{13} & T_{14} \\ T_{21} & T_{22} & T_{23} & T_{24} \\ T_{31} & T_{32} & T_{33} & T_{34} \\ T_{41} & T_{42} & T_{43} & T_{44} \end{bmatrix} \begin{bmatrix} x \\ y \\ z \\ 1 \end{bmatrix}$$

Let us test this matrix operation with two examples.

Example 1 Given a unit cube located at the origin (Figure 2.12) and the following parameter values:

$$roll = 0°$$
$$pitch = 0°$$
$$yaw = -90°$$
$$t_x = 11$$
$$t_y = \frac{1}{2}$$
$$t_z = \frac{1}{2}$$

then:

$$\begin{bmatrix} X \\ Y \\ Z \\ 1 \end{bmatrix} = \begin{bmatrix} 0 & 0 & 1 & -\frac{1}{2} \\ 0 & 1 & 0 & -\frac{1}{2} \\ -1 & 0 & 0 & 11 \\ 0 & 0 & 0 & 1 \end{bmatrix} \begin{bmatrix} x \\ y \\ z \\ 1 \end{bmatrix}$$

The point $(1, 1, 1)$ becomes $(1/2, 1/2, 10)$, and the point $(0, 0, 1)$ becomes $(1/2, -1/2, 11)$, which can be confirmed from Figure 2.12.

Example 2 If a new set of values are assigned as follows:

$$\begin{aligned} roll &= 90° \\ pitch &= 180° \\ yaw &= 0° \\ t_x &= \frac{1}{2} \\ t_y &= \frac{1}{2} \\ t_z &= 11 \end{aligned}$$

then:

$$\begin{bmatrix} X \\ Y \\ Z \\ 1 \end{bmatrix} = \begin{bmatrix} 0 & -1 & 0 & \frac{1}{2} \\ -1 & 0 & 0 & \frac{1}{2} \\ 0 & 0 & -1 & 11 \\ 0 & 0 & 0 & 1 \end{bmatrix} \begin{bmatrix} x \\ y \\ z \\ 1 \end{bmatrix}$$

The point $(1, 1, 1)$ becomes $(-1/2, -1/2, 10)$ and the point $(0, 0, 1)$ becomes $(1/2, 1/2, 10)$, which can be confirmed from Figure 2.13.

So now we have a matrix to convert coordinates in the WCS to the CCS, and a separate matrix for performing the perspective projection. However, there are many ways of positioning the camera, and whatever technique is used, somehow the geometry must be capable of creating the above matrices.

In the following section we examine the problems of ensuring how the camera only sees those objects that are physically in front of it, and within its field of view. And in anticipation of this topic we need to introduce a parameter to control the width of the image – which is defined as W.

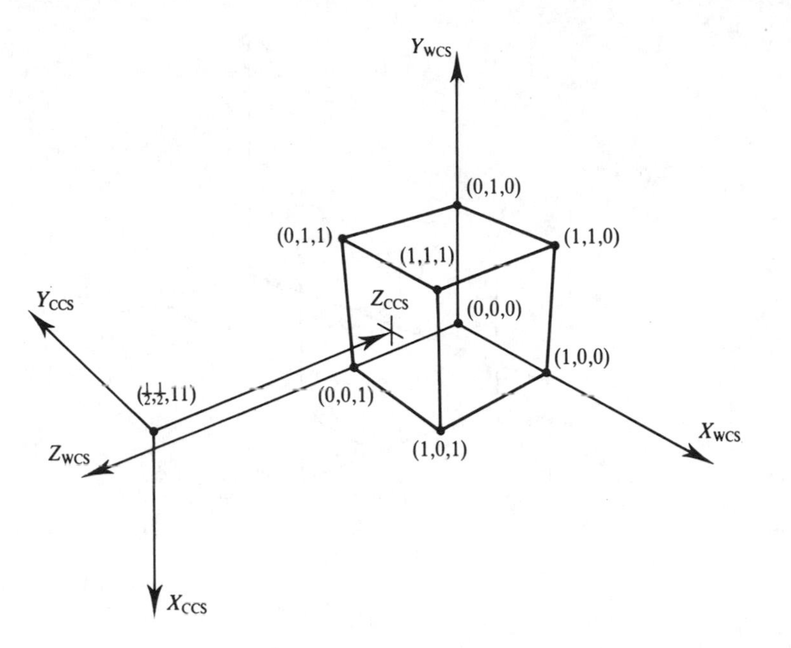

Figure 2.13

This diagram shows the CCS after it has been subjected to a roll of 90°, a pitch of 180°, and a translation of (1/2, 1/2, 11). The point (1, 1, 1) in the WCS has coordinates (−1/2, −1/2, 10) in the CCS, and the point (0, 0, 1) in the WCS has coordinates (1/2, 1/2, 10) in the CCS).

Although we assumed the existence of a viewing screen associated with the camera, it was only included for convenience. For it is also possible to assume that the projection plane is in front of the camera's pinhole without disturbing the action of the projective geometry. Figure 2.14 illustrates this new arrangement.

A further simplification is achieved by scaling the coordinates such that the visible x and y-coordinates range between $-1/2$ and $+1/2$, and a z-coordinate of d becomes $z = 1$. Thus the projection plane is effectively positioned at $z = 1$. The matrix for performing this is:

$$\begin{bmatrix} \frac{1}{W} & 0 & 0 & 0 \\ 0 & \frac{1}{W} & 0 & 0 \\ 0 & 0 & \frac{1}{d} & 0 \\ 0 & 0 & 0 & 1 \end{bmatrix}$$

For example, let $(5, 5, 10)$ be a point in the CCS; $W = 10$, and $d = 10$; which gives a field of view approximately equal to 53°. To convert this to its scaled form we obtain:

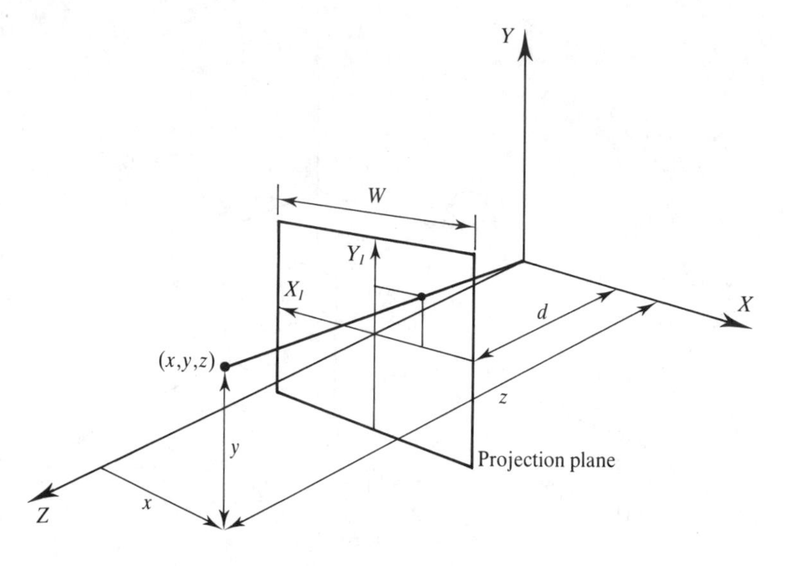

Figure 2.14
The action of the viewing plane in the pinhole camera is identical to the projection plane seen in this illustration. In fact, in this diagram it is easier to see how the perspective projection is formed.

$$\begin{bmatrix} 0.5 \\ 0.5 \\ 1 \\ 1 \end{bmatrix} = \begin{bmatrix} 0.1 & 0 & 0 & 0 \\ 0 & 0.1 & 0 & 0 \\ 0 & 0 & 0.1 & 0 \\ 0 & 0 & 0 & 1 \end{bmatrix} \begin{bmatrix} 5 \\ 5 \\ 10 \\ 1 \end{bmatrix}$$

Similarly, $(-5, -5, 10)$ is scaled to $(-0.5, -0.5, 1)$.

We can now continue and see how these scaled values help the clipping process.

2.3 Clipping the camera's view

A conventional camera can only capture an image of a scene that is physically in front of it and within the field of view of the lens. However, the mathematical camera used in computer graphics effectively 'sees' everything. To appreciate this, just consider a point in the CCS with a negative z-coordinate. When this z-value is substituted into the above perspective projection equations the values of x_i and y_i will have opposite signs to a corresponding point having a positive z-coordinate. If this is allowed, the final image is going to appear very confused, as objects behind the camera will appear upside down and back-to-front, and superimposed upon those in front of the camera.

Obviously, vertices behind the camera have to be removed before they are transformed into a perspective projection, but simply removing those points with a negative z-coordinate will not be sufficient. Edges

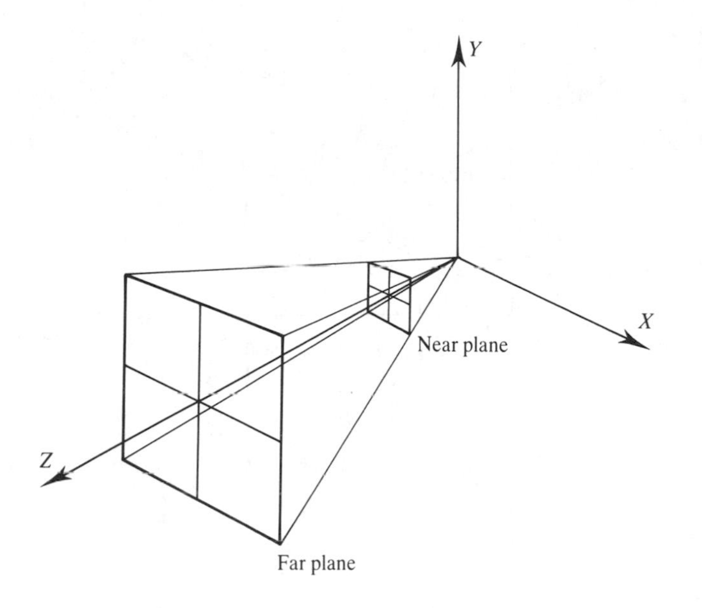

Figure 2.15

The viewing frustum defines the volume containing points visible to the camera. The 'near' plane is used to clip objects too close and behind the camera, while the 'far' plane clips those objects too far to be seen. Four further planes clip objects that are partially or completely out of the camera's field of view.

connecting two vertices must be clipped to reveal their visible portion. There may be other edges that are so far in the distance that they are virtually invisible and can also be clipped. In fact there are three classes of vertices requiring clipping from the scene: vertices too near to the camera, vertices too far from the camera and vertices in front of the camera but outside the camera's field of view. If one delimits the volume of space containing the vertices visible to the camera it will have six planes: two delimiting the 'near' and 'far' planes (sometimes referred to as the *hither* and *yon* planes) and four further planes surrounding the camera's image format.

Figure 2.15 illustrates this configuration, which is called the viewing frustum. To begin with, let us consider the problem of identifying those objects that will be completely invisible to the camera. Assuming that $W = 1$, and the projection plane, where $z = 1$, is the *near* clipping plane, then an object whose z-coordinates are all less than 1 can be totally clipped. What happens in practice is that a parameter is set in the database holding the geometry indicating that it is invisible and should not be rendered. Similarly, objects whose z-coordinates all exceed the distance of the far clipping plane are also invisible. Now we come to the left, right, top and bottom clipping planes. Referring to Figure 2.16a we see a plan view of the frustum, and it can be observed that any point (x_i, y_i, z_i) is invisible when $x_i/z_i \geqslant 1/2$. Similarly, when $x_i/z_i \leqslant -1/2$. These can be rewritten as:

$$2x_i \geqslant z_i$$
$$2x_i \leqslant -z_i$$

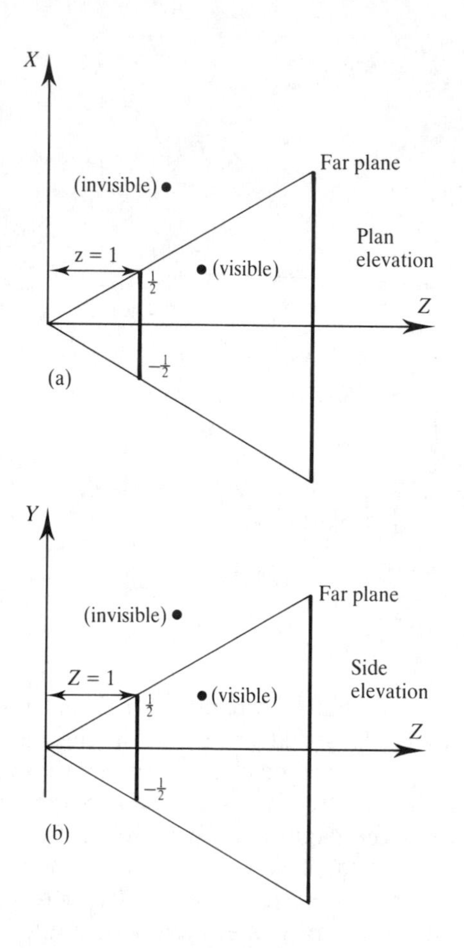

Figure 2.16
The plan elevation of the CCS shows how the side clipping planes determine those points visible and those points invisible to the camera. In the side elevation of the CCS the top and bottom clipping planes form a similar division.

Referring to Figure 2.16b it can also be observed that any point (x_i, y_i, z_i) is invisible when $y_i/z_i \geqslant 1/2$. Similarly, when $y_i/z_i \leqslant -1/2$. These, too, can be rewritten as:

$$2y_i \geqslant z_i$$
$$2y_i \leqslant -z_i$$

Therefore, an object can be completely clipped if all of its vertices satisfy one of the above relationships. If the coordinates have not been scaled to the window size W, then the conditions for invisibility are:

$$\frac{2x_i}{W} \geqslant z_i$$

$$\frac{2x_i}{W} \leqslant -z_i$$

$$\frac{2y_i}{W} \geqslant z_i$$

$$\frac{2y_i}{W} \leqslant -z_i$$

Objects that pass the above tests are either totally or partially visible, and a more rigorous clipping algorithm such as the Sutherland–Hodgman (1974) or the Cyrus–Beck (1978) must be used to identify the visible portions.

So, now we are able to locate a camera in WCS and point it at a collection of objects and compute a perspective view. In fact, five stages are involved in this process:

(1) locate and position the camera;

(2) compute the matrix for converting vertices in the WCS to the CCS;

(3) convert every vertex from the WCS to the CCS using the matrix;

(4) clip away unwanted portions of objects;

(5) perform the perspective transformation.

Thus every time the camera or scene changes, the above five steps must be executed.

A computer animation system must basically provide the animator with a variety of tools for building objects from 3-D vertices and positioning a camera. Further facilities must also exist for moving the objects and the camera in a controlled fashion, and outputting an image at prescribed times.

We have still to discover how objects are constructed and rendered, but before examining these techniques let us complete this review of computer graphics by examining some essential concepts of colour theory.

2.4 Colour theory

This brief review of colour theory is insufficient to cover every aspect of how we perceive images and experience the sensation of colour; nevertheless, some of the important concepts that are relevant to computer graphics are explored, and arguments that still surround this complex subject are deliberately avoided.

When we speak of colour we refer to a sensation associated with images created by the human visual system, which consists of the eyes, the optic nerves and the visual cortex of the brain; perhaps other major areas of the brain are also involved in this process. Words such as 'green', 'blue', 'red', 'light' and 'dark' are used to describe these sensations, and if we attempt to analyse their meaning any further we stumble into the world of philosophy. Therefore, in the following explanations it is accepted that readers also share a common understanding of these words, and they will understand the meaning of descriptions such as 'the sky is blue' and 'the grass is green'.

We know from experience that our sun radiates something we call light, which plays a central role in the process of seeing. Scientists who have studied the nature of light over past centuries have accumulated considerable information about its behaviour. For example, in empty space light travels in straight lines (unless it is deviated by a large mass or passes through a small slit) at the approximate speed of 300 000 000 m/sec. Its transmission can be described by a model of oscillating electric and magnetic waves which undulate sinusoidally and consequently have an associated frequency and wavelength.

Newton demonstrated that when sunlight passes through a prism it is dispersed into the spectrum of colours ranging through red, orange, yellow, green, blue, indigo and violet; the blue end of the spectrum is dispersed more than red. Further experiments have shown that these dispersed colours only differ in their wavelength with red being 700 nm (nanometres), green 520 nm and blue 480 nm.

An accepted model for seeing assumes that when light radiation – with an initial distribution of wavelengths – illuminates a surface, some wavelengths are absorbed while others are reflected. If an observer intercepts this reflected light, a colour sensation is experienced which depends upon the nature of the original light source and the absorption characteristics of the surface. However, although this simple model provides a satisfactory mechanism for describing simple optical phenomena, it does not explain why colour sensations are also dependent upon other colour surfaces adjacent to the observed surface.

One possible construction for the eye could be based upon a receptor, which for every wavelength outputs some special signal – however, this does not seem to be the case. In fact, the eye's retina is constructed from two types of receptors called rods and cones. The rods are active during low levels of illumination, for example at night-time; apparently, they are not very sensitive to wavelength and are excited by the intensity of the incoming light. This explains why very little colour is observed with night vision. However the cones, which are only activated by strong light, divide into three types each having peak sensitivites at three different points in the spectrum.

Figure 2.17 shows the individual photopigment sensitivities to wavelength for an average human eye. These curves reveal that the green- and red-type cones have peak sensitivities around 535 nm and 575 nm respectively, with green being the most sensitive. The blue photopigment is, in comparison, very weak. It is interesting to note that the so-called red-type cone has a peak sensitivity to a wavelength corresponding to the sensation of yellow. However, what is important is the sampling action of the eye. Three photopigments react to overlapping bands of wavelengths, which are translated into electrical signals for final interpretation within the visual

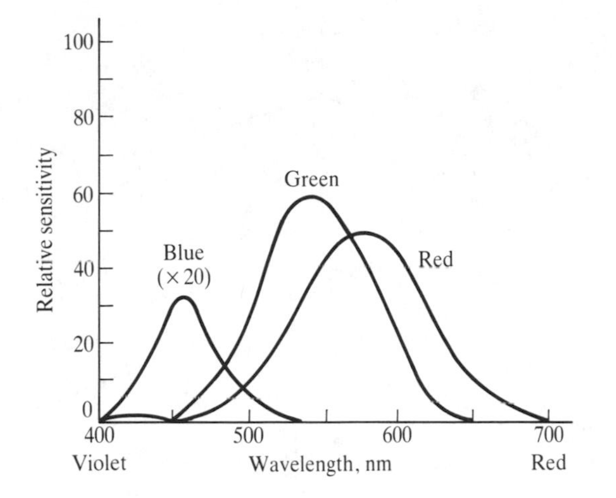

Figure 2.17

These three curves show the relative sensitivity of the human eye to wavelength. Note that the blue curve is magnified by a factor of 20.

cortex; this provides us with the sensations we describe with words such as pale blue, gold and magnolia.

Although these photopigments have been chemically identified, another effect which also adds weight to this mechanism is the ability to match a colour by adjusting the individual intensities of three coloured lamps fitted with red, green and blue filters. Experiments have provided adequate evidence to support a mechanism for colour television and colour computer graphics. This entails describing an image in the form of three colour separations, the red, green and blue components. In television the three colour components are first separated by the television camera and ultimately broadcast as a composite signal, which at the receiving end is decoded into three colour signals to modulate the three electron guns within a cathode ray tube. This encoding and decoding has a detrimental effect upon the final image, in the form of noise and interference.

Another concept introduced in television technology is the idea of pixels or picture elements, for the television screen is divided into a regular matrix of phosphor triads which are activated by the scanning electron guns. If these pixels are small enough, and there are sufficient of them, at an optimum viewing distance the eye will perceive a continuous coloured image. Furthermore, if the screen is continuously repainted at a refresh rate of approximately 50 times a second, the image will be perceived to be of constant intensity, even though in reality it is flickering.

All of these ideas are exploited within computer graphics. To begin with a computer-generated image is built from a matrix of pixels perhaps 1000 by 1000, where each pixel has a red, green and blue component. These ideas will be further developed in Section 2.1.6, so for now let us return to the idea of colour and the way it can be described in an objective manner.

If one accepts the idea of describing a colour in terms of its three additive components, i.e. red, green and blue, one will want to know how

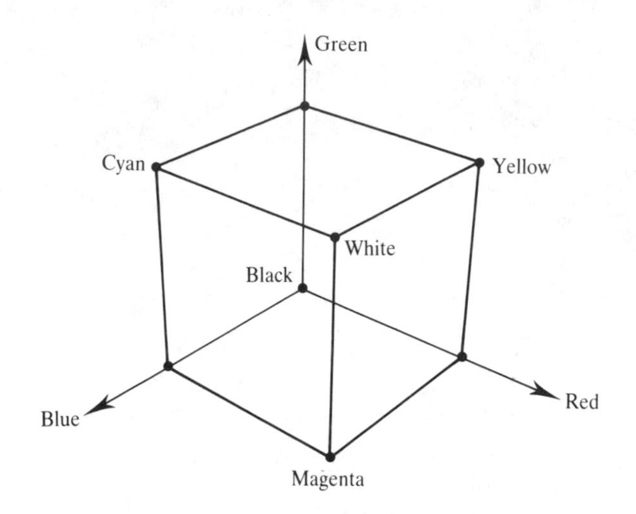

Figure 2.18

The RGB colour space consists of a cube in which the additive primary colours form a set of orthogonal axes. Any point within the cube represents a colour having levels of red, green and blue.

much of these primaries is needed to make a desired colour. This appears to be a real problem, and one that can be appreciated if we construct a set of 3-D axes where each axis corresponds to a primary component. Figure 2.18 illustrates this arrangement where a cubic volume of space identifies the gamut of colours composed from different mixes of red, green and blue (RGB). But where is magnolia? And where is salmon pink? Well, although this RGB colour model is fundamental to display technology, it is not very convenient for identifying positions of colours and how they will be affected if RGB levels are modified.

Another three-dimensional model for organizing colours is known as the hue, saturation and value (HSV) colour space. This employs the parameters hue, saturation and value to define a colour. The term hue returns to the original colour spectrum for its definition using terms such as red, yellow, green, cyan, blue and magenta. Saturation defines how much white light is desaturating the colour, (remember that equal amounts of red, green and blue light create a white light sensation), and value is used to differentiate a light colour from a dark one.

Figure 2.19 illustrates this model and one can immediately see where certain colours should be approximately located. More importantly, the HSV colour model allows a hue to be modified in terms of its saturation and value, something the RGB approach is unable to directly provide. In fact, the two systems are not completely divorced from one another; there are simple algorithms for converting levels of hue, saturation and value to equivalent levels of red, green and blue, and vice versa. If this were not possible, the HSV model would not be useful.

Using the HSV colour model a colour can be represented by three fractions representing hue, saturation and value. The convention for hue is to let zero represent red, 1/6 for yellow, 1/3 for green, 1/2 for cyan, 2/3 for

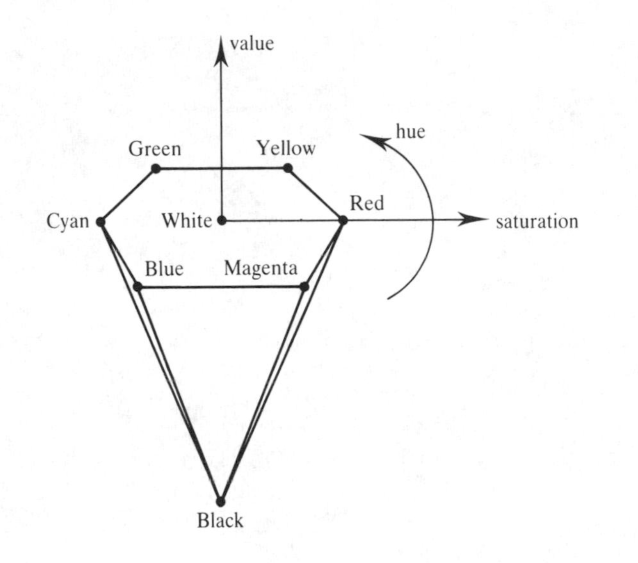

Figure 2.19
The HSV colour space consists of a hexcone where hue is represented by a rotational sweep about the vertical axis; saturation increases for colours located away from the central axis; and value is a displacement along the vertical axis.

blue, 5/6 for magenta and 1 also for red. A colour without any white component is fully saturated with a level of 1, whilst a totally desaturated colour, i.e. a grey, has a level of zero. Value, which represents the lightness of the colour, varies from 0 for black, to 1 for white.

Now that colour can be represented numerically one can anticipate how it could be altered within an animation sequence. For example, an object could be assigned levels of hue, saturation and value, and for certain frames the hue is allowed to increase slightly. When animated, these frames would show the object moving continuously through a controlled range of colours.

An object's colour can be made to change over a period of time by assigning a starting and ending colour, perhaps using RGB notation, and interpolating between them. However, one must be aware that interpolating between a pair of colours specified in RGB will not give precisely the same results as interpolating between the equivalent pair of colours defined in HSV. This is because there is not a linear relationship between the two colour models.

2.5 Computer graphics hardware

2.5.1 Digitizer

Having seen how important Cartesian coordinates are to computer graphics, perhaps the first device we should examine is the digitizer, for this actually generates coordinates in a form acceptable to a computer.

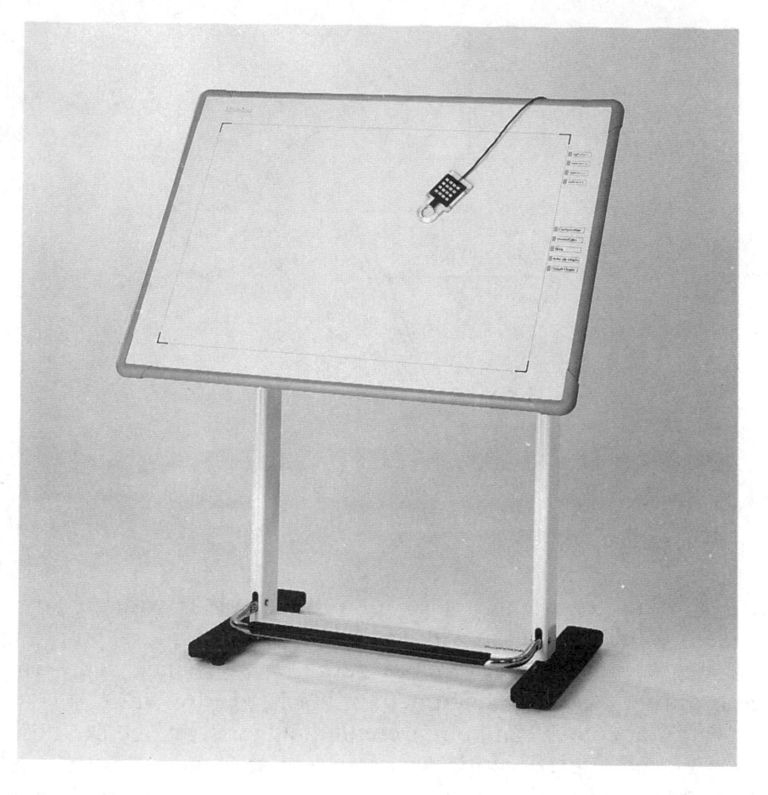

Figure 2.20
This digitizer uses a puck to probe the active area of the device which in real-time supplies the host computer with 2-D coordinates.

Figure 2.20 shows a photograph of a popular digitizer which consists of an active surface, a stylus, and a control unit. The active surface is generally constructed from an accurate matrix of horizontal and vertical wires radiating a low-level electromagnetic field. This field is encoded with signals such that when a stylus is placed in the vicinity of the surface, a coil within the stylus acts as an aerial and returns a signal to the control unit. This in turn decodes the signal and computes the x- and y-coordinates of the stylus and transmits them to the host computer. The actual wires within the digitizer are bonded so that they cannot move and are protected by a laminated surface.

To digitize some design, a program in the host computer must anticipate receiving numbers from the digitizer, upon which is mounted the artwork. Perhaps the program has been designed such that, before digitizing, the user informs the program of the precise location of the origin. This might be placed in the middle of the artwork. Once this has been communicated, the user proceeds to traverse the contours touching the pen at certain points. When the digitizer is operating in a 'point mode', every time the user presses the stylus onto the digitizer, an internal switch is operated which triggers the digitizer's control unit to transmit the current position of the pen. In the 'continuous mode', the system outputs coordinates at a controllable speed while the pen's switch is in an 'on' status.

Typically a piece of artwork consists of a number of distinct contours, and the end of each contour and the beginning of another must be communicated to the host program. While these coordinates are being fed into the computer, the program is constructing a series of coordinate lists that represent a sampled version of the artwork. Obviously if the user operating the digitizer has not accurately followed the contours of the artwork, the internally stored coordinates will reflect these errors.

2.5.2 3-D digitizer

When the surface detail of a solid model needs to be captured, then a 3-D digitizer is particularly useful. The model is first prepared by drawing a network of polygons over the surface, making sure that smaller polygons are used for areas of fine detail. A hand-held probe is then used to identify the vertices of the polygons in some specified sequence. The digitizer employs two small coils positioned within the volume containing the model to radiate a signal which is received by the probe; with this data a processor computes the position of the probe in space which is then sent to a host computer. Software in the host computer can then organize the data so that the original polygons can be reconstructed.

2.5.3 Graph plotter

A graph plotter basically reverses the action of the digitizer in that, if a sequence of coordinates is held within a computer and sent to a plotter, the plotter's pen will trace out on paper or plastic cel, the design encoded by the coordinates. Such plotters are available within a range of sizes that vary from A3 to A0 and can draw with biros, fibre pens or professional drafting pens.

Some graph plotters are able to draw at speeds in excess of 1 m/sec, but this can only be achieved when the lines are relatively long. If the line segments are very short the plotter's motors will be unable to accelerate to the maximum drawing speed, and a much lower average drawing rate will be achieved.

Filling in areas with colour or patterns presents a problem for the pen-based graph plotters, which is why other types of printing devices have evolved that are capable of converting coloured screen images onto paper. Similarly, electrostatic plotters exist (both monochrome and colour) that transform a coordinate file of data into a raster format, such that the final plotted image appears when the paper is finally released from the machine.

2.5.4 Frame store

In an earlier section, it was established that a colour image could be maintained as a matrix of pixels where each pixel held the red, green and blue components. A device for storing such a format is called a frame store or frame buffer. This has a memory element for every pixel's colour, and a popular construction employs one byte of computer memory for this element. This means that to store a full-colour image consisting of 1024 lines, where each line has 1024 pixels, 1 Mb of memory is needed for each colour separation, making a total of 3 Mb in all. When the frame store is connected to a computer, the resident software system can load into it the numbers representing levels of red, green and blue for any pixel. While this is occurring, the frame store memory is being scanned at video rates and the digital signal is converted into an analogue form to drive a colour monitor. Thus the user can observe an image being constructed by the host program.

As a byte of computer memory can store any number between 0 and 255, such numbers can represent the intensity of the red, green or blue components in the store. This means that a pixel can have 256 levels of red, 256 levels of green and 256 levels of blue; together there are $256 \times 256 \times 256$ different colour combinations possible, making approximately 16.7 million in all. This may sound excessive but the special effects industry frequently employs 12 bits per primary colour as their images are transferred to 35 mm cine-film.

Although the individual numbers stored within the pixel's three bytes can represent the primary colour intensities, the numbers are frequently used to indirectly address the final colour through a look-up table as shown in Figure 2.21. As the look-up tables have 256 entries, the frame store values can now be interpreted as positions within the tables which ultimately contain the colour intensities.

At first sight this may not seem to achieve anything, but this indirect reference to the final colour has certain advantages. First, it means that the values held in the tables need not increase linearly one increment at a time, but are adjusted to follow some non-linear law; this procedure is used for fine-tuning gamma correction and controlling any non-linearities that might exist in the system. Second, the tables may be loaded with arbitrary values such that the displayed image loses all of its original colour information; this is called pseudo-colouring and is often found in image processing applications. Third, for certain images, if the entries of the table are moved along one position, recycling those entries that fall off the end of the table, a pseudo-animation effect is created known as look-up table animation.

2.5.5 Colour monitor

A colour monitor is very similar to a television: both employ a cathode ray tube to display the colour image but they differ slightly in the type of input

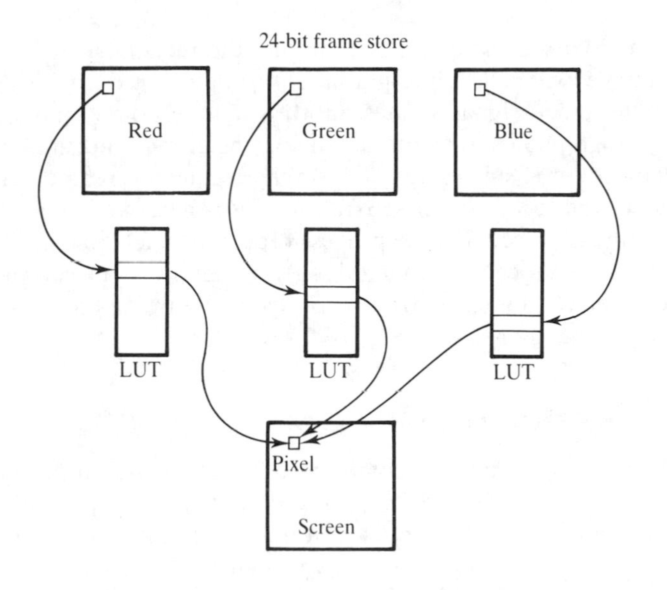

Figure 2.21
Frame stores often employ look-up tables (LUTs) to identify the final intensity of red, green and blue associated with a pixel. This provides a mechanism for extra gamma correction, pseudo-colouring and LUT animation where the table's values are cycled.

signals expected. A television accepts a signal broadcast in a PAL, NTSC or SECAM format, where colour and sound information are encoded together; whereas a monitor will accept the component signals for red, green and blue, and the sound has its own channel. This component approach accounts for the superior image found on monitors.

Some monitors can also display their image in one sweep of the screen, producing 60 or more frames every second. This display mode is called non-interlaced, whereas a television image comprises two interlaced fields to form a single frame. A field is formed from the odd or even raster lines of the image.

2.5.6 Film recorder

Although the majority of computer animation is recorded onto video tape, the quality is not acceptable for large-screen viewing, which is where the medium of film is required. A low-cost film system can be achieved by filming the monitor screen one frame at a time. This requires a light-proof hood to protect the camera and screen from stray reflections. Unfortunately, the image is distorted by the screen's curvature. The monitor may also not be capable of maintaining a constant intensity over long periods of time and the picture may also drift due to temperature changes of components.

In overcoming these drawbacks, special film recorders have been developed with flat screen monitors mounted in a light-proof environment. The monitors, which are monochrome, automatically display the three individual colour separations. For example, the red signal creates a monochrome image which is photographed through a red filter. After this exposure the green signal creates another monochrome image, which in turn is photographed – without advancing the film – and finally the blue component follows suit. Thus the single frame is created from three exposures to the three colour separations. For the next frame, the film is automatically advanced and the process repeated. Such systems can be left to operate automatically, either taking the signals from computer disks storing the coloured images, or directly from the frame store as the computer renders the image.

2.5.7 Workstation

Ten to twenty years ago it was common to find large mainframe computers with perhaps a hundred simultaneous users working on different problems, including computer graphics. Such systems were appallingly slow in comparison with today's computers, but through the advances of miniaturization, computers are now relatively cheap and very small, so much so that microcomputers are no larger than their associated keyboards.

Nowadays, the workstation philosophy brings to the individual user sufficient processing power, disk storage and display technology to fit on or under a desk. The user can design and test programs locally which, if they create graphics, can also be displayed at high speed. Workstations come equipped with a wide range of facilities: some are monochrome while others may display between 256 and 16.7 million colours. Resolution may also vary but is typically in excess of one million pixels.

Exercises and projects

2.1 Derive from first principles the matrix for rotating a point an angle θ about the origin, and the matrix for shearing a point in the x-direction by an angle θ.

2.2 Design and test a program to concatenate two matrices.

2.3 How is it possible to test whether a set of 2-D Cartesian coordinates are in a clockwise or anti-clockwise sequence? (A clue will be found in the way a determinant is evaluated, and its capacity to measure the area of a triangle.)

2.4 What effect does changing a right-handed set of axes to a left-handed system have upon the action of rotation matrices? Support your answer with an example using diagrams.

2.5 Write a program which subjects a set of 3-D coordinates to three rotations about the x-, y- and z-axes.

2.6 Using the formulae stated in Section 2.1.3 to create a perspective projection, write a program to convert a list of 3-D coordinates into a 2-D set. Investigate the effect the image plane distance has on the perspective image. What happens when it is made negative?

2.7 What parameters are needed to control the field of view of the virtual camera, and explain their interaction?

2.8 Explain why edges, rather than single vertices, must be clipped against the viewing frustum.

2.9 Distinguish between the world coordinate system (WCS), the camera's coordinate system (CCS), and the image space (IS) and explain how coordinates in the WCS are converted to the CCS, and finally projected onto the IS.

2.10 Write a program converting coordinates in WCS to the CCS using the matrix developed in Section 2.1.3.

2.11 In the context of Section 2, what computer graphics features should be implemented at a hardware level if fast animation is a priority?

2.12 If red light has an approximate wavelength of 700 nm and blue light 480 nm, to how many octaves of light radiation is the human eye sensitive? (An octave implies a doubling or halving in frequency.)

2.13 What are the benefits of using the HSV colour model over the RGB system?

2.14 Implement the algorithms for converting HSV into RGB and vice versa (see Rogers (1985) or Foley (1990)).

Further reading

Geometric transformations Foley (1990), pp. 201–227, contains a thorough description of geometrical transformations, where 2-D and 3-D transformations are explained using matrix notation. It also explains the role of homogeneous coordinates. Rogers (1990), pp. 61–100, treats the same subject matter to a greater depth and includes some valuable worked examples with good illustrations. Blinn's paper 'Nested transformations and Blobby Man' (Blinn, 1987) is also recommended.

Projections Further concepts of projections are treated in Burger (1989), pp. 181–191, which introduces orthographic, oblique and perspective projections, vanishing points and back projections. Watt (1989), pp. 17–26, also contains an interesting review of perspective projections and considers the role of the camera. However, both Foley (1990), pp. 229–281, and Rogers (1990), pp. 101–206, contain a really rigorous analysis of this subject.

Clipping Those readers who wish to discover more about clipping will find an excellent description in Foley (1990), pp. 271–281. Rogers is also very thorough in *Procedural Elements for Computer Graphics* (Rogers, 1985).

Colour theory Human colour vision is covered in great depth in Boynton (1979) and Gregory (1979), while colour theory is explained in Hunt (1975). Foley (1990), pp. 563–604, also provides an excellent overview for the uses of colour in computer graphics.

Computer graphics hardware Computer graphics hardware has a habit of rapidly becoming dated, and the reader is advised to monitor articles in *Byte* and *Computer Graphics World*.

KEY POINTS

Although this chapter is only intended as a survey of the principles of computer graphics, it does cover the most important concepts relating to computer animation. The following list contains the key points that are carried forward into the following chapters.

- Cartesian coordinate notation is central to the description of objects, light sources and cameras. This notation lends itself to a matrix formulation where a homogeneous form allows a coherent description of scaling, translation, shearing and rotation operations.
- The world coordinate system (WCS) is an axial system which will become the space in which all animations are staged. Within the WCS, the camera's coordinate system (CCS) is oriented to capture a perspective projection of objects which also reside in the WCS.
- The CCS can be oriented in the WCS using a variety of techniques; however, whichever technique is chosen, it is possible to derive a matrix operation to align the CCS with the WCS.
- When the coordinates are subjected to the inverse of the aligning matrix, the perspective projection becomes simple to compute.
- Clipping procedures must be implemented to remove whole or parts of edges invisible to the camera.
- The description of colour employs the three additive primary colours using an RGB colour space; however, the HSV system is an alternate space which is much more intuitive and also related to RGB.
- Although hardware changes continuously, computer animation does depend upon 2- and 3-D digitizers, plotters, frame stores, monitors, film recorders and workstations.

3 Modelling Schemes

In computer animation modelling is closely coupled to the way objects are animated, which implies that the storyboard should identify clearly everything that will happen to them. If a box, for example, is expected to possess a hinged lid, or the sides are to be blown apart at some stage, then this needs to be known when the box is being constructed.

Modelling also calls upon a variety of disparate techniques for building objects such as cars, logos, teapots, fireworks, rain, water, mountains and human beings, which also influences the way they are rendered. A simple strategy is to build things from a collection of straight edges, but this wire frame approach does not contain the vital topological data that enables surface normals, common vertices and individual polygons to be identified.

Objects are constructed using a boundary or volumetric representation. The boundary approach entails constructing a surface skin from triangles, polygons, ruled surfaces or surface patches, while the volumetric approach employs mathematical equations to delimit a precise 3-D volume. When these formal geometric techniques prove inadequate, procedural methods can be applied such as fractals and soft objects; these can be used to build 3-D terrains and flexible structures respectively.

With this requirement for a wide range of modelling strategies, a computer animation system must be capable of supporting these different data sets, which change dynamically while the animation is in progress. This calls for various data structures for storing this hierarchical data.

Introduction

In the real world we know that everything is constructed from atoms, which collect together to form molecules and ultimately form objects such as apples, concrete and sea mist. A computer animator may wish to construct all of these objects within a computer, and one is tempted to ask whether there is a similar building block like the atom for their construction? Unfortunately, the answer is no. The computer's memory can only store electrical codes representing numbers or symbols – these have to be the ultimate building blocks for everything. These numbers and symbols can be employed to represent other structures such as Cartesian coordinates, equations, volumes of space, slopes, surface properties and physical attributes such as tension, softness and velocity, and collectively they provide the tools for modelling a variety of things. There is no universal modelling scheme (at the moment) that allows one to build the wealth of objects encountered in our everyday experience.

To cope with the totally different physical structure of familiar artefacts, computer modelling consists of a very wide range of disparate techniques. For example, the simple cube has six planar sides, eight vertices and twelve edges. (This satisfies Euler's rule which states that for a polyhedron without holes, the number of edges is always two less than the sum of the faces and vertices.) Such an object can be represented in several ways, and perhaps the simplest is to build a definition based upon its corners using Cartesian coordinates. This data can be used to construct the edges, which then form the sides. Finally, the sides can be arranged to define the cube's surface – such a model is known as a boundary representation. But could the same technique be used to model a sphere? Well, the answer is yes, but the sphere would have to be built from a large number of planar surfaces that, hopefully, could be disguised by a shading program.

Another modelling approach for the sphere refers to its equation:

$$x^2 + y^2 + z^2 = r^2$$

where r is the radius and (x, y, z) is any point on the sphere's surface. This implicit method of defining the surface requires that values of x, y and z have to be discovered to satisfy a value of r. This method not only identifies the points on the surface, but can also classify those points inside and outside of the sphere, hence it is used for volumetric modelling schemes.

Consider another example such as fire. Constructing flames from coordinates, edges and planar surfaces doesn't sound practical, and digitizing them could be dangerous! Geometry offers no solution in the form of an equation, therefore another technique has to be found. We will discover later that particle systems and fractals offer useful solutions to this phenomenon.

Finally, consider the problems of modelling the ubiquitous teapot, which has become an icon within the world of computer graphics. The pot has a body, lid, handle and spout, and the last two elements touch the body to form complex curves of intersection. Constructing such curves might prove extremely difficult, however it just so happens that a hidden-surface technique automatically creates them. Now this may seem very useful, and it is, but in achieving these intersection curves the modelling scheme has depended upon the modeller ensuring that the handle and spout physically intersect the body.

If we examined the interior of the teapot we would discover this surplus geometry penetrating the body. We would also discover that the teapot is totally useless for serving tea, as there is no hole in the body for the tea to pass through to the spout! Does it matter? You may ask – it's only a computer model! But in an engineering CAD application the designer may want to compute the weight of the teapot, its centre of gravity, its surface area and possibly its moment of inertia; therefore, it is essential that the physical description of the model be accurate. Surely such information is not needed in computer animation? Well, much depends on how the teapot is to be animated. Obviously, it would be necessary to model the inside of the teapot if an internal journey was planned.

This argument will not be pursued further, for hopefully the reader is beginning to see that modelling is not just concerned with images, it has important ramifications upon how we wish to animate the final object, and how we intend to render the final image. In the rest of this chapter various modelling schemes will be examined with consideration to representing objects and their animation.

3.1 Wire frame

One of the simplest methods of building a 3-D object is to construct it from a collection of lines representing the straight edges that identify its major geometric features. Such a method is known as wire frame, for it appears as though the object is physically constructed from straight pieces of wire. Figure 3.1 illustrates a table built in this wire frame mode.

Because such objects are built from an uncoordinated collection of edges, it can often prove impossible for programs to automatically remove those lines potentially masked by other surfaces. This is because the numerical data does not store information associating edges with their surfaces. Consequently, the wire frame approach is not considered as a valid modelling scheme, although the term is still employed to describe a transparent view of a model constructed from edges.

The idea of defining an object's surface from its edges is still a sound idea, however the data structure (the internal organization of data in the

Figure 3.1
This wire-frame model of a table appears rather confusing as edges that should be invisible are seen as though it was physically constructed from wire. If the model is constructed from polygons, a procedure can be used to hide the invisible lines.

computer) must also be supplied with other information describing how the edges are connected to form boundary surface elements, which leads us into the boundary representation schemes.

3.2 Boundary representation

Boundary representation schemes refer to modelling techniques that construct 3-D objects from surface descriptions rather than from the contained volumes. As a simple example, the cube described above refers to a surface description using the coordinates of the vertices to define edges, which in turn form the surface polygons. This is clearly a boundary representation, as there is explicit geometry to identify any point on the surface of the cube. However, what we do not possess are similar data identifying points that are inside the cube and those points that are outside. Furthermore, although calculating the volume of a cube is a simple calculation, it is not directly computed from this boundary data; considerable manipulation is necessary to reorganize the data to provide such information. In Section 3.3 we will consider other modelling schemes that provide volumetric data at a primary level, with surface data at a secondary level.

3.2.1 Planar polygons

A polygon defines a class of figure constructed from a chain of straight edges. This includes shapes whose boundaries are convex, concave or intersecting, and may or may not be planar. Because of this wide range of constructions most polygonal modelling is performed with planar polygons which can either be convex or concave, although concave polygons do tend

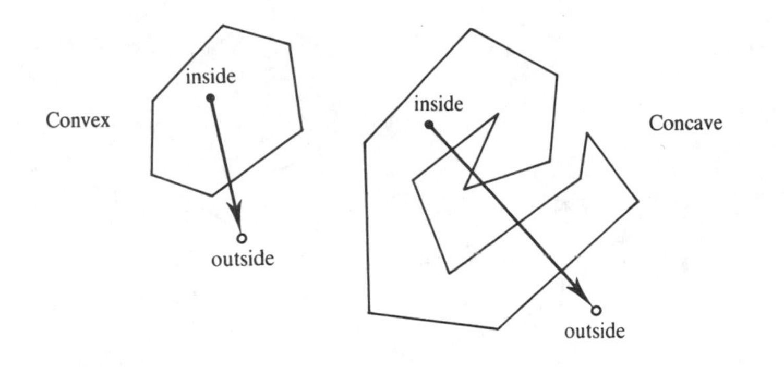

Figure 3.2
Any point within a convex polygon only has to intersect the boundary once to reach the outside, whereas a concave polygon may have a number of intersections depending upon the degree of concavity. This observation is exploited by some computer graphics algorithms.

to complicate matters. For example, with a convex polygon any point contained by the boundary only has to intersect this boundary once to escape outside; whereas a concave boundary can create any number of odd intersections. Figure 3.2 illustrates this effect. Furthermore, any two adjacent edges in a convex polygon can be used as vectors to derive a consistent orthogonal vector to the surface, whereas a concave polygon could reverse the direction of the vector depending upon the enclosed angle between the edges.

These side effects introduced by concave polygons become rather annoying when developing shading algorithms, and are either avoided by not allowing them into the modelling scheme, or by triangulating the polygon; this reduces the polygon to a mesh of triangles which can only be convex and are always planar. For the rest of this section it will be assumed that all polygons are planar, unless specified otherwise, and in general they will be convex.

Building objects using polygons is relatively straightforward as it only requires one to identify important edges and construct the family of facets covering the surface. But in computer animation one must always be aware of how the object is to be animated when it is modelled. To illustrate this last point let us construct the cube to which we have already referred. Figure 3.3 shows its position relative to some coordinate system, and for the sake of simplicity let us assume that each side is one unit in length. For the moment there is no need to think in terms of whether the units of measurement are in centimetres, inches, feet or metres.

The cube could be constructed in a variety of ways and one method would be to store the coordinates of the eight vertices in a table as shown in Figure 3.3. Another table would then reference these vertex entries to form the six boundary polygons. A program can then construct any polygon by extracting the four vertices referenced in the polygon table.

An animation feature that might want to be tried is to squash the cube at vertex 7 with coordinates $(1, 1, 1)$. This vertex could slowly drop downwards, say to $(1, 0.5, 1)$, and could be effected simply by altering the y-entry for vertex 7 from 1 to 0.5 over a specified number of frames. The

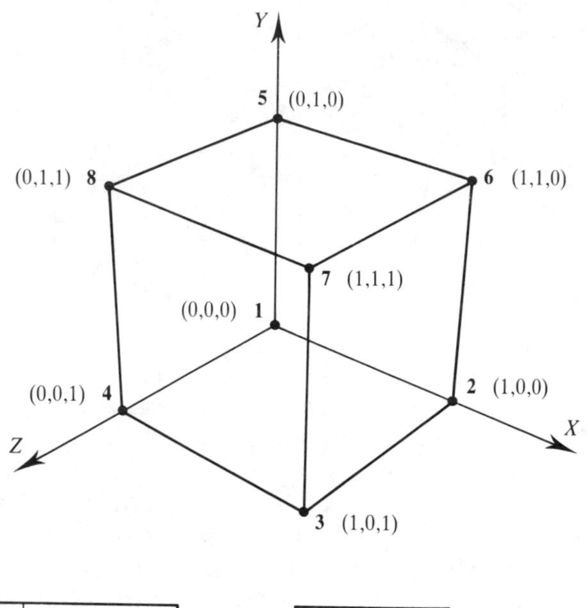

p	*vertices*			
1	1	2	6	5
2	2	3	7	6
3	3	4	8	7
4	4	1	5	8
5	5	6	7	8
6	1	4	3	2

Polygons

v	*x*	*y*	*z*
1	0	0	0
2	1	0	0
3	1	0	1
4	0	0	1
5	0	1	0
6	1	1	0
7	1	1	1
8	0	1	1

Vertices

Figure 3.3

If this unit cube is assigned coordinates as shown, tables can be constructed that relate the six surface polygons with the eight vertices. The two tables show how six polygons forming a cube are stored as a table of vertex entries; e.g. entry 5 in the polygon table shows that the top of the cube is made up from vertices 5, 6, 7 and 8. Note that the vertex groups are in a clockwise sequence as seen from the cube's outside.

renderer program, which actually creates the coloured image, would refer to the two tables and construct the cube's polygons at every frame of the animation, and if the geometry is being altered by the animator, then the final image will reflect these changes. However, one cannot change geometry arbitrarily and hope that the renderer will be able to cope, especially if its calculations assume planar polygons.

If the *y*-coordinate of vertex 7 is reduced, the top polygon of the cube is no longer planar, it is twisted, and it is quite likely that the renderer will compute highlights in the wrong places. Therefore, if one really wanted the top of the cube to squash down at vertex 7, then vertices 8 and 6 must also be moved down to preserve the planarity of the top.

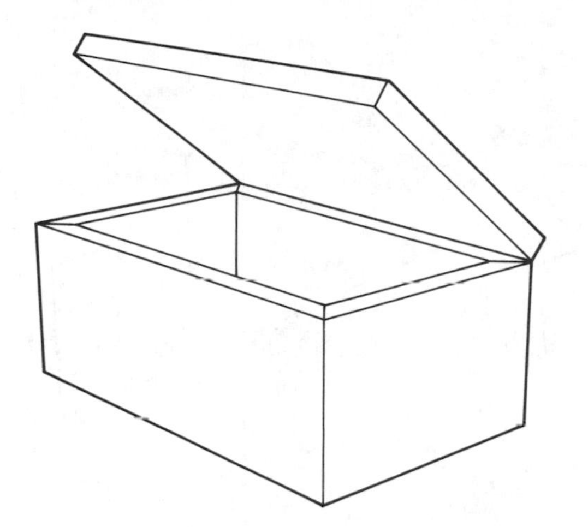

Figure 3.4
If an animation sequence requires that a box has thickness and the top is to be hinged, this geometry must be incorporated in the model from the outset.

In reality the way the cube alters its geometry really depends upon its composition. Just imagine the changes that would occur to a cube built from sponge to one made from clay. Also a cube built from aluminium panels would react totally differently to one made out of paper. Now perhaps one can begin to appreciate how modelling and animation techniques are closely coupled.

Another animation exercise that might be contemplated, is to lift back the top of the cube as though it were hinged at one of the edges. With the proposed modelling scheme this presents serious problems, for not only are the top's vertices shared by the four walls, but the walls have no thickness and therefore the inside does not exist! Constructing a solid box requires that it is modelled as shown in Figure 3.4.

We can see that the animation requirements must be anticipated at the modelling stage, and the renderer must have sufficient geometry to perform its work, part of which entails having access to the edges that form the boundary polygons. In such cases, objects are defined in terms of a hierarchy of polygons built from edges which in turn are built from vertices, and would be represented by three lists of polygons, edges and vertex data.

3.2.2 Extruding

Although the surface polygonal approach provides a convenient method for constructing objects, it can become rather tedious when building complex models. To overcome this tedium, various shortcuts have evolved to aid the building of generic forms. The first such technique is extruding. This automatically constructs a boundary representation by sweeping a cross-sectional shape along an axis to create an extrusion of a given length. Figure 3.5 illustrates a cross-section and the 3-D surface created when it is displaced in the z-direction.

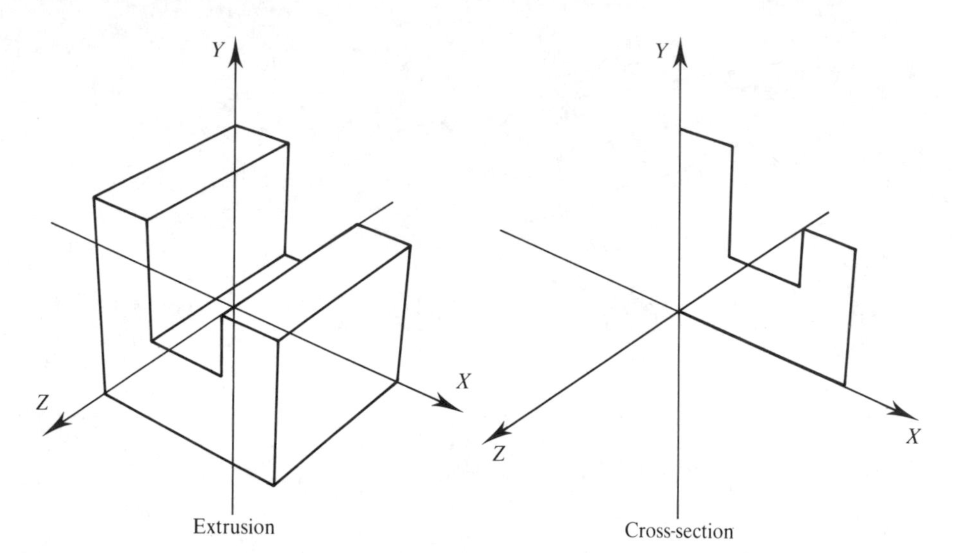

Figure 3.5

The cross-section is used to construct the illustrated 3-D extruded volume, and if it is clockwise, the modelling program will also probably build all of the 3-D polygons with the same sense. Some modelling systems provide facilities to reverse these vertex sequences.

The task of constructing the surface can be achieved automatically by a computer program – all that this requires is the coordinate data describing the cross-section held within a convenient data structure, and the length of extrusion. There is now sufficient geometric information to locate every vertex on the extruded surface. In this building process the program may employ a convention of constructing polygons with a clockwise vertex sense. It may, therefore, expect the master cross-section to be in a clockwise sense. If this is not the case, the extruded surface will be constructed with anti-clockwise polygons, which may be interpreted as being invisible by the renderer. Moreover, some back-facing polygons will appear clockwise and thus visible to the renderer, resulting in an image where the inside of the object is shaded and the outside ignored! For this reason, some commercial modelling systems anticipate such problems by incorporating commands that enable polygon boundaries to be reversed.

A further development of this extruding method is to construct a family of surface polygons at several discrete stages of extrusion, and at each stage the cross-section is rotated. This permits twisted thread-like forms to be modelled. Figure 3.6 illustrates an example of this process.

Perhaps even the size of the cross-section could be changing during this process, or even the shape of the cross-section is turning into another form. Ideally, an extruding program should allow the user to specify the starting and finishing cross-sections (even if the latter is a scaled version of the former), and an angle of rotation applied to the cross-section at each stage of the extrusion. Furthermore, instead of a straight extruding distance, the procedure should allow any 3-D contour to form the centre line of the final object.

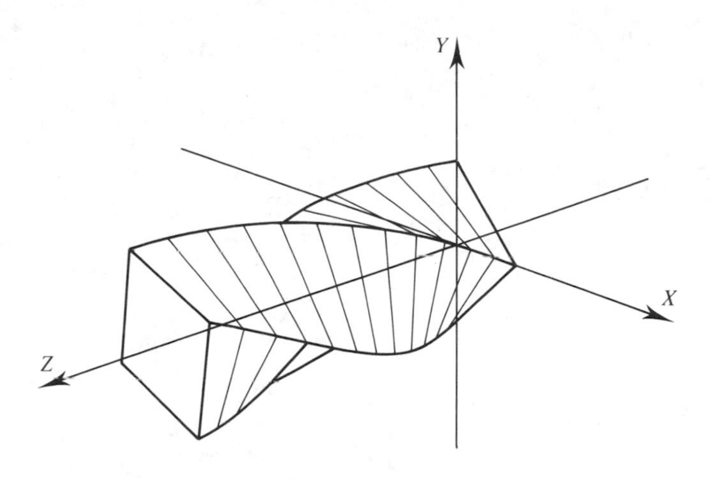

Figure 3.6
This twisted extrusion is achieved by rotating a reference cross-section through a small angle every time it is moved in the *z*-direction.

3.2.3 Surfaces of revolution

Surfaces of revolution help us construct objects such as glasses, spheres, bottles, pepper mills and certain chess pieces. These objects exhibit a symmetry about a central axis. Once more a master 2-D contour is required, however this time it is rotated about one of the 3-D axes to sweep out a surface of revolution. Figure 3.7 shows how a wine glass can be formed from the initial 2-D contour. Notice that the final surface is still constructed from planar polygons, and the actual number depends upon the number of vertices in the original contour and the size of the angle swept at each stage of the construction. The angle step becomes a very useful method of building a wide range of objects from the same contour.

Just like the extrusion program, surfaces of revolution can be built automatically – all that the user needs to specify are the forming contour, the number of increments to be made during the 360° rotation, and the axis about which the rotation is to occur. Such a program will only produce symmetric objects; however, with a slight modification it can be used to create all sorts of asymmetric surfaces. To begin with just imagine the final surface if, while rotating the contour about the reference axis, the axis itself was moving along some closed path. Similarly, imagine the distorted shapes that could be created by actually modifying the master 2-D contour while it was being rotated. Investigating such imaginary forms becomes rather taxing on one's 3-D visualizing faculties, which is why such modelling tools demand a fast interactive computer graphics environment.

3.2.4 Free-form surfaces

No matter where you may be reading this book, a quick glance at your surroundings will confirm that objects in our everyday world are not built from polygons. Perhaps the walls of a room and the floor and ceiling are

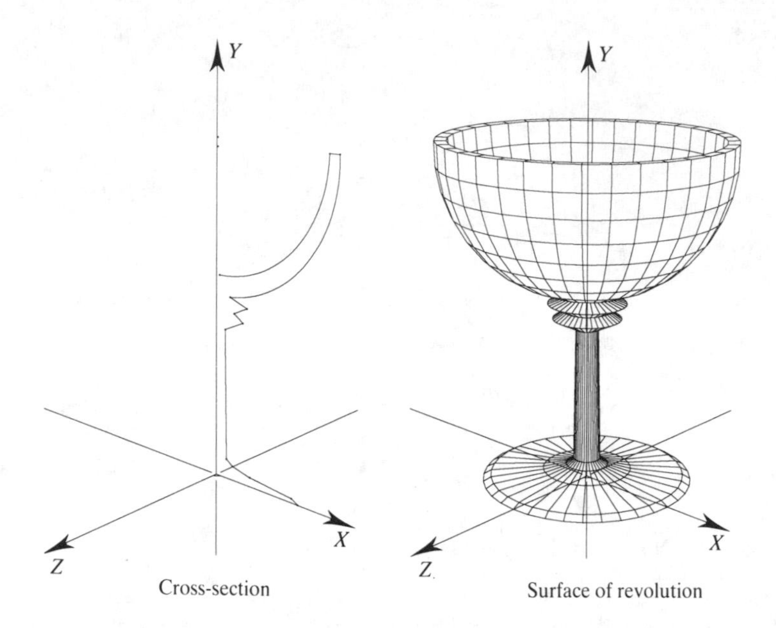

Figure 3.7
If the cross-section is rotated about the *y*-axis in small angular increments, a polygonal surface can be constructed which eventually forms a continuous surface of revolution.

quite large polygons, yet the handle on a door, the form of a telephone and the shape of a flower are collections of complex surfaces that defy an analytic mathematical solution. In computer graphics such shapes are classified as free-form surfaces.

A variety of techniques are available to construct such surfaces, from the use of 3-D digitizers to parametric patches, and many of the techniques only work with a particular type of object. Some of these techniques are described in Chapter 9 which deals with the particular problems of modelling and animation. However, as parametric surface patches have become a universal modelling scheme they will be included in this section.

The design philosophy behind modelling with surface patches is based upon the fact that it would be difficult, if not impossible, to identify the equations describing the surface geometry of a teapot or an apple. However, the problem is greatly simplified if the surface is divided into small areas that individually have a simple geometric solution. This surface patch approach may simplify the initial overwhelming complexity, but it introduces another problem concerning the joins between the patches. For whatever technique is used, the joins have to be invisible to the eye, otherwise there is no point in using them.

We do not always need to visually inspect whether a surface is marked with a join, just sweeping one's hand over a surface quickly reveals any slight discontinuity in the geometry. However, if one's car body has been remodelled by an accident, a quick visual test quickly reveals whether the panel beater has managed to restore the metalwork to its former

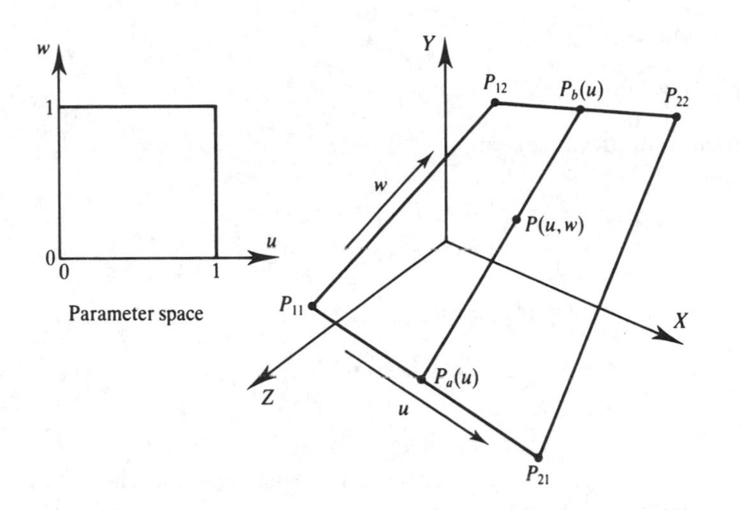

Figure 3.8
The parameter space diagram shows that parameters u and w vary between 0 and 1 and are associated with the bilinear interpolation of the points P_{11}, P_{21}, P_{12} and P_{22}. $P_a(u)$ and $P_b(u)$ are points on two opposite edges, and $P(u, w)$ is a linear interpolation between them.

pristine condition simply by moving one's head and watching how the reflections travel over the repaired area. What we are detecting are changes in the slope of the surface. Therefore if patches are to be positioned against one another, slope continuity must be preserved at these boundaries. For those readers not familiar with the ideas behind 2-D parametric curves, these are covered in Section 7.4.1 which introduces the ideas of Bézier curves.

3.2.5 Bilinear surfaces

Before we embark upon Bézier surface patches, let us first consider the idea of blending together coordinates using linear interpolation. Imagine that we have been given four points in 3-D space as shown in Figure 3.8, and our task is to derive a linear function which identifies any point contained within this patch boundary. First a parameter space diagram is constructed, also shown in the same figure, which relates two parameters u and w with the patch points. Now a linear function which blends together the points P_{11} and P_{21} is expressed as:

$$P_a(u) = (1 - u)P_{11} + uP_{21}$$

where $P_a(u)$ is any point on the line $\{P_{11}, P_{21}\}$.

A similar function for the points P_{12} and P_{22} is:

$$P_b(u) = (1 - u)P_{12} + uP_{22}$$

where $P_b(u)$ is any point on the line $\{P_{12}, P_{22}\}$. The points $P_a(u)$ and $P_b(u)$ can in turn be linearly blended using the second parameter w and the expression:

$$P(u, w) = (1 - w)P_a(u) + wP_b(u)$$

which expands to:

$$P(u,w) = (1-u)(1-w)P_{11} + u(1-w)P_{21} + (1-u)wP_{12} + uwP_{22}$$

which has a matrix form as:

$$P(u,w) = [(1-u)u]\begin{bmatrix} P_{11} & P_{12} \\ P_{21} & P_{22} \end{bmatrix}\begin{bmatrix} (1-w) \\ w \end{bmatrix}$$

Even this can be rearranged to:

$$P(u,w) = [u \quad 1]\begin{bmatrix} -1 & 1 \\ 1 & 0 \end{bmatrix}\begin{bmatrix} P_{11} & P_{12} \\ P_{21} & P_{22} \end{bmatrix}\begin{bmatrix} -1 & 1 \\ 1 & 0 \end{bmatrix}\begin{bmatrix} w \\ 1 \end{bmatrix}$$

It is left to the reader to explore this relationship, where by selecting different values of u and w within the range 0 to 1, the x-, y- and z-coordinates of $P(u, w)$ can be evaluated by substituting the corresponding coordinates for P_{11}, P_{21}, P_{12} and P_{22}.

3.2.6 Ruled surfaces

A ruled surface is developed from a family of straight lines. For example, if we took two rods and fixed them apart in space, we could lace them together with tight pieces of cord which would form a ruled surface. Familiar examples of ruled surfaces are found on cylinders and cones.

The shapes forming the surface need not be straight – they can take on any form. One end might be straight, whilst the other forms a semicircle. The important feature is that points on the two shapes are connected with straight lines.

A convenient method for creating such surfaces is to use a parametric approach where two parametric curves form the boundary shapes, which are then linearly interpolated. As an example, consider the parametric expressions described in Section 7.4.1 for developing a Bézier quadratic curve. If the function $B(1, w)$ computes a 3-D Bézier curve from the control points P_{11}, P_{12}, and P_{13}, and the function $B(2, w)$ computes a similar Bézier curve from the control points P_{21}, P_{22}, and P_{23}, then the ruled surface can be defined as:

$$P(u,w) = (1-u)B(1,w) + uB(2,w)$$

where $0 \leqslant u \leqslant 1$ and $0 \leqslant w \leqslant 1$.

By selecting values for w the corresponding points on the two Bézier curves can be computed. These in turn can then be used to identify points along a connecting line by selecting suitable values for u, as shown in Figure 3.9.

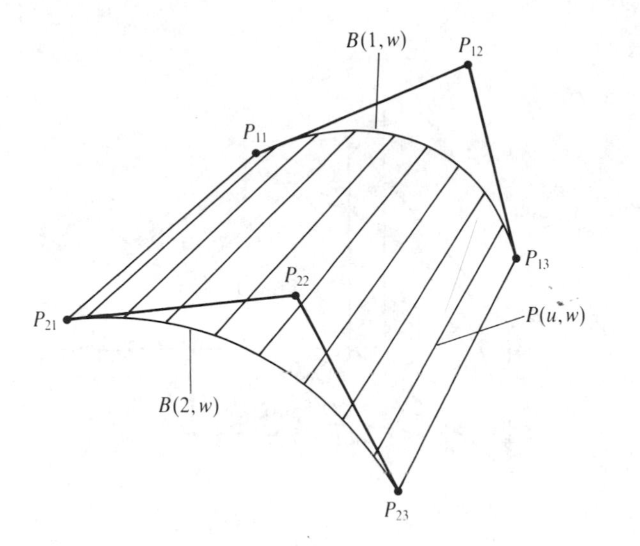

Figure 3.9
This lofted surface is formed from two quadratic Bézier curves. If $B(1, w)$ and $B(2, w)$ are the two Bézier functions, then they can be linearly interpolated to create any point $P(u, w)$.

3.2.7 Bézier surface patches

Section 7.4.1 introduces the geometry of Bézier curves and describes how such curves are computed with the aid of functions that, when supplied with a parameter, provide explicit positions of points on the curve. These positions are based upon the location of certain control points, which in the case of a quadratic curve is three, and for a cubic curve is four. Figure 3.10 illustrates two such curves.

To construct a quadratic Bézier surface patch, nine control points are needed in the form of a 3 × 3 matrix. Any point on the associated Bézier surface can be calculated by specifying the values of two parameters that vary over the range 0 to 1. If these parameters are labelled u and w,

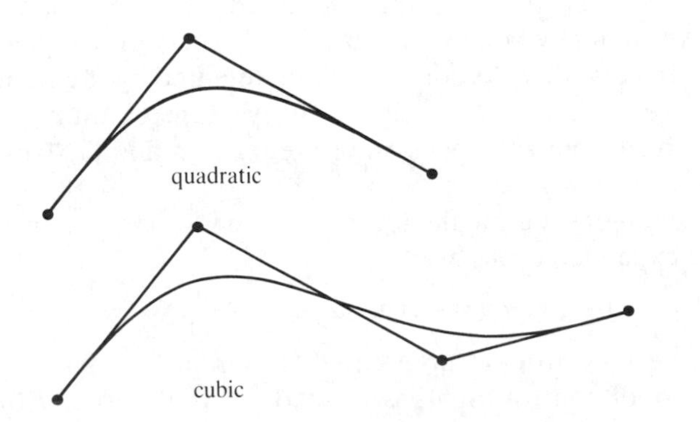

Figure 3.10
These two Bézier curves require three control points for a quadratic curve and four control points for a cubic curve.

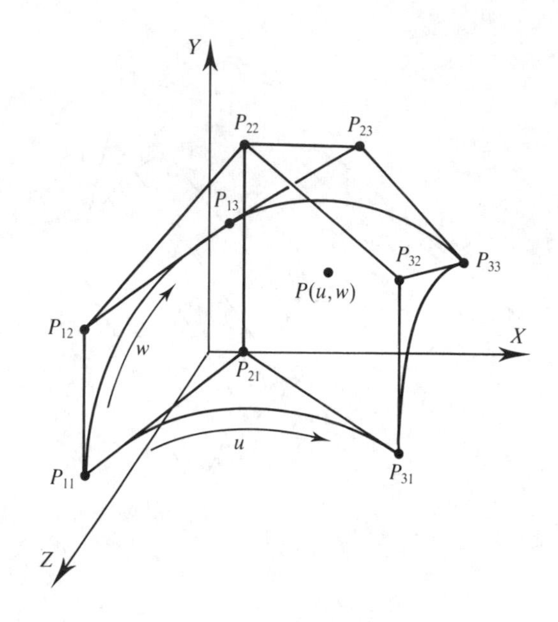

Figure 3.11
This diagram illustrates the nine control points used to develop a quadratic Bézier surface patch which touches the four corner points P_{11}, P_{31}, P_{13} and P_{33}. Any point $P(u, w)$, where the parameters u and w vary between 0 and 1, can be derived by evaluating the matrix operations described in the text.

and the control points referenced as shown in Figure 3.11, then any point $P(u, w)$ can be found by evaluating the x-, y- and z-components of the control points as follows:

$$P(u,w) = [(1-u)^2 \; 2u(1-u) \; u^2] \begin{bmatrix} P_{11} & P_{12} & P_{13} \\ P_{21} & P_{22} & P_{23} \\ P_{31} & P_{32} & P_{33} \end{bmatrix} \begin{bmatrix} (1-w)^2 \\ 2w(1-w) \\ w^2 \end{bmatrix}$$

or re-arranged as:

$$P(u,w) = [u^2 \; u \; 1] \begin{bmatrix} 1 & -2 & 1 \\ -2 & 2 & 0 \\ 1 & 0 & 0 \end{bmatrix} \begin{bmatrix} P_{11} & P_{12} & P_{13} \\ P_{21} & P_{22} & P_{23} \\ P_{31} & P_{32} & P_{33} \end{bmatrix} \begin{bmatrix} 1 & -2 & 1 \\ -2 & 2 & 0 \\ 1 & 0 & 0 \end{bmatrix} \begin{bmatrix} w^2 \\ w \\ 1 \end{bmatrix}$$

Table 3.1 illustrates how $P(u, w)$ is computed for certain values of u and w where we see that any point on a quadratic Bézier surface patch is derived from summing together the control points weighted by the terms generated by the above matrices; the weights always sum to unity as they were initially derived from an expansion of the terms u and $(1 - u)$, which also sum to unity.

If instead of squaring the terms for a quadratic relationship, they are cubed, the expanded terms are:

$$(1-u)^3, (1-u)^2 3u, (1-u)3u^2, u^3$$

which can be used to develop a cubic Bézier surface patch. This time a 4×4 matrix of control points is needed, and any point $P(u, w)$ can be

Table 3.1

u	w	P_{11}	P_{21}	P_{31}	P_{12}	P_{22}	P_{32}	P_{13}	P_{23}	P_{33}
0.0	0.0	1	0	0	0	0	0	0	0	0
1.0	0.0	0	0	1	0	0	0	0	0	0
0.0	1.0	0	0	0	0	0	0	1	0	0
1.0	1.0	0	0	0	0	0	0	0	0	1
0.5	0.0	1/4	1/2	1/4	0	0	0	0	0	0
0.0	0.5	1/4	0	0	1/2	0	0	1/4	0	0
1.0	0.5	0	0	1/4	0	0	1/2	0	0	1/4
0.5	1.0	0	0	0	0	0	0	1/4	1/2	1/4
0.5	0.5	1/16	1/8	1/16	1/8	1/4	1/8	1/16	1/8	1/16

found by evaluating the x-, y- and z-coordinates of the control points as follows:

$$P(u,w) = [(1-u)^3 \; 3u(1-u)^2 \; 3u^2(1-u) \; u^3] \begin{bmatrix} P_{11} & P_{12} & P_{13} & P_{14} \\ P_{21} & P_{22} & P_{23} & P_{24} \\ P_{31} & P_{32} & P_{33} & P_{34} \\ P_{41} & P_{42} & P_{43} & P_{44} \end{bmatrix} \begin{bmatrix} (1-w)^3 \\ 3w(1-w)^2 \\ 3w^2(1-w) \\ w^3 \end{bmatrix}$$

This again can be re-arranged as:

$$P(u,w) = [u^3 \; u^2 \; u \; 1] \begin{bmatrix} -1 & 3 & -3 & 1 \\ 3 & -6 & 3 & 0 \\ -3 & 3 & 0 & 0 \\ 1 & 0 & 0 & 0 \end{bmatrix} \begin{bmatrix} P_{11} & P_{12} & P_{13} & P_{14} \\ P_{21} & P_{22} & P_{23} & P_{24} \\ P_{31} & P_{32} & P_{33} & P_{34} \\ P_{41} & P_{42} & P_{43} & P_{44} \end{bmatrix} \begin{bmatrix} -1 & 3 & -3 & 1 \\ 3 & -6 & 3 & 0 \\ -3 & 3 & 0 & 0 \\ 1 & 0 & 0 & 0 \end{bmatrix} \begin{bmatrix} w^3 \\ w^2 \\ w \\ 1 \end{bmatrix}$$

Thus with only nine control points for a quadratic blend, and 16 for a cubic blend, one can define a continuous patch of space whose geometry can be modified by adjusting one or more of the control points. This is a powerful modelling tool – nevertheless, remember that a patch approach will only function if the slope continuity can be preserved from one patch to another.

Although it is not very difficult to imagine an undulating surface, measuring its slope in three dimensions is another thing, therefore it might be useful to return to 2-D Bézier curves to see how the characteristic of slope can be defined.

Consider, then, the quadratic Bézier curves illustrated in Figure 3.12. It can be shown that the slope of the curve at P_1 is equal to the slope of the first span P_1 to P_2, and the slope of the curve at P_3 is equal to the slope of the last span P_2 to P_3. Therefore, to maintain slope continuity across two Bézier curve segments, one must ensure that the slope of the trailing control point span matches the leading control point span of the

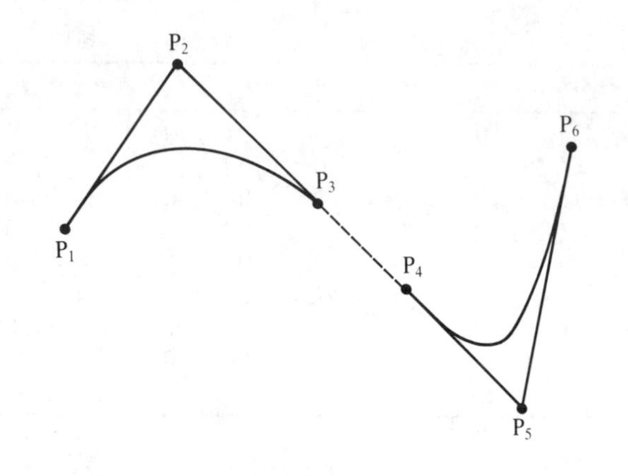

Figure 3.12
It can be shown that the slope of the curve at P_1 is equal to the slope of the line $\{P_1, P_2\}$. Similarly, at P_3 the slope is equal to the slope of the line $\{P_2, P_3\}$. For slope continuity to be preserved across the two curve segments, the slope of $\{P_2, P_3\}$ must equal the slope of $\{P_4, P_5\}$.

second curve. Similarly, it can be shown that in three dimensions slope continuity across surface patches can be maintained if:

(1) the control points at the boundary between the two patches are identical, and

(2) the polygons formed by the control points at the boundary edge are coplanar for both patches.

These conditions are shown in Figure 3.13 for two bicubic Bézier surface patches.

To construct a surface built from a patchwork of Bézier surface patches, one is required to identify the number and position of the patches and adjust the control points until the required surface is achieved. This sounds to be a visually complex task, and it is, but with the aid of a graphics workstation and the right modelling tools, it becomes relatively easy.

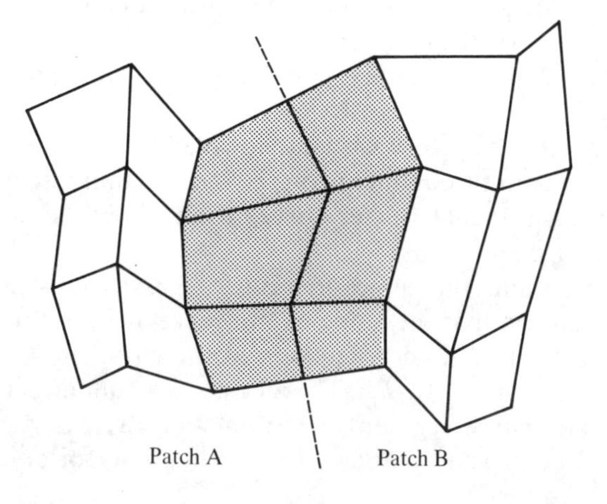

Figure 3.13
To guarantee that the slope continuity is maintained across patches *A* and *B*, the boundary vertices must be coincident and the shaded polygons coplanar. For first-order slope changes, the centre two polygons need not be planar.

A modern workstation is now capable of providing real-time manipulation of the 3-D control points, and it is also capable of displaying the associated Bézier curves, so that when a control point is moved the Bézier curve is immediately computed and redrawn.

As a final example, take the case of modelling a sphere from cubic Bézier surface patches – this can be achieved with eight patches, where one patch is used to model one octant of the sphere. There is, however, a slight problem concerning accuracy, for the cubic Bézier patch as described is unable to precisely match the geometry of the sphere; there is a small error well below 0.1%. If this cannot be tolerated then another type of Bézier surface patch called a rational Bézier can be employed, which matches the sphere's geometry precisely.

3.2.8 Coons bicubic surface patches

A Coons bicubic surface patch employs cubic blending functions for developing surface geometry. These blending functions are covered in Section 7.3.2 where they are described in an animation context. Basically, given two values N_1 and N_2, and corresponding rates of change S_1 and S_2, a blended value $N(t)$ can be computed from:

$$N(t) = [t^3 \quad t^2 \quad t \quad 1] \begin{bmatrix} 2 & -2 & 1 & 1 \\ -3 & 3 & -2 & -1 \\ 0 & 0 & 1 & 0 \\ 1 & 0 & 0 & 0 \end{bmatrix} \begin{bmatrix} N_1 \\ N_2 \\ S_1 \\ S_2 \end{bmatrix}$$

where $0 \leqslant t \leqslant 1$.

However, this technique can also be developed to compute points on a 3-D surface patch as follows:

$$Q(u, w) = [U]\ [C]\ [P]\ [C]^{\mathrm{T}}\ [W]^{\mathrm{T}}$$

(Note: $[C]^{\mathrm{T}}$ is the transpose of $[C]$ which changes every element $C_{row,col}$ into $C_{col,row}$.)

where

$$[U] = [u^3 \quad u^2 \quad u \quad 1]$$

$$[C] = \begin{bmatrix} 2 & -2 & 1 & 1 \\ -3 & 3 & -2 & -1 \\ 0 & 0 & 1 & 0 \\ 1 & 0 & 0 & 0 \end{bmatrix}$$

$$[C]^{\mathrm{T}} = \begin{bmatrix} 2 & -3 & 0 & 1 \\ -2 & 3 & 0 & 0 \\ 1 & -2 & 1 & 0 \\ 1 & -1 & 0 & 0 \end{bmatrix}$$

$$[W] = [w^3 \quad w^2 \quad w \quad 1]$$

$$[P] = \begin{bmatrix} P(0,0) & P(0,1) & P_w(0,0) & P_w(0,1) \\ P(1,0) & P(1,1) & P_w(1,0) & P_w(1,1) \\ P_u(0,0) & P_u(0,1) & P_{uw}(0,0) & P_{uw}(0,1) \\ P_u(1,0) & P_u(1,1) & P_{uw}(1,0) & P_{uw}(1,1) \end{bmatrix}$$

The elements of the last matrix need some explanation. The four terms in the top left-hand corner are position vectors storing the coordinates of the four vertices of the surface patch. The four terms in the top right-hand corner are the slopes of the patch corners with respect to the parameter w, and the four terms in the lower left-hand corner are the slopes of the patch corners with respect to the parameter u. The four terms in the lower right-hand corner are called the twist vectors, which control the propagation of the corner slopes into the rest of the patch. Effectively, the twist vectors force the surface patch to become more convex or concave, whilst preserving the corner tangents.

The Bézier patch requires the positions of control points to manipulate the geometry of the surface, but the Coons patch requires that this is achieved by adjusting the tangents at the four corners, together with selecting suitable values for the twist vectors.

3.2.9 B-spline surface patches

In Section 3.2.7 we saw how a matrix of control points can be used to define a 3-D Bézier surface patch, and if any one of these points is modified, then the entire patch surface is disturbed. The reason for this global disturbance stems from the Bézier algorithm calculating the coordinates of any surface point from varying proportions of all the control points. However, if the algorithm is modified to cater for any size matrix of control points, and only references those points that are necessary to compute the associated surface portion, then the B-spline algorithm is created. A consequence of this modification is that whereas the Bézier algorithm employs a parameter varying between 0 and 1, the B-spline algorithm requires a string of parameter values determined by the number of control points and the type of curve – i.e. whether it is quadratic, cubic or quartic. These parameter values are called a knot vector.

The knot vector values also influence the nature of the surface, as they are used in the algorithm to vary the influence a control point has on the final geometry. If the knot values are spaced equally, then the algorithm will employ them accordingly, and if the values have an irregular or non-uniform spacing, the influence of the control points is modified and results in the surface being pushed and pulled locally.

Another useful feature of the B-spline approach is that knot vector values can be repeated – this has the effect of emphasizing the existence of a control point, which is useful for forming cusps. A control point can even be repeated a number of times, which also pulls the curve towards it.

Just as the Bézier algorithm has a rational form, the B-spline too can be represented as a ratio of two polynomials; this allows B-splines to accurately construct arcs and complete circles. The success of B-splines has now resulted in some workstation manufacturers incorporating these algorithms at a very low level in the machine's architecture. And to ensure that these systems have the greatest flexibility, the B-spline algorithm is implemented to cater for the non-uniform spacing of knots, and the rational form for describing arcs and circles. Such B-splines are known as non-uniform rational B-splines (NURBS).

The main design advantage of B-splines is that when a control point is moved it only influences the local portion of the curve sensitive to the cluster of points containing this point. This is a useful feature when designing complex shapes, and is best undertaken with the aid of a high-performance workstation capable of displaying B-spline curves in real-time.

Patches can be further shaped by cutting away specified portions; the shape of this surface can also be a spline, and such surfaces are called 'trimmed surfaces'. Most commercial CAD systems employ trimmed surfaces as they are a vital modelling strategy, especially for the automotive industry in the design of car bodies

3.3 Volumetric representation

As mentioned earlier in this chapter, volumetric modelling schemes construct objects from a set of 3-D primitive volumes rather than attempt to create a boundary skin to enclose a desired volume. The two major approaches are constructive solid geometry (CSG) and spatial subdivision schemes. The latter technique does have limited applications in commercial computer animation, although it is becoming increasingly important as a fundamental technique in scientific and medical visualization.

A consequence of these alternative schemes is that they influence the algorithms needed to generate the final image, and the range of animation effects that are possible. First, let us examine the ideas behind CSG.

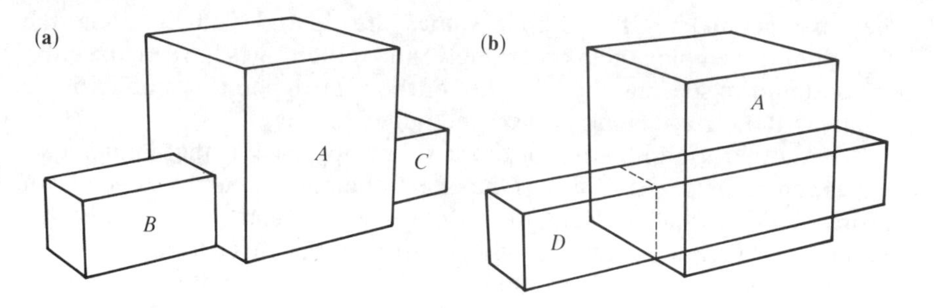

Figure 3.14
This structure could be imagined to be built from three blocks *A*, *B* and *C*. But if *B* has the same dimensions as *C*, then the two blocks *B* and *C* can be replaced by a single block *D*. In a CSG environment the assembly is defined by the union of *A* and *D*.

3.3.1 Constructive solid geometry

Constructive solid geometry or set-theoretic modelling (an alternative name) attempts to build an object from a small set of 3-D forms such as a box, sphere, cylinder, cone, torus and a helix. This might appear to be an impossible task, and in some applications it is, as it would be impractical to model a human face using this technique. Therefore, in general, it is only used for building scenes that have an inherent geometric form. For example, certain mechanical components such as a car engine's piston, a cylinder head, or various architectural structures are candidates for a CSG representation.

One of the unusual features of this technique is the ability to add and subtract volumes, and also to identify a volume of space that is shared by two intersecting primitives. Let us start by examining the union operation which effectively combines two objects together.

For example, say we needed to build the object shown in Figure 3.14a. We can see that it consists of three block elements A, B and C, but if B and C are identical, then perhaps the object can be imagined to consist of two intersecting blocks A and D, as illustrated in Figure 3.14b. Using the notation of CSG, the final object is constructed from the union of A and D as shown in the tree diagram in Figure 3.15.

As another example, consider the object shown in Figure 3.16a – basically it is a block containing a hole. This can be defined using the difference operation which effectively subtracts one volume from another, and is shown in Figure 3.16b together with its tree diagram.

Finally, the intersection operation identifies the volume shared by two intersecting objects. Figure 3.17a illustrates an object which can be specified by the common space shared by the two objects A and B in Figure 3.17b. It is left to the reader to investigate how more complex structures can be built using the union, intersection and difference operations.

The above scheme seems to be powerful, and it is, yet in order for it to work, a mechanism is needed to implement it within a computer environment, which is where geometry and mathematics come in.

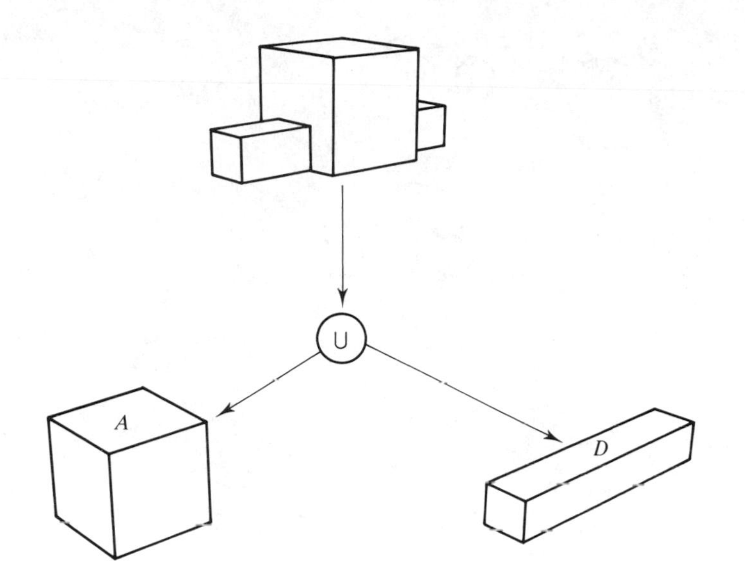

Figure 3.15
Using CSG, the top object can be defined as the union (U) of the two blocks *A* and *D*.

(a)

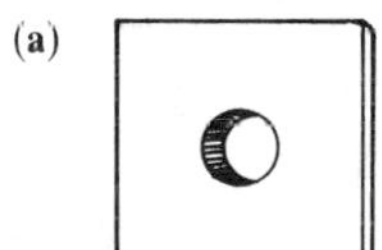

(b)

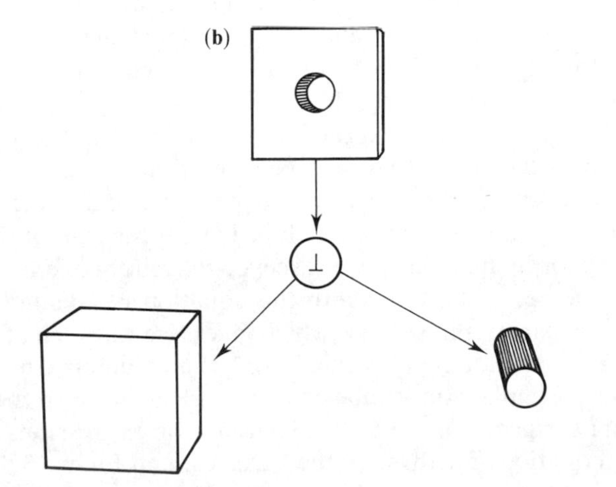

Figure 3.16
(a) A CSG definition for the block containing a hole is a cylinder *B* subtracted from the cuboid *A*, and is represented by the difference operation.
(b) The difference operation is shown as a Boolean tree structure.

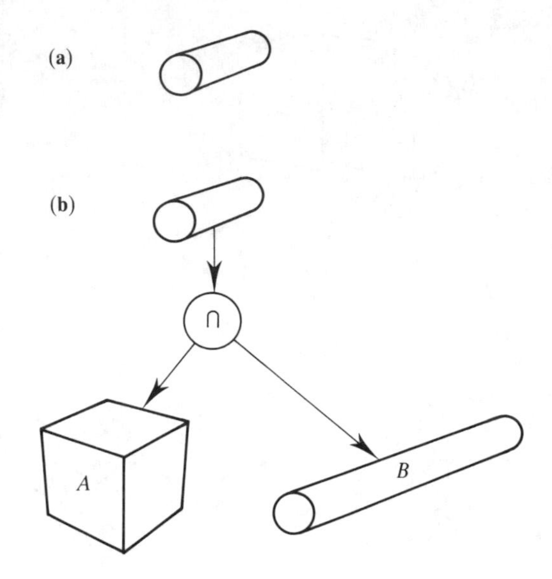

Figure 3.17
(a) The short cylinder can be formed by trimming a longer cylinder with a cube; this effectively identifies the volume of intersection. (b) The intersection operation is shown as a Boolean tree structure.

Although there is an equation for a sphere, there is no equivalent equation for a box; however, it is possible to derive one from other equations. Consider the equation for a plane:

$$ax + by + cz + d = 0$$

If specific values are chosen for a, b, c and d such as:

$$a = 0, b = 0, c = 1 \text{ and } d = 0,$$

then the equation becomes:

$$0x + 0y + z = 0$$

There are an infinite number of points that satisfy this equation, and no matter what the values of x and y are, z must always be zero. Geometrically, this equation defines a planar surface coincident with the x- and y-axes where $z = 0$, as shown in Figure 3.18.

If we investigate the expression on the left-hand side of the equation, once more we notice that, irrespective of the values of x and y, if the value of z is positive, the expression is positive, and if the value of z is negative, the expression is negative. Plotting out the sign of the expression for various coordinate values, we discover that the space is partitioned in two by the plane, separated where the equation is satisfied. Figure 3.18 illustrates this partitioning effect, which gives rise to two half-spaces. CSG exploits space partitioning for constructing the volumetric primitives.

As an example, a unit cube can be constructed from the intersection of six planar surfaces. Figure 3.19a illustrates the expressions derived from the planar equations for three of the surfaces, and Figure 3.19b illustrates

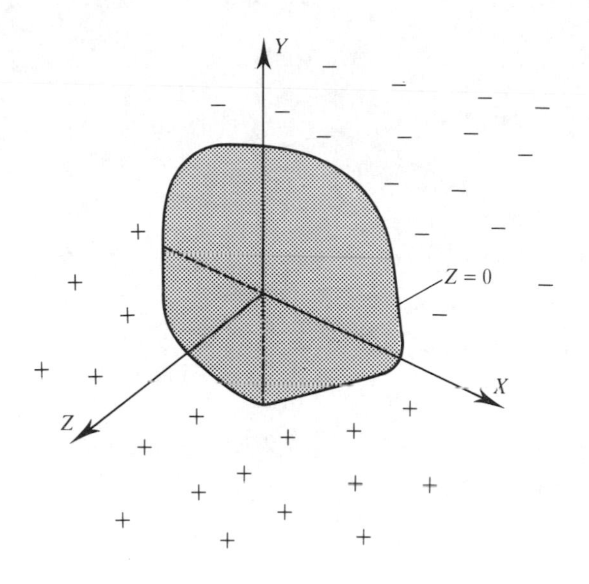

Figure 3.18
This surface is described by the equation $0x + 0y + z = 0$, which is only satisfied when $z = 0$. The plane effectively divides space into two half spaces.

the other three surfaces. Notice that the expressions have been arranged such that their positive half-space is inside the cube's volume. Any point (x, y, z) will be inside or on the cube's surface if all six expressions provide a zero or positive value:

$$
\begin{aligned}
0x + 0y + z &\geqslant 0 \\
0x + y + 0z &\geqslant 0 \\
x + 0y + 0z &\geqslant 0 \\
0x - y + 0z + 1 &\geqslant 0 \\
-x + 0y + 0z + 1 &\geqslant 0 \\
0x + 0y - z + 1 &\geqslant 0
\end{aligned}
$$

For example, let us substitute the point $(1, 1, 1)$ (which is a vertex of the cube) in the above expressions. Evaluating them produces: 1, 1, 1, 0, 0, 0 which are zero or positive, confirming that the point is not inside. However, the point $(2, 1, 1)$, which is outside the cube, produces values: 1, 1, 2, 0, -1, 0 which contains a negative value, confirming that the point is outside. A renderer can now exploit this effect to identify points that lie on the object's surface.

Another powerful feature of CSG modelling schemes relates to the ability to examine the interior of an object (assuming that it has been modelled). This is achieved by intersecting the object with a cutting plane to divide it in two, then it would be possible to view detail that only existed on one side of this surface. This lends itself to an animation effect whereby a journey can be taken through the object revealing its changing cross-sectional detail.

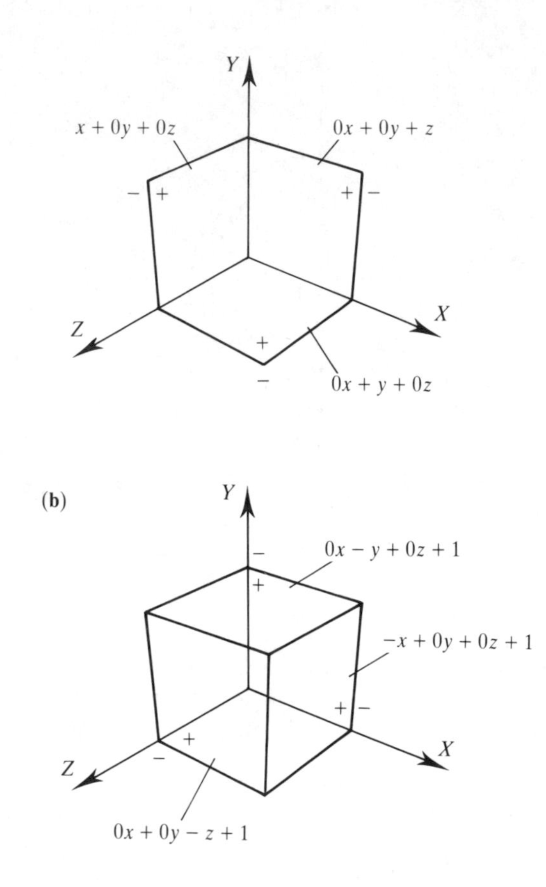

Figure 3.19

The three expressions in (a) are positive for all points having positive coordinate values, while the expressions in (b) are positive for all coordinate values lower than 1. The six expressions can be used to identify whether a point is in the interior or the exterior of the cube.

In this brief description of CSG the reader may gain the impression that there are severe limitations on the structures it can model, but the work of William Latham (Latham, 1989) clearly demonstrates that CSG is very flexible, and capable of modelling artefacts that other schemes would find extremely difficult.

3.3.2 Spatial subdivision

Spatial subdivision modelling algorithms attempt to construct 3-D objects from a family of nested box volumes or from a volume of space divided into voxels. For example, the cube of space illustrated in Figure 3.20 can be divided into eight smaller cubes which in turn can be divided into another eight, without any real limit. Such a spatial division can be represented by a tree diagram as shown in the same illustration, which also identifies the volumes with numbers. The tree diagram, which is known as an octree, is used to describe the object's geometry by recording those space divisions that are totally occupied by the object or are further divided.

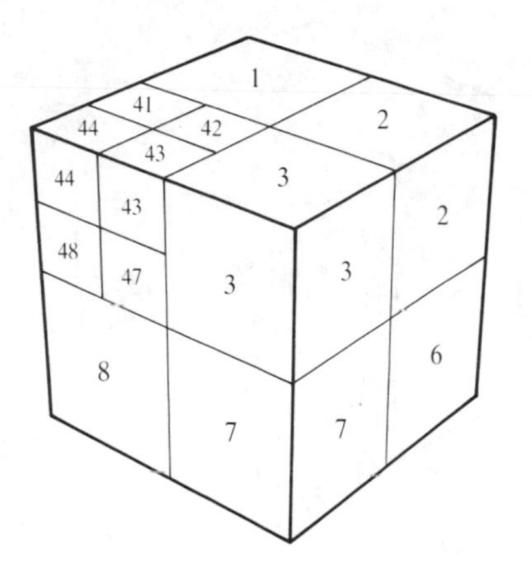

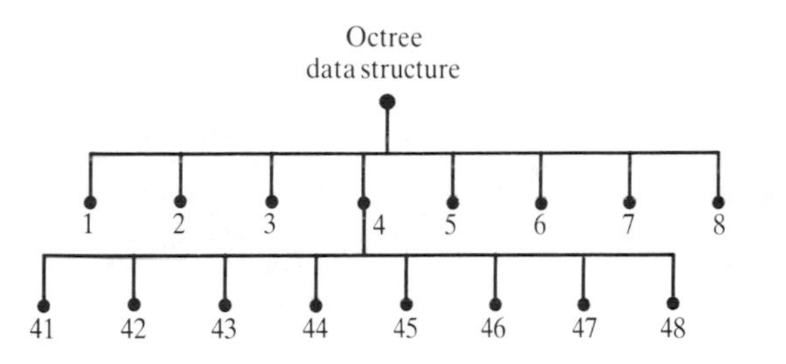

Figure 3.20

A cube can be partitioned into eight sub-cubes, which in turn can be divided into smaller cubes. This is the octree subdivision scheme for 3-D modelling and can be extended to any depth of subdivision. The data structure is represented by a tree which records the status of each cube in terms of whether the octree element is full or empty.

Figure 3.21 illustrates how a simple block object can be represented by an octree. The finer the detail becomes, the deeper the tree becomes, which raises important questions concerning complexity and memory storage. However, the scheme is still relatively young and open to further research.

The other space partitioning scheme assumes that a volume of space is divided into a number of volume elements called voxels, the 3-D equivalent of a pixel. These volumes are of identical size and can be in one of two states – they are either full or empty, there is no intermediate level.

Voxel schemes have proved very useful in the 3-D representation of structures that have been scanned with the aid of a CT scanner as used in medical diagnosis. Each voxel is assigned a value representing the type of material it encodes (for example, bone, flesh or fat) and, with the aid of special shading programs, images can be generated depicting internal views of the volume. A very powerful visualization tool for surgeons is created when certain classes of voxels are made transparent and others opaque; this enables only the bone structure to be revealed. Animated sequences of

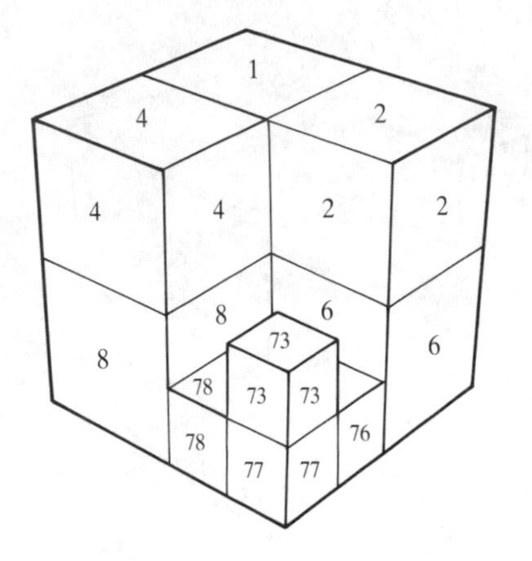

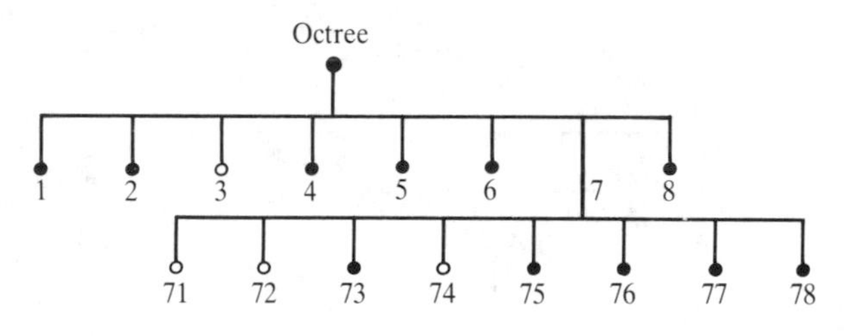

Figure 3.21
This object can be represented by the octree which identifies those volume elements that are full or empty.

voxel data sets are very useful in medical teaching as they provide an accurate insight into the internal structure of the human body without undertaking surgery.

3.4 Procedural modelling

So far we have examined the standard techniques for representing objects that are a part of our everyday lives, such as cars, tables, buildings, teapots and flying logos. However, there are many other things that will cause problems if we attempt to model them from polygons, patches or voxels. For instance, how can we model snow and rain? And what about modelling and animating waves breaking on a sandy beach? And what about mountains, trees, hair, fire, mist and electric fields? The list is endless, and finding modelling schemes capable of describing such phenomena will keep computer graphic researchers busy for many years to come. However, there are some other schemes worth examining just so that they can be identified, and later we will apply them to specific applications and explore the ramifications in an animation environment.

Procedural modelling encompasses a class of techniques that involve a computer procedure to compute the geometry of some form. For example, if we want to model a mountain it is obviously going to be impossible to precisely describe every ridge, cliff and valley. Furthermore, it is totally out of the question to position every boulder, rock and pebble. But if we delegate these design decisions to a procedure, then this can supply us with a solution that hopefully meets our requirements. Even if it does not, the procedure can be arranged such that it will accept certain parameters that will influence its modelling behaviour. So in the following sections we will examine how procedures can be used to create fractal surfaces and soft objects.

3.4.1 Fractals

In this section, some of the essential ideas behind fractals will be reviewed to identify those concepts relevant to computer animation. Hopefully, you will then be able to pursue the subject in other texts and research papers, if you so wish.

One of the first concepts worth exploring is that of dimension. We all know and accept that our physical world appears to be three-dimensional – but what is really meant by this parameter? One answer stems from the fact that the geometric descriptions of things that exist in our universe can be described by a geometry requiring three measurements (coordinates) to fix points in space. Such a space is called Euclidean if the laws for measuring distances, areas and volumes are linear. This does not seem to be the case when very large distances are involved, especially when astronomers attempt to measure and describe the gross characteristics of our universe; but for everyday measuring tasks, our immediate space seems to be three-dimensional and linear.

Another important concept to the world of fractals is that of self-similarity. This is a property belonging to some shapes which, when magnified, appear to reveal the same detail found in the original shape. A winter snowflake pattern is a good example: its crinkled edges also appear to consist of similar crinkles when scaled under a magnifying glass. However, these similar crinkles stop appearing as the magnification power is increased. One quickly leaves the gross detail of the water crystal structure behind and moves into new types of detail.

In the abstract world of mathematics virtually anything is possible. Indeed, over the centuries mathematicians have constructed a variety of imaginary forms that are only now being understood through the development of fractals. So before we look at some of these abstract concepts, let us see if there are any other familiar artefacts that possess the property of self-similarity.

One object we are all familiar with is the cube. This is self-similar as it can be constructed from eight similar cubes scaled by a factor of a half.

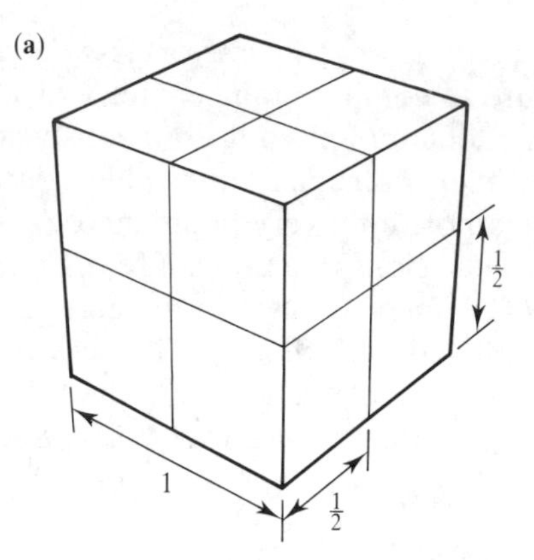

Figure 3.22
The idea of self-similarity can be demonstrated to exist in a cube, square and a line. In (a) a cube can be replaced by eight similar cubes scaled by a factor of a half. In (b), a square can be replaced by four similar squares scaled by a factor of a half; and in (c), a line can be replaced by two similar lines scaled by a factor of a half.

Figure 3.22a illustrates this relationship. What we now need is a formula to relate dimension (3) with the number of self-similar parts (8) and the scaling factor (1/2), but before this is stated, let us examine the one- and two-dimensional cases.

A square is also self-similar as it too can be described in terms of itself. Figure 3.22b shows that a square is equivalent to four self-similar squares that have been scaled by a factor of half. Once more, we would like to discover a relationship between the dimension (2), the number of self-similar parts (4) and the scaling factor (1/2).

Finally, a straight line segment is self-similar as it is equivalent to two self-similar line segments that have been scaled by a factor of a half, as shown in Figure 3.22c. Similarly, we require to discover the relationship between the dimension (1), the number of self-similar parts (2) and the scaling factor (1/2).

Now we are in a good position to find a relationship between dimension, self-similar parts and scaling factor. Table 3.2 lists the information discovered from the three examples.

Table 3.2

Dimension	Self-similar parts	Scaling factor
D	N	S
1	2	1/2
2	4	1/2
3	8	1/2

The rule linking these three parameters together is:

$$N = 1/S^D$$

where N is the number of self-similar parts, S is the scaling factor and D is the dimension. Rearranging this formula provides a definition of dimension in terms of self-similar parts and scaling factor:

$$D = \log(N)/\log(1/S)$$

This is verified by substituting $N = 8$ and $S = 1/2$, which gives $D = 3$. The reader can confirm that the other two conditions also hold. So now we have a useful way of defining dimension which, in fact, takes us into the world of fractals.

A first example of a fractal is discovered in the mathematical snowflake curve (the von Koch curve) which can be formed by replacing line segments by four similar line segments that have been suitably scaled, as shown in Figure 3.23. The scaling factor S of the replaced line segments is 1/3, while there are four similar line segments. Therefore, $S = 1/3$ and $N = 4$, which implies that:

$$D = \log(4)/\log(3) = 1.2619\ldots$$

This fractional value for dimension initially seems surprising, but remember it no longer relates to anything that physically exists in our universe; it is a mathematical construct and the term 'dimension' cannot be used to replace the original meaning of dimension which has a topological association. And to avoid this confusion it is often referred to as the 'fractal' or 'similarity dimension'. Nevertheless, although the snowflake curve is still a curve with a topological dimension of one, it has this strange property in that its fractal dimension of 1.2619... indicates that it is an entity that has both 'line' and 'area-like' qualities – it is a fractal. In fact, there exists a class of space-filling curves that have a topological dimension of one, yet have a fractal dimension of two, as the curves take up all of the available space in a plane.

There is no mathematical function that supplies the x- and y-coordinates of the snowflake curve – they have to be derived algorithmically,

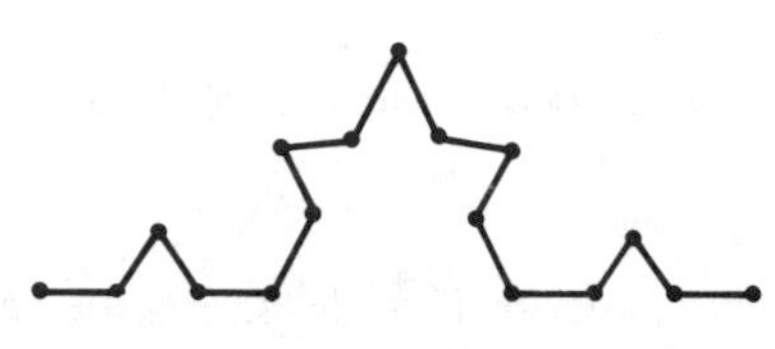

Figure 3.23

The snowflake curve can be created by replacing every line segment by four smaller segments scaled by a factor of 1/3. This makes its similarity dimension approximately 1.262.

normally in the form of a computer program. Fractals are generated by procedures, and a reasonably simple program is capable of drawing a snowflake curve to various levels of detail.

Bearing in mind that pure fractals are imaginary constructs of mathematicians, and have infinite recursive levels of detail, the only way that they can be manipulated within a computer is as an approximation. Moreover, if fractal forms appear to exist in nature they will never exhibit the precise self-similarity which is a feature of their theoretical form, therefore they are called 'statistically self-similar'. Consequently, the fractal-like shapes employed in computer graphics are necessarily 'cheats' or, as Richard Voss refers to them, 'fractal forgeries' (Voss, 1985).

Although the snowflake curve is interesting, it has limited applications in computer animation; so how useful are fractals? Well, they become extremely useful when we move to three dimensions and introduce random numbers. For example, consider the triangle shown in Figure 3.24a: this can be replaced by four smaller triangles derived from the mid-points of the original edges. They have also been displaced by a random amount which reflects the fractal dimension required in that it is proportional to the edge lengths. Thus the surface can be made as crinkly as needed by repeatedly subdividing smaller triangles into even smaller triangles. Figures 3.24b and 3.24c illustrate these stages. Figure 3.25 illustrates a fractal surface that has had certain heights set to some common value to create a pseudo-mountain and associated seascape. Once more, it is a simple exercise to develop a program that can create a fractal landscape based upon some initial height characteristics, and a similarity dimension to control the surface detail.

Another way of exploiting fractals in computer graphics is to create arrays of numbers that have been generated using a subdivision process,

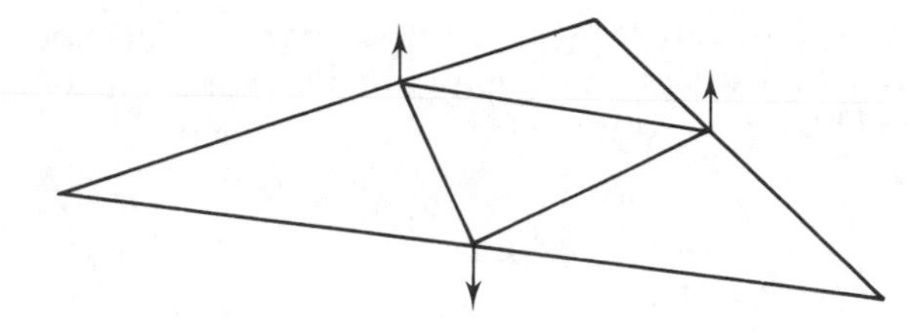

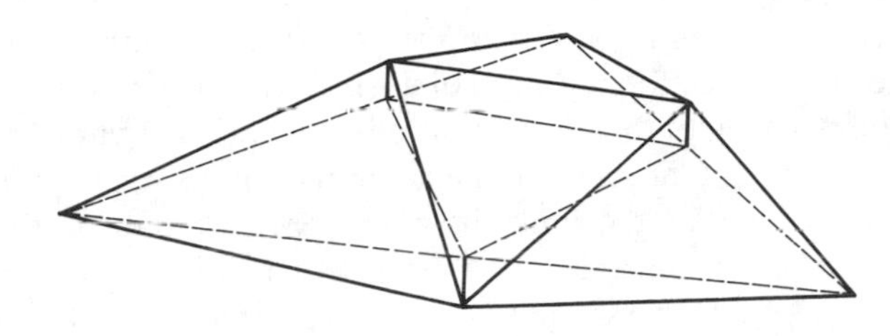

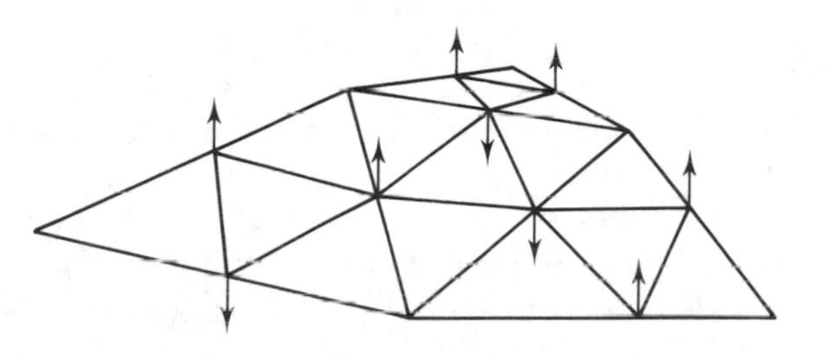

Figure 3.24
Mid-point displacement provides a useful method for creating fractal terrains by repeatedly dividing triangles into smaller triangles and introducing random off-sets proportional to the similarity dimension required.

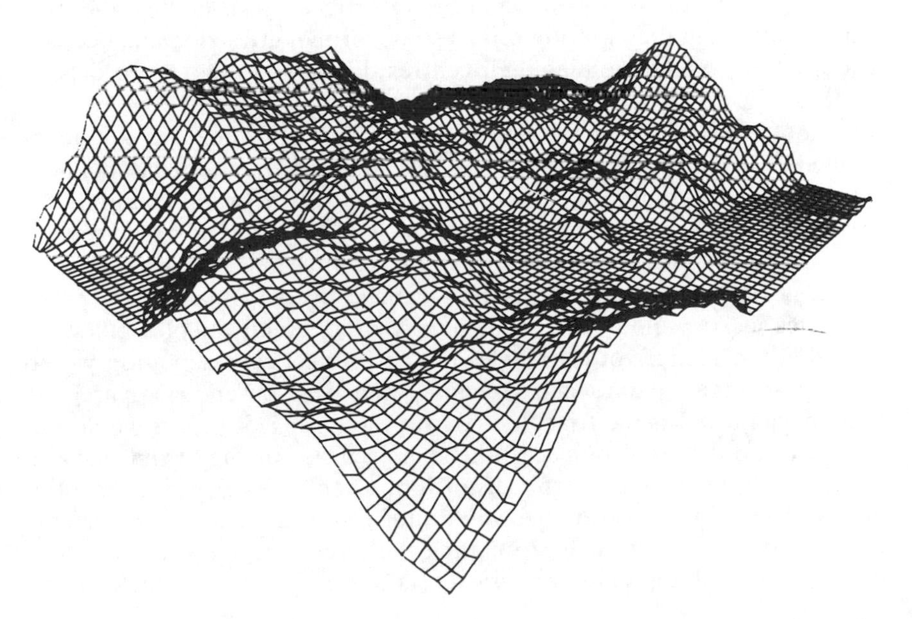

Figure 3.25
This mountain is built from a fractal mid-point division technique and has had certain height values fixed to a common level to create a seascape.

which are then used as texture maps to represent mists and clouds. Modern commercial animation systems normally provide modelling tools for creating fractal terrain, and for forming fractal texture maps.

3.4.2 Soft objects

A useful way of describing soft objects is by way of a physical example. Imagine that an electrically charged sphere is suspended from the ceiling in the middle of a room and cannot move, and we possess a meter which measures the strength of the radiated electric field. This meter can be used to plot out the strength of the electric field by placing it at various positions and taking readings. One way of performing this operation is to take measurements at points a constant distance apart, perhaps in the form of regular cubic lattice. From this 3-D matrix of readings we could plot out surfaces of constant electric strength – such 'isosurfaces' would appear as a collection of concentric spheres with high readings in the centre and lower readings as one moved away from the sphere.

If a second charged sphere is introduced, touching the first one, and the same measuring experiment repeated, one would discover a different family of isosurfaces consisting of two offset intersecting spheres. However, at the point of intersection, instead of finding a precise boundary between the spheres, one would detect a 'soft' blend where one electric potential adds to the second. If one of the spheres is slowly moved relative to the other, the original isosurface will reflect this change by appearing to stretch to maintain one continuous surface. But, at some point, the one surface will divide into two separate isosurfaces surrounding the two spheres, although they will still reflect some form of attraction and become distended along a line joining their centres. Figure 3.26 shows this experiment as 2-D cross-sections.

Soft objects do not require electric charges; they are implicitly defined by equations describing a scalar field. Such equations can define a sphere, cylinder, ellipsoid, torus and a plane which, when combined at various distances, can be used to construct a wide variety of structures.

As the isosurface is created from the additive and subtractive effects of scalar fields, the same procedure can be used to manipulate other attributes such as colour. For example, say a red, green and blue ball were placed at the vertices of a triangle, the soft object representation would initially be three separate balls (assuming they were far enough apart). As they moved towards the triangle's centre, the three isosurfaces would not only become distorted by each other's presence, but they would absorb their neighbour's colour at this distortion. Eventually, the level of influence reflected by the isosurface would move from three separate surfaces to one soft elastic surface encapsulating the three objects, with the colour distributed according to their physical relationship.

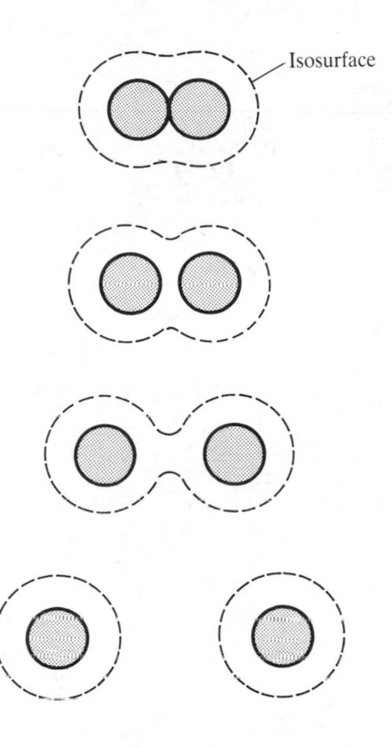

Figure 3.26
This sequence of 2-D cross-sections show how an isosurface is influenced by the relative positions of two objects. If the objects move too far apart, one single isosurface forms into two, which still reflect the existence of the other until they move far enough apart for their mutual influence to be insignificant.

This type of modelling lends itself to the animation of fluids, especially when simulating wet sticky substances, as these can be modelled by a system of spheres appropiately positioned to create one continuous bumpy isosurface. In particular, the work of Yoichiro Kawaguchi is outstanding in the use of meta-balls for creating animated, textured, dynamic structure. Bob and Geoff Wyvill have also used soft objects to model and animate a wide variety of traditional cartoon characters to develop a style that is peculiar to this approach (Wyvill, 1989). Plate 1 shows an example of soft modelling animation.

Although the term 'soft objects' has been used to describe the process of modelling from scalar fields, other terms have also been used by different researchers such as 'equipotential surfaces', 'iso-valued surfaces', 'iso-valued contour surfaces', 'isosurfaces', 'implicit surfaces', 'contour surfaces', '3D contouring' and 'meta-surfaces'.

3.4.3 Procedural manipulation

Procedural techniques can also be used to manipulate coordinate data for creating 3-D objects, and one example is found in transforming 2-D data sets into 3-D structures. Figure 3.27 shows a map of the world which when digitized is an *xy*-coordinate file but, by adding an extra *z*-coordinate where $z = 0$, is quickly turned into a 3-D planar lamina that can be

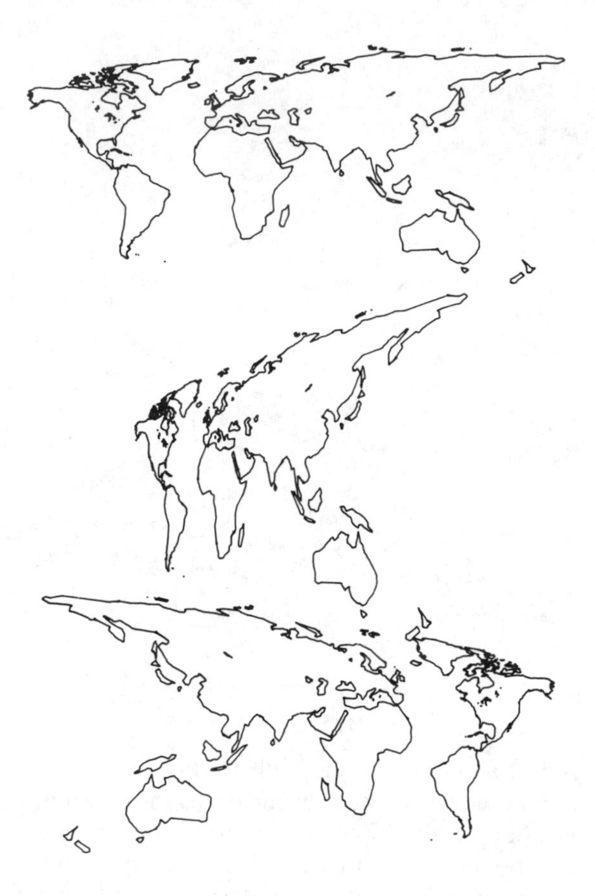

Figure 3.27

The top view shows a world map digitized as a file of 2-D coordinates. By assigning a *z*-coordinate of zero for each vertex, a 3-D lamina is created. The two lower images show the map rotated in space.

manipulated like any other 3-D object. Two such perspective views are shown in the same illustration.

Another manipulative technique is to wrap the design around some form such as a cylinder or a sphere, which are worth considering in greater depth. In the case of the cylinder, we need to define the 2-D design as a map addressed by coordinates u and v, and then find mapping functions to transform them into a point (x, y, z) on the cylinder. Given the following conditions shown in Figure 3.28 where:

r is the radius of the cylinder
h is the height of the cylinder
$0 \leqslant u \leqslant 1$
$0 \leqslant v \leqslant 1$

then the angle θ is given by:

$$\theta = 2\pi u$$

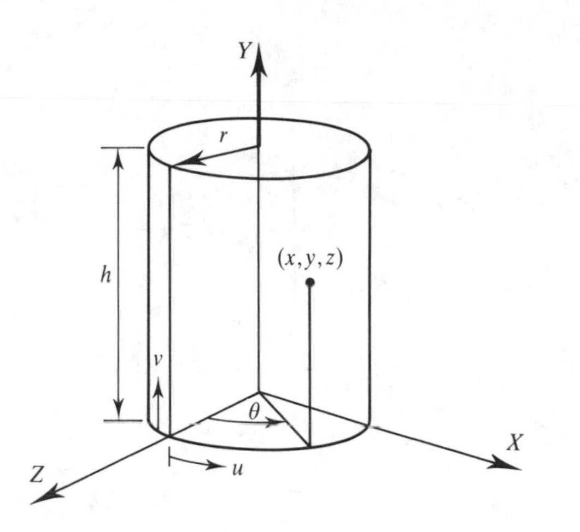

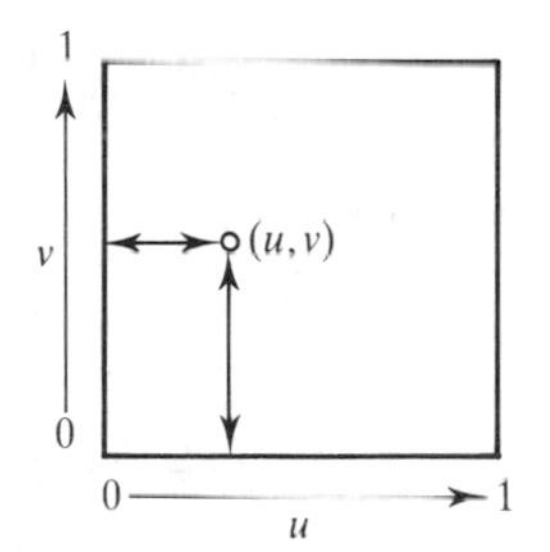

Figure 3.28
Any 2-D image addressed by coordinates (u, v) can be mapped to a point (x, y, z) on a cylinder using the functions shown in the text.

and the values of x, y, and z are:

$$x = r\sin(u), \qquad y = vh, \qquad z = r\cos(u).$$

These functions are easily verified by substituting some test values.

The other useful function maps a point (u, v) to a point (x, y, z) on a sphere. The geometry for this operation is illustrated in Figure 3.29 where a sphere of radius r has its centre located at the origin. Once more we have a 2-D map addressed by uv-coordinates where u controls the longitude, and v the latitude. The longitudinal angle θ is given by:

$$\theta = 2\pi u$$

and the angle of latitude ϕ is given by:

$$\phi = \pi(v - 0.5)$$

therefore the values of x, y, and z are:

$$x = r\sin(\theta)\cos(\phi), \qquad y = r\sin(\phi), \qquad z = r\cos(\theta)\cos(\phi).$$

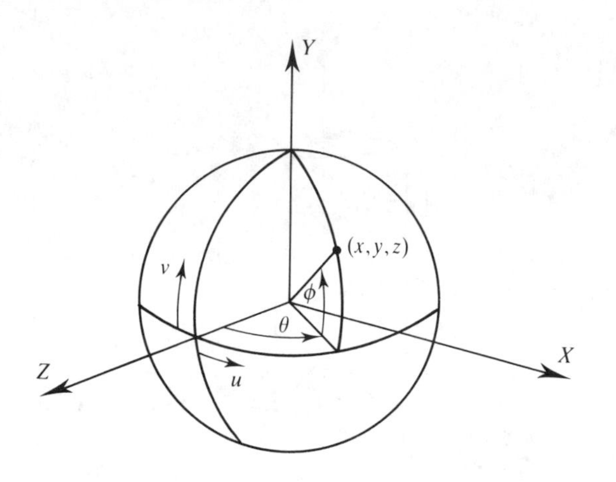

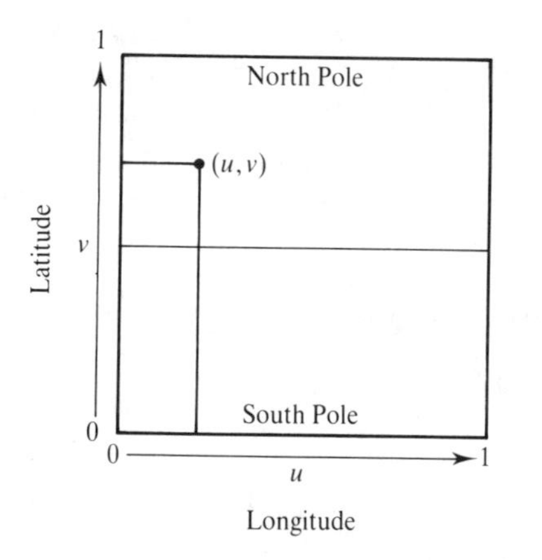

Figure 3.29
Any 2-D image addressed by coordinates (u, v) can be mapped to a point (x, y, z) on a sphere using the mapping functions shown in the text. Note that the mapping operation distorts the image as it approaches the north and south poles.

These functions can be tested with some values of u and v.

To begin with, let us examine the extremes of v. When $v = 0$ or 1, $\cos(\phi) = 0$, confirming that the north and south poles have zero x- and z-coordinates. If we now test the functions as follows:

$$u = 0.25, \quad v = 0.75, \quad r = 1.$$

the values of x, y and z are:

$$x = 0.707, \quad y = 0.707, \quad z = 0.0$$

which can be verifed visually from Figure 3.29. Another combination,

$$u = 1, \quad v = 0.25, \quad r = 1$$

produces values of x, y and z as:

$$x = 0.0, \quad y = -0.707, \quad z = 0.707$$

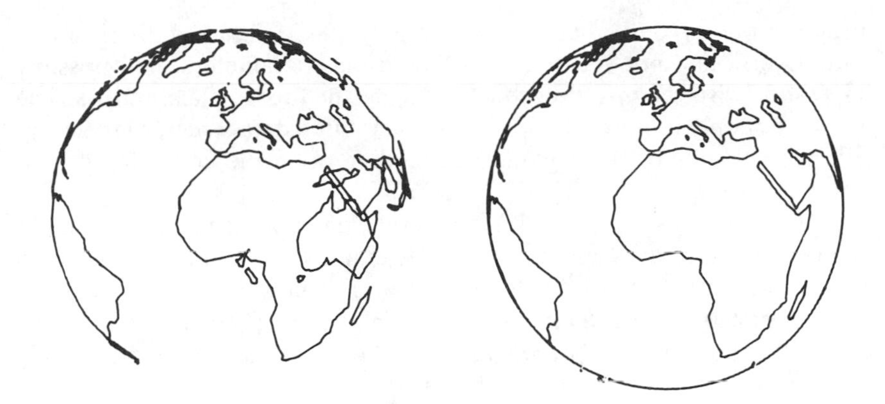

Figure 3.30
The left-hand image shows a world map after the wrapping operation, and the right-hand image shows the same map with hidden lines removed and a boundary circle drawn.

which again can be confirmed visually from Figure 3.29.

If these functions are now applied to the world map shown in Figure 3.27, we obtain the 3-D object shown in Figure 3.30. The left image is shown transparent, whilst the right image has been enclosed by a circle and hidden lines removed. One must not forget that this image is nothing more than a collection of lines and therefore cannot be rendered, however, the 2-D map could be transformed into a mesh of triangles and subjected to the same spherical wrapping. This would create a true 3-D boundary skin which could be rendered.

3.5 Data structures

Programming languages provide a variety of mechanisms for organizing data structures such as: multi-dimensional tables, binary-trees, lists, rings, quad-trees, and octrees. In computer graphics applications, these data structures are used for storing data associated with objects, light sources and the camera. The camera's parameters are relatively easy to store, as this might only involve data controlling its position and orientation, and perhaps its focal length. The light source data could be stored in a two-dimensional table, where for each table entry, the light source type (point, directional and spot), intensity, colour, position, direction, attenuation factor and cone angle can be assigned where needed. As this involves a relatively small amount of data it would be acceptable to declare an array capable of maintaining a maximum of fifty lights, which should be more than adequate for most purposes.

Storing objects however, is a different problem, for there is no unified system for describing their 3-D geometry. Objects constructed from planar polygons need to reference their vertices, edges, surface normals, reflectance coefficients, transparency, roughness and gloss coefficient. Objects built from surface patches, however, will still need to retain surface property data, but instead of polygons, will need to maintain control vertices, knot vectors, tension and bias parameters, and possibly slope and twist vectors. Procedural objects such as fractals and particle systems not only require a building program, but a data structure to accept different versions of these models depending upon the controlling parameters.

Objects constructed from articulated elements such as a hand might also need to store axes about which the elements rotate, and further data may be needed to control the degree of rotation allowed for each axis.

In constructive solid geometry systems, implicit equations are used to describe the geometric primitives and will require a data structure totally different from polygonal-based systems.

This diverse range of data types is further complicated by the dynamic nature of the objects, in that collections of primitive elements are frequently combined to construct some final complex assembly. Even during an animation sequence the animator may wish to deliberately remove various elements.

Unfortunately, there are no universal solutions to these problems as they frequently depend upon the available facilities for defining data structures in the source language. FORTRAN, Pascal, C, C++ and LISP provide programmers with individual environments where features such as dynamic arrays and garbage collection are either left totally in the hands of the programmer, or supported by automatic system tools. However, it is worth mentioning that hierarchical data structures are vital to supporting many of the concepts encountered in computer animation.

We have already seen in Section 3.2.1 that vertex, edge and polygonal data can be stored in tabular form, which can be easily mapped into arrays. However, the same data structure would not support objects such as octahedrons, tetrahedrons, cylinders and dodecahedrons without some modification. The main problem concerns how many edges a polygon is allowed to have, and some modelling systems impose a maximum limit on the user. One could even build everything from triangles which simplifies matters, but this introduces extra edges that serve no real role in describing the object's boundary, which may, or may not, be seen as a disadvantage.

As an illustration, let us consider a hypothetical data structure which, although incomplete, will serve as a useful vehicle to mention some of the issues associated with storing graphical data. To begin with, let us assume that we have access to a memory cell capable of storing eight values (Figure 3.31a). The first entry stores a code called *Cell_Type* which describes the application of the cell. For instance, one type of cell may be used for storing lists of facet data defining the surface. Another type might contain colour information for a facet, and so on. The codes can also be used by the interrogating procedures to confirm the type of cell they are accessing. One entry called *Next_Cell* will be used to point to another cell of the same type so that linked lists of indefinite length can be created.

Plate 1 This image illustrates the style of model that can be created using soft objects. Notice how colour has been associated with different parts of the train, and how the colours blend together.
Courtesy: Brian and Geoff Wyvill.

Plate 2 The single tree employs a growth model for developing the system of branches, with leaf texture created by tiles containing holes. The forest scene shows how effective this model is in simulating the level of detail associated with such scenarios. Notice how the use of a haze model establishes a realistic sense of depth.
Courtesy: Gordon Selley, Coventry Polytechnic and Rediffusion Simulation Ltd.

Plate 3 This marketing image of a display cabinet was modelled using Alias, and incorporates extensive texture mapping to achieve the high level of realism. It is a perfect example of how powerful software in the hands of creative designers can create incredibly delicate scenes.
Courtesy: Deilcraft Furniture Inc. and Semania Luk Cheung, Design Vision Inc., Toronto.

Plate 4 This image is taken from the animation 'Enter the Elgin'. The project involved very complex models and employed extensive use of texture, bump, displacement, opacity and specular mapping. The lighting demanded special attention in order to create a mysterious and haunting ambience.
Courtesy: Alias Research Inc., Semania Luk Cheung, Design Vision Inc., Toronto. Copyright: Alias Research Inc. 1990.

Plate 5 This presentation image of a Japanese hotel lobby was prepared for a Toronto interior designer. It was modelled using Alias and shows how sensitive design skills can be used to create realistic interior scenes.
Courtesy: Yabu Pushelberg and Semania Luk Cheung, Design Vision Inc., Toronto.

Plate 6 Ray tracing provides an ideal environment for implementing motion blur, and in this image one can see how the motion of the ball has been blurred, together with its shadow.
Courtesy: Stewart McEwan, Electric Image Ltd.

Plate 7 By computing the circles of confusion that arise from parts of the scene being out of focus, it is possible to create depth of field effects. This image was created using ray tracing software.
Courtesy: Stewart McEwan, Electric Image Ltd.

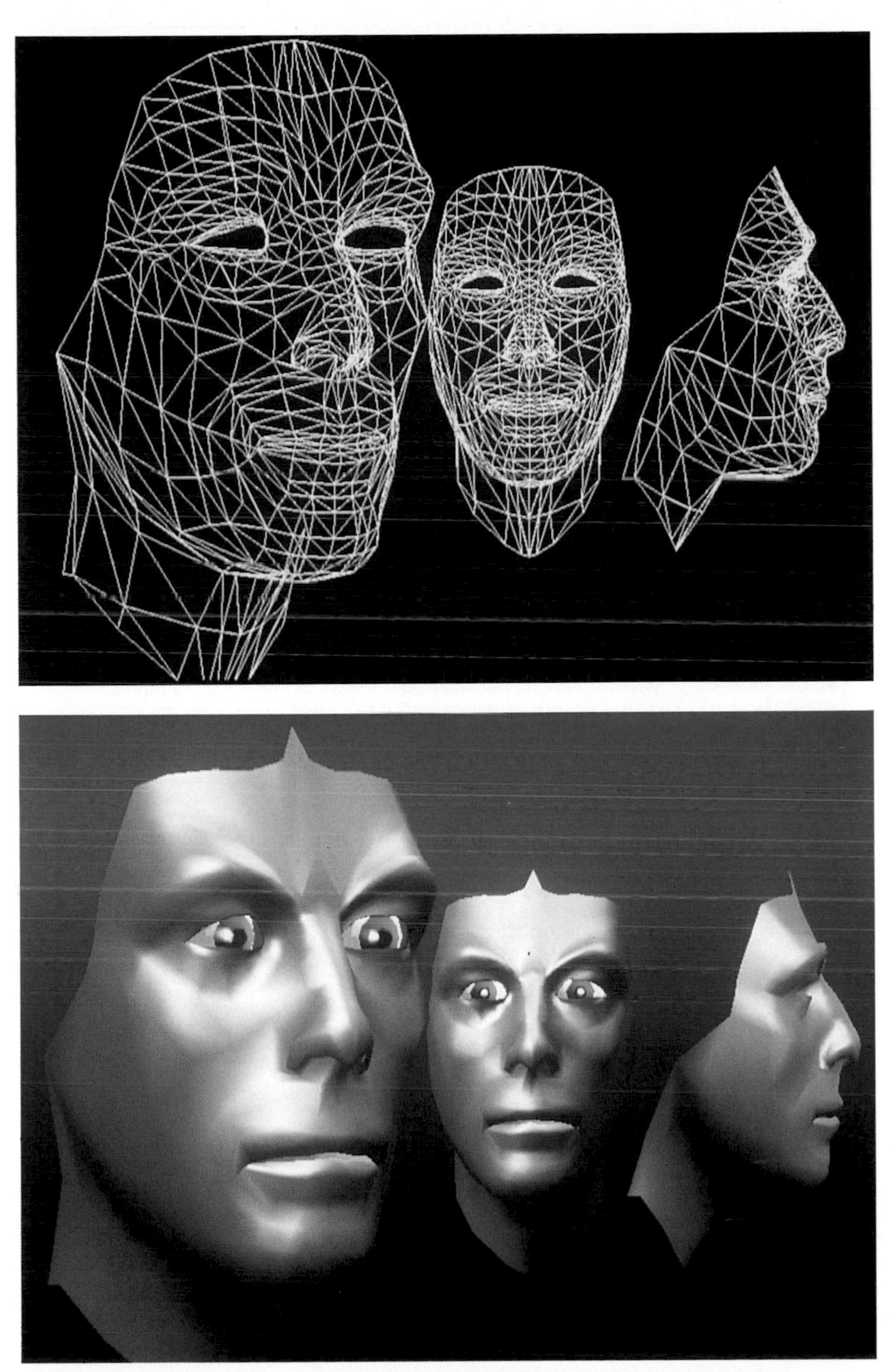

Plates 8 and 9 These two images are from Keith Waters' research into facial expression. The line drawings illustrate the polygonal mesh needed to support the detail of the face, and the rendered images demonstrate the effectiveness of this approach in creating realistic human expressions.
Courtesy: Keith Waters.

Plate 10 Even when 'Eurythmy' was first released in its line-test form, one could immediately see the extraordinary level of dynamics that had been captured by the animators. When it was finally rendered, it was obvious that computer animation had reached a watershed in its ability to create such powerful animation.
Courtesy: Michael Girard and Susan Amkraut.

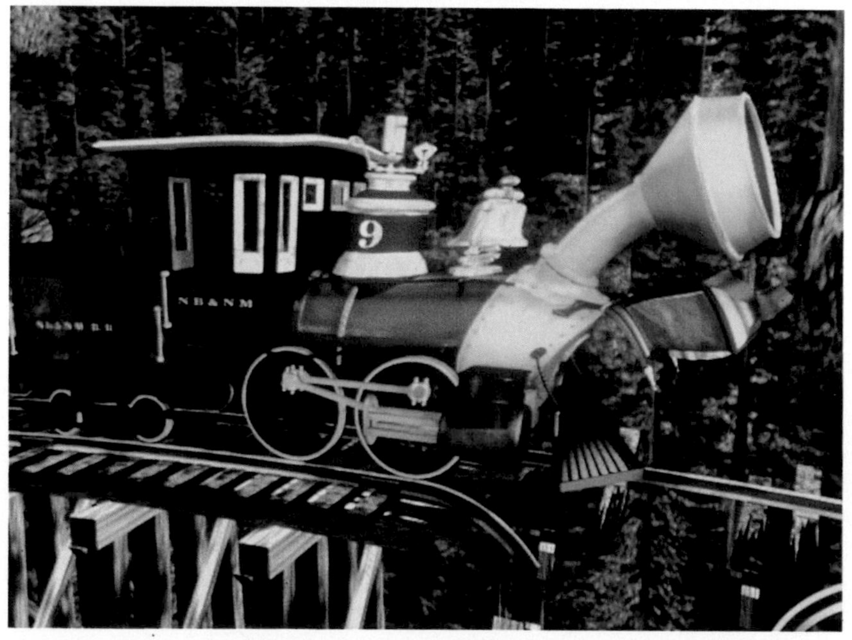

Plate 11 'Locomotion' is a landmark in the history of computer animation in its creative use of free-form deformation. FFDs provided the animation tools for bending the model with a degree of flexibility one normally only associates with traditional cartoon animation.
Courtesy: Pacific Data Images Inc.

Plates 12 and 13 These two scenes are taken from the opening title sequence for BBC Television Breakfast News, and they illustrate the range of special effects that are employed in such sequences. The software was developed in-house and was implemented upon an AT&T Pixel Machine.
Courtesy: BBC Television and Infynity Computer Animation Ltd.

Plate 14 This image is taken from an advertisement for Harp Lager and shows a computer-generated model composited onto live action using Quantel's Harry digital editing system. The model was created using Alias and employs environment maps to form the realistic surface reflections.
Courtesy: Guinness Ltd., Irish International Ltd. and The Moving Picture Company Ltd.

Plate 15 This scene from a commercial for Twister Fries is an excellent example of the creative effort that goes into high-quality adverts. The image was composited using Quantel's Harry edit system and shows a seamless combination of a computer-generated twisted coil of water with live action.
Courtesy: Lamb Weston, Wight Collins Rutherford Scott and The Moving Picture Company Ltd.

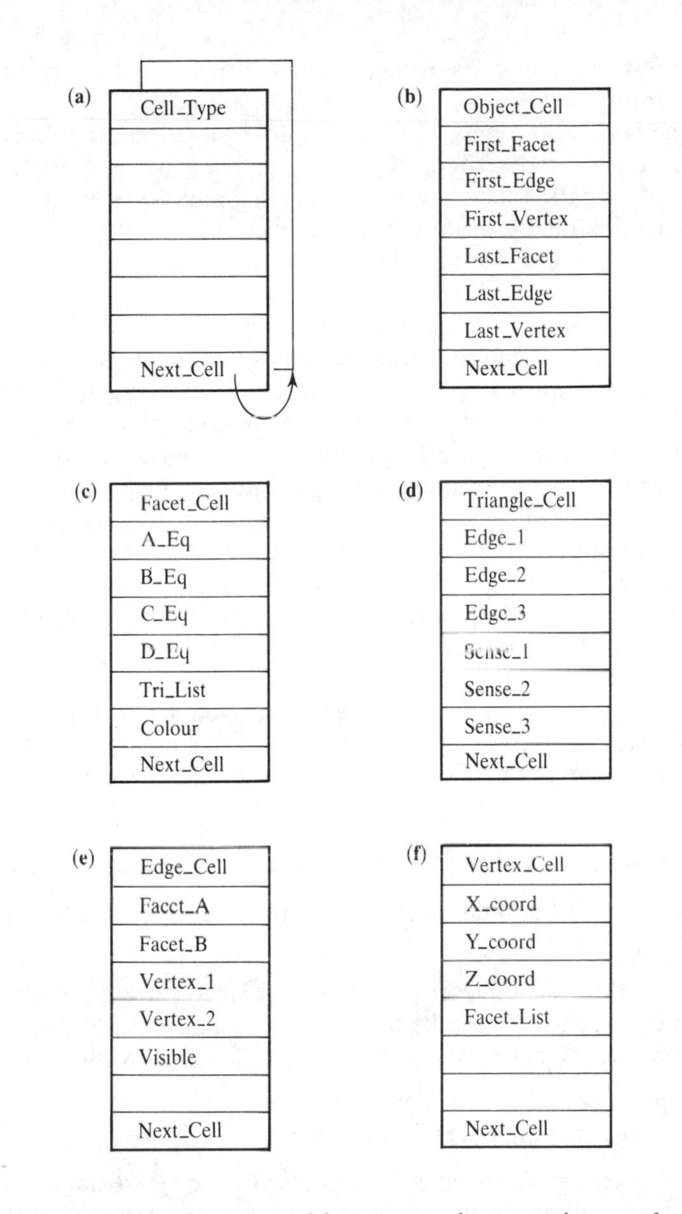

Figure 3.31
These six diagrams show the typical contents of a graphics data structure. The first entry in each cell identifies the cell type, and the last entry provides a link to the next cell in the linked list. The entries for the cells are explained in the text.

When an object is accessed by a procedure a pointer value is supplied to identify an *Object_Cell* (Figure 3.31b). This contains six pointers: three pointing to the lists of facets, edges and vertices, and three to the last cells in these lists. The first three pointers permit the object to be traversed either on a facet, edge or vertex basis, and the last three pointers provide quick access to the data structure when new elements are being loaded. The facet traversal will be used in back-face removal and rendering; the edge traversal will be used in clipping, and the vertex traversal will be used when the object is scaled, rotated or translated. The *Next_Cell* pointer could point to another cell storing parameters such as colour, gloss, roughness and transparency.

The *Facet_Cell* (Figure 3.31c) contains four parameters derived from the plane equation describing the facet; this will be used for back-face removal, illumination calculations, texture mapping and ray tracing. It also contains a pointer to the list of triangles forming the facet. The *Colour* entry points to an extra cell storing colour information that overrides the object colour.

The *Triangle_Cell* (Figure 3.31d) contains three pointers to the edges forming the triangle, and three binary values that indicate the sense of the edge. These are required as the object's facets share edges, and the triangles need to be formed in a consistent clockwise or counter-clockwise sense.

The *Edge_Cell* (Figure 3.31e) points to the two facets associated with it and the two vertices forming the edge. The *Visible* parameter controls whether the edge is formed from the triangulation process, or whether it could ever be seen on the object's silhouette.

Finally, the *Vertex_Cell* (Figure 3.31f) stores the x-, y- and z-coordinates of the vertex, and a pointer to the facet list which identifies the facets sharing this vertex. This last feature is needed to compute the average normal for smooth shading.

There are many other features to this data structure; hopefully, however, this example demonstrates the amount of detail needed to organize the wide range of data used in computer animation programs.

Exercises and projects

3.1 Distinguish between boundary representation and solid modelling schemes.

3.2 Using three tables described in Section 3.2 to store the polygon, edge and vertex data, describe how a 3-D pyramid would be stored using the tables. What must one do to alter the height of the pyramid?

3.3 Explain why different data structures are needed to store objects constructed from polygons or patches.

3.4 Write a program which builds a 3-D cylinder by extruding an n-sided polygon vertically up the y-axis. Design your program to accept parameters for the number of sides, radius and cylinder height.

3.5 Explain the action of a procedure which constructs the surface of revolution by rotating a single contour about the vertical y-axis.

3.6 Implement the expression for bilinear interpolation in Section 3.2.5 in the form of a computer procedure.

3.7 Implement the quadratic Bézier surface patch algorithm shown in Section 3.2.6 and test it for different values of u and w.

3.8 Implement the cubic Bézier surface patch algorithm shown in Section 3.2.6 and test the effect a single control point has on the entire surface.

3.9 Explain the philosophy behind modelling free-form surfaces from surface patches.

3.10 Why is slope continuity important when modelling with Bézier surface patches, and how is it maintained?

3.11 What benefits are there in modelling with NURBS rather than with Bézier surface patches?

3.12 Explain how spatial subdivision schemes are used in modelling.

3.13 Using the technique of mid-point subdivision, write a program which transforms a single edge into a 'crinkled' contour by applying random displacements. Explore the effect the displacement has upon the nature of the line.

3.14 Using the technique of mid-point subdivision, write a program which transforms a single 3-D tile into a pseudo-fractal landscape by applying random displacements. Explore the effect the magnitude of the displacements have upon the nature of the surface.

3.15 Implement the wrapping functions for a cylinder and a sphere used in Section 3.4.3 and test them with some 2-D examples

Further reading

Boundary representation Apart from the technical papers listed in the reference index the reader is referred to Rogers (1990), pp. 247–375, which includes a thorough survey of space curves, cubic splines, parabolic blending, Bézier curves, B-spline curves and rational B-splines. This chapter also includes worked examples that are very useful as an aid to understanding these techniques. Foley (1990), pp. 471–529, contains a smaller chapter but very illuminating. Farin (1988), concentrates on curves and surfaces in CAD and provides an alternative survey of this highly mathematical subject. Barsky's book *Computer Graphics and Geometric Modelling using Beta Splines* provides an in-depth treatment of this subject (Barsky, 1988). Piegl produced a survey on NURBS (Piegl, 1987b) which was published in *IEEE Computer Graphics and Applications*.

Volumetric representation CSG and octrees are briefly examined in Foley (1990), pp. 533–562, and those readers who wish to pursue the subject to a greater depth are recommended to refer to the reference section. *Computer Aided Geometric Design* published by North-Holland will also be a useful journal.

Procedural modelling Perhaps the references for this section will be the best source of discovering more about fractals, soft objects and other procedural techniques; especially papers presented at SIGGRAPH conferences and published in *IEEE Computer Graphics and Applications*. The books by Peitgen, Richter and Saupe (Peitgen, 1986; 1988) provide an excellent treatment of fractal sets.

Data structures Two excellent papers by H. Samet will be found in *IEEE Computer Graphics and Applications* which survey the range of data structures employed in computer graphics (Samet, 1988; 1988b). *Data Structure Techniques* (Standish, 1980) also gives a good introduction to the subject.

KEY POINTS

Modelling forms a major part of any animation project, and the animator must always model an object using a scheme that allows it to be animated and rendered. More techniques that have special applications are covered in Chapter 9, but the basic strategies are listed below.

- Any data set describing an object must contain the 3-D geometry together with explicit or implicit data from which edges, surfaces and surface normals can be computed.
- Basically two modelling strategies are employed in computer animation – namely boundary representation (B-rep) and volumetric representation. Out of the two, B-rep is able to meet the animator's needs for modelling most objects.
- The majority of 3-D models eventually become reduced to a collection of planar convex polygons, which are easy to render.
- Free-form surfaces can be constructed from a collection of Bézier surface patches, B-spline surfaces or NURBS, which enable spheres, toroids and ellipsoids to be modelled precisely.
- Other surface patch descriptions also exist and include: bi-linear surfaces, ruled surfaces and Coons patches.
- Constructive Solid Geometry (CSG) provides an elegant system where Boolean operators manipulate computer graphic primitives to build complex structures.
- Procedural modelling plays an important role in modelling structures such as fractals and soft objects. Fractals have become very useful for modelling arbitrary 3-D terrain, and the implicit surfaces of soft objects have been useful for the modelling of liquids and bendy structures.
- Data structures are vital to the success of a computer animation system as they maintain a wide range of data types that change dynamically while an animation program is being executed.

4 Rendering

In order to create a coloured view of a collection of 3-D objects, rendering algorithms are required to describe the physical behaviour of light in the real world. This chapter describes how simple illumination models are used to simulate the action of point, directional and spot light sources. Specific examples are then numerically evaluated to show how simple vector theory is used to determine angles required in the illumination calculations.

Reflection models are then examined to see how surfaces interact with incident light energy by analysing the ambient, diffuse and specular components. Equations are developed for these three lighting components showing how the final colour value is determined for a pixel. Other effects are also covered such as intensity fall-off with distance, light balancing, shadows and negative light.

Using these illumination and reflection models Gouraud shading can be used for rendering flat and smooth-shaded diffuse objects, while Phong shading introduces specular highlights. Various strategies are then examined for creating images with hidden surfaces correctly removed. These include the painter's algorithm, scan-line, z-buffer, A-buffer, zz-buffer and the single scan-line depth buffer algorithm. Finally, the ideas behind ray tracing and radiosity are reviewed.

Introduction

We have already seen that there are various modelling strategies for describing the shape of objects, and so far we have not associated any physical attributes to these objects such as colour, roughness, transparency or translucency. The rendering process which creates the final coloured image requires both geometry and attribute data to perform this task.

We also know from personal experience that in order to see something it must either be self-luminous, such as the sun or a television screen, or be illuminated by some light source. Therefore, computer animation systems must be able to cater for a variety of different types of light sources which can be altered in intensity and colour, and placed at different positions in the WCS.

To develop a coloured image the renderer needs to know the colour of every object, how its surfaces reflect light and the nature of the illuminating light sources. During the rendering process the relative positions of objects must be preserved, and surfaces invisible to the observer must not appear in the final scene. Overall, rendering is quite a time-consuming and complex process, which is why considerable research work has been undertaken in this area. Fortunately, there are many excellent texts describing this subject – consequently this section will only address the basic principles behind the major topics.

4.1 Illumination models

Illumination models refer to the various types of light sources that can be simulated within computer graphics; these attempt to model the various types of light sources that we find in the real world. The sun is the most important light source to our own lives, for it not only illuminates our world but also heats it.

In our homes, lighting fixtures include ceiling fittings, wall lights, spot lights, strip lights and diffusing panels. Rooms also have windows that let in natural light from outside. Therefore if a renderer is going to be able to compute the light levels upon the surfaces comprising our objects, it will require accurate data relating to the various modes of illumination, and Plate 3 shows what can be achieved when a creative designer is given the right computer graphics tools.

Simulating reality is obviously going to present some daunting problems. Just imagine the complex reflections that take place within a typical living-room. Perhaps there is a central light hanging from the ceiling radiating light in all directions. Some light is radiated towards the ceiling, which is generally white, and reflects most of the light down into the room. The rest of the light radiates out towards the walls and floor which absorb some of this energy and reflects the rest. The television might be on and creates a continuous pattern of coloured light throughout the room which varies depending on the nature of the programme. The windows in the room allow in daylight which may enter from all angles, depending on the surfaces in the vicinity of the window. The dynamics of these illumination levels are obviously complex, and only in the last decade or so have been simulated with ray tracing and radiosity.

Simulating real light sources is therefore going to be a compromise between rendering time and the level of realism one is prepared to accept. It would be impossible to mimic the behaviour of every ray of light leaving a lamp and take into account its loss of intensity, surface absorption, refraction, reflection and interference patterns that occur in natural situations. Therefore, we must expect that some computer-generated images will not appear natural. This might be because subtle shadows are missing; the intensities are not balanced; or that surfaces appear plastic-like, when they are supposed to be metallic or some other material. In the rest of this sub-section we will explore the basic types of light sources available to computer animators.

4.1.1 Point light sources

The point light source is the simplest source of illumination to model, as one only has to specify its position in space together with its intensity and colour. Its position presents no problems as all this entails is identifying a suitable place in the WCS such that it will illuminate the important parts of a scene. When one light source is insufficient, extra lights can be introduced at strategic positions. However, a method is needed to encode its colour and intensity.

In Section 2.1.6 we saw that frame stores are used to hold a colour image in the form of its three primary colours: red, green and blue. This component approach to handling colour means that the renderer has to create three colour intensities for each pixel – one for each additive primary colour. This also implies that light sources can be imagined as consisting of three coloured lights in the same position, and their intensities are adjusted to create the required colour. For example, if a pure yellow light source is needed, the blue component will be set at zero and the red and green components adjusted to give the required intensity. Thus in general, a light source will require six parameters, the x-, y- and z-coordinates of its location, and the three numbers defining the primary colour intensities; the latter would be decimal numbers with a maximum value of one.

Specifying the colour of a light source using levels of red, green and blue is rather cumbersome, therefore it is quite normal to find the hue, saturation and value notation being employed at the user interface. The

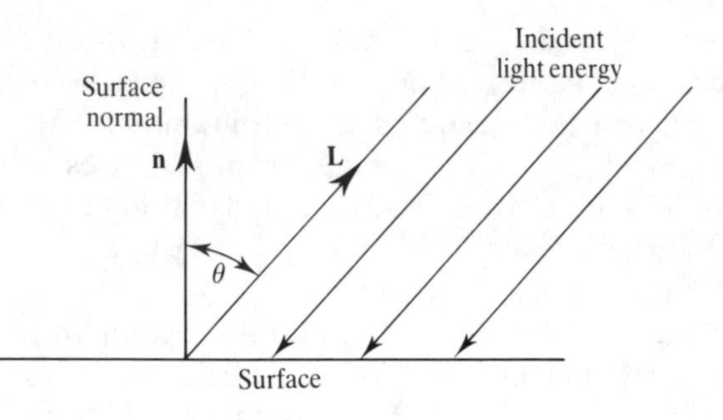

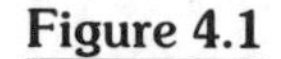

Figure 4.1

When light is incident to a surface, its intensity is proportional to the angle it makes with the surface normal; in this case the angle θ.

values of H, S and V are then internally converted to equivalent values of R, G and B.

As an example, let us consider the illumination characteristics of a point light source positioned at (0, 10, 0) and a point on the ground plane. Now the incident light energy per unit area is proportional to the cosine of the angle contained between the incident light direction and the surface normal (Figure 4.1). Therefore to compute the incident light energy at any point (x, y, z) we need to know the surface normal at this point, and a vector towards the light point. For the ground plane the surface normal **n** is equal to:

$$\mathbf{n} = \begin{bmatrix} 0 \\ 1 \\ 0 \end{bmatrix}$$

To compute the light energy incident at any point (x, y, z) from a point light source located at P (p_x, p_y, p_z), the vector **s** representing the incident light is therefore equal to:

$$\mathbf{s} = \begin{bmatrix} p_x - x \\ p_y - y \\ p_z - z \end{bmatrix}$$

and the angle θ between the vectors **s** and **n** is found using the dot-product operation:

$$\mathbf{s} \bullet \mathbf{n} = |\mathbf{s}|\ |\mathbf{n}| \cos(\theta)$$

where $|\mathbf{s}|$ is the magnitude of **s**, $|\mathbf{n}|$ is the magnitude of **n**, and the dot-product is equal to:

$$\mathbf{s} \bullet \mathbf{n} = (s_1 n_1 + s_2 n_2 + s_3 n_3)$$

In this example $|\mathbf{n}| = 1$, therefore we can rewrite the dot-product expression as:

$$\cos(\theta) = \frac{\mathbf{s} \bullet \mathbf{n}}{|\mathbf{s}|} = \frac{((p_x - x)0 + (p_y - y)1 + (p_z - z)0)}{|\mathbf{s}|}$$

$$= \frac{p_y}{|\mathbf{s}|}$$

$$= \frac{10}{|\mathbf{s}|}$$

Therefore, imediately underneath the light source (i.e. the origin) $\theta = 0°$ and the intensity is a maximum; but at a point $(10, 0, 0)$, $\cos(\theta) = 0.707$, therefore the incident intensity is attenuated to 70.7%.

Now although the above example was simplified by the nature of the horizontal ground plane, one can see that as long as a surface normal is available, it is possible to compute the incident light energy upon any surface, no matter how it is oriented.

4.1.2 Directional light sources

The sun – which is approximately 94 million miles from the Earth – is for all intents and purposes a directional light source. Its great distance means that light rays arriving at a small patch on the Earth's surface are virtually parallel and are of the same intensity. This means that directional light sources can be specified in terms of a colour, intensity and a direction which is encoded in the form of a unit vector **s**. The angle between this vector and a surface normal is then used by the renderer to determine the quantity of light energy actually striking an inclined surface. For example, to model the sun in an overhead position the light direction **s** would be represented as the unit vector:

$$\mathbf{s} = \begin{bmatrix} 0 \\ -1 \\ 0 \end{bmatrix}$$

Thus the direction of the sunlight vector **s** is orthogonal to the ground. But as we have just seen, in calculating the light energy incident upon a surface, the vector for the incident light was directed towards the light source. Therefore, the vector **s** must be reversed to:

$$\mathbf{s} = -\begin{bmatrix} 0 \\ -1 \\ 0 \end{bmatrix}$$

Now if the surface normal **n** of the ground plane is:

$$\mathbf{n} = \begin{bmatrix} 0 \\ 1 \\ 0 \end{bmatrix} \quad \text{(i.e. vertically upwards)}$$

we can once more compute the angle between the two vectors using the dot-product operation:

$$\mathbf{s} \bullet \mathbf{n} = (0 + 1 + 0) = 1$$

and as both $|\mathbf{s}|$ and $|\mathbf{n}|$ equal unity:

$$\mathbf{s} \bullet \mathbf{n} = \cos(\theta) = 1$$

which means that the angle between the two vectors is 0°.

If the sun's direction is changed to:

$$\mathbf{s} = -\begin{bmatrix} 0.707 \\ -0.707 \\ 0.0 \end{bmatrix} = \begin{bmatrix} -0.707 \\ 0.707 \\ 0.0 \end{bmatrix}$$

then the angle between $\mathbf{s}$ and $\mathbf{n}$ becomes:

$$\mathbf{s} \bullet \mathbf{n} = 0.707$$

Therefore, $\cos(\theta) = 0.707$, and $\theta = 45°$. Thus the original intensity of the sunlight is effectively reduced by a factor of 0.707 at the ground plane.

Thus it is a simple operation to show the illumination effects of a sun effectively moving across the sky, as this only requires for the direction vector to be animated in a controlled way.

4.1.3 Spot light sources

As the name suggests, a spot light simulates the behaviour of a conventional spot light which creates a controlled beam of light in the shape of a cone; these are also called directed light sources. The minimum range of parameters required to model this light source include position, intensity, colour and spot angle; however, extra realism can be introduced by including a function which attenuates the light intensity towards the boundary of the spot light to create a soft edge. The cosine function can be used to create this type of attenuation.

For example, if a spot light has the following features:

Position: (p_x, p_y, p_z)

Direction: $\mathbf{s} = \begin{bmatrix} s_x \\ s_y \\ s_z \end{bmatrix}$

Cone angle: ϕ

then a point (x, y, z) falls within the cone of illumination if the angle θ between the direction vector $\mathbf{s}$ and a vector $\mathbf{u}$ from the spot light to the sample point, is less than or equal to $\phi/2$.

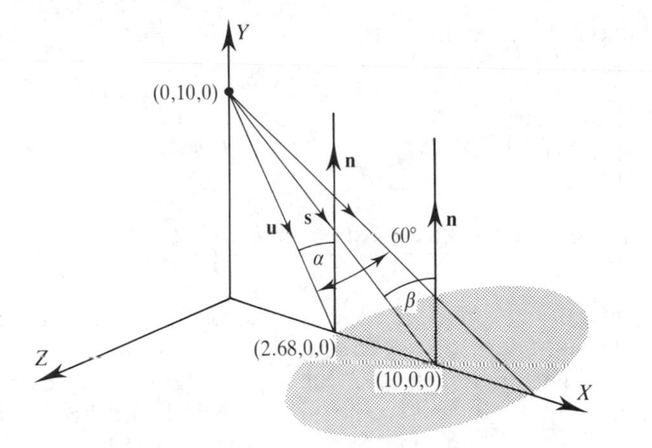

Figure 4.2
A spot light is located at (0, 10, 0) and directed to the point (10, 0, 0). As the angle of incidence is 45°, its effective intensity is reduced by cos(45), which is 0.707. Where the spot's footprint intersects the *x*-axis at (2.68, 0, 0) the intensity is 0.966.

Therefore if **u** is given by:

$$\mathbf{u} = \begin{bmatrix} x - p_x \\ y - p_y \\ z - p_z \end{bmatrix}$$

then θ is given by:

$$\theta = \cos^{-1}\left(\frac{\mathbf{s} \bullet \mathbf{u}}{|\mathbf{s}|\,|\mathbf{u}|}\right)$$

Let us test this with the following data:

Position: (0, 10, 0)

Direction: $\mathbf{s} = \begin{bmatrix} 0.707 \\ -0.707 \\ 0.0 \end{bmatrix}$

Cone angle: 60°

The point (10, 0, 0), which should be in the centre of the spot's footprint, as shown in Figure 4.2, is evaluated as follows:

$$\mathbf{u} = \begin{bmatrix} 10 - 0 \\ 0 - 10 \\ 0 - 0 \end{bmatrix} = \begin{bmatrix} 10 \\ -10 \\ 0 \end{bmatrix}$$

$$\theta = \cos^{-1}\left(\frac{7.07 + 7.07 + 0.0}{14.14}\right) = \cos^{-1}(1) = 0°$$

which is as expected.

The point $(2.68, 0.0, 0.0)$, which should be on the edge of the footprint, reveals:

$$\mathbf{u} = \begin{bmatrix} 2.68 - 0 \\ 0 - 10 \\ 0 - 0 \end{bmatrix}$$

$$\theta = \cos^{-1}\left(\frac{0.707 \times 2.68 + 0.707 \times 10 + 0}{10.35}\right) = \cos^{-1}\left(\frac{8.965}{10.35}\right) = 30°$$

which is equal to half the cone angle and is therefore illuminated.

As we now have access to the vector **u** for any light ray, we can compute the light energy incident at a point (x, y, z) by calculating the angle between **u** and the surface normal **n**. In fact, the direction of **u** must be reversed as it represents light leaving the source. In the case of the point $(10, 0, 0)$ and a vertical surface normal **n**, the cosine of the enclosed angle β is given by:

$$\cos(\beta) = \frac{-\mathbf{u} \bullet \mathbf{n}}{|\mathbf{u}|\,|\mathbf{n}|} = \frac{10}{14.14} = 0.707$$

Therefore the light intensity at this point is 0.707 of the spot's intensity. Similarly, for the point $(2.68, 0, 0)$ the cosine of the enclosed angle α is:

$$\cos(\alpha) = \frac{10}{10.35} = 0.966$$

and the light intensity is much brighter at 0.966 of the spot's intensity.

4.1.4 Other features of light sources

Intensity fall-off with distance

We know from experience that the intensity of light decreases with distance: in fact, the relationship is an inverse-square law. This means that if an observed intensity is measured at a distance of one metre, at two metres the intensity will be a quarter of the original. Experiments have shown that a good approximation can be achieved by dividing the incident light intensity by $(d + k)$, where d is the distance of the observer from the illuminated surface and k is some suitable constant. However, as calculating d involves a square-root and three squaring operations, this inverse term is dropped when high-speed rendering is required.

An alternative decay function (Comninos, 1991) based upon empirical observations is:

$$F(d) = R^d$$

where d is the distance from the light source, and R is a decay parameter. For example, if at 2 units from a light source the intensity is attenuated by 0.5, then R needs to be set accordingly. In fact, R is computed as follows:

$$R = atten^{(1/d)}$$

This ensures that when $d = 2$, and $atten = 0.5$, then $R = 0.707$; therefore $F(2) = 0.5$. And when $d = 3$, $F(3) = 0.353$. Thus specific levels of attenuation can be associated with any light source to create a desired effect.

Balancing illumination levels

When multiple light sources are used, it is quite probable that some surfaces can become saturated with light and are rendered as one constant colour. This means that an animator will have to spend some time adjusting the various intensities to achieve an acceptable balance. There are no real short cuts in achieving this, apart from experience and trial and error; it can be simplified, however, by ensuring that objects are only illuminated by selected light sources.

Shadows

Although shadows occur naturally in our real world, in the virtual world of computer graphics they have to be calculated during the rendering process. When these calculations are not undertaken, the illumination model allows for light rays to illuminate a surface and all other surfaces behind the first as if it did not exist. Obviously this is bound to create strange visual anomalies, and is a major cause for computer-generated images looking unnatural.

Negative light

An interesting aspect of computer light sources is that, as their intensity is defined in terms of a positive number by making their sign negative instead of adding illumination to a surface, they can remove illumination and create a source of 'darkness'. Although this has limited applications, it is, nevertheless, an interesting feature and is very useful for creating soft shadow effects.

4.2 Reflection models

Reflection models are used to describe the way incident light reflects from a surface – and taking a simplistic approach, there are three types of light reflection we need to consider: ambient, diffuse and specular. Ambient light simulates the level of constant light that can be thought to exist due to multiple reflections, while diffuse light is created by surfaces whose roughness causes any incident light to be reflected equally in all directions. Specular light refers to light reflected by polished surfaces and creates a highlight of the illuminating light source and surrounding environment.

The colour of an object is determined by the nature of the illuminating radiation and the proportions that are absorbed and reflected. In general, the light we receive from the sun is an equal mixture of all visible frequencies, though strictly speaking it does depend upon the time of the day and weather conditions. This balanced mixture of frequencies causes a white sensation to be experienced, so that when we talk of white paper, we really mean a surface that reflects light radiation of all frequencies; and when we describe a tomato as red, it really implies that when a tomato is illuminated with white light (i.e. all frequencies), the tomato absorbs most frequencies and reflects some others that create a red sensation in the brain's visual cortex.

In Section 2.1.5 a case was put forward to show how the sensation of colour could be explained by the eye sampling the visible spectrum in the red, green and blue portions. This model can be extended to allow the renderer to construct an image from the red, green and blue components. This means that light sources are considered as radiating three components: red, green and blue. Surfaces, on the other hand, have three reflection coefficients which specify the fractional amount of red, green and blue light reflected. In this way it is possible to simulate the interaction of coloured objects with coloured lights.

Dividing light behaviour into these three categories is a gross simplification and is responsible for some computer-generated images appearing too synthetic. Consequently, other reflection models have been developed which are capable of creating some very realistic images. Readers who wish to explore this subject to a greater level of technical background are advised to read the recommended references.

4.2.1 Ambient light

If we imagine a normal room illuminated by a ceiling lamp and perhaps exposed to daylight through a window, many of the internal surfaces will appear to have a constant level of illumination modulated by other smaller intensity changes. This environment can be simulated by assuming that there is a background level of illumination, upon which are superimposed other light intensities. In fact there is no overall level of illumination that permeates the entire room, for each surface is illuminated by light energy that has achieved some natural level of equilibrium through many levels of absorption and reflection; nevertheless, it is a reasonable compromise and is a useful model.

This constant level of light is called the ambient component. It has no source as it represents the light energy arriving from all directions. However, in order to be able to control its impact upon different objects, surfaces are assigned a parameter which decides the proportion of the ambient light is reflected back towards the observer.

In calculating the total light seen by the observer, the ambient component is represented by:

$$I_a K_a$$

where I_a is the incident ambient intensity and K_a is a parameter associated with a surface to control the proportion reflected away from the surface. As described above, this expression must be evaluated for the red, green and blue portions of the spectrum.

For example, if $I_a = 0.25$ and the three values for K_a are 0.5, 0.5, and 0.0 for red, green and blue respectively, then the ambient components are computed as:

$$I_{\text{amb(red)}} = 0.25 \times 0.5 = 0.125$$
$$I_{\text{amb(green)}} = 0.25 \times 0.5 = 0.125$$
$$I_{\text{amb(blue)}} = 0.25 \times 0.0 = 0.0$$

However, this assumes that the colour of the ambient light is white, which might not be the case. If coloured ambient light is required then three separate values of I_a must be specified as follows:

$$I_{\text{amb(red)}} = I_{a\text{(red)}} \times K_{a\text{(red)}}$$
$$I_{\text{amb(green)}} = I_{a\text{(green)}} \times K_{a\text{(green)}}$$
$$I_{\text{amb(blue)}} = I_{a\text{(blue)}} \times K_{a\text{(blue)}}$$

Naturally, these need specifying by the animator, but it means that during an animation sequence the intensity and the colour of the ambient light can be changing under the automatic control of the computer.

4.2.2 Diffuse reflection

The rough surfaces found on carpets, most textiles and papers result in any incident light being reflected in random directions. This means that when these surfaces are observed, they appear to have a constant intensity no matter the position of the observer, though their brightness does change when their orientation with the light source alters. Such reflection is termed diffuse. To simulate such behaviour within a computer graphics environment does not entail knowing where the observer is, but knowing the angle between the light source and the surface.

Consider the case when a directional light source is immediately above a surface: incident light will be reflected back into the environment in various random directions. However, if a surface is positioned such that the light rays strike it at 45°, then the effective incident illumination is reduced by a factor of 0.707. If, in the limiting case, the angle was increased to 90°, theoretically the surface would not receive any incident light at all. Figure 4.1 illustrates this effect. In calculating this diffuse component the renderer must introduce this cosine term to attenuate the surface intensity – this law is known as Lambert's law, after the scientist who investigated the behaviour of light.

The diffuse term for one light source is then calculated by:

$$I_i K_d (\mathbf{L} \bullet \mathbf{n})$$

where I_i is the intensity of the light source, K_d is a fractional constant associated with a surface to control the proportion of diffuse light reflected, **L** is the vector directed towards the light source, and **n** is the normal vector of the surface. Remember that this diffuse expression must be evaluated three times for the red, green and blue components.

4.2.3 Specular reflection

A smooth or polished surface produces specular reflections, which include the perfect reflections we see in windows and mirrors, and the reflections of light sources that we see in other surfaces that are not so smooth. Ray tracing was developed to calculate the reflections of the environment seen in surfaces and will be described later. So in this section we will examine the conditions under which it is possible to see reflections of light sources in smooth surfaces.

Personal experience of using mirrors and handling polished surfaces teaches us that the position of the observer relative to the surface is important. In fact, two laws of specular reflection state that the angles of incidence and reflection are equal, and that the incident ray, reflected ray and surface normal at the point of reflection, all lie in a plane. Figure 4.3 illustrates these laws.

As computer graphic light sources are theoretical points, it would be unrealistic for the renderer to make all reflections of light sources appear as a single bright pixel, especially when physical light sources have a finite size and reflections become smeared by various degrees of surface roughness. Consequently, the renderer must attempt to simulate this behaviour. A neat approximation to this smearing effect can be created by allowing the observer to see a specular reflection even when it is not located at an optimum position. In fact, as Figure 4.4 illustrates, if the angles of incidence and reflection are θ, and the error angle is ϕ, then the specular component can be computed by the following expression:

$$I_i K_s \cos^g(\phi)$$

where I_i is the intensity of the incident light, K_s is the colour-independent specular coefficient, ϕ is the error angle, and g is a term that determines the gloss of the surface. A value of $g = 10$ creates a rough plastic effect, whereas a value of 150 creates a very small highlight, typical for a highly polished surface.

In order to compute ϕ, θ must be known, therefore the expression is also written as:

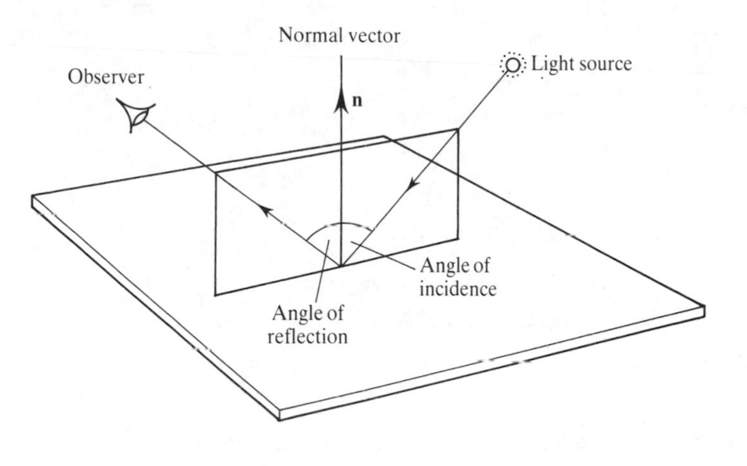

Figure 4.3
Two laws of optics are exploited in computing specular reflections: the first states that the angle of reflection equals the angle of incidence, while the second states that at the point of reflection, the incident ray, the reflected ray and the normal vector lie in the same plane.

$$I_i K_s (\mathbf{R} \cdot \mathbf{V})^g$$

where the cosine term is replaced by the dot-product of the vectors **R** and **V**; **R** is the unit vector representing the reflected ray, and **V** is the unit vector directed towards the viewer. Unfortunately, computing **R** is not that simple, therefore **R** • **V** is computed indirectly as follows using the unit light vector **L**:

$$\begin{aligned}\mathbf{V} \cdot \mathbf{L} &= \cos(2\theta + \phi) \\ &= \cos(2\theta)\cos(\phi) - \sin(2\theta)\sin(\phi) \\ &= \cos(\phi)(\cos^2(\theta) - \sin^2(\theta)) - 2\sin(\theta)\cos(\theta)\sin(\phi)\end{aligned}$$

and

$$\begin{aligned}\mathbf{n} \cdot \mathbf{V} &= \cos(\theta + \phi) \\ &= \cos(\theta)\cos(\phi) - \sin(\theta)\sin(\phi)\end{aligned}$$

Combining the two equations reveals that

$$\mathbf{R} \cdot \mathbf{V} = 2(\mathbf{n} \cdot \mathbf{L})(\mathbf{n} \cdot \mathbf{V}) - \mathbf{V} \cdot \mathbf{L}$$

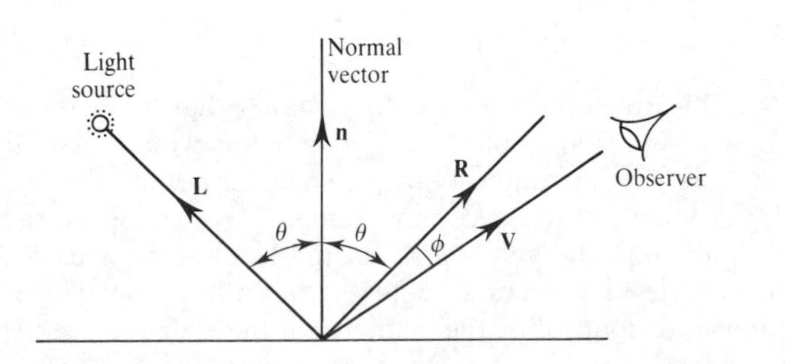

Figure 4.4
In order to create specular reflections at positions slightly off-axis to the optimum optical path, Phong shading incorporates a cosine term of the error angle ϕ, and raises this to some power to control the size of the specular highlight.

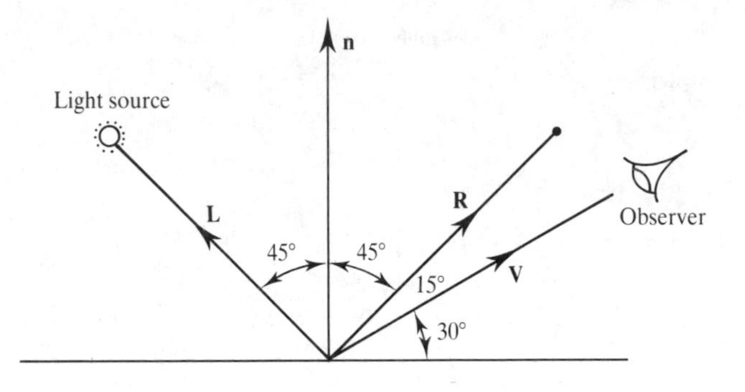

Figure 4.5

This diagram shows an observer misaligned with the reflection vector **V** by 15°. If the gloss term is 1 the observer will see the light attenuated to 0.966; if the gloss factor is 10, the attenuation is 0.707, and if the gloss factor is 100, the attenuation is 0.0314.

therefore the original specular expression can be written as:

$$I_i K_s (2(\mathbf{n} \cdot \mathbf{L})(\mathbf{n} \cdot \mathbf{V}) - (\mathbf{V} \cdot \mathbf{L}))^g$$

We can test this relationship by substituting some sample values:

$$\mathbf{n} = \begin{bmatrix} 0 \\ 1 \\ 0 \end{bmatrix}$$

$$\mathbf{L} = \begin{bmatrix} -0.7071 \\ 0.7071 \\ 0.0 \end{bmatrix}$$

$$\mathbf{V} = \begin{bmatrix} 0.866 \\ 0.5 \\ 0.0 \end{bmatrix}$$

Then:

$$\mathbf{n} \cdot \mathbf{L} = 0.7071$$
$$\mathbf{n} \cdot \mathbf{V} = 0.5$$
$$\mathbf{V} \cdot \mathbf{L} = -0.2588$$
$$2(\mathbf{n} \cdot \mathbf{L})(\mathbf{n} \cdot \mathbf{V}) - (\mathbf{V} \cdot \mathbf{L}) = 2 \times 0.7071 \times 0.5 + 0.2588 = 0.966$$

Figure 4.5 illustrates this geometry and shows that the error angle is 15°, whose cosine is indeed 0.966. Now if $g = 1$, this would mean that with an offset angle of 15°, the intensity of the specular component would still be very high at 96.6% of the maximum value. This would give rise to a large surface highlight. However, if $g = 10$, the level reduces to 70.7%, and if $g = 100$, the level reduces to 3.14%, thus the value of g provides an excellent way of controlling the diameter of the specular highlight.

4.2.4 The complete reflection expression

This simple reflection model has three components for ambient, diffuse and specular reflections, each of which has three colour samples. The total light reflected by a surface can be expressed as the sum of these components, which is:

$$I = I_a K_a + [I_i K_d(\mathbf{L} \cdot \mathbf{n}) + I_i K_s(\mathbf{R} \cdot \mathbf{V})^g]$$

but is only for one light source, therefore the expression in brackets must be computed for every light source within the animation environment.

The virtual nature of these light sources and objects means that liberties can be taken with the laws of physics. For example, a light source can be set such that it is only associated with a certain group of objects. There is also nothing to prevent the animator from placing light sources inside other objects. Any parameter can be changed at will during an animation sequence, and this level of flexibility might seem amazing; however, it must be appreciated that rendering is still a time-consuming operation, and it may be impossible to explore all of the possibilities open to the animator.

4.3 Shading techniques

In the previous section we saw how the ideas of diffuse and specular reflection, together with the simplistic notion of ambient light, enabled us to devise a model for calculating light levels upon surfaces. In this section we will develop these ideas to create shaded views of 3-D objects, and we should keep in mind that the realism of the shading will only be as good as the original illumination model permits.

Although there are different ways of storing a shaded image, for simplicity, the existence of a 24-bit frame store will be assumed, where each additive primary colour is held to a precision of 8 bits. Furthermore, shading algorithms will be described assuming that hidden-surface removal procedures will ensure that surfaces are rendered into the frame store in the correct sequence.

As the shading programs output their colour intensities to a frame store, they introduce two types of error into the image. The first is caused by colour intensities being held as integers, for even though an intensity may be computed as 230.45, for example, it has to be rounded to 230 if it is to be stored in the frame store. Thus the colouring will be subjected to a quantization error. The second source of error is much more important, and is caused by the image being constructed from a myriad of sampled points.

The problem is easily appreciated by referring to Figure 4.6 which depicts an edge of a polygon together with the sample points of the pixels.

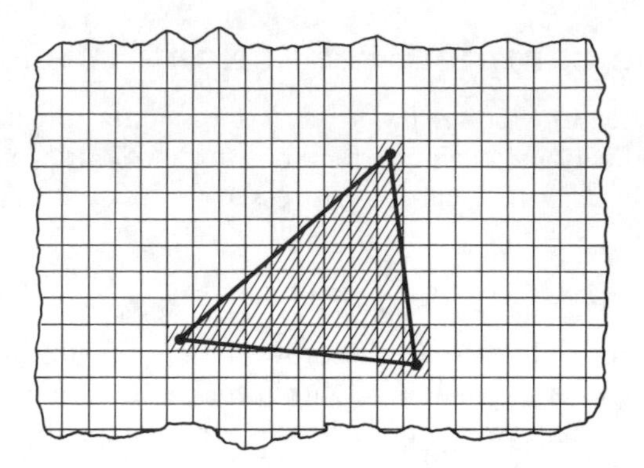

Figure 4.6

If a pixel's intensity is set according to whether or not its centre is covered by a polygon, a ragged staircase effect results called aliasing. This artefact can be made visually acceptable by anti-aliasing procedures which effectively soften the boundary edges with appropiate intensity levels determined by different filtering strategies.

Where those sample points miss the polygon the pixel is unaffected; however, if the sample point even just hits the polygon, the pixel is set to the same intensity of another pixel which was totally covered by the polygon. As one can see from Figure 4.6, the polygon's edge is jagged, which is often referred to as 'staircase aliasing'. This is because the sampling process has deduced erroneous information from the original scene.

As this produces such noticable errors in the image, there has been considerable research effort to identify efficient anti-aliasing procedures and, as one might expect, these increase rendering times. Now it is not vital for a computer animator to understand every available anti-aliasing technique, so for the moment it will be sufficient for the reader to appreciate the existence of aliasing, its causes and the techniques that are available to clean up the image. The subject of aliasing and anti-aliasing, both spatial and temporal, will be addressed in Section 5.1.

4.3.1 Gouraud shading

Henri Gouraud made the first major contribution to shading algorithms (Gouraud, 1971) by proposing a linear interpolation technique for blending colours across a planar surface. He suggested that the eye could be deceived into accepting surface colour intensities that had been blended from a few samples. This algorithm can be quickly appreciated by examining Figure 4.7, which shows a 3-D triangle illuminated by a single point light source. This implies that the vertices A, B and C will each have different light intensities, as the incident light rays of a close light source subtend slightly different angles to the surface normal. In the case of a light source at infinity, the incident rays would be parallel, and the angles of incidence would be identical.

If the light intensities at the three vertices of a small triangle are I_a, I_b and I_c, then it seems reasonable to assume that along the edge joining vertices A to B the light intensity changes linearly from I_a to I_b. This means

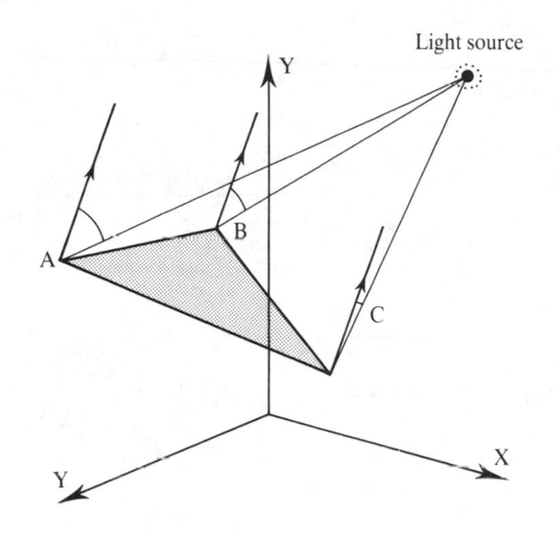

Figure 4.7
If a light source is relatively close to this triangle, incident light rays will subtend different angles at the vertices A, B and C. Gouraud shading interpolates these intensities along the edges and throughout the triangle's interior to create a continuous diffuse shading effect.

that the interpolation can be made in the image space using the x- and y-coordinates of the vertices (Figure 4.8). For instance, if the three vertices A, B and C had image space coordinates of:

$$A(x_a, y_a), \quad B(x_b, y_b), \quad \text{and} \quad C(x_c, y_c)$$

then the intensity I_L at a point (x_L, y_s) is given by a linear interpolation using y_a, y_c and y_s:

$$I_L = \frac{I_a(y_s - y_c) + I_c(y_a - y_s)}{y_a - y_c}$$

Similarly, for the right-hand edge, the intensity I_R at a point (x_R, y_s) is given by a linear interpolation using y_a, y_b and y_s:

$$I_R = \frac{I_a(y_s - y_b) + I_b(y_a - y_s)}{y_a - y_b}$$

Now we have the intensity I_L on the left-hand side of the triangle and I_R on the right-hand side of the triangle, therefore it also seems reasonable to linearly interpolate between them to compute an intensity I_s at (x_s, y_s) using x_L, x_R and x_s:

$$I_S = \frac{I_L(x_R - x_s) + I_R(x_s - x_L)}{x_R - x_L}$$

We now have a light intensity I_s for a position (x_s, y_s) on some raster, and by processing the triangle on a scan-line basis we can Gouraud shade the triangle.

We have already discovered that coloured images can be created by separating the image into the additive primary component colours, red, green and blue, which can be stored individually within a 24-bit frame

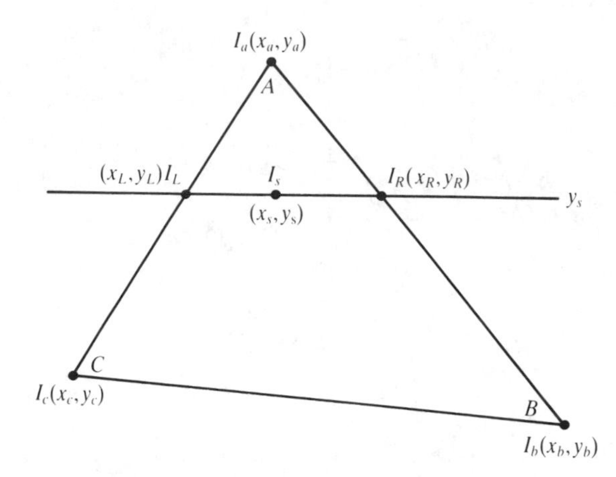

Figure 4.8
Gouraud shading derives pixel intensities by sampling the incident illumination at the vertices of this triangle to give I_a, I_b and I_c. These are then linearly interpolated along the edges to produce I_L and I_R, which are in turn interpolated across the enclosed pixels to compute I_s.

store. So to produce a full-colour image using Gouraud shading, the algorithm has to supply the interpolated pixel intensities for red, green and blue light. If the individual polygons defining an object are shaded using this technique, the final image will obviously appear as though it was constructed from a faceted surface, which is why it is often called 'faceted' or 'flat shading'.

Gouraud also suggested an extension to the technique where a 3-D model could be shaded such that it appeared smooth, though in reality was still constructed from a collection of planar surfaces. To achieve this, one must ensure that the light intensity associated with any vertex must be identical for every surface sharing this vertex. For example, vertex V in Figure 4.9 is shared by the four triangles A, B, C and D, and because these triangles have different orientations, they will reflect different amounts of light when illuminated; consequently the triangles will retain their straight boundaries.

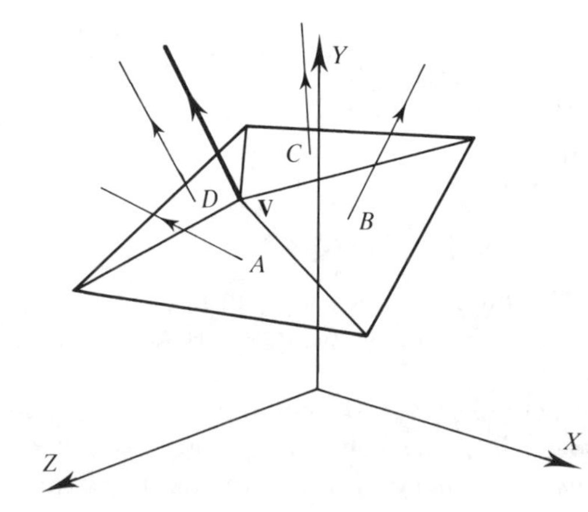

Figure 4.9
Each triangle in this diagram has its own surface normal, and in order to create smooth Gouraud shading an average surface normal is created at the shared vertex. This guarantees that, independent of the triangle being rendered, edges will always have the same intensities and therefore be invisible in the final scene. However, if there are large changes in the surface normals, the intensity changes on either side of the edge are detected by the eye and create visible Mach bands.

Smooth Gouraud shading replaces the four surface normals associated with vertex *V* into an average surface normal, which is then used for light intensity calculations. This ensures that no matter which triangle is being shaded, a consistent light intensity is computed at the shared vertex, and results in a common light intensity along any shared edge between two triangles. If the light levels are identical along these edges, the eye has no way of distinguishing between the two surfaces, and a triangular mesh appears as a continuous surface, apart from its silhouette, where the triangle's edges are still visible. However, the eye does possess some very sophisticated image processing features that enhance changes in light intensity; this is employed for highlighting edges in everyday scenes. Consequently, if the light intensities change rapidly at an edge boundary in a computer-generated image, the eye emphasizes it and creates what are called Mach bands.

4.3.2 Phong shading

Where Gouraud shading generally assumes a diffuse reflecting surface, Phong shading (Phong, 1973) simulates a polished surface by adding specular reflections to the diffuse component. Once more it is an approximation to what in reality is a very complex phenomenon, but in practice it creates some very acceptable images.

To compute the specular component, Phong shading algorithms need to retain a knowledge of the geometric relationships between observer, object and light source. For only when certain angles hold between these elements will a specular highlight be observed. Central to the specular calculation is the surface normal at the incident light ray as shown in Figure 4.3, and as Figure 4.4 shows, the observer is still allowed to see an attenuated highlight even when the angle of observation is not precisely equal to the angle of reflection. For flat-shaded planar surfaces the surface normal is constant, therefore Phong shading evaluates the additional specular component that must be added to the ambient and diffuse component.

To compute this specular component we need to derive a normal vector for every pixel rendered, which could involve considerable geometric computation; but Phong's approach provides a compromise whereby this normal is interpolated in the image space using average normals at the polygon's vertices. As an example, consider the triangle *ABC* in Figure 4.10, where the normals $\mathbf{n}_a$, $\mathbf{n}_b$ and $\mathbf{n}_c$ are average normals computed from the surface normals sharing a common vertex. We can now linearly interpolate $\mathbf{n}_a$ and $\mathbf{n}_c$ to produce $\mathbf{n}_L$ using the values of y_a, y_c and y_s (Figure 4.11):

$$\mathbf{n}_L = \frac{\mathbf{n}_a(y_s - y_c) + \mathbf{n}_c(y_a - y_s)}{y_a - y_c}$$

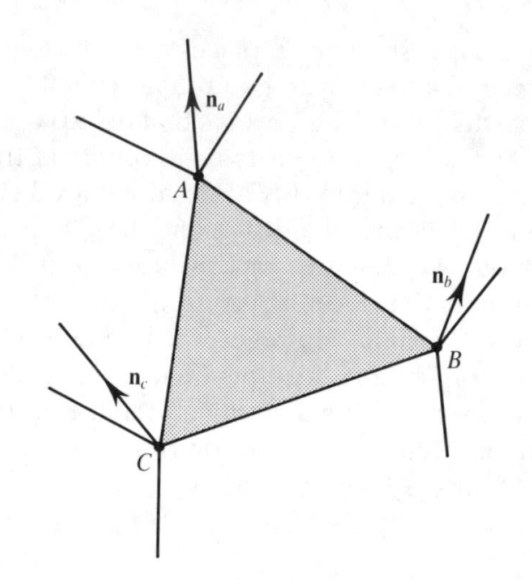

Figure 4.10
In this mesh of triangles the vertices have been assigned average normals; these are interpolated in Phong shading to create smooth specular shading.

A similar expression can be given for $\mathbf{n}_R$:

$$\mathbf{n}_R = \frac{\mathbf{n}_a(y_s - y_b) + \mathbf{n}_b(y_a - y_s)}{y_a - y_b}$$

Therefore, just like Gouraud shading, we can linearly interpolate between these two normals $\mathbf{n}_L$ and $\mathbf{n}_R$ to compute $\mathbf{n}_s$:

$$\mathbf{n}_s = \frac{\mathbf{n}_L(x_R - x_s) + \mathbf{n}_R(x_s - x_L)}{x_R - x_L}$$

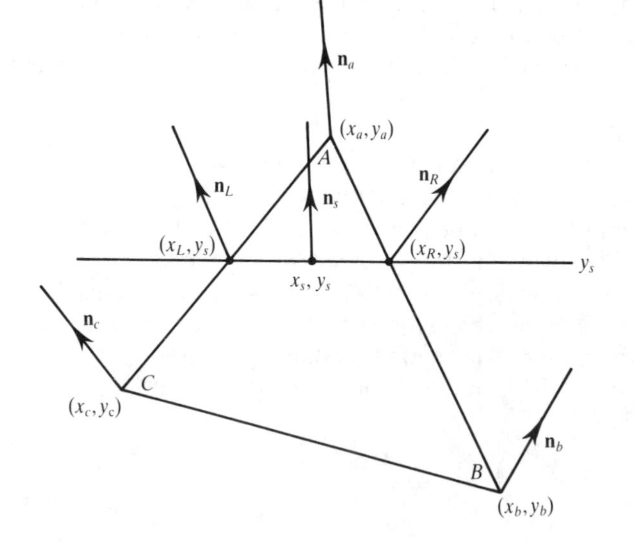

Figure 4.11
Phong shading derives pixel intensities by first computing the average surface normals $\mathbf{n}_a$, $\mathbf{n}_b$ and $\mathbf{n}_c$ at the three vertices. These are then linearly interpolated along the edges to produce $\mathbf{n}_L$ and $\mathbf{n}_R$, which are in turn interpolated across the enclosed pixels to compute $\mathbf{n}_s$. This final vector is substituted into the specular reflection expression shown in the text.

We now have a pseudo-surface normal $\mathbf{n}_s$ which can be substituted into the specular reflection component:

$$I_i K_s(2(\mathbf{n}_s \bullet \mathbf{L})(\mathbf{n}_s \bullet \mathbf{V}) - (\mathbf{V} \bullet \mathbf{L}))^g$$

Although Phong shading produces some very acceptable images, they are still unrealistic, as neither Phong or Gouraud shading consider the optical effects of shadows, multiple reflections, colour bleeding and mirror surfaces. These effects, and others, are described in later sections.

4.4 Hidden-surface techniques

Hidden-surface algorithms ensure that when a scene is rendered, objects closer to the camera will hide more distant ones. Now this is a phenomenon that occurs naturally in the real world, as we – with our sense of vision – receive light waves that interact with opaque and transparent objects. In our computer environment, objects are described using a variety of modelling techniques, and basically are held as collections of numbers. Spatial relationships are also held numerically in the form of coordinates, and therefore the masking of an object by another has to be teased from this data and used to aid the rendering process.

Many real-world objects have a rigid structure that prevents one object penetrating another; some, like liquids and gases, allow objects to pass through them; some are elastic and can adjust their shape when they come in contact with others. These effects cannot be associated with our simple numerical models; they must be deliberately designed into the animation system as procedures incorporating our knowledge of the physical world.

The numerical nature of computer models also causes other problems: imagine, for example, the case of two or more objects that coexist in the same volume of space. In reality, one object normally displaces another when it is moved into the same space, although liquids and gases (because of their molecular structure) can share a common space – whereas inside a computer an object is translated to another position in the WCS by modifying its coordinate values. If this modification causes it to move inside another object, it will have to be resolved by the hidden-surface removal algorithm. Some techniques are unable to cope with this, whereas others are able to resolve the spatial conditions and create effects that are physically impossible. This is another exciting aspect of computer animation where the numerical nature of the animation environment provides a virtual world where physical impossibilities become possible.

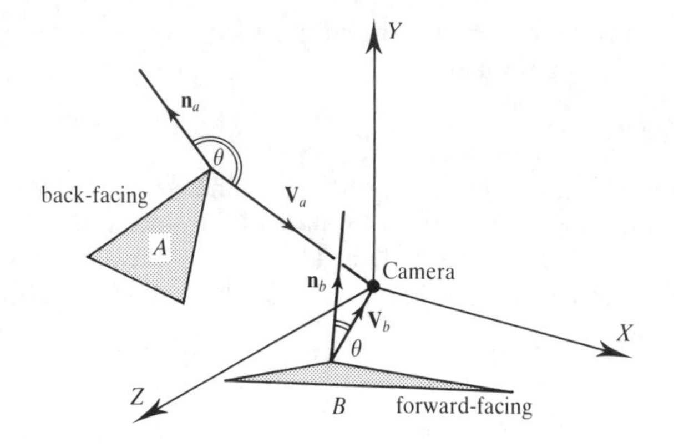

Figure 4.12
Hidden surfaces can be detected by computing the angle subtended from the camera to the surface normal. In polygon A, the angle is less than 90° and is visible; however the angle to B exceeds 90° and is invisible.

4.4.1 Back-face removal

A simple form of hidden-surface removal is to ignore those surfaces facing away from the camera. For instance, convex objects such as a cube, sphere, cylinder, tetrahedron, octahedron, icosahedron and a dodecahedron, back-face removal creates a natural solid image. However, if one of these objects is placed in front of another, they will have a wire frame appearance. Nevertheless, by removing back faces a scene is greatly simplified and the renderer's task is made easier.

Any planar polygon can be tested for a back-facing condition by computing the dot product of its surface normal with the view vector as shown in Figure 4.12. Polygon B is forward-facing and therefore visible as the vectors $\mathbf{n}_b$ and $\mathbf{V}_b$ contain an angle less than 90°; however, polygon A is back-facing as the angle between $\mathbf{n}_a$ and $\mathbf{V}_a$ exceeds 90°.

Most hidden-surface removal algorithms employ this form or polygon pre-processing; however, in a ray-tracing strategy back-facing polygons must not be culled as they may be seen in a reflection. Similarly, in radiosity, although back-facing polygons are invisible to the camera, they still take part in diffuse reflection processes, and must not be removed.

4.4.2 Painter's algorithm

If a collection of 3-D polygons is maintained in an arbitrary sequence and are then selected one at a time and rendered into a frame store, the final image cannot be expected to reflect a true picture of the 3-D scene. Probably what will happen is that some polygons that are relatively close to the camera will be rendered into the frame store, only to be partially masked by more distant ones later on. Such an effect will appear bizarre, however it can be avoided if the original polygons are sorted in a depth sequence such that the first polygon to be rendered is the furthest, and the last polygon is the nearest. This mimics a simplistic approach to landscape painting where the artist develops the canvas by first painting the sky, followed by the mountains, then the fields and trees, and finally decorating the scene with the foreground objects – hence the name of this technique.

Sorting polygons into depth sequence is not always that easy especially when one has to resolve situations where, for example, an oblong polygon passes through the centre of a circular ring. One end of the oblong might be in front of the ring, whereas the other end will be behind the ring; therefore the sorting process will be unable to resolve the question of priority. This problem is resolved by breaking the offending polygons into smaller elements. The Painter's algorithm is not very popular as it suffers from other restrictions such as its inability to handle inter-penetrating objects and anti-aliasing.

4.4.3 Scan-line algorithm

The scan-line algorithm is basically concerned with computing the pixels associated with one line of the image in the frame store, and by applying the algorithm for every raster, which may be several hundred times, the complete scene can be rendered. In general, the process begins with the top scan-line and proceeds a line at a time until it reaches the bottom, at which point the image is released. Some image generator systems are capable of achieving this cycle in just a few milli-seconds, which provides the mechanism for real-time animation.

To compute the pixel intensities for one scan-line, the algorithm initially sorts the visible objects into a vertical sequence so that it can keep a record of which object intersects a specific scan-line. It then analyses those surfaces that intersect the current line and resolves depth priority by considering small portions of the polygons relevant to this raster. In this way it can handle inter-penetrating objects, and implement anti-aliasing strategies.

4.4.4 Z-buffer

The z-buffer algorithm provides a very elegant mechanism for removing hidden surfaces – unfortunately, it suffers from various deficiencies such as its inability to handle transparent surfaces and support anti-aliasing. Nevertheless, because of its simplicity it is very useful, and is often implemented in hardware and found on many graphics workstations.

The z-buffer is actually a memory element for storing depth information for every pixel in the frame store, and is initially primed with some very large number. When the first polygon is rendered, the depth of the polygon is computed at every pixel affected and, as these depths will be smaller than the initial value, they will be used to overwrite the z-buffer. The frame store is loaded with corresponding colour intensities. As further polygons are rendered in an arbitrary sequence, their depths are compared with those currently held, and if they are nearer than these, then they too will overwrite the z-buffer and the frame store. If the pixel depths are found to be greater than the current values this would imply that the polygon is more distant than the previously held surface, and therefore invisible; consequently, these pixels would not be updated and the surfaces would remain hidden. Continuing in this manner, the z-buffer algorithm can accept polygons in any sequence and handle the intersection of objects at a pixel level.

Unfortunately, as there is no mechanism for retaining the opacity of a surface it is unable to handle transparency. For instance, say a 50% transparent polygon has just been rendered and the next polygon is found to be located behind this one. Because the program does not retain opacity data it is unable to show this new polygon attenuated by the transparent surface, however, dithering can help overcome this problem. Similarly, it cannot anti-alias the scene as there is no facility to retain a list of those polygons that impact upon a pixel.

4.4.5 A-buffer

The A-Buffer algorithm (Carpenter, 1984) was developed at Lucasfilm Ltd and inherits its name from its ability to render an image with anti-aliasing using an area-averaged accumulation technique. Central to the algorithm is the concept of bit masks associated with a pixel, which are maintained for the current raster line; these record the impact a polygon has upon any pixel on this raster, and are used to control the final colour of a pixel which contains one or more partially masking polygons.

The algorithm operates by first identifying those surfaces that impact upon the current raster and, by taking one of these in any sequence, it keeps a record of whether it completely or partially masks any of the pixels. The greater its cover, the more influence it has on the pixel's final colour. By storing in the buffer the depth of the surface at this pixel, any surface that is rendered later on can be compared against this depth, and if it is more distant it may be totally or partially masked by the nearer surfaces. This is the simple mechanism for hidden-surface removal.

4.4.6 ZZ-buffer

The zz-buffer (Salesin, 1989) derives its name from the z-buffer as it uses z-depth measurements to resolve hidden-surface removal. It also partitions the rendered scene into a matrix of rectangular cells, where each cell has the ability to retain a list of every polygon that touches a pixel within its domain, and by how much. The list also records the opacity of the polygon and therefore can handle many layers of transparent surfaces. As polygons are input in an arbitrary sequence, lists begin to develop for each cell which are allowed to grow and collapse. For example, say that a particular cell holds a list of transparent surfaces, and the next polygon rendered completely covers the cell, this means that the current list is no longer of any use and can be restarted with this latest polygon. Eventually, when every polygon has been processed, the lists can be rendered to reveal the final image and, due to the spatial independence of the cells, can be given to a multi-processor environment.

4.4.7 Single scan-line depth buffer

As the name suggests, the single scan-line depth buffer is a hybrid algorithm. Its action is based upon the scan-line approach to rendering where the final image is rendered one raster at a time. Where the z-buffer algorithm requires a depth buffer for every pixel on the display device, this approach only requires a depth buffer for the current raster. This means that there is a dramatic saving in memory storage, and allows the depth buffer to have a greater resolution. For example, every pixel could be divided into 16 sub-pixels and dynamic lists maintained for the polygons impacting upon them. This hybrid strategy enables the scan-line depth buffer algorithm to support transparency and anti-aliasing.

4.5 Ray tracing

Ray tracing simulates some of the optical properties of light to determine the frame store pixel intensities. In fact, the basic algorithm is only capable of determining the colour values for one pixel, which means that the program must be executed several hundred thousand times to construct the entire image. This has advantages in that it lends itself to running on multi-processor computers, but also implies that the database has to be replicated for each processor, which may not be practical.

The action of ray tracing can be appreciated by imagining a matrix of holes as shown in Figure 4.13 to represent the pixel positions of a graphics display screen. Here we see the camera directed along the z-axis receiving light rays through the holes, and as long as there are a sufficient number of them (say a million) and they are close together, then the incident light through the holes can be used to fix the pixel intensities in the frame store.

By selecting any hole corresponding to a pixel, it is possible to trace back into the object space the geometric path of the incoming light ray; in fact, by converting this ray into a vector, it is possible to test for an intersection with a surface in the database. One of three things can now occur: first, there are many intersections with objects; second, there are no object intersections, but an intersection with a light source; third, there are no intersections whatsoever. In the last case the ray-tracing algorithm has to be given a value which could be background colour influenced by

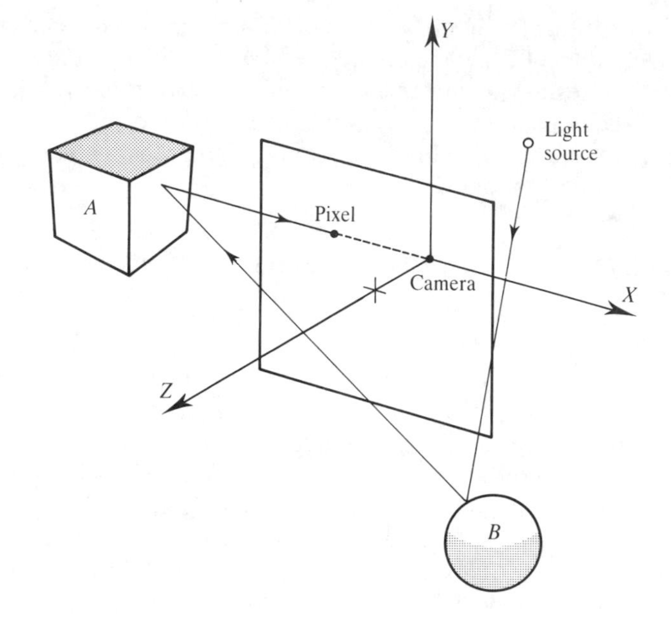

Figure 4.13

In ray tracing, an image is formed by tracing the optical origins of rays which pass through the sample points of the pixels. In this example, the ray seen by the camera has emanated from the light source, reflected off object *B*, and in turn reflected off object *A*. Thus the camera will record a scene where *A* reflects an image of *B*, which in turn reflects the original light source.

atmospheric absorption. In the case of a light source intersection, the ray tracer must compute the light intensity seen by the observer, and take into account the nature of the light source, i.e. whether it is a point, area, directional or spot source, and perhaps even incorporate some form of atmospheric absorption depending upon the light source distance.

The case where the light ray intersects with surfaces is more complex, and only some of the conditions that could prevail will be examined. For instance, the hidden-surface problem is resolved by identifying the surface that provides the nearest intersection, and if this is opaque, other surfaces can be ignored. If this nearest surface was a polished reflecting surface, the ray it was reflecting into the camera must have had an origin, and it is this optical path that is traced back into the database. By tracing back several levels of reflection the pixel's intensity can be influenced by the colour of reflections seen in various surfaces. Not only can these realistic specular reflections be computed, but ray tracing provides a simple method for computing shadows and refractions.

4.6 Radiosity

It is interesting to observe in natural scenes how most surfaces tend to be diffuse reflectors unless they are wet, when they also become specular reflectors. However, one of the most important features of natural scenes is provided by the complex inter-reflections of light that occur when collections of surfaces are in close proximity. These reflections give rise to subtle shading that fade imperceptibly into shadows.

Radiosity is a global illumination model that attempts to simulate these multiple reflections by first dividing surfaces into small patches which will become the sample points at which diffuse reflection occurs. Each patch is then compared with every other patch to identify whether a reflection can actually occur. Where this is possible, the relative orientations of the patches are used to define a form-factor parameter, which represents the fractional radiant energy leaving one patch and arriving at the other. These form factors are substituted into the family of simultaneous equations describing the diffuse optical world of the database, and the equations solved to identify a steady-state condition which satisifies this environment. Once this steady-state condition has been obtained, the light intensities of the original patches can be computed and interpolated across the surface to reveal the subtle shadings.

Although considerable time is required to solve the simultaneous equations, once the patch radiosities have been solved, on some processors the image can be rendered in real-time. And as the technique is view-independent, it means that virtual reality applications such as architecture and interior design can interact with very realistic images. However, this does assume that none of the objects are disturbed in the scene, as this would alter the radiosity values.

Recent research into radiosity has shown how specular reflections can be incorporated, and how the radiosity values can be evaluated using a progressive refinement technique. This enables an approximate image to be created very quickly; then, over a further period of time, the image settles down to a steady-state condition.

Exercises and projects

4.1 Compare the action and definition of point, directional and spot light sources.

4.2 Distinguish between ambient, diffuse and specular light behaviour.

4.3 If a surface colour is defined using HSV values, describe how these can be used to control the reflection coefficients in the diffuse shading model.

4.4 Implement a procedure for rendering triangles using Gouraud shading.

4.5 Modify the procedure from Project 4.4 to create Phong shading.

4.6 Implement the z-buffer algorithm and test it with polygons that penetrate one another.

Further reading

Rendering Perhaps the most useful book to address the rendering process is Watt (1989) which covers reflection models, illumination models, ray tracing, radiosity as well as various aspects of realism. It also refers to key papers that the reader will find useful to obtain a deeper understanding of this fascinating subject. Foley (1990), pp. 721–813, gives a superb treatment of the subject with excellent descriptions of ray tracing and radiosity. The *Renderman Companion* (Upstill, 1989) also provides an interesting insight into all aspects of rendering. Rogers (1985) also covers rendering with good descriptions of hidden-surface algorithms.

Probably the best book on ray tracing is *An Introduction to Ray Tracing* (Glassner, 1989) as it includes chapters written by Eric Haines, Pat Hanrahan, Robert Cook, David Kirk, Paul Heckbert and Andrew Glassner. In 1986, Hall published a paper *A Characterization of Illumination Models and Shading Techniques* (Hall, 1986) which provides a unique overview of the subject.

SIGGRAPH, Eurographics and CG technical papers will still be the best source for state-of-the-art topics in rendering.

KEY POINTS

The renderer creates the coloured images that eventually form the final animation. In achieving this, it relies upon accurate geometry describing the 3-D models, together with the illumination models describing the light sources, and the reflection models that describe how surfaces reflect, transmit and refract light.

- Light sources can be point, directional, spot and ambient and possess attributes such as position, intensity, colour and angle, with other features such as attenuation and directional characteristics.
- Simple reflection models reduce the local lighting calculations to ambient, diffuse and specular components which have three components (red, green and blue) and allow the effects of coloured lights and coloured surfaces to be simulated.
- The ambient component is a constant light term which represents the background light level and accounts for approximately 20% of the total illumination of an object.
- The diffuse component is computed using Lambert's cosine law, where the reflected diffuse light is independent of the observer, but dependent upon the cosine of the incident angle.
- The specular term is dependent upon the angle of incidence and the error angle the observer makes with the reflected ray. The size of the specular highlight is controlled by a gloss term.

- Two popular shading techniques are Gouraud's algorithm where light intensities are linearly interpolated across a polygon, and Phong shading which linearly interpolates average surface normals across a polygon.
- The use of average surface normals enable an object to appear smooth, as the eye is deceived by the intensity changes that change imperceptibly across edge boundaries. However, Mach bands are detected if there is a large change in the average normals.
- Hidden-surface removal algorithms begin with back-face removal followed by techniques such as the painter's algorithm, the scan-line algorithm, the z-buffer, the A-buffer, the zz-buffer and the single scan-line depth buffer which is a hybrid of the previous approaches.
- Ray tracing is a global illumination technique which renders an image on a pixel-by-pixel basis. For any pixel, an imaginary light ray arriving at this point is traced back into the object space to discover its origins. It provides accurate descriptions of specular phenomena, but is forced to make assumptions about the behaviour of multiple diffuse reflections.
- Radiosity is a global illumination technique which computes the radiosities for small patches of a surface. These describe the steady-state diffuse reflection conditions that exist within an environment. It is view-independent, and allows the scene to be rendered very quickly (sometimes in real-time) by linearly interpolating the light intensities of the small patches. Progressive refinement techniques introduce an adaptive algorithm which refines the image over a period of time.

5 Realism

Objects rendered with Gouraud and Phong shading often look synthetic as they lack the natural features we associate with objects in the real world. Therefore in this chapter we examine some of the techniques that are employed in modern renderers to improve the realism of the final image. One of the first problems to resolve are the aliasing artefacts caused by the sampling nature of pixel-based displays. This is a complex subject and it is not vital that a computer animator should understand the fine detail of these algorithms, therefore no analytic rigour is used to support this subject.

The chapter describes the process of texture mapping which provides the most effective way of increasing realism. The problems of mapping flat texture maps onto planar surfaces is discussed, and how cylindrical and spherical mapping functions can create non-linear mappings. Further topics include bump mapping, shadows, motion blur, depth of field, solid texturing, opacity mapping and environment mapping. Finally, the RenderMan system is introduced, as this provides an integrated environment where all of the above features are available.

Introduction

Chapter 4 reviewed some popular shading and hidden-surface removal techniques that are capable of rendering scenes with some success; the radiosity approach perhaps being the most realistic. Realism can be further enhanced by a plethora of extra effects which have resulted from research projects undertaken throughout the world during the past decade. Such realism can include the modelling of mirages, refraction by transparent objects or even the simulation of smoke. In this chapter, only some of the major subjects that have a first-order influence on the fidelity and realism of the rendered image will be considered, and even then, only at a superficial level.

5.1 Anti-aliasing

Anti-aliasing techniques are concerned with minimizing the visual artefacts introduced by the scene sampling methods for constructing a computer-generated image. Such artefacts are associated with edges of polygons where 'staircase' jagged pixels appear as illustrated in Figure 5.1, and the display of thin objects which are really beyond the resolving capacity of pixel-based systems. Other visual anomalies appear in the form of moiré patterns when detailed texture is displayed, which become extremely annoying when the texture is moving. This last effect is very common in conventional television images, especially on clothing containing fine woven patterns.

One obvious technique for reducing aliasing is to increase the number of samples taken within a pixel area; for example 4, 9, 16 or more sub-pixel samples, which can be used to influence the intensity of the pixel. By associating different numerical weights with these samples, the intensity can be related, through various functions, to the pixel's masking by a polygon. When a number of polygons impact upon the same pixel, their

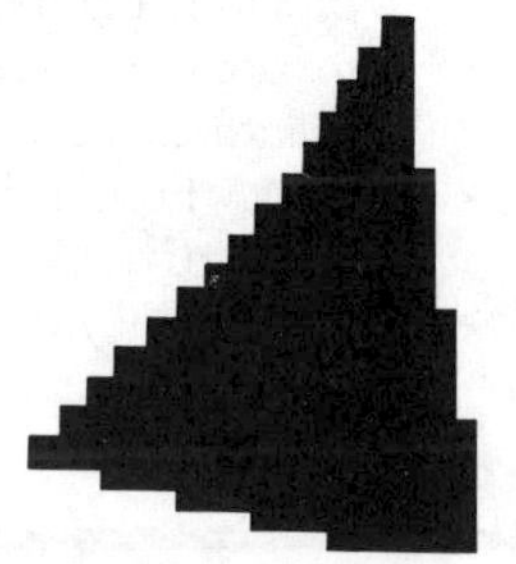

Figure 5.1
The familiar aliasing artefact of jagged edges is introduced when polygons are rendered without computing whether they completely or partially cover a pixel.

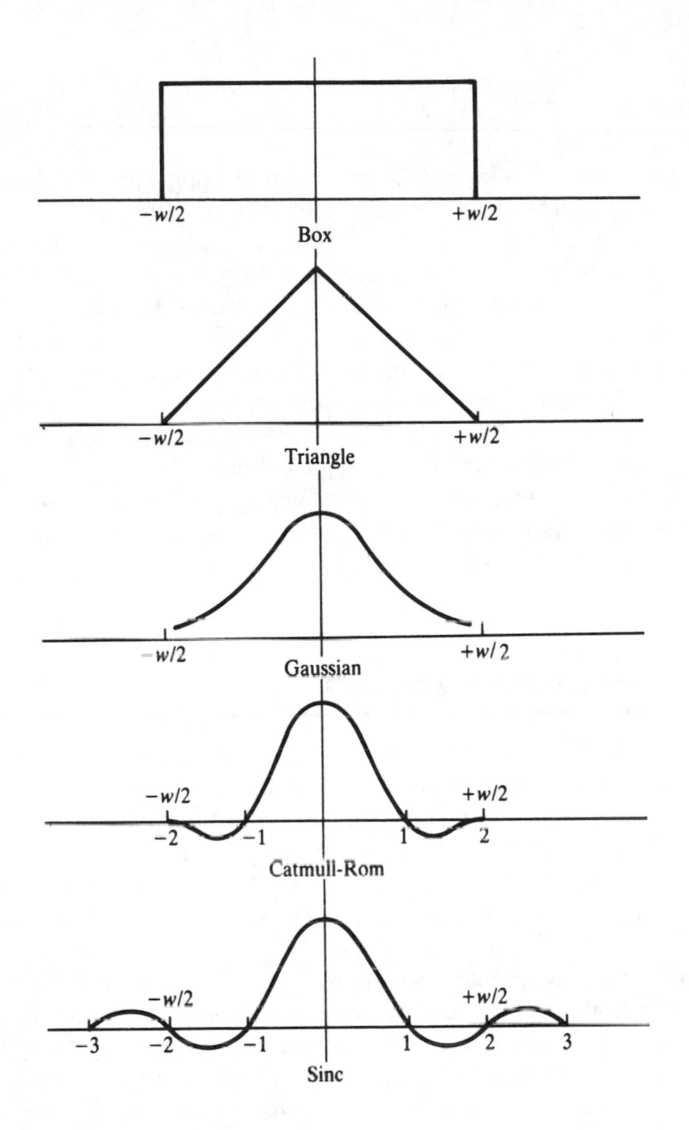

Figure 5.2
These five filter functions illustrate the different weights that can be in operation over one or more pixel widths. As one proceeds from the *box* towards the *sinc* function, the anti-aliasing improves, but extra processing time is required.

individual contributions to the final colour can be computed using this technique. The weights associated with the pixel samples are derived from filter shapes such as triangle, box, Catmull-Rom, sinc and Gaussian, as illustrated in Figure 5.2.

The number of samples and assigned weights will naturally have an influence on the efficacy of the strategy, and will ultimately be reflected in the processing required to undertake this extra computation. Unfortunately, no matter how many samples are made, there could always be detail in the scene which will give rise to aliasing. Another approach, which is not so obvious, is to sample different positions within a pixel on a random basis; this randomizing of sample points, called stochastic sampling (Dippe, 1985), creates visual noise which does not appear so objectionable to the human visual system.

There are other approaches to anti-aliasing, yet whichever technique is used, extra processing time is required, and this may not be thought to be worthwhile especially during the early stages of an animation project. The artefacts discussed above are the result of sampling the image space at discrete positions, consequently the effect is frequently referred to as 'spatial aliasing'. Another form of aliasing, which is well-known in animation, is called 'temporal aliasing'; this arises when a moving object is sampled at different points in time, and causes effects such as rotating wheels to reverse in direction as their speed increases. As it was first noticed in early movies involving stage coaches, the effect is sometimes called the 'wagon-wheel' effect. Not much can be done to alleviate this effect apart from attempting to blur the rotating object before its onset; this is examined further in Section 5.5.

5.2 Texture mapping

One very simple method of increasing image realism is to cover 3-D models with texture detail, perhaps derived from some external source. The texture is normally held as a matrix of pixels known as a texture map, which may be 24 bits deep for full-colour images. The map is addressed using coordinates in exactly the same way as any 2-D area, and to avoid confusion with spatial coordinates, the labels assigned to the horizontal and vertical axes are u and v. Consequently, the term '*uv*-coordinates' is frequently employed in texture mapping.

The mapping of the texture onto the surface can be accomplished in a variety of ways, and it should be appreciated from the beginning that it is impossible to lay any flat design upon most non-planar surfaces without the design being distorted in some way, therefore it is highly likely that some form of distortion will creep in. Much depends upon the nature of the object's surface geometry.

For example, if a planar polygon is to be mapped with texture, then somehow the pixels associated with this polygon must be assigned colour intensities from the texture map. However, because the polygon can have an arbitrary orientation, different parts of the surface will receive different portions of texture. Figure 5.3 shows a texture map addressed with *uv*-coordinates, and another diagram illustrating how a pixel's footprint is projected back onto the polygon. The polygon also references a set of axes to control the orientation of the texture. Now if the texture map is to completely cover the polygon, we need to map the pixel's footprint back into the texture space. This is possible because the polygon provides us

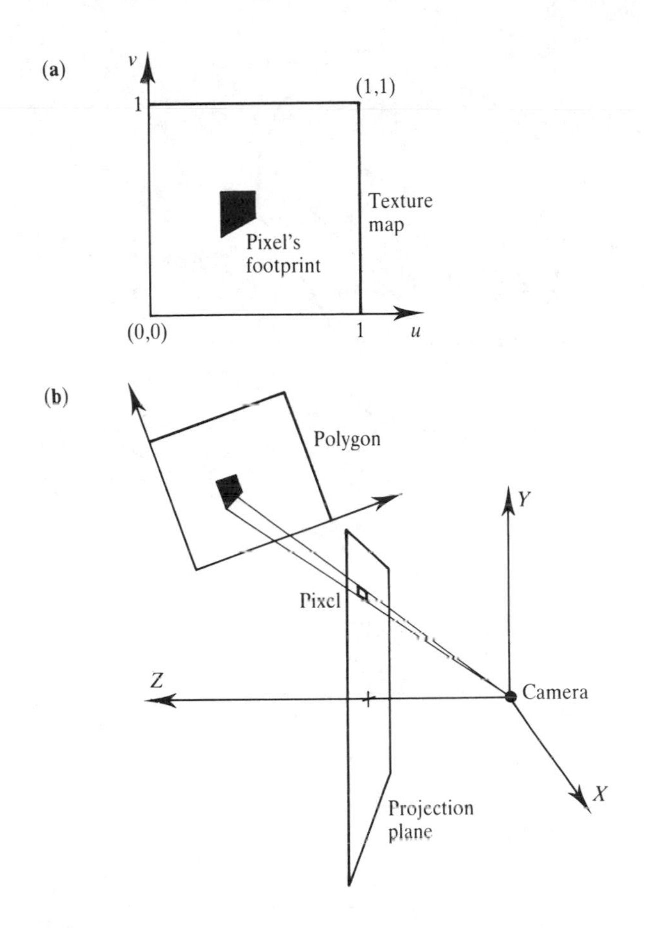

Figure 5.3
A texture map is conventionally addressed using *u* and *v* coordinates to distinguish them from the *x*-, *y*- and *z*-coordinates associated with 3-D space descriptions. In this diagram a pixel's footprint is projected back onto a polygon, which in turn has to be mapped into the texture space. This filtered value of the pixel's footprint in the texture map is then assigned to the pixel.

with the necessary 3-D geometry contained in vertex values and its surface normal. The next stage involves identifying those elements of the texture map covered by the footprint, and if this is not performed accurately will introduce flickering aliasing artefacts when the polygon moves.

There are three conditions that must be addressed by the renderer. First, if the polygon is very close to the camera, the pixel's footprint could be smaller than a texture element (texel); second, as the polygon recedes, the footprint shape will cover one or two texels; and third, when the polygon moves into the distance, the footprint could cover the entire texture map. Obviously, a renderer must be able to handle all three cases, but the techniques employed are beyond the scope of this text. Nevertheless, the geometry of mapping onto a plane, cylinder and sphere will be examined.

To map texture onto a planar surface, a mechanism is first needed to align the texture with the surface; this can be accomplished by associating an axis with the surface which aligns with an axis on the texture map.

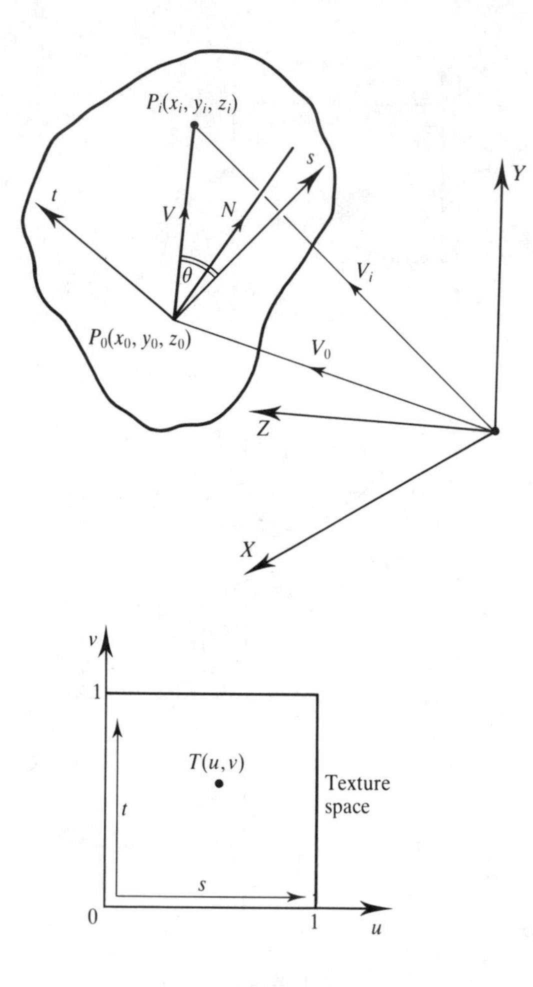

Figure 5.4
When texture is mapped onto an arbitrary plane, a mapping function is required to relate the point $P_i(x_i, y_i, z_i)$ to $T(u, v)$. These functions are shown in the text.

Second, a point on the surface is needed to fix the $T(0,0)$ point of the texture map. And third, a scaling factor k will control how the scale of the texture relates to the size of the surface.

Figure 5.4 illustrates an arbitrary surface which is to be mapped with the texture from the texture map addressed by u and v. The vector **S** on the surface will align with the u-axis of the texture, and the point $P_0(x_0, y_0, z_0)$ will align with $T(0,0)$ on the texture. If the following conditions exist:

N is a unit vector normal to the planar surface
S is a unit vector orthogonal to **N**
$P_0(x_0, y_0, z_0)$ is a reference point on the plane mapped to $T(0,0)$
$P_i(x_i, y_i, z_i)$ is a point to be mapped into $T(u, v)$
k is a scaling term for the texture

then

$$\mathbf{V}_i = \mathbf{V}_0 + \mathbf{V}$$

where

$$\mathbf{V} = \begin{bmatrix} x_i - x_0 \\ y_i - y_0 \\ z_i - z_0 \end{bmatrix}$$

Then

$$\mathbf{V} \cdot \mathbf{S} = |\mathbf{V}|\,|\mathbf{S}|\cos(\theta)$$

but

$$ku/|\mathbf{V}| = \cos(\theta)$$

And as $|\mathbf{S}| = 1$

$$\mathbf{V} \cdot \mathbf{S} = uk$$

therefore

$$u = \mathbf{V} \cdot \mathbf{S}/k$$

Similarly,

$$v = \mathbf{V} \cdot \mathbf{T}/k$$

where the vector **T** is given by the cross product of **N** and **S** and is equal to:

$$\mathbf{T} = \begin{bmatrix} N_2S_3 - N_3S_2 \\ N_3S_1 - N_1S_3 \\ N_1S_2 - N_2S_1 \end{bmatrix}$$

This technique only relates to the mapping of single points on a plane to the texture map, and does not consider the anti-aliasing strategies that must be implemented when the pixel's footprint is evaluated.

Let us now consider the geometry of cylindrical mapping as shown in Figure 5.5. Here we see a cylinder with radius r and height h. The point $P_i(x_i, y_i, z_i)$ will be mapped into the texture space as $T(u, v)$, and the inverse mapping functions are:

$$v = y_i/h$$
$$\theta = \cos^{-1}(z_i/r)$$

and if θ is expressed as a ratio of 2π,

$$\theta' = \cos^{-1}(z_i/r)/2\pi$$

Now if $x \geqslant 0$ then $u = \theta'$, else $u = 1 - \theta'$.

These functions can be tested as follows:

If $P_i = (0, 0, r)$, then $\theta' = 0$, and $u = 0$
If $P_i = (r, 0, 0)$, then $\theta' = 0.25$, and $u = 0.25$
If $P_i = (0, 0, -r)$, then $\theta' = 0.5$, and $u = 0.5$
If $P_i = (-r, 0, 0)$, then $\theta' = 0.25$, and $u = 0.75$

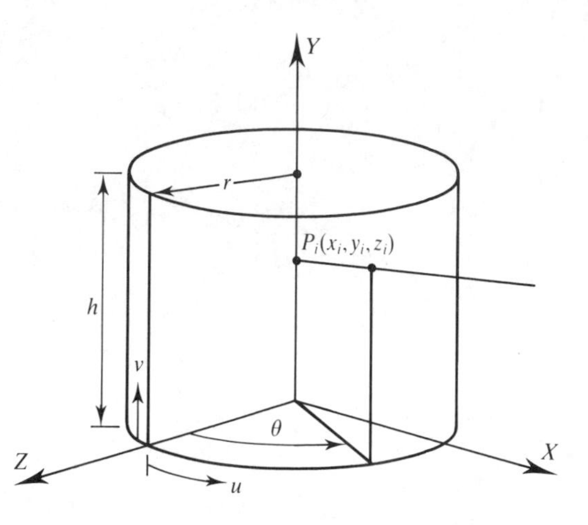

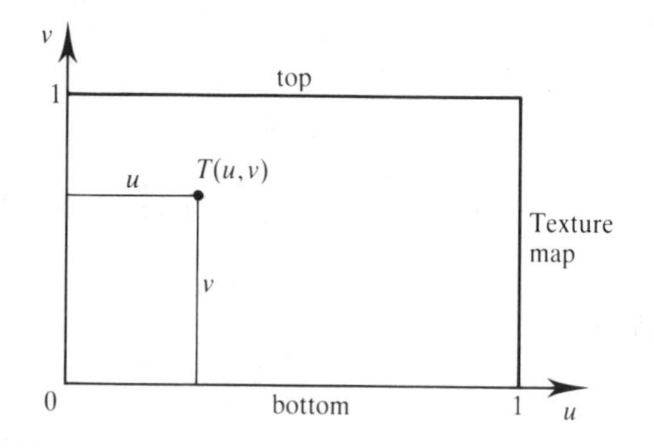

Figure 5.5
When texture is mapped onto a cylinder, a mapping function is required to relate a point $P_i(x_i, y_i, z_i)$ to $T(u, v)$. These functions are shown in the text.

These can be verified with reference to Figure 5.5.

Spherical projection is also very useful in texture mapping especially for creating artificial planets. For if one prepares a texture map containing coloured surface detail it is possible to map it onto the surface of a sphere using the following technique.

Figure 5.6 shows a texture map addressed by coordinates u and v, and a sphere of radius r addressed by latitude and longitude coordinates. When a pixel's footprint is projected onto the sphere we need to compute the uv-coordinates for the four corners of the pixel to determine its colour. For this we need functions that will convert any point on the sphere into a point on the texture map. Obviously the texture will be distorted when it is mapped onto the sphere, as we can see that all texels having a v-coordinate of 0 are mapped onto the south pole, while all texels having a v-coordinate of 1 are mapped onto the north pole. But this can be compensated for when the texture is painted.

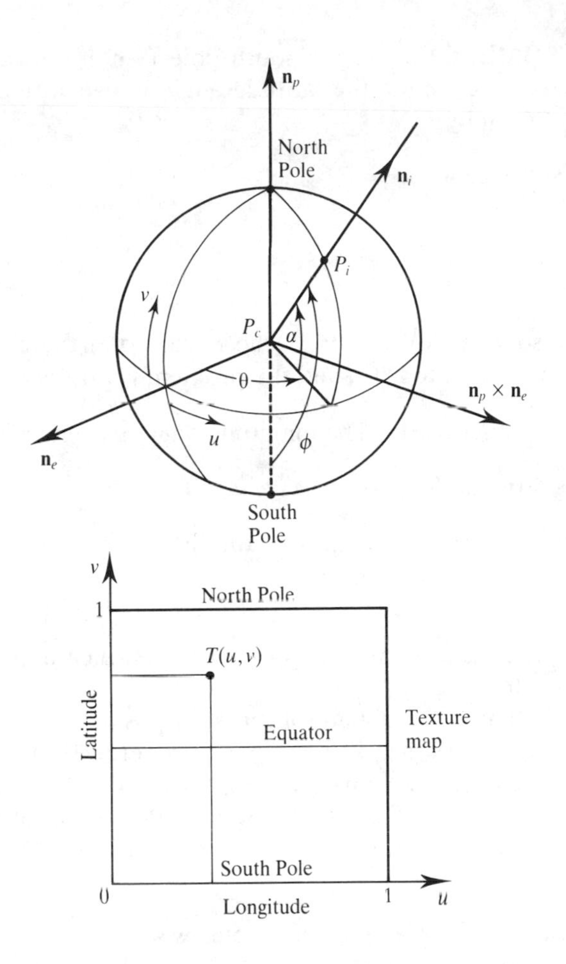

Figure 5.6

When texture is mapped onto a sphere, a mapping function is required to relate a point $P_i(x_i, y_i, z_i)$ to $T(u, v)$. These functions are shown in the text.

To begin with, the sphere requires a position and orientation, so let the following parameters control this:

$\mathbf{n}_e$ is a unit vector normal to a zero reference point on the equator
$\mathbf{n}_p$ is a unit vector orthogonal to $\mathbf{n}_e$ and normal to the north pole
P_i is the point (x_i, y_i, z_i) to be mapped to $T(u, v)$
$\mathbf{n}_i$ is a unit vector normal to P_i
P_c is the centre of the sphere (x_c, y_c, z_c)
r is the radius of the sphere.

Then

$$\mathbf{n}_i = \begin{bmatrix} (x_i - x_c)/r \\ (y_i - y_c)/r \\ (z_i - z_c)/r \end{bmatrix}$$

Compute v (latitude) As the south pole ($-\mathbf{n}_p$) is to be mapped to $v = 0$, we need to compute the latitude angle between $\mathbf{n}_i$ and the south pole, which is given by:

$$\phi = \cos^{-1}(-\mathbf{n}_p \bullet \mathbf{n}_i)$$

therefore

$$v = \phi/\pi$$

If $v = 0$ (the south pole) or $v = 1$ (the north pole) there is no need to compute u; this can set to zero, and the problem is finished.

Compute u (longitude) The longitude angle θ is given by:

$$\theta = \cos^{-1}((\mathbf{n}_e \bullet \mathbf{n}_i)/\sin(\phi))$$

and if $\phi = \pi/2$ (the equator) then θ becomes:

$$\theta = \cos^{-1}(\mathbf{n}_e \bullet \mathbf{n}_i)$$

When $\mathbf{n}_i = \mathbf{n}_e$ (i.e. coincident) then $\theta = 0$ or 2π, which implies that θ will eventually have to be scaled by $1/2\pi$.

However, another problem concerns the position of $\mathbf{n}_i$ relative to the plane containing $\mathbf{n}_e$ and $\mathbf{n}_p$. This can be discovered by taking the cross product of $\mathbf{n}_p$ and $\mathbf{n}_e$ (Figure 5.6) and computing the dot product with $\mathbf{n}_i$. If this angle exceeds zero it is on the same side as this normal vector, otherwise it is on the opposite side.

Thus:

$$u = \theta/2\pi \qquad \text{if } (\mathbf{n}_p \times \mathbf{n}_e) \bullet \mathbf{n}_i > 0 \qquad \text{otherwise}$$
$$u = 1 - \theta/2\pi$$

Let us test this with an example:

$$\mathbf{n}_e = \begin{bmatrix} 0 \\ 0 \\ 1 \end{bmatrix}$$

$$\mathbf{n}_p = \begin{bmatrix} 0 \\ 1 \\ 0 \end{bmatrix}$$

$$\mathbf{n}_i = \begin{bmatrix} 0.707 \\ 0.707 \\ 0.0 \end{bmatrix}$$

Compute v (latitude)

$$\begin{aligned}\phi &= \cos^{-1}(-[0\ 1\ 0] \bullet [0.707\ 0.707\ 0.0]^T) \\ &= \cos^{-1}(-0.707) \\ &= 2.356(135°) \\ v &= 0.75\end{aligned}$$

Compute u (longitude)

$$\begin{aligned}\theta &= \cos^{-1}\left(\frac{[0\ 0\ 1] \bullet [0.707\ 0.707\ 0.0]^T}{\sin(2.356)}\right) \\ &= \cos(0/0.707) \\ \theta &= \pi/2\,(90°)\end{aligned}$$

Compute the cross product $\mathbf{n}_p \times \mathbf{n}_e$ For two vectors $\mathbf{v}$ and $\mathbf{w}$, where:

$$\mathbf{v} = \begin{bmatrix} v_1 \\ v_2 \\ v_3 \end{bmatrix} \quad \text{and} \quad \mathbf{w} = \begin{bmatrix} w_1 \\ w_2 \\ w_3 \end{bmatrix}$$

the cross product is given by the vector:

$$\begin{bmatrix} v_2w_3 - v_3w_2 \\ v_3w_1 - v_1w_3 \\ v_1w_2 - v_2w_1 \end{bmatrix}$$

Therefore, $\mathbf{n}_p \times \mathbf{n}_e$ is given by:

$$\begin{bmatrix} 1 - 0 \\ 0 - 0 \\ 0 - 0 \end{bmatrix} = \begin{bmatrix} 1 \\ 0 \\ 0 \end{bmatrix}$$

therefore

$$[1\ 0\ 0] \bullet \begin{bmatrix} 0.707 \\ 0.707 \\ 0.0 \end{bmatrix} = 0.707$$

This is greater than zero, therefore:

$$u = \frac{\pi/2}{2\pi} = 0.25$$

We see that the uv-coordinates for this point on the sphere are $u = 0.25$, and $v = 0.75$.

The above three mapping functions form the basis for projecting texture onto objects and are normally standard features of professional renderers. Plate 4 illustrates the level of detail that can be achieved using texture mapping.

5.3 Bump mapping

Bump mapping was developed by James Blinn (Blinn, 1978c), and increases realism by introducing a pseudo-surface patterning effect which gives the appearance that the surface is covered with a 'bumpy' surface texture such as leather or concrete. The bump map is introduced into the computer system either from a video source or the output from a paint program, or computed using some algorithm. During the rendering stage the intensity levels of this image are used to disturb the surface normal when computing specular highlights. This results in a surface that appears to be covered in a mottled texture which creates highlights and shadows, and emphasizes the 'bumpy' effect.

5.4 Shadows

Shadows are found wherever there are light sources and objects, and provide us with important visual cues to aid our interpretation of the 3-D physical world. The lack of shadows in many computer-generated images is one reason why they fail to appear convincing; frequently it is difficult to determine whether an object is resting on a floor or floating above it, simply because a vital shadow is missing.

The reason for their omission is due to the time needed for their computation, especially when the scene is complex and there are several active light sources. However, we have already seen that ray tracing can reveal some very acceptable shadows, and radiosity develops shadow zones caused by objects in close proximity. These techniques are not always available, however, and even when they are, they might not provide the type of imagery required by the animator. Consequently, shadow algorithms have been developed as add-on effects which can be incorporated with other rendering algorithms.

Consider the following solution for computing shadows. Figure 5.7 shows a scene where a single light source illuminates an object that casts a shadow onto the ground; photographing the scene is a camera. If one imagines being positioned at the light source, it becomes possible to construct a shadow map of visible surfaces from this viewpoint. This map

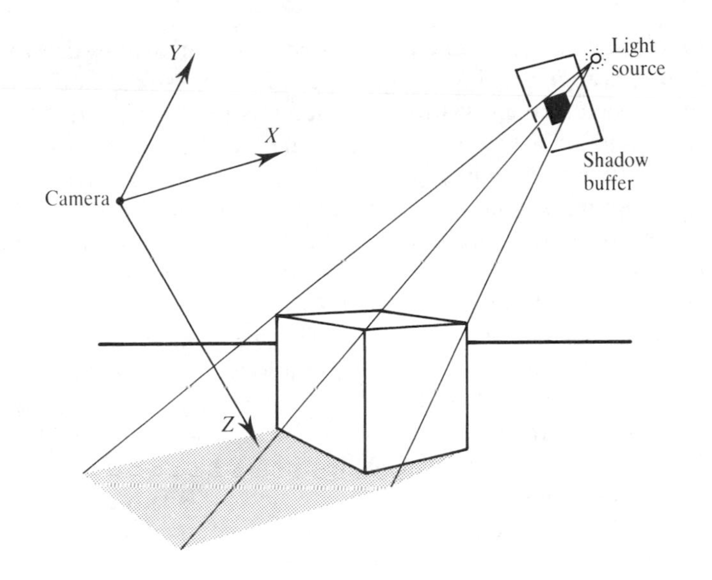

Figure 5.7
To speed up the process of detecting shadows, a shadow map can be created for each light source illuminating a scene by storing the depths of surfaces nearest to the light source in a light buffer. Points visible to the camera may be visible or invisible relative to the light source: when they are visible to the light source, they are illuminated, but when they are invisible, they are in shadow.

stores the depths of surfaces from the light source, somewhat similar to the z-buffer algorithm. From the position of the camera, one can investigate every pixel of the scene to see whether it is illuminated, or in shadow. This can be discovered by selecting a pixel and projecting its footprint onto the nearest surface. This position in space is then tested to see whether it is visible using the light source's depth map: if it is not, then the pixel is in shadow or else it is illuminated. This technique is used to speed up shadow calculations in ray tracing and scanline renderers. Although the technique is simple to implement, it fails if the camera is too close to the shadows, or the resolution of the buffer is coarse.

5.5 Motion blur

Motion blur is probably a phenomenon with which we are all familiar, and is frequently found on photographs where subjects have been moving too fast for the camera's shutter speed. A car, for example, travelling at 30 mph (50 kph) covers approximately 1.5 ft/sec (0.46 m/sec), but if the camera's shutter is operating at 0.01 sec, during this period it only covers a distance of 0.176 in (0.447 cm), which might not be noticable. Yet someone waving their arms about could easily exceed speeds of 1.5 ft/sec (0.46 m/sec), and cause a blurred photograph. Such blurring is also found in cine films and television, and recent developments in camcorder technology have produced video cameras with shutter speeds in the order of 0.001 sec, which virtually eliminates image blur.

In traditional cel animation, where each image is drawn, back-painted and photographed for projection at 24 frames/sec, motion blur will not occur as each image is stationary when it is photographed. This means that if the animator wishes to accentuate the motion of a character, it will have to be deliberately blurred using a drawing or painting technique.

In computer animation, the virtual camera has no physical shutter speed; it records a status of the world space at an instant in time, therefore motion blur cannot arise. Consequently, when these images are animated, one loses the sense of motion associated with cine and video animation, as the individual images are too precise. To meet these drawbacks, techniques have been developed whereby motion blur is deliberately introduced during rendering. One technique developed by Andrew Glassner uses 'spacetime ray tracing' to blur objects in motion (Glassner, 1988). The renderer is based upon a ray tracing algorithm which is extended to create the 3-D volume swept out by a moving object; this is then sampled with extra rays over a small period of time to simulate an open shutter.

Steve Upstill describes another technique employed in RenderMan which uses a time-varying parameter approach (Upstill, 1989). This involves identifying those objects to be blurred and the motion to which they are subjected and, rather than describe each scene at the different moments when the shutter is open, the objects are described several times by the parameters controlling their motion. The parameters are then interpolated over the shutter time to move the object, during which time it is sampled to develop the final blurred image. There are other approaches to motion blur which are listed in the reference section of this text. Plate 6 shows a ray-traced scene incorporating motion blur.

5.6 Depth of field

Depth of field, like motion blur, is another attribute associated with camera technology, but this time it is associated with the camera's lens system. Once more, personal experience with a conventional camera reminds us that, in general, the lens has to be focused upon a subject to obtain a sharp image. However, some cameras do exist that employ a fixed-focus lens, which is only capable of realizing sharp images over a useful distance for the majority of images taken.

The depth of field of a lens describes the distance in the object space over which the focused image is 'reasonably' sharp. It is a function of the lens aperture, in that the smaller the aperture, the greater the depth of field. This feature is exploited by photographers for isolating objects within a scene by keeping them in sharp relief against a blurred (out of focus) background.

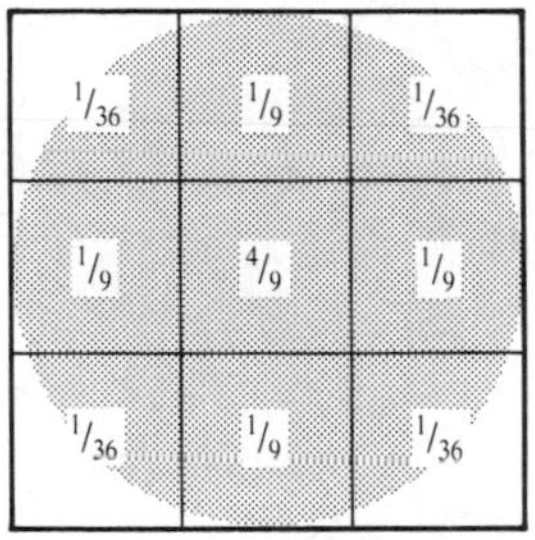

$^1/_{36}$	$^1/_9$	$^1/_{36}$
$^1/_9$	$^4/_9$	$^1/_9$
$^1/_{36}$	$^1/_9$	$^1/_{36}$

Figure 5.8

If a circle of confusion covers a 3×3 pixel matrix, the intensities can be distributed as shown.

The pinhole camera model described in Section 2.1.3 is the basis for capturing perspective images within a computer and, as it does not employ a lens, there is no associated depth of field, and everything is always in perfect focus. So if the blurring caused by depth of field is required, it must be deliberately introduced by the renderer.

A depth of field effect can be created by simulating the action of a lens which focuses a point in its object space onto an image screen when the following relationship is satisfied:

$$1/d_o + 1/d_i = 1/f$$

where d_o is the object distance, d_i is the image distance, and f is the focal length of the lens. However, if f is constant, then different values of d_o will require complementary values of d_i to satisfy the lens equation. But as the image screen distance is fixed, points in the object space will either focus perfectly upon the image screen or create circles of confusion.

Potmesil and Chakravarty proposed that the diameter of this circle of confusion C_d could be specified by the following formula:

$$C_d = (1 - d/d_i)f/n$$

where d is the distance of the image plane from the lens and n is aperture stop number (Potmesil, 1982). Values of f and d_i are as specified above in the lens equation. When the diameter of this circle of confusion is computed, the light intensity for this sample point is spread over surrounding pixels. For example, if the diameter of the circle covers a 3×3 pixel square, the light intensities could be distributed as shown in Figure 5.8. It is this spreading of light values that creates the image blurring effect.

In RenderMan (Upstill, 1989), the user can select a depth of field by supplying the system with the focal length of the lens, its aperture, and the distance at which the image appears in perfect focus – the renderer should then blur the image accordingly. Plate 7 shows a scene rendered with a depth of field.

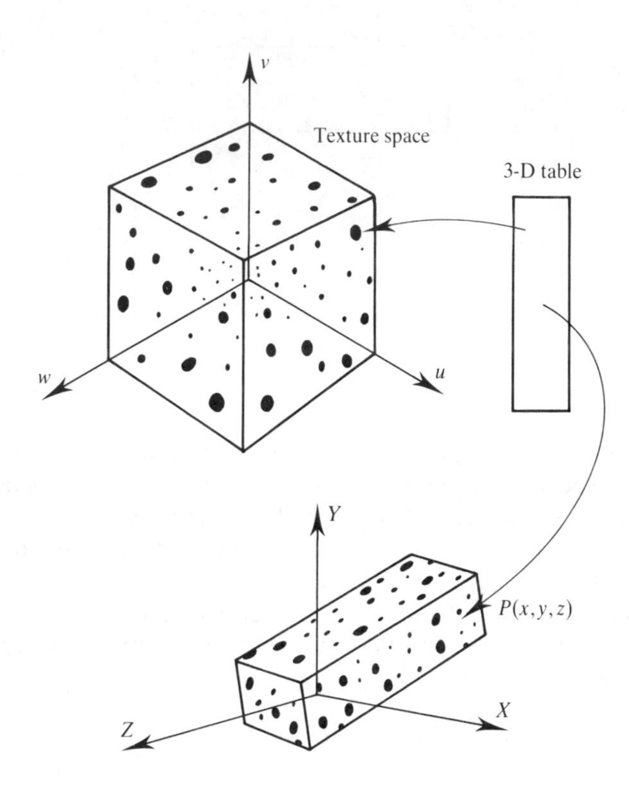

Figure 5.9

In this example, a table locates the position and size of spherical bubbles permeating a unit volume of space. When an object is rendered using solid texture, points on its surface are used to access the table to discover whether it is covered by a bubble or a background colour. If the object has cut-away portions, the exposed surface will reveal a continuous solid texture effect.

5.7 Solid texture

One disadvantage with texture mapping is the distortion that occurs when it is wrapped around a complex surface, resulting in patterns that should remain spatially consistent, becoming stretched. Solid texture (Peachey, 1985) overcomes this problem by defining the texture pattern in terms of mathematical functions or procedures that explicitly define what texture exists in any point of 3-D space. Naturally, the technique cannot be used for mapping photographs and other images upon objects, but it is extremely effective for creating surface textures such as marble, stone, wood grain, composite and abstract patterns.

The algorithm is best illustrated by describing how an object could be covered with random circular spots of colour. To begin with, a mechanism is needed to locate the position and size of these spots throughout a volume of space. This can be achieved with a table of random *xyz*-values that reference the bubble radius located at this point. When the object is rendered, the surface geometry provides the precise 3-D location viewed at a pixel, which is used to search the table to discover whether the pixel is covered by a coloured spot or by a background colour. This geometry is illustrated in Figure 5.9. No matter how complex the object may be, the volumetric nature of the texture ensures that the spots appear correctly distributed over the surface.

Wood grain effects can be simulated by defining a volume of space which contains parallel slices of alternate colour, or with concentric cylinders. Such definitions can be specified through simple functions which, when interrogated by a renderer, reveal which colour should cover the associated pixel. An interesting effect emerges if the object is moved, which results in the texture pattern sliding over the surface.

5.8 Environment mapping

Although reflections from polished surfaces can be distracting, they are vital to the correct rendering of chrome-plated objects such as knives and forks, and other highly polished materials. Ray tracing can easily compute these precise optical reflections, but is rather an expensive approach and also introduces aliasing through its sampling strategy. An alternative technique is through the use of environment maps, which assist in modelling the world surrounding a polished object to create visually acceptable reflections.

To illustrate this technique, imagine that a chrome-plated spoon has to be animated and composited with video images taken in a real kitchen. Ideally, one should see different reflections of this kitchen as the spoon moves about, but rather than model the entire kitchen within the computer, an environment map can be created which effectively performs this operation. The map consists of six photographs taken from the centre of the kitchen with the camera directed toward the four walls, the ceiling and the floor. The camera may have to be fitted with a wide-angle lens to capture every surface. If these six images are now input to the animation system and addressed such that they effectively enclose the space used by the spoon, a ray-casting technique can determine which part of the map is seen by the viewer. Plate 14 shows a scene rendered using this technique.

When a model has to reflect other synthetic models within the animation system, the environment must be constructed from this source data. This also implies capturing the maps from the centre of the object reflecting this environment, although the object is not part of this operation. RenderMan provides two facilities for building these maps either using the above cubic surface, or with a spherical map. In the latter case, because distortion is inevitable when mapping between flat and spherical surfaces, these environment maps are often created using an electronic paint system, whereby an artist can pre-distort the image to compensate for the distortion introduced by the mapping function.

5.9 Opacity mapping

Transparency effects are easily implemented within a ray tracing environment, as objects can be declared transparent and assigned an index of refraction. However, within other rendering schemes, opacity mapping provides an effective method for creating variable transparency effects. Basically, it consists of making an opacity map (or transparency map which is just the inverse) whose values control the degree of opacity given to the associated surface portion. It is subjected to the same inverse mapping functions to determine the pixel's footprint, and when an opacity value is computed this will control the level of opacity assigned for the surface at this pixel. Anything behind the surface will be visible depending upon the degree of opacity. The renderer still assumes that a surface exists and will create specular highlights given the right optical conditions.

5.10 RenderMan

In the previous sub-sections, some of the important issues affecting synthetic image realism have been described which include shading, texture mapping, bump mapping, illumination, anti-aliasing, opacity mapping and environment mapping. These techniques appeared at different times in the evolution of computer graphics, from different researchers and were, in general, incompatible with one another.

Bill Reeves and Pat Hanrahan, as part of the Lucasfilm group, designed a software interface for the REYES machine, which was being developed by Tom Porter, Adam Levinthal, Mark Leather and Jeff Mock, to render the highly complex images that were becoming a feature of their work. This software interface was the first version of RenderMan. With the participation of many other people, the software specification developed into the current product.

RenderMan provides a scene description methodology where objects, scenes, lights and cameras can be defined and manipulated coherently through procedure calls within conventional programming languages. It also provides the user with powerful interfacing tools for constructing 3-D objects including extrusions, swept surfaces, Bézier and B-spline surface patches. RenderMan's most important feature is the distinction it makes between the modelling and the rendering domains. A user knows that when a model is built it can be rendered using the various features of the shading language.

The success of RenderMan in providing a standard means of defining synthetic 3-D scene description depends upon the willingness of various manufacturers to implement the interface for their products. This has already begun to happen, and there is a good chance that RenderMan is here to stay for some time.

Exercises and projects

5.1 Distinguish between spatial and temporal aliasing, giving examples of each.

5.2 What effect will the resolution of a shadow map have upon the quality of shadows computed using this technique?

5.3 Explain the difference between texture mapping and solid texture.

5.4 Explain why shadows are a natural feature of ray tracing but have to be explicitly calculated in many other rendering procedures.

5.5 Implement the inverse texture mapping functions described in Section 5.2.

Further reading

Realism Realism is a subject that advances in leaps and bounds with every SIGGRAPH conference, where papers appear on every aspect of this subject. Many of the ideas presented in these papers may never find their way into books, and conference proceedings will be the only source for this information. The reference index contains most of the recent articles to appear in the proceedings of SIGGRAPH, Eurographics and CG, and *IEEE Computer Graphics and Applications (CG&A)*. Amanatides surveyed the subject in 1987 and published a paper in *IEEE CG&A* (Amanatides, 1987a). Blinn's column in *IEEE CG&A* is worth following, especially the articles on aliasing, anti-aliasing and texture mapping (Blinn, 1989a; 1989b; 1989c; 1990a). Although the paper is old, Crow's paper 'Survey of antialiasing techniques' (Crow, 1978) is useful, so too are his later papers (Crow, 1984; 1986). Heckbert's paper 'A survey of texture mapping' published in *IEEE CG&A* (Heckbert, 1986) is also a useful paper to acquire.

KEY POINTS

Modern renderers incorporate a variety of extra features that permit the creation of photo-realistic images. These consist of implementations of more accurate reflection models and various mapping strategies that introduce real-world images.

- Renderers base their image data upon samples of the geometric database made at the screen resolution – this sampling process introduces image artefacts referred to as aliasing.

- Anti-aliasing strategies must be introduced to filter out artefacts such as jaggies and moiré patterns in textured scenes.
- Texture mapping enables painted texture or photographic texture to be mapped onto arbitrarily-oriented surfaces. Planar surfaces and cylinders will not introduce any distortion, however, spheres and toroids will distort the texture by the very nature of their geometry.
- Bump mapping uses the texture map to modulate the surface normal during rendering for creating a pseudo-bumpy surface effect.
- Shadows do not occur as a natural bi-product of the rendering process: they can be computed using shadow volumes formed by a light source interacting with an object, or with shadow buffers, which have limitations of resolution.
- Motion blur simulates the effect of objects moving while the camera's shutter is open, and depth of field simulates the out-of-focus effects found in a normal lens.
- Solid texture employs a procedural technique for introducing a decorative texture on surfaces, where texture functions define the distribution of explicit texture patterns in space which can be applied to any arbitrary surface without distortion.
- Environment mapping simulates the effect of reflective surfaces reflecting their surrounding environment. This can be effected by the use of six maps arranged in the form of a box.
- Opacity mapping techniques are used in the modelling of semi-transparent objects. The map's values modulate the surface's opacity at different parts of the surface.
- RenderMan provides a unique environment for describing the modelling and rendering domain. Some manufacturers have implemented interfaces for accepting RenderMan descriptions.

6 Traditional Animation

Introduction

6.1 History of animation

This chapter is relatively short as its sole purpose is to reveal the background of traditional animation and prepare us for the later chapters that address specific topics in computer animation. What is interesting to discover, though, is that many people have been attempting to create animated images for well over a century, and today's work in computer animation is just a continuation of this process. It has engaged the activities of a wide range of personalities including scientists, engineers, inventors and artists; it has also created totally new professions for people to pursue, not to mention a thriving animation industry that depends heavily upon the television industry.

Today we see the emergence of computer animation which will ultimately have a tremendous impact upon traditional animation techniques but, until there are technological processes that offer real benefits over traditional methods, the labour-intensive approach of back-painting cels will continue. However, one can see a day in the future when computer animation will become so simple and cost-effective, that it will have a dramatic effect upon the animation industry.

Introduction

'To give life to or cause to come alive' is my dictionary's definition for animation, and in the context of cartoon animation this is achieved by an animator creating a sequence of drawings which, when viewed in rapid succession, create an illusion of continuous life-like movement. In fact, animation techniques extend beyond the source imagery of drawings – they include clay models, puppets, and shapes cut from paper. Nevertheless, they all exploit the human visual system's ability to integrate a sequence of individual images into a sensation of visual continuity.

The point at which a sequence of images stops flickering and is seen as a coherent image, is called the fusion frequency. This depends upon the brightness of the images, and is in the region of 40 Hz. Cine film, for example, is projected at 24 frames/sec, and a rotating blade interrupts each image two or three times to create an effective refresh rate of 48 Hz or 72 Hz, which is needed in cinemas to prevent flicker occurring on their large bright screens.

PAL television also exploits this integrating process by displaying 25 images every second; in fact, if the refresh rate were 25 Hz one would detect flicker. However, in reality, each image frame is composed of two fields consisting of the odd and even raster lines. These two fields are displayed alternately and effectively double the refresh rate to 50 Hz. In the USA, the NTSC television standard employs a similar process, but the refresh rate is approximately 60 Hz – it is in fact 59.94 Hz. Computer animation is also based upon these well-established principles and simply introduces the computer as the source of the images. The computer's introduction is not arbitrary; it brings many advantages, and also some disadvantages, which are the subjects of the following chapters.

In this introduction it is worth mentioning that computer animation is still relatively young, and has had very little opportunity to develop a history of usage to compare with traditional animation. It is therefore understandable that interfaces have still not evolved which solve all of an animator's problems. This is just a question of time, and developing future systems can be very exciting, even though it involves learning and understanding concepts which are not directly associated with the pure design aspects of animation.

6.1 History of animation

Animation has been around in one form or another for over 150 years; some of the important landmarks are listed below:

1824 Peter Roget presented his paper 'The persistence of vision with regard to moving objects' to the British Royal Society.

1831 Dr Joseph Antoine Plateau and Dr Simon Ritter constructed a machine called a phenakistoscope which produced an illusion of movement by allowing a viewer to gaze at a rotating disk containing small windows, behind which was another disk containing a sequence of images. When the disks were rotated at the correct speed, the synchronization of the windows with the images created an animated effect.

1834 Horner developed the zoetrope from Plateau's phenakistoscope.

1872 Eadweard Muybridge started his photographic compilation of animals in motion.

1887 Thomas Edison started research work into motion pictures.

1889 Thomas Edison announced his kinetoscope which projected a 50 ft length of film in approximately 13 seconds.

1889 George Eastman began the manufacture of photographic film strips using a nitro-cellulose base.

1895 Louis and Auguste Lumière issued a patent for a device called a cinematograph capable of projecting moving pictures.

1896 Thomas Armat designed the vitascope which projected the films of Thomas Edison; this machine had a major influence on all subsequent projectors.

1906 J. Stuart Blackton made the first animated film called 'Humorous phases of funny faces'.

1908 Emile Cohl produced a film depicting white figures on a black background.

1908 Winsor McCay produced an animation sequence using his comic strip character 'Little Nemo'.

1909 Winsor McCay produced a cartoon called 'Gertie the Trained Dinosaur' consisting of 10000 drawings.

1913 Pat Sullivan created an American cartoon series called 'Felix the Cat'. J.R. Bray devised 'Colonel Heeza Liar', and Sidney Smith created 'Old Doc Yak'.

1915 Earl Hurd developed cel animation.

1917 The International Feature Syndicate released many titles including 'Silk Hat Harry', 'Bringing Up Father', and 'Krazy Kat'.

1923 Walt Disney extended Max Fleischer's technique of combining live action with cartoon characters in the film 'Alice's Wonderland'.

1926 Lotte Reiniger produced the first feature-length animated film called 'Prince Achmed'.

1927 Warner Brothers released 'The Jazz Singer' which introduced combined sound and images.

1928 Walt Disney created the first cartoon with synchronized sound called 'Mickey Mouse'.

1943 John and James Whitney produced 'Five Abstract Film Exercises'.

1945 Harry Smith produced animation by drawing direct onto film.

1957 John Whitney used 17 Bodine motors, 8 Selsyns, 9 differential gear units and 5 ball integrators to create analogue computer graphics.

1961 John Whitney used differential gear mechanisms to create film and television title sequences.

1964 Ken Knowlton, working at Bell Laboratories, started developing computer techniques for producing animated movies.

In the 1960s, computer graphics was starting to blossom and it was already obvious to many researchers that there was a potential application in the field of animation. It was left to the enthusiasm of these people to develop systems that could take some of the tedium away from traditional animation techniques. It has really only been during the last decade that computer animation has been able to demonstrate that the technology has really something unique to offer.

In general, the 1960s was a time for computer graphics to become established, and for many of the subjects that were to become major areas of research to be identified. The 1970s was a period of intense research and many important answers were discovered to fundamental technical problems. The 1980s saw computer graphics taken from the research laboratory into the commercial domain, where it made significant in-roads in the areas of architecture, engineering CAD, medicine, graphic design and even animation.

No one would claim that any of these systems were perfect; users often had to struggle with far-from-friendly interfaces, which had been designed by computer scientists for computer scientists. Data files would mysteriously disappear, programs could malfunction, and certain activities needed hours instead of minutes to arrive at some trivial result. In spite of these inevitable teething problems, modern systems can at last perform tasks which would be unthinkable without the assistance of computer technology.

So, although it is very easy to criticize the quality of animation from this period, it must be borne in mind that some projects were undertaken under conditions that promised very little chance of success and yet, after several months or one or two years of very hard work, there appeared a few seconds of animation that moved the subject another step forward.

What is obvious to everyone in the industry is that, although programmers may possess extraordinary skills in developing software, they cannot be expected to possess similar skills in graphic design and animation. This has stimulated animation companies to employ both animators and software programmers who, as a team, can stimulate the synthetic forms of computer graphics into some semblance of life. Achieving this requires that each party understands the other's needs, which means developing a mutual appreciation of unusual techniques and new terms. It is also worth mentioning that there are some truly gifted people working in computer animation who possess extraordinary programming skills and artistic sensitivities.

Central to the world of character animation are the techniques of squash and stretch, slow-in and slow-out, arcs, anticipation and exaggeration. And central to the world of computer graphics are the techniques of coordinate geometry, vectors, parametric curves and software engineering. Applying the tools of computer graphics to solve the sensitive needs of the animator is no mean task; the programmer must appreciate the importance of an animation technique, and somehow develop an insight into why and how it is used. The animator must expect some form of compromise in the way the programmer will be able to implement the technique using a keyboard, screen menus and data tablet. Together, though, they can make for original and exciting 3-D computer animation, which is the subject of the following sections.

Further reading

Traditional animation *The Animator's Handbook* (White, 1986) is a very useful introduction to traditional animation; it covers everything from inbetweening and run cycles to exaggerated action and backgrounds.

KEY POINTS

Traditional animation has a long history extending back over 150 years. The production process still relies upon some well-established ideas which are listed below.

- Animation effects exploit the eye's characteristic of persistence of vision.
- When a sequence of discrete images are projected, the observer will detect a continuous visual sensation given an adequate refresh rate.
- The point at which flickering subsides is called the 'fusion frequency' and is in the region of 40 Hz. Television screens are refreshed at 50 Hz where each new image is formed from the odd or even raster lines.
- Film is projected at 24 Hz but is interrupted by a blade to produce an effective refresh rate of 48 or 72 Hz.
- Earl Hurd developed cel animation in 1915.
- Walt Disney created Mickey Mouse in 1928.

- Computer animation begins in earnest during the 1960s.
- Rendering and modelling algorithms were developed in the 1970s.
- Image realism and convincing computer animation were further extended in the 1980s.

7 Computer Animation Tools

Mathematics plays a central role in any computer animation system, and one of the skills of the system designer is to hide as much of it as possible from the animator, whose task is concerned with images and movement. However, in spite of the excellent commercial computer animation systems on the market, there are always situations when one needs to develop a program to realize some new effect, and this may need an understanding of some useful mathematical techniques. Consequently, this chapter illustrates the ideas behind linear and non-linear interpolation which play an important part in the dynamics of animation. In particular, the use of formulae, external data and random numbers can be used for creating movement, but blending techniques provide a powerful method for smoothly changing a parameter from one state to another. In this section quadratic, cubic, Hermite, and parabolic blending are illustrated. Finally, the chapter explores the ideas behind Bézier and B-spline curves with practical examples to illustrate their usage in computer animation.

Introduction

In traditional animation, virtually everything must be created with pencil, paper and the innate skill of the animator, although there are times when rotoscoping (tracing images from film or video) provides a helping hand in achieving some complex movement. In computer animation, many of the animator's techniques have been committed to computer programs, and the animator's skill is now measured in how well he or she can control these programs to create a desired effect. For example, in cel animation, changing one contour into another is a relatively simple operation. The first and last key frames are initially drawn on separate sheets of paper and are inbetweened by an assistant, called an 'inbetweener'. If the movement between the first and last images is linear, the inbetweener's task is to calculate the equal distances moved for each frame and draw the inbetween frames accordingly. However, in reality non-linear movements are more likely, and the inbetweener's task is made slightly more complicated.

In calculating these inbetween frames, the inbetweener employs a chart to control the rate at which the animation moves towards a key frame – these are an important aid to creating realistic walk cycles, eye movements and other subtle movements. Similar tools must be available within the computer animation environment; in fact a plethora of tools is available, some replicating traditional tools, and others that are peculiar to the world of computer animation. Let us examine some of these and see how they are employed.

7.1 Representing attributes numerically

An attribute is any feature or quality associated with the things that comprise the computer animation environment. Examples are hue, saturation, value, height, depth, width, gloss, angular velocity, coordinates, transparency, translucency, field-of-view, focal length, tension and atmospheric absorption levels. All of these may be used to describe the cameras, objects and lights associated with an animation sequence, and all of them, without exception, are stored numerically within the computer. Some of the numbers may be decimal, as in the case of the x-, y- and z-coordinates of a vertex, which can also be negative. Numbers representing levels of hue, saturation and value are always positive with an upper limit of 1, whereas levels of red, green and blue in a frame store are represented by positive integers, with a typical range of 0 to 255.

It is up to the animation software to ensure that these numbers retain their integrity, as illegal values might cause havoc in the system. For example, the distance between two points can only be a positive number –

a negative distance has no physical meaning (apart from its usage in Cartesian coordinates). Similarly, dimensions such as height, width and depth are also positive quantities, and although a modelling program might accept a negative value for a depth, there is no guarantee that something valid will result.

The integers loaded into a frame store must never be allowed to exceed their range, as unpredictable effects will result. This requires that renderers must continuously monitor the red, green and blue intensities being computed to prevent overflow conditions.

Translating physical attributes into numbers might appear to be a disadvantage but, on the contrary, this is a perfect notation for the computer, even though it may cause some inconvenience to human users. For when animation programs have access to numerical descriptions, anything can be changed into anything with incredible speed, which makes computer animation possible and useful.

Imagine, for one moment, any piece of computer animation with which you are familiar. No matter how the animation had been produced, whether with a commercial animation system or with a system of FORTRAN or C++ programs, each frame results from the status of various parameters held within the computer's memory. The entire animation sequence was produced by changing these parameters in an orderly fashion to achieve some desired visual effect. Attributes can be changed in a variety of ways, including the use of formulae, interpolation, externally derived data or even randomly, and these methods are now examined in some detail.

7.2 Animating numbers

For thousands of years man has attempted to understand and explain the physical world: from the motion of a swinging pendulum, to the movement of stars. Mathematics is the language that has evolved to describe such physical behaviour, although it has also developed into a language for describing abstract and impossible worlds. Mathematics can be considered as a language of rules for manipulating numbers, which are frequently associated with physical systems. For example, when a heavy object is suspended beneath a spring, it is possible that the spring's stiffness and the object's mass allow the system to oscillate freely at some resonant frequency. Mathematical techniques provide a mechanism for calculating this frequency without having to build the system. In fact, current research into the animation of physical systems employ such mathematical techniques.

Mathematics also provides solutions to problems where two or more numerical values are known, from which it is possible to determine some underlying pattern. For example, say we have been given the position of

three different points on a plane that should lie on a circular arc; a simple formula enables us to calculate the radius and the circle's centre. This type of geometrical reasoning is vital to computer graphics.

If, for the moment, one ignores how an animator is interfaced to an animation system, then changing numbers becomes the key to successful animation. If only the values representing the attributes describing objects, lights and cameras can be changed correctly, then the problem is solved. So the real issue revolves about the dynamics of numbers.

7.2.1 Linear interpolation

In computer animation we are frequently faced with the problem of knowing that an object is located at point $P_1(x_1, y_1, z_1)$ at frame F_1, and at point $P_2(x_2, y_2, z_2)$ at frame F_2, and the object has to be moved from P_1 to P_2 as the frame count proceeds from F_1 to F_2. Computing these inbetween values is called interpolating, and when they have equal spacings, the term linear interpolation is used.

If we introduce a new concept in the form of a parameter t, computing the interpolated values becomes extremely easy. The parameter t varies between 0 and 1, and the intermediate positions are then specified by $P(x, y, z)$ as follows:

$$x = (1 - t)x_1 + tx_2$$
$$y = (1 - t)y_1 + ty_2$$
$$z = (1 - t)z_1 + tz_2$$

where $0 \leqslant t \leqslant 1$.

A quick examination of these statements confirms that when t equals zero, $P(x, y, z)$ is equal to P_1, and when t equals 1, $P(x, y, z)$ is equal to P_2. And when t takes on any other value between 0 and 1, $P(x, y, z)$ is set to the corresponding linear interpolated position. However, something has to control the value of t, and in this example it will be the current frame number F, which starts with a value of F_1 and finishes at F_2. The following rule for computing t ensures that when F equals F_1, t equals zero, and when F equals F_2, t equals *1*:

$$t = \frac{F - F_1}{F_2 - F_1}$$

The graph of this relationship is shown in Figure 7.1.

The steps in the animation sequence can be summarized as follows. For frames between and including F_1 and F_2:

(1) Compute t using F, F_1 and F_2.

(2) Compute $P(x, y, z)$ using t, P_1, and P_2.

(3) Display the object at $P(x, y, z)$.

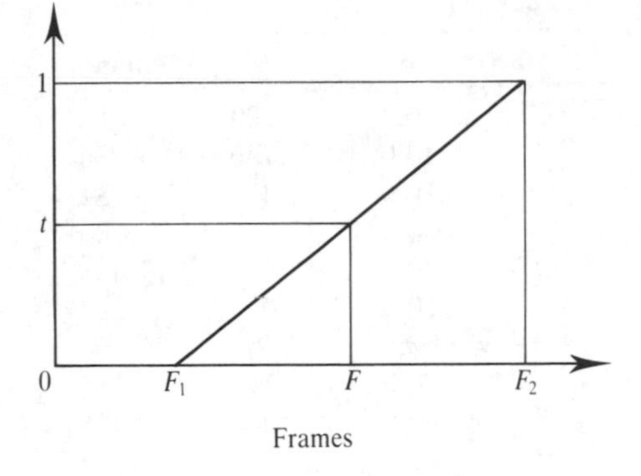

Figure 7.1
This straight-line graph depicts a linear relationship between F, as it changes from F_1 to F_2, and t as it changes from 0 and 1.

As the frame count F increases, so does t, therefore the object will move from P_1 to P_2, as required.

Obviously this form of linear interpolation can be applied to any pair of quantities, whether they be colours, speeds, positions, angles or coordinates. Another aspect of interpolation is the non-linear type which enables us to alter the spacing between the interpolated values; this type of movement is vital to animation and is considered in the next section.

7.2.2 Non-linear interpolation

Newton's first law of motion states that 'every particle remains at rest or moves with uniform motion in a straight line unless or until acted upon by an external force'. However, Nature has arranged that uniform motion rarely happens, for there is always something to get in the way and prevent such linear behaviour. A rolling ball is eventually brought to rest by frictional forces, and a rifle's bullet has to ultimately succumb to the force of gravity and the drag of air resistance. Even when we want to move an object, it does not immediately change to the desired speed; its mass resists the propelling force resulting in the object being accelerated to a new velocity.

Now these movements are non-linear and are well documented in the form of laws, which enable them to be incorporated within a computer program to accurately control the movements of objects. However, it is going to be impossible to simulate everything using physical and mathematical laws, so we will have to discover other techniques that approximate this behaviour.

One very useful non-linear effect is created by the sine function whose graph is in the form of a smooth undulating wave. When the parameter of the function is altered in linear steps, it creates a sequence of non-linear values. This can be used for blending one number into another. For example, say we needed to interpolate between N_1 and N_2 such that the initial rate is fast, but slows down until at the end of the sequence the

Table 7.1

Frame	θ	N	Change
1	0.0	10.000	–
2	10.0	11.736	1.736
3	20.0	13.420	1.684
4	30.0	15.000	1.580
5	40.0	16.428	1.428
6	50.0	17.660	1.232
7	60.0	18.660	1.000
8	70.0	19.397	0.737
9	80.0	19.848	0.451
10	90.0	20.000	0.152

rate of change falls to zero. This can be achieved using the sine function over the period of 0° to 90°, and can be expressed as:

$$N(t) = (1 - t)N_1 + tN_2$$

where $t = \sin(\theta)$ and θ varies from 0° to 90°. Table 7.1 shows the interpolated values between $N_1 = 10$ and $N_2 = 20$ occurring over 10 frames.

The last column indicates the change in N and shows that between frames 1 and 2 there is a relative change of 1.736, whereas between frames 9 and 10, this has reduced to 0.152, confirming the non-linear effect. The numerical values in Table 7.1 are also shown graphically in Figure 7.2.

If we are not satisfied with the animation created by the sine function, then other functions can be explored such as a square-law relationship, which can be implemented by declaring N as follows:

$$N(t) = N_1 + (N_2 - N_1)t^2$$

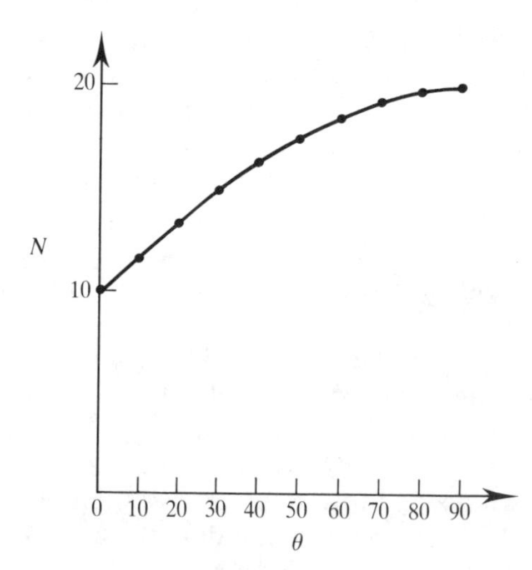

Figure 7.2
This graph shows how a non-linear interpolation can be achieved between $N = 10$, and $N = 20$, using a sine interpolant. The values are listed in Table 7.1.

Table 7.2

Frame	t	N	Change
1	0.0	10.0	–
2	0.1	10.1	0.1
3	0.2	10.4	0.3
4	0.3	10.9	0.5
5	0.4	11.6	0.7
6	0.5	12.5	0.9
7	0.6	13.6	1.1
8	0.7	14.9	1.3
9	0.8	16.4	1.5
10	0.9	18.1	1.7
11	1.0	20.0	1.9

This creates values of N as shown in Table 7.2 with t varying from 0 to 1 in equal steps.

Notice that the rate of change in N begins very slowly at 0.1, and finishes with a final increment of 1.9. The graph of this data is shown in Figure 7.3.

Obviously one could explore a whole range of functions to create different animation effects, but hopefully these two examples are sufficient to demonstrate how non-linear interpolation can be used to simulate the slow-in and slow-out movements used in traditional animation.

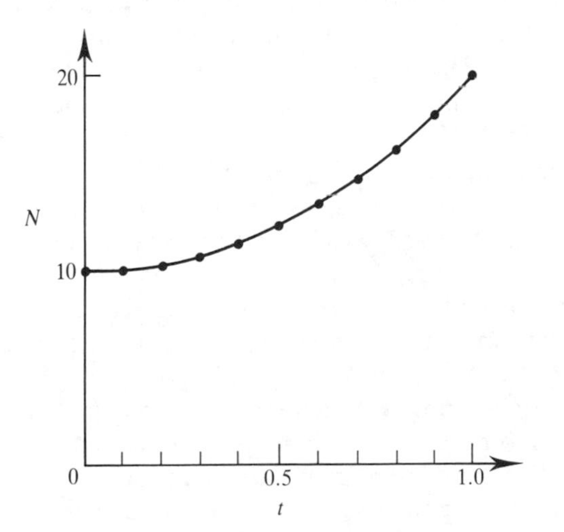

Figure 7.3
This graph shows how a non-linear interpolation can be achieved between $N = 10$ and $N = 20$, using a quadratic interpolant. The values are listed in Table 7.2.

7.2.3 Formulae

Mathematical formulae are essential for controlling movements that have a precise regularity or a well-defined form. For example, the hands of a clock rotate at a constant angular velocity; the swinging arm of a metronome has a regular beat; and a bouncing ball traces out parabolas that decay as the ball loses its energy through friction, overcoming air resistance and creating noise and heat. This type of behaviour can be animated by employing the equations used in mechanics, physics and science.

As a very simple illustration let us consider the problem of animating an object which rotates about the origin by a fixed radius, and at the same time undulates up and down. Rather than associate absolute values to the radius, speed and undulation height, let us declare parameters which can be adjusted to provide a range of animations. Useful parameters would be:

F is the current frame number.
R is the radius of rotation.
θ is the angle rotated by the object per frame of animation.
H is the amplitude of the sinusoidal undulations.
N is the number of undulations per rotation.

The motion of the object is illustrated in Figure 7.4, and can be described by defining the three coordinates as follows:

$$x = R\sin(F\theta)$$
$$z = R\cos(F\theta)$$
$$y = H\sin(NF\theta)$$

The x- and z-coordinates control the rotation about the origin on the ground plane, while the y-coordinate ensures that the object undulates up and down with a wave motion of amplitude H. The $F\theta$ term ensures that as the frame count F increases, the angle rotated by the object is automatically generated. The $NF\theta$ term for the y-coordinate can be understood as follows: if $N = 1$, then during one rotation the object will rise and fall exactly once, and if $N = 2$, then it will rise and fall twice during one revolution. The rotation will be in an anti-clockwise sequence about the y-axis, but can be reversed by making θ negative.

The object is now animated by computing x, y and z for each frame and translating it to this position before it is rendered. The animation can be further embellished by allowing the object to tumble about its own centre while performing the above rotation. This tumbling action would be performed prior to translating the object to the point (x, y, z).

This example brings out a very important technique in problem-solving, which is to reduce a problem into several components and resolve them individually. Coordinate geometry is an ideal mathematical tool for determining these components, and one should always attempt to analyse

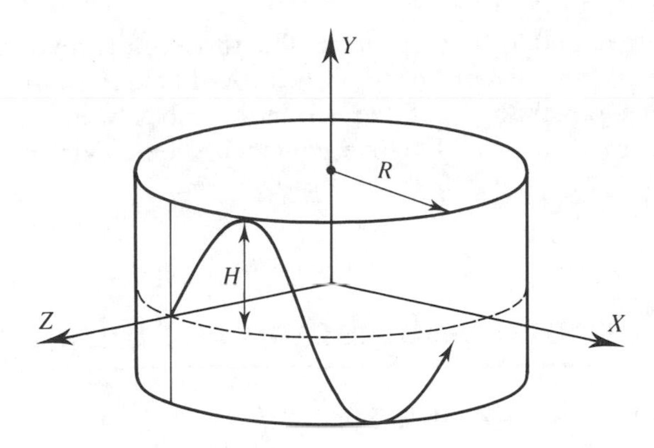

Figure 7.4
The path of this object is such that, while it rotates about the *y*-axis, it is also subjected to a sinusoidal vertical displacement.

any geometrical problem by thinking in terms of parametric expressions that generate the separate *x*-, *y*- and *z*-coordinates.

7.2.4 External data

There will be occasions when external data has to be input to control an animation sequence; this might be in the form of a special curve a camera has to follow, or the variation in size associated with an object. A good example for the latter technique is in the simulation of a human heart beating. Having modelled the heart from cross-sectional geometrical data, further medical data might be available describing how certain parts of the heart move in space. This data can be input and used to manipulate the 3-D model. Basically, there are no limits to the type of data that can be input to an animation program, as long as an input path exists in the animation system.

7.2.5 Random numbers

Random number generators provide a useful source of numerical data: when instructed, these programs supply a random number within a specified range, having a uniform distribution. In fact, these programs are often called pseudo-random number generators as they usually have a cycle which repeats itself over and over again. This cycle is not a problem as it is normally very long, perhaps in the order of tens of thousands of numbers.

An application of random numbers is in the assignment of random rotations which could be associated with a large number of objects. Take a situation where 1000 cubes have to be shown rotating in space about their own centres, and each cube must have a random motion within a given range. A simple solution would be to store for each cube three random numbers representing the angular rotations about the *x*-, *y*- and *z*-axes in an array – 3000 numbers in all. The final scene is created by taking one

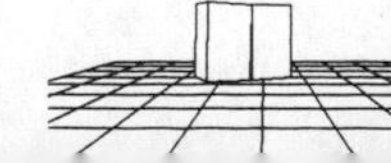

cube at a time, and subjecting it to the three individual accumulated rotations. Even the positions of the cubes could be determined randomly, but there is a possibility that two or more cubes would intersect one another – yet even this could be overcome with some extra programming.

7.3 Parametric blending techniques

A vital facility in any animation system is the ability to make adjustments to a parameter without introducing an obvious visual discontinuity, or disturbing other parts of the sequence that have just been perfected. We will now see how parametric blending techniques can be used to provide alternative interpolation techniques.

Unfortunately, some of the mathematics is beyond the scope of this text and is not included. Therefore we will concentrate on some of the fundamental ideas to provide the reader with a feel for the potential of the technique in an animation environment. Ambitious readers may wish to research some of the following topics to a greater technical depth in the recommended references.

7.3.1 Quadratic and cubic blending

In Section 3.2.6, Bézier surface patches were described as a strategy for modelling free-form surfaces. In this section we will examine the same parametric techniques, but use them for blending any numeric quantity, whether it represents a Cartesian coordinate or even a light intensity.

In previous sections, the use of a parameter t has played an important role in developing expressions for incorporation within an animation program, and is frequently used to control a linear interpolation as follows:

$$N(t) = (1 - t)N_1 + tN_2$$

where $0 \leqslant t \leqslant 1$ and $N(t)$ is an interpolated value between N_1 and N_2, depending on t's value as it varies between 0 and 1.

Now it is no coincidence that the terms $(1 - t)$ and t sum to unity, as the interpolation process works by taking a fraction of one value, and adds it to one minus that fraction of the second value. So this must apply to any other blending operation we design.

If we wanted a quadratic blending (square law), this can be achieved by squaring the $(1 - t)$ and t terms to create the following blending expression:

$$N(t) = (1 - t)^2N_1 + t^2N_2$$

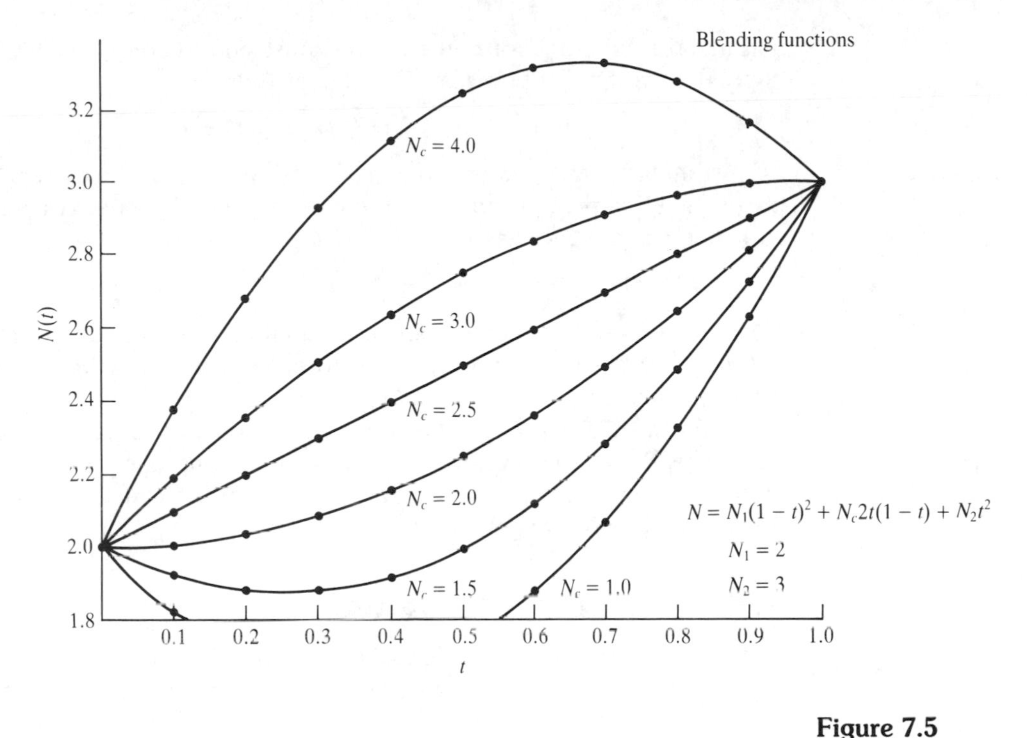

Figure 7.5
This family of curves arises by altering the value of N_c in the parametric equation: $N = N_1(1-t)^2 + N_c 2t(1-t) + N_2 t^2$ where $N_1 = 2$, $N_2 = 3$ and $0 \leqslant t \leqslant 1$.

However, when the terms in t are expanded, we find that they no longer sum to unity, in fact an extra term $2t(1 - t)$ is missing, which must be included in the blending expression as:

$$N(t) = (1 - t)^2 N_1 + t^2 N_2 + 2t(1 - t)$$

Now the interesting thing about this extra term is that when t equals zero or one, the term's value is also zero, therefore it has no influence at the extremes of the blending process. It obviously must have some impact upon the way the blend proceeds from N_1 to N_2, therefore its impact could be further controlled by multiplying it by some extra value N_c, as follows:

$$N(t) = (1 - t)^2 N_1 + t^2 N_2 + 2t(1 - t) N_c$$

The effect of N_c can be seen in Figure 7.5 which shows the blends between two numbers for different values of N_c. Notice that certain values of N_c allow the blended value to fall below N_1 and even overshoot N_2, which may, or may not, be a useful feature. There are also limits to the type of blend created by different values of N_c, but further flexibility can be introduced by employing a cubic function. If we cube the $(1 - t)$ and t terms we have:

$$N(t) = (1 - t)^3 N_1 + t^3 N_2$$

and like the quadratic form, the t terms must sum to unity, which will only happen if two further terms are included as follows:

$$N(t) = (1 - t)^3 N_1 + t^3 N_2 + 3t(1 - t)^2 + 3t^2(1 - t)$$

Similarly, these extra terms have no influence at the extreme limits of the blending process, and they too can be scaled by two extra values to control their influence as follows:

$$N(t) = (1 - t)^3 N_1 + t^3 N_2 + 3t(1 - t)^2 N_c + 3t^2(1 - t) N_d$$

Needless to say, there are now so many combinations for values of N_c and N_d that it is left to the reader to explore the effect they have upon the blending curves between N_1 and N_2.

As with all of these blending operations, it is very difficult to anticipate the shape and effect of these functions upon a sequence of animation, therefore it is vital that they are interfaced to the animator through an interactive graphics interface.

7.3.2 Hermite blending

In the quadratic and cubic blending functions described in the previous section, control of the function was effected through assigning values to N_c and N_d. Choosing these values, especially in the cubic version, can present problems to the animator when attempting to balance the rate at which the blend starts and finishes. And, as animated movement is so sensitive to the rate at which it is started and terminated, perhaps these are qualities that can also be blended. This is the idea behind Hermite blending, where cubic functions can be used to blend two values N_1 and N_2, together with another pair S_1 and S_2 which control the rate at which the blends start and end respectively. The process can be represented in a matrix form as:

$$N(t) = [t^3 \quad t^2 \quad t \quad 1] \begin{bmatrix} 2 & -2 & 1 & 1 \\ -3 & 3 & -2 & -1 \\ 0 & 0 & 1 & 0 \\ 1 & 0 & 0 & 0 \end{bmatrix} \begin{bmatrix} N_1 \\ N_2 \\ S_1 \\ S_2 \end{bmatrix}$$

The best way to visualize what is happening here is to construct a graph where the parameter t is represented by the horizontal axis, and the numerical scale by the vertical axis. If both axes have the same scale, then S_1 and S_2 will be the slopes of the blend function at $t = 0$ and $t = 1$ respectively.

Let us discover how this operates by interpolating $N_1 = 1$ and $N_2 = 2$ with different combinations of S_1 and S_2. In Table 7.3 N has been computed for different values of S_1 and S_2, and various values of t. These blends are also shown in Figure 7.6. The graphs show that when the slopes S_1 and S_2 are both equal to 1, a linear interpolation occurs – which is what

Table 7.3

t	Values of N S1 = 1, S2 = 1	S1 = 0, S2 = 0	S1 = 2, S2 = 0
0.0	1.0	1.00	1.00
0.1	1.1	1.03	1.19
0.2	1.2	1.10	1.36
0.3	1.3	1.22	1.51
0.4	1.4	1.35	1.64
0.5	1.5	1.50	1.75
0.6	1.6	1.65	1.84
0.7	1.7	1.78	1.91
0.8	1.8	1.90	1.96
0.9	1.9	1.97	1.99
1.0	2.0	2.00	2.00

one might expect. When both slopes are zero, the blend function gently moves away from its starting value, interpolating intermediate values, and at the same time anticipating that it must arrive at N_2 with the same speed with which it left N_1; this it does very effectively. The last example shows how the blend must 'jump' away from N_1, and also anticipate a very gentle 'arrival' at N_2.

The Hermite blend offers a very useful technique for a computer animation environment which must be able to simulate the slow-in, slow-out (also referred to as easing or fairing) movements so vital to animation. However, animation is not always concerned with interpolating between a

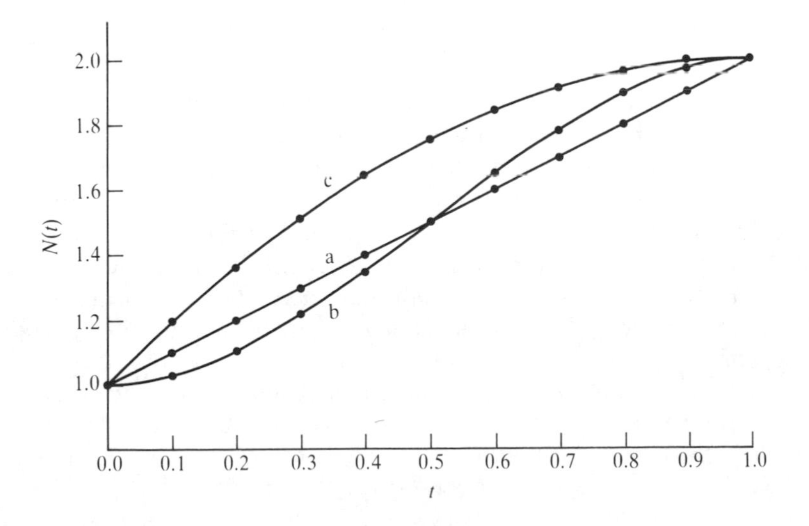

Figure 7.6
These three curves show the Hermite blending function applied between the values of 1 and 2 with different slope conditions at the two ends. Curve (a) has end slopes of 1 and 1; curve (b) has end slopes of 0 and 0; curve (c) has end slopes of 2 and 0. The values are listed in Table 7.3.

pair of values. An animator will frequently need to blend between a series of values associated with specific key frames, and it is vital that continuity is maintained over this sequence. This is arranged by the animator adjusting the slopes at these key frame values to create the required dynamics. One must remember, however, that the slopes relate the change in value to the interpolating parameter of the animation; therefore, when linking two sequences having different frame counts, care is needed to match the slopes on the basis of change in value per frame.

The technique can be further extended to introduce a sense of bias to the blend curve – this gives the impression that the curve leans forwards or backwards. Tension is another quality that can be incorporated and effectively 'tightens' or 'loosens' the attack of the curve as it approaches a key value. Appreciating some of the non-mathematical terms used to describe the Hermite blending function will obviously be very difficult for the animator unless the technique is implemented graphically.

7.3.3 Parabolic blending

Parabolic blending is a technique which enables a large number of values to be continuously interpolated, and like Hermite blending, the control values are included in the interpolated sequence. For example, say we need to interpolate between a sequence of values N_1, N_2, N_3, N_4, N_5 etc., using a cubic function. The interpolated value $N(t)$ is given by:

$$N(t) = [t^3 \quad t^2 \quad t \quad 1] \begin{bmatrix} -0.5 & 1.5 & -1.5 & 0.5 \\ 1.0 & -2.5 & 2.0 & -0.5 \\ -0.5 & 0.0 & 0.5 & 0.0 \\ 0.0 & 1.0 & 0.0 & 0.0 \end{bmatrix} \begin{bmatrix} N_1 \\ N_2 \\ N_3 \\ N_4 \end{bmatrix}$$

where $0 \leqslant t \leqslant 1$.

The range of $N(t)$ will only be between N_2 and N_3 and to obtain the next portion of the blend, the process must be repeated for N_2, N_3, N_4 and N_5, with t varying between 0 and 1. Therefore the entire interpolation is constructed from a sequence of segments which possess slope continuity at the joins. A consequence of this technique is that the values between N_1 and N_2 are not generated, nor are they generated between the last pair of values. However, if two extra 'phantom' values are added at the front and at the end of the value sequence, these end condition problems disappear.

Let us examine the technique with an example where we require to interpolate the values 1, 3, 6, 2, 1. First of all, the values will be extended to include the first and last terms twice, so that they become 1, 1, 3, 6, 2, 1, 1. Applying the above matrix operation to the first four gives us:

Table 7.4

t	N(t)
0.0	1.000
0.1	1.115
0.2	1.256
0.3	1.421
0.4	1.608
0.5	1.813
0.6	2.032
0.7	2.264
0.8	2.504
0.9	2.751
1.0	3.000

$$N(t) = [t^3 \quad t^2 \quad t \quad 1] \begin{bmatrix} -0.5 & 1.5 & -1.5 & 0.5 \\ 1.0 & -2.5 & 2.0 & -0.5 \\ -0.5 & 0.0 & 0.5 & 0.0 \\ 0.0 & 1.0 & 0.0 & 0.0 \end{bmatrix} \begin{bmatrix} 1 \\ 1 \\ 3 \\ 6 \end{bmatrix}$$

which provides the values shown in Table 7.4 and Figure 7.7 as t varies from 0 to 1.

The next blend sequence can be computed by replacing the values 1, 1, 3, 6 by 1, 3, 6, 2, and for the remaining blends 3, 6, 2, 1 and 6, 2, 1, 1. These have been computed and tabulated in Table 7.5. The blended sequence can be seen by scanning down the second column, followed by the third and so on. Graphically they are represented by the curve shown in Figure 7.8, which plots the values against a horizontal linear parameter

Table 7.5

	Sequences of N1, N2, N3, N4			
t	**1, 1, 3, 6**	**1, 3, 6, 2**	**3, 6, 2, 1**	**6, 2, 1, 1**
0.0	1.000	3.000	6.000	2.000
0.1	1.115	3.291	5.870	1.774
0.2	1.256	3.648	5.600	1.592
0.3	1.421	4.047	5.220	1.448
0.4	1.608	4.464	4.760	1.336
0.5	1.813	4.875	4.250	1.250
0.6	2.032	5.256	3.720	1.184
0.7	2.264	5.583	3.200	1.132
0.8	2.504	5.832	2.720	1.088
0.9	2.751	5.979	2.310	1.046
1.0	3.000	6.000	2.000	1.000

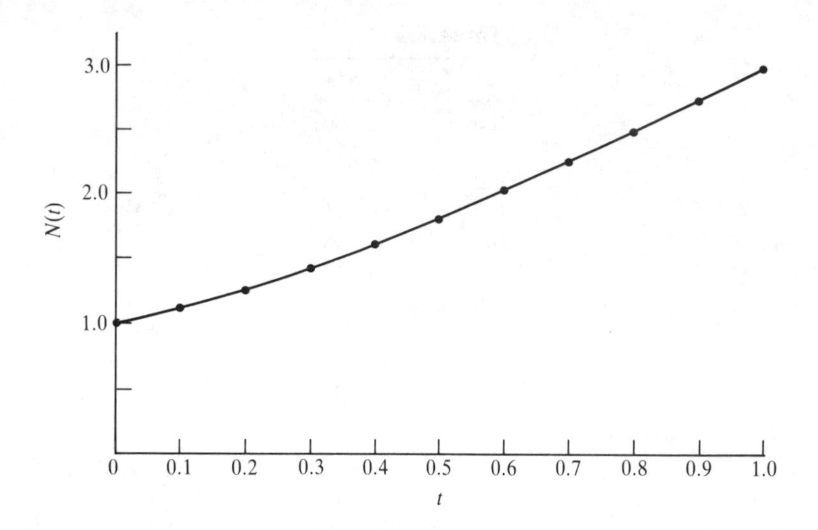

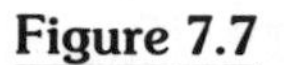

Figure 7.7
This graph shows the effect of a parabolic blending function that created the data listed in Table 7.4.

axis. The duplication of the first and last values was rather arbitrary, but other values can be inserted which will provide a mechanism for controlling the slope of the interpolated values at the start and end.

An extension of the technique enables the concept of 'tension' to be introduced – this controls the tangent of the curve as it passes through the control values. This is conveniently incorporated by introducing a tension parameter T into the matrix as follows:

$$\begin{bmatrix} -T & 2-T & T-2 & T \\ 2T & T-3 & 3-2T & -T \\ -T & 0 & T & 0 \\ 0 & 1 & 0 & 0 \end{bmatrix}$$

The original matrix is equivalent to a value of T equal to 0.5, and when T equals 1, it creates the following matrix:

$$\begin{bmatrix} -1 & 1 & -1 & 1 \\ 2 & -2 & 1 & -1 \\ -1 & 0 & 1 & 0 \\ 0 & 1 & 0 & 0 \end{bmatrix}$$

It is left to the reader to chart the effect the parameter T has on the curve shape.

As one can imagine, it is not a difficult exercise to implement this in a computer program and, as we shall see in Section 7.4.3, it provides a useful basis for defining spline space curves.

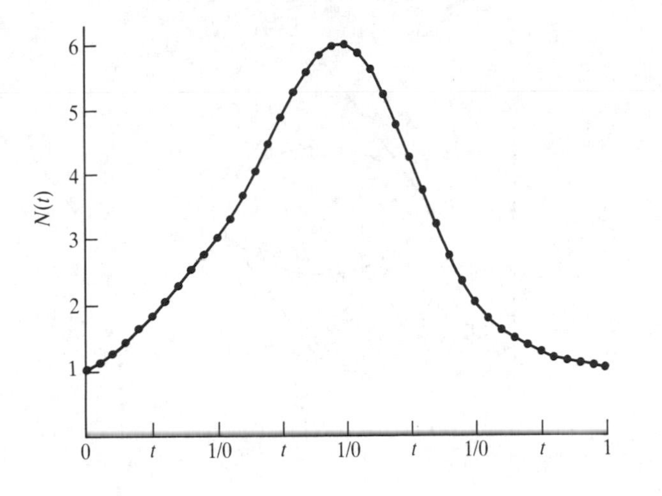

Figure 7.8
Parabolic blending can be used to blend over a range of numbers, and in this diagram we see how the technique interpolates the sequence 1, 3, 6, 2, and 1.

7.4 Space curves

So far, this chapter has considered various methods for blending sequences of numerical values that can be used for animating any attribute within an animation environment; however, as animation is naturally concerned with the spatial position of objects, lights and cameras, it is essential that similar techniques are available to effect and control these spatial manoeuvres. Such techniques provide various methods for defining 3-D space curves which can be used as flight paths for objects, lights and cameras.

Three-dimensional curves having a circular, elliptical, parabolic or a cubic form can be represented by employing the relevant mathematical formulae, but free-form curves describing some arbitrary path in space require a different approach. In fact, they exploit the blending procedures already covered, and are used specifically to blend Cartesian coordinates which ultimately create a 3-D space curve.

In the following sub-sections, we will investigate some of the more important techniques relevant to computer animation.

7.4.1 Bézier curves

In Section 7.3.1, the concepts behind quadratic and cubic blending were introduced, and we saw how it was possible to interpolate between a pair of numeric values using blending functions which included one or two control values. These influenced the nature of the blend interpolating between the boundary values, and it was quite difficult to predict their influence without drawing a family of graphs. Now we will discover a visual interpretation of their action in their role in Bézier curves.

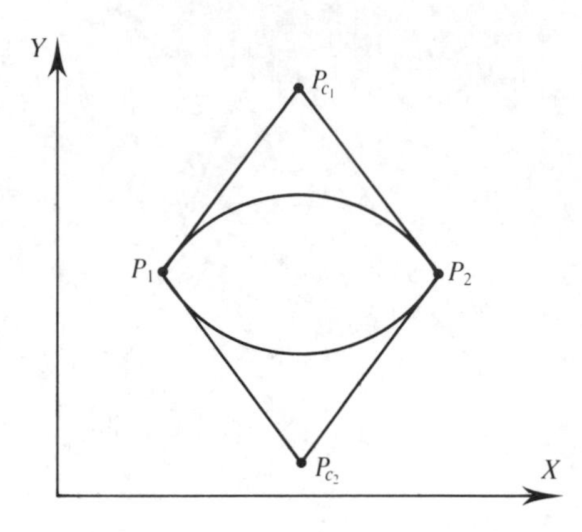

Figure 7.9
To construct a quadratic Bézier curve between the two points P_1 and P_2, the central control point P_c is located at a suitable position to derive the desired curve. In this diagram the positions of P_{c_1} and P_{c_2} show their influence in determining the curve's shape.

Let us begin with a 2-D quadratic Bézier curve whose form is specified in terms of two parametric expressions describing the x- and y-coordinates of any point on the curve. If the two end points of the curve are P_1 and P_2, with coordinates (x_1, y_1) and (x_2, y_2) respectively, then any point $P(t)$, where t is a parameter between the limits 0 and 1, has coordinates $(x(t), y(t))$ defined as follows:

$$x(t) = (1 - t)^2 x_1 + t^2 x_2 + 2t(1 - t)x_c$$
$$y(t) = (1 - t)^2 y_1 + t^2 y_2 + 2t(1 - t)y_c$$

where (x_c, y_c) are the coordinates of a control point which affects the shape of the curve between P_1 and P_2. Figure 7.9 shows the shape of a quadratic Bézier curve with two different control points. The terms in the parameter t were derived from the algebraic evaluation of expressions having the following form:

$$(a + b)^2 = a^2 + b^2 + 2ab$$

and if $a = (1 - t)$, and $b = t$, we obtain the above expressions for $x(t)$ and $y(t)$.

A natural extension is to introduce a third expression to define the value of $z(t)$, which creates a 3-D quadratic Bézier space curve. The role of the control point now has a spatial interpretation, in that it acts as a point towards which the curve is attracted, yet never quite touches.

The action of a single control point limits the range of curves that can be created, however, by using cubic blending functions, two control points become available, giving extra flexibility. Taking a 3-D example, consider two points P_1 and P_2 with coordinates (x_1, y_1, z_1) and (x_2, y_2, z_2) respectively, with control points (x_c, y_c, z_c) and (x_d, y_d, z_d). Then any point $P(t)$ on the curve will have coordinates $(x(t), y(t), z(t))$ defined by the expressions:

$$x(t) = (1 - t)^3 x_1 + t^3 x_2 + 3t(1 - t)^2 x_c + 3t^2(1 - t)x_d$$
$$y(t) = (1 - t)^3 y_1 + t^3 y_2 + 3t(1 - t)^2 y_c + 3t^2(1 - t)y_d$$
$$z(t) = (1 - t)^3 z_1 + t^3 z_2 + 3t(1 - t)^2 z_c + 3t^2(1 - t)z_d$$

The terms in t were derived from the algebraic evaluation of the following expression:

$$(a + b)^3 = a^3 + b^3 + 3a^2b + 3ab^2$$

where $a = (1 - t)$ and $b = t$.

Once more the action of the control points is to attract the curve on its journey between the boundary points, with the extra point providing the ability to flex the curve and create a wider range of paths.

There are a number of interesting features of these curves, the first of which, concerns the direction the curve at the boundary points. When the curve first leaves the starting point P_1, it 'heads' for the first control point, but is immediately diverted from this goal by the influence of any second control point and P_2. Nevertheless, the initial slope of the curve is equal to the slope of the line connecting P_1 with the first control point. Similarly, as the curve arrives at P_2, it becomes coincident with the line connecting P_2 with its neighbouring control point. Being able to control the starting and ending slopes enables any number of these curve segments to be joined together, where the end slope of one segment matches the start slope of an adjoining segment. Thus, long Bézier space curves can be constructed using this piecewise approach.

A second feature relates to the global nature the control points have upon the overall curve, in that if a control point is moved to another position, then the entire shape is modified; although in a piecewise construction, only the local segment is affected.

A third observation is that the curve does not pass through its control points, although it would if they had been aligned such that they rested on a straight line connecting P_1 with P_2. Fourthly, the convex polygon created by the control points (i.e. the convex hull), will always contain the Bézier curve.

A final feature of these curves concerns the distribution of points on the curve in relation to the parameter t. For instance, how are the points $P(0.0)$, $P(0.1)$, $P(0.2)$, $P(0.3)$, ... $P(1.0)$ spaced? Well, they are not positioned at equal distances along the curve, which may or may not be a problem; in fact, their non-linear distribution might be highly desirable in simulating the gentle fairings needed in camera movements. If a linear distribution is needed, this can be effected by constructing a table of coordinate values for the curve, together with entries showing the chord length along the curve for these points. To calculate the position of a point, say half-way along the curve, the table is searched for this value. If it does not exist – which is more than likely – the nearest two values are accessed and linearly interpolated to reveal the required value. Naturally, the number of entries in the table must be sufficient to prevent the interpolation process introducing any obvious sampling errors.

One must also be careful of discontinuities between point spacing on one piecewise segment when it joins another segment, for there is nothing to automatically guarantee that $(P(1.0) - P(0.9))$ on the first segment will equal $(P(0.1) - P(0.0))$ on the second segment.

7.4.2 B-spline curves

B-spline curves are a generalization of Bézier curves and allow a curve to be constructed from any number of control points such that, when they are adjusted, only a local span of the curve is influenced. Remember that this was not the case with Bézier curves, whose control points had a global impact upon curve shape. Where the Bézier algorithm employs a parameter t which varies from 0 to 1, the B-spline algorithm requires a list of parameter values that plot the progress of the parameter as the curve is developed.

We already know that to linearly interpolate between a pair of values N_1 and N_2 we use the following expression:

$$N(t) = (1 - t)N_1 + tN_2$$

where t is constrained between 0 and 1, but say we need to linearly interpolate between several values $N_0, N_1, N_2, N_3, \ldots N_n$. One method of achieving this is to create a sequence of parameter values that can be associated with the numbers listed in Table 7.6.

where $t_0 \leqslant t_1 \leqslant t_2 \leqslant t_3 \leqslant \ldots t_n$

We now need a mechanism to compute any value $N(t)$ by employing blending functions $B_0(t)$, $B_1(t)$, $B_2(t)$, $B_3(t)$ etc. such that:

$$N(t) = B_0(t)N_0 + B_1(t)N_1 + B_2(t)N_2 + B_3(t)N_3 + \ldots B_n(t)N_n$$

However, we do not want dozens of separate functions, ideally we want one function that adjusts itself depending upon the value of its parameter t. For the moment, let us assume that this will be possible and take a closer look as to how the interpolation process will be performed.

We know in linear interpolation that the interpolated value is derived from two portions: one whose value is reducing, and another whose value is increasing; this is the action of the terms $(1 - t)$ and t. In the above situation during the parameter span t_1 to t_2, the effect of N_0 must reduce, while that of N_1 must increase. These actions can be computed as follows:

Blend out N_0 while $t_1 \leqslant t \leqslant t_2$

$$\frac{t_2 - t}{t_2 - t_1} N_0$$

Table 7.6

values	N_0	N_1	N_2	N_3	–
parameters	t_0	t_1	t_2	t_3	t_4

Blend in N_1 while $t_1 \leqslant t \leqslant t_2$

$$\frac{t - t_1}{t_2 - t_1} N_1$$

Similarly, during the parameter span t_2 to t_3, N_1 must be blended out, while N_2 is blended in. These actions can be computed as follows:

Blend out N_1 while $t_2 \leqslant t \leqslant t_3$

$$\frac{t_3 - t}{t_3 - t_2} N_1$$

Blend in N_2 while $t_2 \leqslant t \leqslant t_3$

$$\frac{t - t_2}{t_3 - t_2} N_2$$

The observant reader will see a pattern evolving, which is vital if a simple algorithm is to be identified. To see how this pattern can be exploited, let us attempt to develop a general-purpose definition of a blending function B by first constructing the function for the value N_1. This will have two portions as follows:

$$\frac{t - t_1}{t_2 - t_1} + \frac{t_3 - t}{t_3 - t_2}$$

and if this is written for any value N_i, we have:

$$\frac{t - t_i}{t_{i+1} - t_i} + \frac{t_{i+2} - t}{t_{i+2} - t_{i+1}}$$

Now the blending function $B(t)$ must be supplied with the current value of i so that it knows which values of t to use, and it must also be given the current value of t otherwise it will be unable to evaluate the linear expression above. Armed with these two values, it must now be capable of proving that when t is between the range t_1 to t_2 the blending value for N_0 is zero, as only proportions of N_1 and N_2 are needed for this calculation.

All of this is possible, as we shall see; but while we are at it we might as well incorporate quadratic and cubic blending, which we know is achieved by squaring or cubing the parameter terms. Rather than attempt to explain in words what is rather a long-winded description, the final definition of the blending function is given without a complete proof:

$$B_{i,k}(t) = \frac{t - t_i}{t_{i+k-1} - t_i} B_{i,k-1}(t) + \frac{t_{i+k} - t}{t_{i+k} - t_{i+1}} B_{i+1,k-1}(t)$$

where $B(t)$ is a recursive function (it references itself), with parameters i, k and t, where:

i references the control values and parameters.
k is the order of the blending function,
$=2$ for linear blending,
$=3$ for quadratic blending, and
$=4$ for cubic blending.
t is the blending parameter.

The recursive action of $B_{i,k}(t)$ is terminated by the following condition:

$$B_{i,1}(t)\{ = 1, \text{ if } t_i \leq t < t_{i+1}$$
$$\{ = 0, \text{ otherwise}$$

The list of parameter values is called a knot vector, and there must be a sufficient number to match the control values and permit the action of a linear, quadratic or cubic blend (or higher). In fact, if there are $m + 1$ control values (this method of describing the number is used as the control values are numbered from N_0, N_1, N_2, to N_m), then the knot vector must contain $m + k + 1$ knots. For example, if 5 ($m + 1$) values are to be B-splined with a cubic blend ($k = 4$) then the knot vector will have nine entries.

In reality, the control values are two- or three-dimensional coordinates, which when blended provide a B-spline space curve. As already mentioned, when one of the control points is moved, only that local portion of the curve is affected. Futhermore, the values of the knots also permits the user to influence the shape of the curve.

Perhaps the B-spline's greatest strengths are in its ability to use any number of control points; the extra flexibility provided by knots; and the possibility of expressing the algorithm in a rational form (the ratio of two polynomials) to create perfect arcs. The B-spline technique also ensures that the curve has first- and second-order slope continuity at the knot positions, which permits it to be used to construct long complex space curves.

The above algorithm is often quoted in technical articles and books describing B-spline curves, and even though it is simple to program, it is slow and not very popular. Hence the existence of the matrix method:

$$P(t) = 1/6 \; [t^3 \;\; t^2 \;\; t \;\; 1] \begin{bmatrix} -1 & 3 & -3 & 1 \\ 3 & -6 & 3 & 0 \\ -3 & 0 & 3 & 0 \\ 1 & 4 & 1 & 0 \end{bmatrix} \begin{bmatrix} N_0 \\ N_1 \\ N_2 \\ N_3 \end{bmatrix}$$

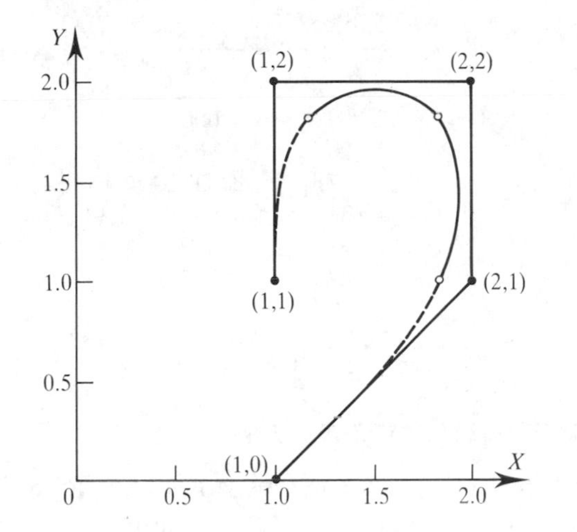

Figure 7.10
These five control points are needed to construct the two central portions of this cubic B-spline curve; but if the first and last points are repeated three times in the matrix evaluation, then the end segments can be developed and become part of the curve.

where for a given value of t, constrained between 0 and 1, and four values N_0, N_1, N_2 and N_3, $P(t)$ lies on a cubic curve.

When the values N_0, N_1, N_2 and N_3 represent the x-, y-, or z-coordinates of the control points in space, the values computed by $P(t)$ form a segment of the cubic B-spline curve. Graphically, the control values become control points, and if they are connected to create the largest convex polygon possible, i.e. its convex hull, then the B-spline curve will always exist within this boundary.

To illustrate the action of the above matrix, consider the following sequence of 2-D control points $(1,1)$, $(1,2)$, $(2,2)$, $(2,1)$ and $(1,0)$, as shown in Figure 7.10. This also displays two segments of the B-spline created by first using the control points $(1,1)$, $(1,2)$, $(2,2)$ and $(2,1)$, and then using $(1,2)$, $(2,2)$, $(2,1)$ and $(1,0)$. The starting and ending segments cannot be computed as there is insufficient geometry, but if the curve has to pass through the first and last control points, then these can be repeated three times to create the sequence $(1,1)$, $(1,1)$, $(1,1)$, $(1,2)$, $(2,2)$, $(2,1)$, $(1,0)$, $(1,0)$ and $(1,0)$. If the matrix is then applied to this sequence six times, taking in turn four neighbouring control points, the complete curve is obtained as shown in Figure 7.10.

The starting and ending coordinates between these segments are tabulated in Table 7.7; as one can see, the first and last curve segments are very short, and yet they still require the parameter t to vary between 0 and 1. In fact for each segment, as t increases in linear steps, the chord length of the space curve varies in a non-linear fashion which might, or might not, be desirable. However, if equal chord steps are required along the curve, the same technique can be employed, as explained in the previous section.

Table 7.7

X	Y
1.000	1.000
1.000	1.167
1.167	1.833
1.833	1.833
1.833	1.000
1.167	0.167
1.000	0.000

7.4.3 Catmull-Rom spline

One method of classifying spline curves is to divide them into two categories: those that pass through their control points, and those that do not. The former class of curve is known as an interpolating spline, while the latter is called an approximating spline.

In the previous section we saw that the B-spline algorithm generates a curve that only approaches its control points, and is therefore an approximating spline. The Catmull-Rom spline, however, is an interpolating spline as it exploits the parabolic blending technique described in Section 7.3.3, and generates cubic curve segments that actually pass through the control points.

As an illustration, consider the 2-D control points $(1,0)$, $(0,1)$, $(1,3)$, $(2,1)$, and $(3,2)$. These can be substituted in the following matrix operation to generate the x- and y-coordinates of the cubic spline. Remember that the first segment of the curve is produced by taking the first four control points, and the second segment is developed by leaving out the first control value, and selecting the next four points.

Table 7.8

t	1st segment		2nd segment	
	x	y	x	y
0.0	0.000	1.000	1.000	3.000
0.1	0.019	1.175	1.100	2.949
0.2	0.072	1.400	1.200	2.808
0.3	0.153	1.653	1.300	2.600
0.4	0.256	1.920	1.400	2.344
0.5	0.375	2.188	1.500	2.063
0.6	0.504	2.440	1.600	1.776
0.7	0.637	2.663	1.700	1.506
0.8	0.768	2.840	1.800	1.272
0.9	0.891	2.958	1.900	1.097
1.0	1.000	3.000	2.000	1.000

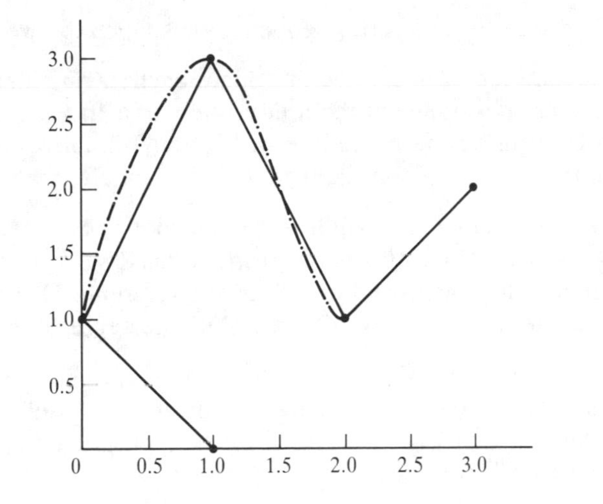

Figure 7.11
Given four control points, the Catmull-Rom spline is capable of deriving a spline between the inner two points. In this diagram five control points have been used to create the two inner segments with slope continuity at their join.

$$P(t) = [t^3 \quad t^2 \quad t \quad 1] \begin{bmatrix} -0.5 & 1.5 & -1.5 & 0.5 \\ 1.0 & -2.5 & 2.0 & -0.5 \\ -0.5 & 0.0 & 0.5 & 0.0 \\ 0.0 & 1.0 & 0.0 & 0.0 \end{bmatrix} \begin{bmatrix} P_1 \\ P_2 \\ P_3 \\ P_4 \end{bmatrix}$$

where $P(t)$ will have coordinates (x, y) given that P_1, P_2, P_3 and P_4 are four 2-D control points. As before, t varies between 0 and 1 for each curve segment.

Table 7.8 shows the corresponding values of $P(t)$ for the two curve segments for different values of t, and the curve is shown in Figure 7.11. Although this example is two-dimensional, a three-dimensional space curve is easily developed simply by introducing the z-coordinate. Furthermore, the idea of 'tension' as explained in Section 7.3.3, can also be implemented.

Exercises and projects

7.1 What are the problems associated with devising an automatic procedure for shape inbetweening?

7.2 Design a program to inbetween a pair of 2-D contours. The procedure should accept the reference contours in the form of coordinate lists with the same number of vertices, together with a parameter varying between 0 and 1, which specifies the degree of transformation. The inbetweened shape should be output by the procedure in the same format as the input shapes.

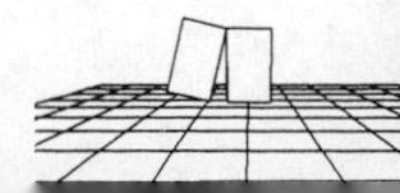

7.3 Explain the effect of vertex sequence on shape inbetweening.

7.4 If four different shapes, one unit high, each having identical vertex counts, are positioned at the four corners of a 10×10 square, write a program using the procedure in Section 7.2 above, to create the 100 inbetween shapes in the form of a rectangular matrix.

7.5 Write a program which will linearly interpolate between two sets of HSV values and output the corresponding RGB triplet. The input parameters for the procedure will be the reference HSV triplets, and a parameter between 0 and 1 controlling the degree of interpolation.

7.6 Design a program which will add a random value between given limits to the x- and y-coordinates of any shape stored as two lists of coordinates. Explore the use of such a program to increase the roughness of a contour.

7.7 Using the expressions stated in Section 7.3, design a procedure to interpolate between any two values using a quadratic blend function.

7.8 Implement the Hermite blending algorithm explained in Section 7.3.2 and explore the effects of the two slope parameters.

7.9 Implement the parabolic blending algorithm explained in Section 7.3.3 and, using the same input data, confirm that it creates the values shown in Table 7.5.

7.10 Modify the parabolic blending program from Exercise 7.9 to include a tension parameter, and explore its effect on the nature of the blend.

7.11 Design a quadratic Bézier curve drawing program using the algorithm shown in Section 7.4.1, and explore the effect the central control point has upon the shape of the curve.

7.12 Design a cubic Bézier curve drawing program using the algorithm shown in Section 7.4.1, and explore the effect the two central control points have upon the shape of the curve.

7.13 Given two end points $(1, 0)$ and $(0, 1)$, identify the central control point for a quadratic Bézier curve to create an approximate 90° arc of a circle. Compute the error deviation from a true arc for different points along the curve.

7.14 Develop the algorithm from Exercise 7.13 above for a cubic Bézier curve.

7.15 Design a cubic Bézier space curve to create a 3-D curve around any four control vertices.

7.16 Using the algorithm from Exercise 7.14, show how slope continuity can be maintained between two separate curve segments.

7.17 Implement the B-spline matrix algorithm from Section 7.4.2 and confirm the values of Table 7.7.

Further reading

Computer animation tools The topics for this section can be pursued further in Foley (1990), pp. 478–516, Burger (1989), pp. 241–282, Rogers (1990) and Farin (1988).

KEY POINTS

To animate the virtual world of objects, light sources and cameras requires a plethora of techniques to change their respective attributes. Ultimately, these revolve around the manipulation of numerical quantities representing these attributes and consist of the following techniques.

- Linear interpolation provides the simplest method of changing one value into another in equal steps over a specified period of time.
- Non-linear interpolation is required to simulate changes that occur in a non-uniform way, and are required to produce slow-in/slow-out movements and dynamic camera moves.
- Mathematical formulae are easily implemented into programs to control the movement of objects that have to obey precise laws.
- Random numbers are very useful in forming data sets where range, rather than a precise value, is important. Such 'stochastic' approaches are employed in texturing, arbitrary vibrations and the random disturbance of geometric data.
- Parametric blending provides a coherent methodology for quadratic, cubic, Hermite and parabolic blending algorithms.
- Space curves are needed to control the path of an object, camera or light source, and are often implemented using Bézier curves, B-spline curves and Catmull-Rom splines.
- All piecewise approaches must be sensitive to the dynamics of changes from one boundary condition to another.

The 3-D Animation Environment

The 3-D animation environment is concerned with the world coordinate system, the world as seen from the camera's viewpoint, how objects are manipulated and the dynamics of lights. The WCS has already been an important concept in previous sections, and in this chapter we investigate its relationship with the object coordinate system (OCS), and how objects are positioned and instanced within the WCS. Similarly, we have already seen how a perspective view of the WCS is achieved from the camera's frame-of-reference, and now we will examine techniques for animating the camera. This will involve the use of polar coordinates, space curves, and inbetweening.

Virtually anything associated with an object can be dynamically modified or physically animated, and in this chapter we will consider the problems of colour control, shape and object interpolation, the interpolation of position and rotation. As the latter is very important in animation, emphasis is placed upon the interpolation of roll, pitch and yaw angles and quaternions, which are beginning to appear in technical papers on computer animation. The chapter concludes with a discussion on the practical issues for lighting animated scenes.

Introduction

Central to any animation sequence, whether using traditional techniques or computer graphics, is the need for a storyboard, which consists of a sequence of drawings identifying the salient scenes of a plot. It also contains other information relating to the timings of movements and scene lengths, the different backgrounds that may be called for, and perhaps the key characters in the story. Further illustrations are needed for the characters to provide the animator with a clear picture of these individuals from all angles. In the case of the traditional approach where the images are hand-drawn, the animator must be able to anticipate the final visual effect, as redrawing it over again is not a practical alternative. In computer animation, on the other hand, last minute alterations in camera movements, lighting levels and colour changes are all possible, without totally upsetting vital costings which are important commercial considerations.

In the following sections it will become increasingly obvious to the reader that the flat world of the traditional animator is totally different to the virtual three-dimensional world created by computer graphics. It would be wrong to say that one is better than the other – they are different, and offer the animator unique alternatives in manipulating images. One very powerful feature of hand-drawn cartoons is the immediacy of the technique – just a few marks on a sheet of paper are all that is needed to create a cartoon figure. Repeating this process several times will quickly generate a 'living' animated character.

Compare this with a computer graphics approach. Before anything can take place a 3-D computer model has to be constructed; it has to be positioned within a world coordinate system which also contains a virtual camera to observe the animation. Somehow the model must be manipulated to perform the required movement, and finally, when all of this has been achieved, the images must be recorded onto film or video tape for viewing. Workstations already exist that are capable of playing back in near real-time, previously rendered scenes using their bit-blit facilities; this permits the rapid display of coloured images that have been loaded from disk into the computer's memory. And as computer technology advances, computer graphics will rapidly move towards a real-time mode of working.

In comparison to an animator's pencil and paper, the computer graphics approach seems rather cumbersome, and perhaps it is, but its strength lies in its flexibility. Its virtual nature, where objects, attributes, positions, movements, lights and camera paths are controlled by parameters, enable anything to be altered at the 'flick of a switch'. The computer provides an imaginary world where anything can happen, if only there is a program to do it. To create this imaginary world we must return to the ideas of Cartesian coordinates and construct a frame of reference for all future work.

8.1 The world coordinate system

The world coordinate system (WCS) is the three-dimensional stage for our piece of animation. It is the space where models are placed, together with any instances (copies); lights are positioned to illuminate our objects; and cameras are manoeuvred to observe all that happens. A right-handed space is used throughout this text, although a left-handed system will work just as well, so long as the convention is appreciated by other modules within the computer graphics system.

Some systems will actually require the user to build models in an object coordinate system (OCS), then with suitable user commands they are placed at their correct positions in the WCS. In reality, though, it should be remembered that these models are nothing more than lists of coordinates, control points or perhaps collections of equations. They reside within the computer's memory, and for display purposes are accessed and subjected to translation, scaling and rotation operations; it is these actions that place them at their correct positions in the WCS. When a copy of the same object is required, instead of replicating the coordinate data, the original object is referenced and subjected to a different set of translation, scaling and rotation operations. These would be in the form of one or more matrices, or a single matrix representing the concatenated operation. This instancing process can save considerable amounts of memory, especially when the objects are complex. An advantage of this approach is that when the original coordinate data for the object is altered, all the instances automatically reflect these changes.

As an example, consider the situation where a cube has been created in its local OCS such that the origin is at its centre (Figure 8.1). If an instance of this cube is required at (x_p, y_p, z_p) in the WCS, and twice size, then the matrix operations will consist of an initial scale of two, followed by a translation. Any point (x, y, z) will then be subject to the following matrix operations to transform it to (x', y', z'):

$$\begin{bmatrix} x' \\ y' \\ z' \\ 1 \end{bmatrix} = \begin{bmatrix} 1 & 0 & 0 & x_p \\ 0 & 1 & 0 & y_p \\ 0 & 0 & 1 & z_p \\ 0 & 0 & 0 & 1 \end{bmatrix} \begin{bmatrix} 2 & 0 & 0 & 0 \\ 0 & 2 & 0 & 0 \\ 0 & 0 & 2 & 0 \\ 0 & 0 & 0 & 1 \end{bmatrix} \begin{bmatrix} x \\ y \\ z \\ 1 \end{bmatrix}$$

which concatenates to:

$$\begin{bmatrix} x' \\ y' \\ z' \\ 1 \end{bmatrix} = \begin{bmatrix} 2 & 0 & 0 & x_p \\ 0 & 2 & 0 & y_p \\ 0 & 0 & 2 & z_p \\ 0 & 0 & 0 & 1 \end{bmatrix} \begin{bmatrix} x \\ y \\ z \\ 1 \end{bmatrix}$$

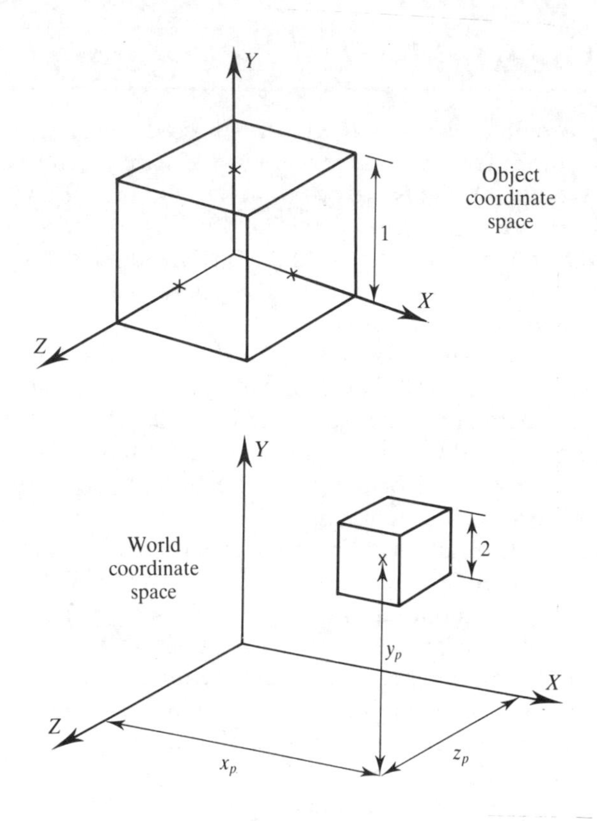

Figure 8.1

Objects are generally modelled in their own local OCS and then transferred to the WCS using some form of matrix operation. In this case, a box is first scaled by 2, and then translated by (x_p, y_p, z_p).

Thus, this single matrix and a reference to the original cube is all that is needed to represent this scaled and translated cube.

One must appreciate that the scaling operation is always with respect to the local origin and not to some other point, such as the centre of an object. To illustrate this effect consider a case in two dimensions (Figure 8.2) where a rectangle is displaced from the origin. If the rectangle's coordinates are scaled by two, as follows:

$$\begin{bmatrix} x' \\ y' \\ 1 \end{bmatrix} = \begin{bmatrix} 2 & 0 & 0 \\ 0 & 2 & 0 \\ 0 & 0 & 1 \end{bmatrix} \begin{bmatrix} x \\ y \\ 1 \end{bmatrix}$$

the rectangle is scaled, but it is also translated – which might not have been expected. Consequently, when scaling is required relative to some specific point (x_c, y_c), the coordinates are first translated by $(-x_c, -y_c)$ then scaled s_c and finally translated (x_c, y_c). In matrix form this consists of:

$$\begin{bmatrix} x' \\ y' \\ 1 \end{bmatrix} = \begin{bmatrix} 1 & 0 & x_c \\ 0 & 1 & y_c \\ 0 & 0 & 1 \end{bmatrix} \begin{bmatrix} s_c & 0 & 0 \\ 0 & s_c & 0 \\ 0 & 0 & 1 \end{bmatrix} \begin{bmatrix} 1 & 0 & -x_c \\ 0 & 1 & -y_c \\ 0 & 0 & 1 \end{bmatrix} \begin{bmatrix} x \\ y \\ 1 \end{bmatrix}$$

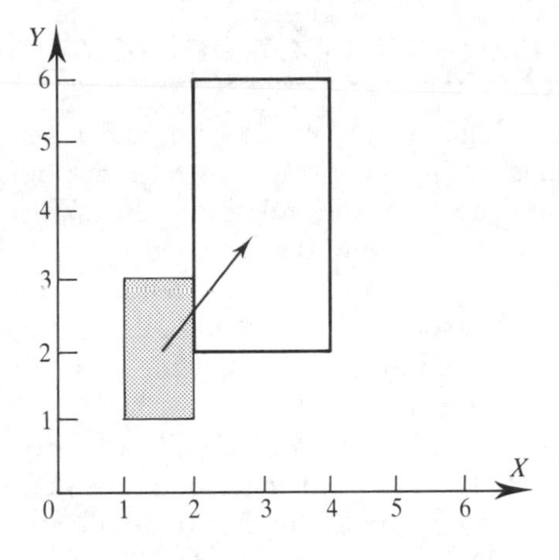

Figure 8.2
The scaling operation is relative to the origin, and in this example we see that when the small rectangle is doubled in size, it is also translated by an amount proportional to its distance from the axes.

which concatenates to:

$$\begin{bmatrix} x' \\ y' \\ 1 \end{bmatrix} = \begin{bmatrix} s_c & 0 & x_c(1 - s_c) \\ 0 & s_c & y_c(1 - s_c) \\ 0 & 0 & 1 \end{bmatrix} \begin{bmatrix} x \\ y \\ 1 \end{bmatrix}$$

thus when $s_c = 2$, $x_c = 1.5$, and $y_c = 2$, the matrix operation becomes:

$$\begin{bmatrix} x' \\ y' \\ 1 \end{bmatrix} = \begin{bmatrix} 2 & 0 & -1.5 \\ 0 & 2 & -2.0 \\ 0 & 0 & 1 \end{bmatrix} \begin{bmatrix} x \\ y \\ 1 \end{bmatrix}$$

and when the rectangle in Figure 8.3 is scaled by the above matrix, one sees that the scaling is symmetric about the point (1.5, 2.0).

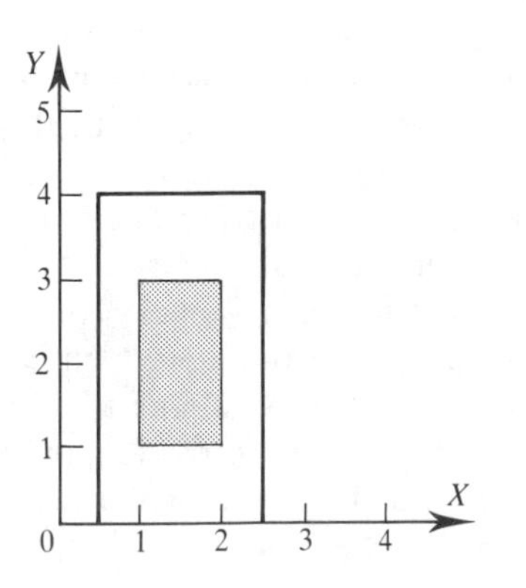

Figure 8.3
Scaling can be made relative to any point if the operation includes an initial translation, followed by the scaling operation, followed by a compensating translation operation. In this case the rectangle is scaled relative to the point (1.5, 2.0).

8.2 The camera coordinate system

In real life, taking a single picture with a camera is a simple operation; it is nothing more than choosing a convenient position, pointing the camera in the right direction, focusing and releasing the shutter. Many modern cameras will even underake the task of focusing for the photographer. However, if you have ever attempted to use a home video camera, you will know of the problems associated with holding the camera steady, keeping the subject in view, maintaining focus while you and the subject are moving.

The concept of a camera in the WCS allows views of this world to be captured by fixing its location and focal point, which must provide sufficient geometric data to create the matrix that will convert coordinates in the WCS to the CCS. Fixing the position and orientation of the camera can employ any method so long as this vital geometry is available; this may employ Cartesian coordinates or polar coordinates, or a mixture of the two.

Moving the camera to a new position creates another viewpoint, and one of the requirements of a computer animation system is to provide the animator with useful commands to effect such continuous moves. Before we address these problems, we will examine some of the basic modes of locating and orienting the camera within the WCS.

8.2.1 Cartesian and polar definitions

Perhaps the simplest method of defining the position and orientation of a camera is by specifying its view position and a focal point using Cartesian coordinates, where (x_c, y_c, z_c) fixes the viewing position C, and (x_f, y_f, z_f) locates the focal point F. (The term **focal point** does *not* have the same meaning as used in photography, but identifies a point along the camera's line of sight which normally becomes the centre of the image on the screen.) These two points only identify how an axis is positioned in space, and do not cater for a rotational angle. Therefore, one can either assume that the camera will always be held in an upright position, or that an extra parameter will control the degree of roll about this axis. Figure 8.4 illustrates this configuration. A simple method of introducing roll is to apply a rotation to the camera's coordinates when they are computed.

One of the major drawbacks with the Cartesian definition is that rotational camera movements, which are very common, become difficult to specify, hence the use of polar coordinates which provide two useful modes of operation. The first mode initially aligns the CCS with the WCS, it is then subjected to two rotations to provide pan and tilt, and is finally translated by (x_c, y_c, z_c). This is equivalent to a pan-and-tilt head on a tripod, as it keeps the camera in an upright position. Roll can be

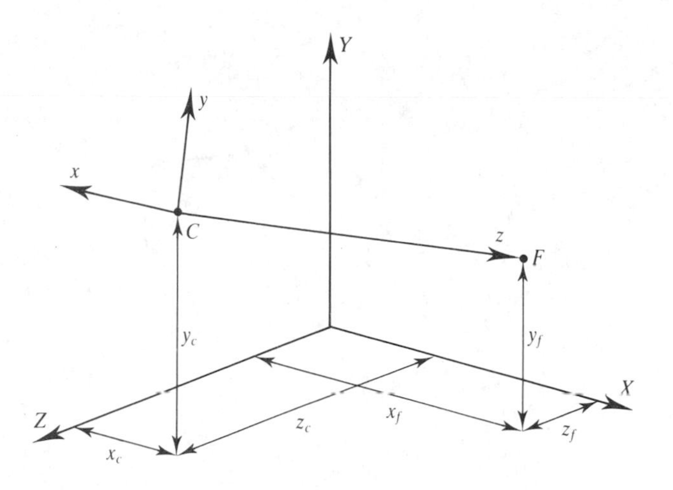

Figure 8.4
A virtual camera can be located in the WCS by fixing its position at $C(x_c, y_c, z_c)$ and its focal point at $F(x_f, y_f, z_f)$, with its x-axis parallel with the x–z ground plane.

introduced by rotating the final perspective projection, in the same way that the camera would be rotated, or it can be included as a basic axial rotation. This definition was described in Section 2.2. Obviously, this method of location is only useful when one requires that the camera is animated along a known trajectory, and has to move through specified angular rotations, for there is no mechanism for ensuring that the camera is directed towards any point in the scene.

When it is vital that the camera must be directed towards a known point then a second mode is employed, which requires that the CCS is initially aligned with the WCS, and then subjected to two rotations to provide pan and tilt. It is then translated such that it is a certain distance from the focal point (x_f, y_f, z_f). Where the first method requires five parameters: (x_c, y_c, z_c) and two angles, the second requires six parameters: (x_f, y_f, z_f), distance and two angles. The latter technique enables a camera to track a moving target by a fixed distance, as the focal point can be any point on the target; for where ever it goes, the camera is forced to follow. Figure 8.5 illustrates both of these methods.

8.2.2 Animating the camera

Modern cine camera techniques are constrained by the physical size of the camera and the manual methods of adjusting focus, both of which have created a style of film-making with which we have become familiar. Every time the camera is moved to a new position it must be refocused, light levels recomputed, areas of shadow and highlights adjusted to ensure that the film is exposed correctly. However, the flexibility offered by the computer animation camera frees the animator from all of these constraints. To begin with, there is no need to pull focus, as there are no lenses

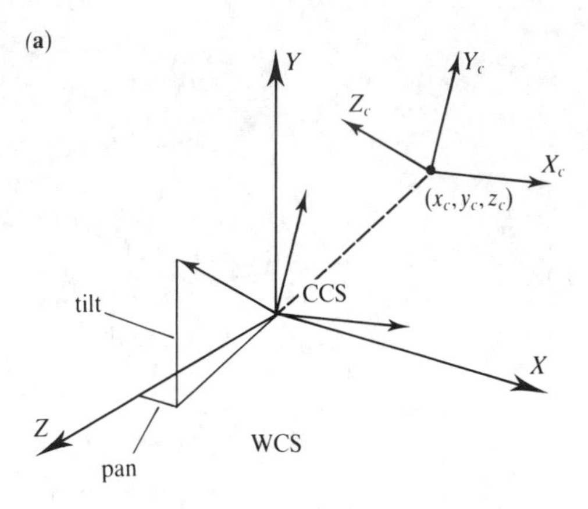

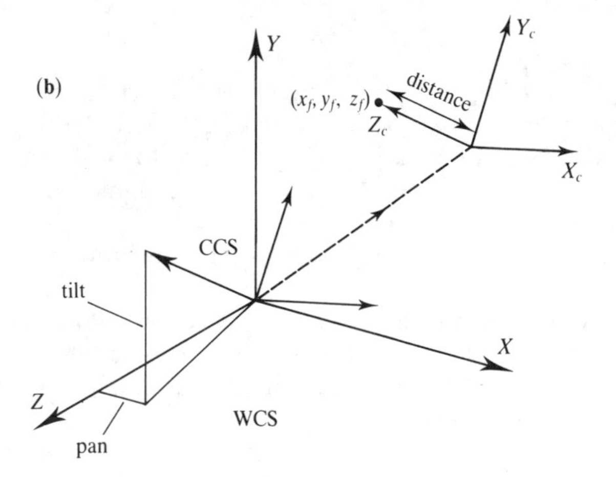

Figure 8.5
A virtual camera can be positioned in the WCS using a variety of techniques. In (a) the the camera's axial system is initially aligned with the WCS and then rotated to introduce pan and tilt; finally it is translated by (x_c, y_c, z_c) to locate it at some convenient position. When the camera is required to be a specified distance from some focal point, the pan and tilt operations are followed by an appropriate translation, as shown in (b).

associated with the computer's camera – although the effect can be simulated. Secondly, the camera has no mass or size, and it can be positioned anywhere and moved around at any speed.

This degree of freedom exposes computer animation to all types of abuse, especially in the form of roller-coaster animated fly-throughs, where the viewer is taken on high-speed journeys and subjected to tedious rolls and zooms as tumbling logos flash past. Directors of such sequences have failed to appreciate the lessons that have been learnt over the past 80 years concerning the art of cine photography. It is an art form requiring a sensitivity to motion, composition, perspective and depth of field that are all intimately coupled with the visual message behind the images. So with these thoughts in mind, let us examine how some of the blending techniques covered in Chapter 7 can be used to animate the virtual camera.

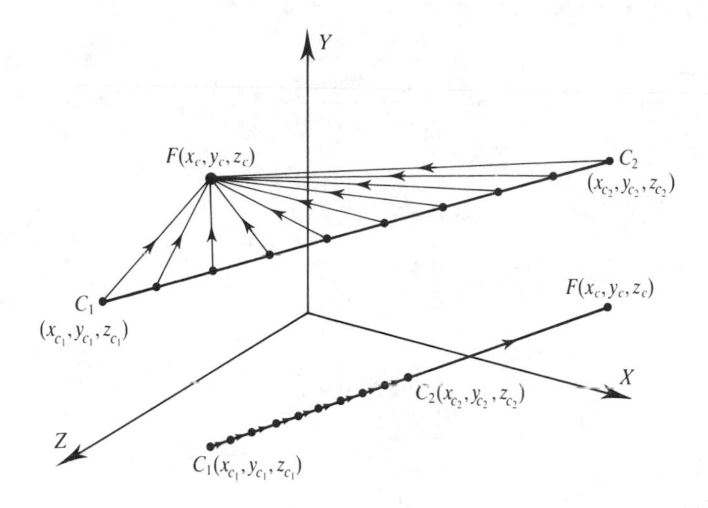

Figure 8.6
These two camera moves can be simulated by keeping the focal point fixed at (x_c, y_c, z_c) and moving the camera from C_1 to C_2 using linear interpolation.

In the Cartesian definition of the camera, we are concerned with the starting and finishing location and focal point of the camera, and perhaps any roll to be applied during the move. If the camera's position is defined by the point C with coordinates (x_c, y_c, z_c), and its focal point F with coordinates (x_f, y_f, z_f), then it can be moved from position $C_1(x_{c1}, y_{c1}, z_{c1})$ to $C_2(x_{c2}, y_{c2}, z_{c2})$ with a common view point by linearly interpolating the coordinates as follows:

$$x_c = (1 - t)x_{c1} + tx_{c2}$$
$$y_c = (1 - t)y_{c1} + ty_{c2}$$
$$z_c = (1 - t)z_{c1} + tz_{c2}$$

where t is a parameter that varies from 0 to 1 as the current frame number changes from one key frame to another. This move causes the camera to remain directed towards the same point throughout the manoeuvre, and as the camera moves in a straight line from C_1 to C_2, its distance from the viewpoint will change. In fact, the relative positions of C_1 and C_2 determine whether the move is a track-in or -out, or even a fixed-focus slide. Figure 8.6 illustrates two moves made possible using this approach.

As the interpolation is linear with respect to t, which also probably has a linear relationship with the current frame, this causes the camera to move with a constant speed between C_1 and C_2. This might be desirable, as the sequence could be eventually edited into some other animation sequence; but if the movement needs to be faired, such that there is a gentle take-up of speed and a final reduction of speed, then a non-linear interpolation must be employed. Such techniques have already been discussed in Chapter 7 and would replace the linear terms in the above expressions. If the focal point was also changing, then this too would be interpolated to create a tracking camera movement. Naturally, it is expected that something is happening at this moving focal point.

Table 8.1

t	hermite
0.0	0.000
0.1	0.028
0.2	0.104
0.3	0.216
0.4	0.352
0.5	0.500
0.6	0.648
0.7	0.784
0.8	0.896
0.9	0.972
1.0	1.000

Rotational movements are best controlled using polar coordinates, and as an illustration let us consider the case where the camera is required to pivot about itself 360°. While it is rotating in the horizontal plane, it must also be tilting upwards so that on completion it is elevated at an angle of 30°. Furthermore, all of the movements must be faired.

An effective method for blending values both at the start and at the end is to use either a sinusoidal function, or Hermite blending as described in Section 7.3.1. Let us examine the latter technique. To begin with, the blended value is given by:

$$N(t) = [t^3 \quad t^2 \quad t \quad 1] \begin{bmatrix} 2 & -2 & 1 & 1 \\ -3 & 3 & -2 & -1 \\ 0 & 0 & 1 & 0 \\ 1 & 0 & 0 & 0 \end{bmatrix} \begin{bmatrix} 0 \\ 1 \\ 0 \\ 0 \end{bmatrix}$$

where the last column of numbers $(0, 1, 0, 0)$ is composed of $(0, 1)$ being the numeric range of the blend, and $(0, 0)$ being the slopes at the start and end. This operation could be represented by the function:

$$N(t) = hermite(0, 1, 0, 0, t)$$

which returns the value of $N(t)$. Table 8.1 shows these values for different values of t.

Inspection of the values of $hermite(0, 1, 0, 0, t)$ confirms that they move from zero very slowly; pass through 0.5 when t equals 0.5; and move gently towards 1 as t approaches 1. This means that if we scale the function by any other value, the same form of blend will be applied to this value.

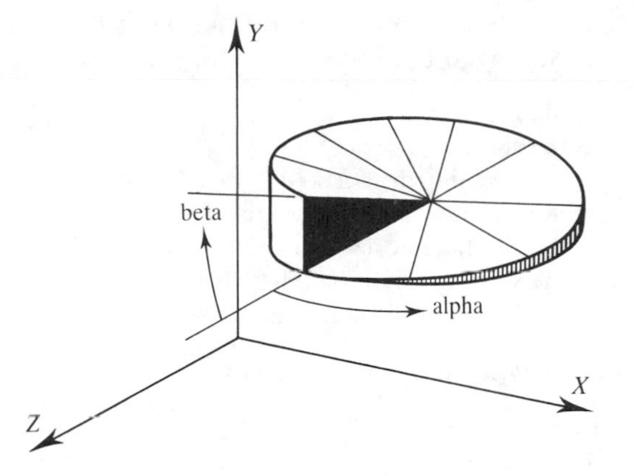

Figure 8.7
By simultaneously interpolating the pan and tilt angles associated with a virtual camera it can move as shown by this trajectory. If a Hermite blending scheme is employed, then the moves can be cushioned at the start and end.

If the horizontal angle of the camera is controlled by *alpha*, and the elevation angle by *beta*, the camera's orientation can be described by:

$$alpha = 360 \, hermite(0, 1, 0, 0, t)$$
$$beta = 30 \, hermite(0, 1, 0, 0, t)$$

The parameter t would be computed from the current frame number F and the key frame values F_1 and F_2 using the following expression:

$$t = \frac{F - F_1}{F_2 - F_1}$$

Substituting F, F_1 and F_2 to derive t, which in turn produces $hermite(0, 1, 0, 0, t)$, enables *alpha* and *beta* to be computed; these are substituted into the polar definition of the camera to cause the camera to move as shown in Figure 8.7. During this move the camera's position has been assumed to be stationary, yet there is no reason why it could not have been moving, making very sophisticated movements, though employing very simple blending functions.

Another situation where polar coordinates are useful is when the focal point is known, and the camera has to remain a fixed distance from it, yet at the same time perform a horizontal and elevational rotation. This arises when the camera has to track a moving object by a given distance, and also gyrate about it. This movement is also easy to specify as it is just a question of isolating the variables and applying the required blends. In this case the focal point (x_f, y_f, z_f) is known and a tracking distance d is specified; all that needs to be computed are the horizontal and elevation angles as in the previous example.

Let us embellish this camera move by incorporating a faired tracking movement. We now have the focal point moving, the camera rotating and elevating, and simultaneously approaching the object. Once more we can employ Hermite blending to fair the movements using the function $N(t)$ as described above. So, given the following information:

(x_f, y_f, z_f) is the focal point
d_1 is the starting distance
d_2 is the finishing distance
$alpha_1$ is the starting horizontal angle
$alpha_2$ is the finishing horizontal angle
$beta_1$ is the starting elevation angle
$beta_2$ is the finishing elevation angle

the parameters d, *alpha* and *beta* can be computed by:

$$\begin{aligned} u &= hermite(0, 1, 0, 0, t) \\ d &= (1 - u)d_1 + ud_2 \\ alpha &= (1 - u)alpha_1 + u\,alpha_2 \\ beta &= (1 - u)beta_1 + u\,beta_2 \end{aligned}$$

Remember that the function *hermite* returns a value between 0 and 1, and is non-linearly interpolated with respect to t, which is derived from the current frame value and the two key frame values over which the camera move is applied.

This last example demonstrates how easy it is to develop general-purpose computer programs to undertake a variety of camera moves – as, by incorporating the above algorithm into an animation system, an animator can simply enter the starting and finishing values for d, *alpha*, *beta* and key frame values, to automatically generate their faired values for different frames.

Once more we discover how important it is for the animator to be interfaced to the animation environment through an interactive graphics workstation; this would enable all of the above information to be communicated to the system via a few menu operations and some graphical commands. One final example will illustrate how a space curve can be used to act as a flight path for the camera – this could be any type of curve construction including B-splines and Bézier curves, and the latter will provide an excellent basis for this example.

If a cubic Bézier curve is chosen, then the two central control points can be employed to 'bend' the curve into the desired shape. A function is then needed to derive the x-, y- and z-coordinates from the control points using a parameter t. Given the control points $C_1(x_{c1}, y_{c1}, z_{c1})$, $C_2(x_{c2}, y_{c2}, z_{c2})$, $C_3(x_{c3}, y_{c3}, z_{c3})$ and $C_4(x_{c4}, y_{c4}, z_{c4})$, and the function $bezier(v_1, v_2, v_3, v_4, t)$, where v_1, v_2, v_3 and v_4 are the control values and t is the standard parameter, then the coordinates of any point $C(x, y, z)$ on the curve can be specified by:

$$\begin{aligned} x &= bezier(x_{c1}, x_{c2}, x_{c3}, x_{c4}, t) \\ y &= bezier(y_{c1}, y_{c2}, y_{c3}, y_{c4}, t) \\ z &= bezier(z_{c1}, z_{c2}, z_{c3}, z_{c4}, t) \end{aligned}$$

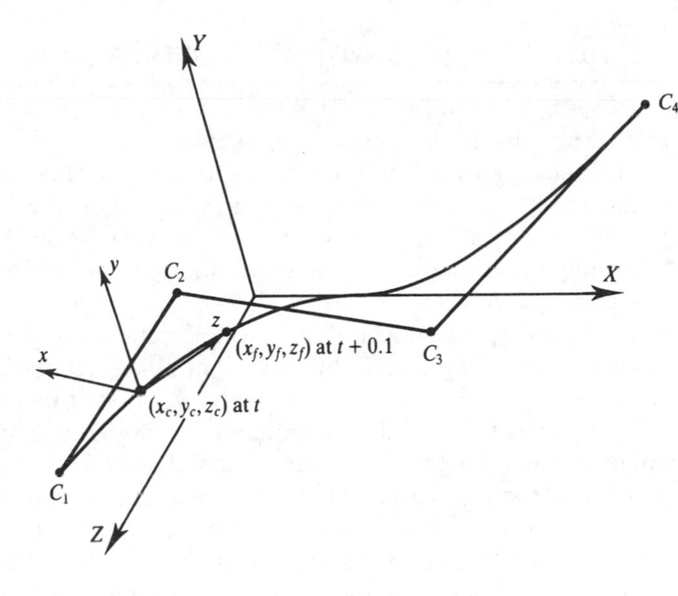

Figure 8.8
This cubic Bézier curve locates the virtual camera's position and focal point by the parameter values t and $t+0.1$ respectively. The camera has valid positions over the range $0 \leq t \leq 0.9$; while the focal point is between $0.1 \leq t \leq 1.0$. The camera can be driven outside of these limits, but direct control over its speed has been lost.

The point $C(x, y, z)$ can become the position of the camera, but it will need a focal point; this may be some fixed position, or even an interpolated value between two other positions. It could even be another position on a second Bézier curve; however, an interesting case is when the focal point is located somewhere further along the same curve. This position can be determined by incrementing t by some amount, say 0.1; this would mean that the focal point $F(x_f, y_f, z_f)$ can be computed by:

$$x_f = bezier(x_{c1}, x_{c2}, x_{c3}, x_{c4}, t + 0.1)$$
$$y_f = bezier(y_{c1}, y_{c2}, y_{c3}, y_{c4}, t + 0.1)$$
$$z_f = bezier(z_{c1}, z_{c2}, z_{c3}, z_{c4}, t + 0.1)$$

This implies that the camera's position can only exist for parameter values between 0.0 and 0.9, and the focal point can only exist for parameter values between 0.1 and 1.0, which should not impose any severe restrictions upon this technique. This geometry is shown in Figure 8.8. In fact, even when t goes negative, or exceeds 1, the function *bezier* will still return a value, but it might not be exactly what was expected! Whether the flight path creates the desired effect will only be discovered when a line-test is made, nevertheless, it is extremely simple to implement and very effective.

An alternative approach is to introduce a fifth control point (x_{c5}, y_{c5}, z_{c5}) beyond (x_{c4}, y_{c4}, z_{c4}) as follows:

$$x_f = bezier(x_{c2}, x_{c3}, x_{c4}, x_{c5}, t)$$
$$y_f = bezier(y_{c2}, y_{c3}, y_{c4}, y_{c5}, t)$$
$$z_f = bezier(z_{c2}, z_{c3}, z_{c4}, z_{c5}, t)$$

8.3 Animating an object's attributes

In Chapter 3 we saw that a wide variety of modelling schemes are available for constructing the various objects that are of interest to us, from polygons to fractals. Each technique relies upon some form of mathematical description to define an object, and as this description has a numerical representation in the computer's memory, modifying these numbers results in corresponding changes in geometry.

Let us take a simple example of animating a cube rotating in space: first we need the geometry that forms the eight vertices, six sides and twelve edges. This may be developed interactively, created manually, or automatically generated by a system command; much depends upon the user's animation environment. However, when the cube is created, a number of other facts must be supplied before the animation can proceed.

For example, where will the cube be positioned in the WCS? Where will the camera be located, and where will its focal point be? What is the colour of the cube? Where are the light sources, and what are their colours? Is the cube a diffuse or specular reflector? Is the cube to be rotated about the x-, y- or z-axis? What is the angular rotation applied to the cube for each image? Will the angular speed of the cube increase from rest and stabilize at a constant angular velocity? So many questions for the animator to consider – however, when values are supplied, the animation system can then allow the animator to explore an infinite number of variations based upon this scenario.

To create the animation, the system will refer to the instructions supplied by the animator and create the first view of the cube. It will then rotate the coordinates of the eight vertices by a specified amount and render another view. By repeatedly modifying the cube's geometry and rendering a new image a sequence of different images will be created. If these can be created at about 50 Hz, the cube will appear to rotate upon the display screen. When the rendering time does not permit for real-time display, the images could be transferred to video tape or video disk, and played back at the video rate.

But what if the cube's colour has to change from red through green and blue, and back again to red in one rotation? Well, this can easily be achieved by instructing the system to associate an initial value of hue, saturation and value to the cube and modify this at each frame. Remember that the decimal numbers encoding these colour parameters range from zero to one, with a convention that a hue of 0.0 equals red, 0.333 equals green and 0.666 equals blue, and 1.0 returns back to red. The first frame starts with a hue of 0.0, and a red cube is rendered. Before each frame is produced, the cube's hue parameter is increased by a value such that in one rotation the value has reached 1.0. When the renderer returns to colour in the next image, it discovers a new value for its hue, which ensures that each rendered image appears as a new colour. However, if the cube is allowed to continue rotating indefinitely, the value of hue will quickly exceed 1.0; therefore the animation script must ensure that as soon as the value of hue exceeds 1.0, it must be reduced by 1.0 before being allowed to proceed.

The above operation is a very simple exercise, though it demonstrates the activities needed to develop very complex animation sequences. The example also shows that basically anything can be changed while the cube is rotating. The saturation and value of the cube could also be varying; the size of the cube could be altering as if it were breathing; some of its vertices could be manipulated to create a distorted object; and the surface finish of the cube could also be changing. In fact, the sky's the limit.

So, altering the attributes of an object does not seem to be a complex operation (which is true), though what can be extremely difficult is changing them in such a way that the animation appears life-like. This is when the animator requires access to an interface which provides the same level of flexibility as that provided by a pencil, paper and years of experience. Remember that in 3-D computer animation the animator has lost the direct control he or she had over the image. The virtual world of computer graphics basically says 'create a world of objects, lights and cameras, and manipulate them with the aid of various tools, tricks and general skulduggery, and I will show you the result. If it is not to your liking, then have another go'. Now this method of working is far removed from the directness of pencil and paper. Nevertheless, when it is mastered, it offers the user so many benefits that the sacrifice of learning new skills is completely rewarded.

So the real problem surrounding the animation of objects is not so much what can be animated, but what techniques are used to perform the animation, and how the animator interfaces to them. Another problem that also arises is whether these techniques can be applied to every type of modelling technique. Well, unfortunately they cannot – however, we will have to wait until Chapter 9 to discover this.

8.3.1 Interpolating shape

Interpolating between a pair of numbers is a trivial exercise and can be achieved either with a straight-forward linear interpolant or with a non-linear function such as parabolic blending or Hermite interpolation. However, if these numbers actually represent Cartesian coordinates, then the interpolated values must also encode some geometric shape. This is the idea behind shape or object interpolation which enables a 2-D shape or 3-D object to undergo a metamorphosis into another shape or object. It is also a mechanism to mimic the inbetweening action employed in traditional animation. The technique is best understood with a 2-D example which is translated to the 3-D domain by adding the extra z-coordinate.

Table 8.2

Vertex no.	A		I(0.5)		B	
	x	y	x	y	x	y
1	1.0	1.0	2.5	1.0	4.0	1.0
2	2.0	1.0	3.0	1.5	4.0	2.0
3	1.0	2.0	2.5	2.5	4.0	3.0

Table 8.2 lists the x- and y-coordinates of two shapes A and B, and for convenience they have the same number of vertices. If we employ a linear interpolant with the parameter t, then any interpolated shape I can be computed by:

$$I(t) = (1 - t)A + tB$$

where this is applied to the x- and y-coordinates. In the same table, the interpolated shape computed by $I(0.5)$ is also listed, and the three shapes A, B and $I(0.5)$ are drawn in Figure 8.9.

Notice from the illustration that the interpolated vertices lie on the straight lines connecting corresponding vertices, and that by changing the value of t any interpolated shape can be created. It will be appreciated that the vertex sequence of shapes A and B is vital, for if one sequence is reversed then the interpolated shapes will appear to undergo a twisting action, which may not be desirable. Furthermore, as the length of shape A is 2.4142 and that of shape B is 2.0, then the intermediate shape lengths will, in general, be different.

When the key shapes do not have the same number of vertices, for example, one shape having 10 vertices and another 120 vertices, a strategy is needed to decide how a vertex in one shape is mapped into a corresponding position in the other. This might be based upon the relative vertex position or upon the chord length in the shapes. A further complication arises when the two key shapes are composed from different numbers of separate line segments. In this case a strategy is required to decide which segment breaks into smaller segments to satisfy the requirements of the final guiding shape. Such problems demand careful planning when writing computer programs, especially when they have to cater for two- and three-dimensional data sets.

The above example obviously works in two dimensions, but will it work in three dimensions? The answer is yes if we are only considering a chain of vertices, as all that is needed is to incorporate the third z-coordinate into the calculations. However, if the geometric data assumes the existence of surfaces then there are problems, as there is no guarantee that surface planarity can be maintained during the interpolation process. And if surfaces become twisted on their journey from one object to another, this could cause problems for the renderer and the hidden-surface removal algorithm.

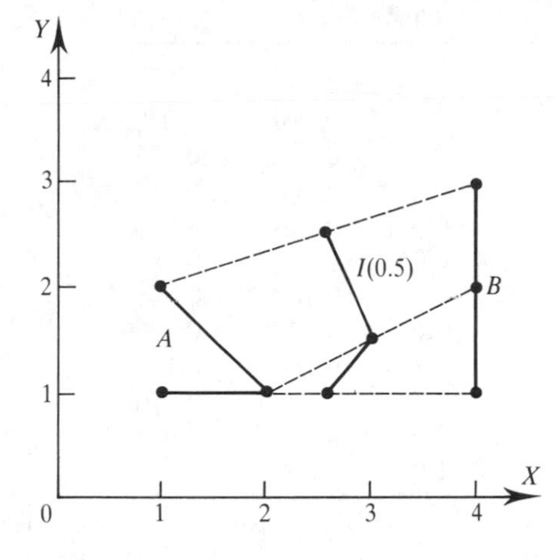

Figure 8.9
The key shapes A and B have been linearly interpolated to produce the shape I which occurs when the controlling parameter equals 0.5.

There is no reason why shape interpolation should be restricted to shape data, as it can equally be applied to the control vertices associated with parametric curves such as Bézier curves. Just consider two cubic Bézier curves S and T controlled by their respective control points $\{S_1, S_2, S_3, S_4\}$ and $\{T_1, T_2, T_3, T_4\}$; whether they are two- or three-dimensional does not matter. An interpolated set of control points $\{C_1, C_2, C_3, C_4\}$ can be derived from the former points using any interpolation technique, which can be then employed to derive the interpolated Bézier curve. The technique could also be applied to the control points forming a surface patch, which would enable one patch to be interpolated into another. However, if this technique is applied to multi-patch objects, continuity problems will arise between one patch and another.

8.3.2 Interpolating position

We know that any data set can be repositioned in space by adding a value to the x-, y- or z-coordinates and, given an object A which has been modelled such that its coordinates imply an origin at the centre of its volume, it can be moved from $P_1(x_1, y_1, z_1)$ to $P_2(x_2, y_2, z_2)$ by the following matrix operation:

$$\begin{bmatrix} A'_x \\ A'_y \\ A'_z \\ 1 \end{bmatrix} = \begin{bmatrix} 1 & 0 & 0 & x(t) \\ 0 & 1 & 0 & y(t) \\ 0 & 0 & 1 & z(t) \\ 0 & 0 & 0 & 1 \end{bmatrix} \begin{bmatrix} A_x \\ A_y \\ A_z \\ 1 \end{bmatrix}$$

where:

(A'_x, A'_y, A'_z) are the translated coordinates of A for any value of t;
(A_x, A_y, A_z) are the original coordinates of A;
$(x(t), y(t), z(t))$ are the translations to be applied to A; and

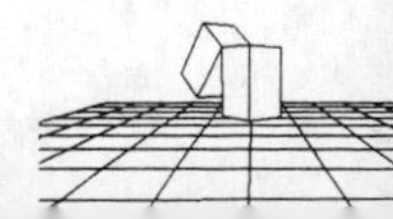

Table 8.3

t	hermite	inc
0.0	0.000	0.028
0.1	0.028	0.076
0.2	0.104	0.112
0.3	0.216	0.136
0.4	0.352	0.148
0.5	0.500	0.148
0.6	0.648	0.136
0.7	0.784	0.112
0.8	0.896	0.076
0.9	0.972	0.028
1.0	1.000	

$$x(t) = (1 - t)x_1 + tx_2$$
$$y(t) = (1 - t)y_1 + ty_2$$
$$z(t) = (1 - t)z_1 + tz_2$$

where $0 \leqslant t \leqslant 1$. This technique preserves the original coordinate data of A and computes a translated version A' which moves from P_1 to P_2 in equal steps as t is changed from 0 to 1. By employing a non-linear interpolant, the translation can be given any type of slow-in or slow-out fairing.

An alternative approach is to actually modify the coordinate data of the object such that its coordinates are modified at each frame of the animation by certain increments. When the movement is linear the increments are easily computed, but non-linear movements mean that they are different for each frame, and must ensure that the object is accurately placed at its final position. This can be illustrated by examining just the x-coordinate of a translation movement.

Given that an object must be translated by 1.0 unit in ten frames with slow-in and slow-out fairings, then a Hermite blend can be used to effect this movement. In Section 8.2.2, such a blend was used to interpolate between 0 and 1 with start and finishing slopes set at zero, and was represented by the function $hermite(0, 1, 0, 0, t)$. This can be used to compute the increments to be applied to the object at each frame. Basically what is needed is the difference between two successive parameter values, as expressed by:

$$inc = hermite(0, 1, 0, 0, t + step) - hermite(0, 1, 0, 0, t)$$

where *step* is the parameter increment for each frame and *inc* is the resulting increment to be applied to the moving object. Table 8.3 shows the increments in the function when step is 0.1. If the column of *incs* is summed, the total is 1.0, which guarantees that if the object is translated in the x-direction by these increments, it will eventually be translated by one unit after ten frames.

One of the advantages of the first technique, where a secondary object is created for each frame, is that it can be rotated about its OCS and scaled about its local origin, whereas in the second approach rotations and scaling operations must be performed about a local set of axes that must follow the object, which in turn must also undergo the same geometric operations applied to the object.

8.3.3 Interpolating rotation

Rotation in two dimensions is easy to imagine as it only occurs about a single point, whereas in three dimensions an object can be subjected to any combination of three axial rotations, which can be difficult to visualize. In Section 2.1.1 the rotation matrix was given for rotating a 2-D point about the origin, and in Section 2.1.2 three matrices were given for rotating vertices about one of the three principal axes. We will now apply the latter in a practical example.

A typical problem concerns spinning an object from rest until it obtains a constant angular velocity. So, consider a cube modelled such that its centre is located at the origin, and which has to be animated from rest in ten frames such that on the tenth frame its angular velocity about the vertical y-axis is one revolution every second. If it is assumed that the frame rate is 25 Hz and it must rotate 360° in a second, then its final angular velocity per frame must be:

$$14.4 = 360/25 \ [°/\text{frame}]$$

Once more, the Hermite blending function can be used to generate the non-linear steps for the angular rotations by having a starting slope of zero degrees, and say a finishing slope of 40°, i.e. $hermite(0, 14.4, 0, 40, t)$. This produces the values for different values of t as shown in Table 8.4.

Inspection of these values shows that as t increases in linear steps, the Hermite function slowly accelerates from very small increments to a final increment of 3.643(14.4 − 10.757). If these are now used to rotate the coordinates of an object at each frame, the animated sequence will show the object spinning from rest, gaining momentum until on the tenth frame it is spinning at 14.4° per frame which becomes its constant angular velocity. Fairing in this rotation could have equally been achieved using a cosine function, a cubic Bézier curve, or even a Catmull-Rom spline algorithm.

The final animation starting at frame F_{start} can then be represented by this matrix operation:

$$\begin{bmatrix} x' \\ y' \\ z' \\ 1 \end{bmatrix} = \begin{bmatrix} \cos(h) & 0 & \sin(h) & 0 \\ 0 & 1 & 0 & 0 \\ -\sin(h) & 0 & \cos(h) & 0 \\ 0 & 0 & 0 & 1 \end{bmatrix} \begin{bmatrix} x \\ y \\ z \\ 1 \end{bmatrix}$$

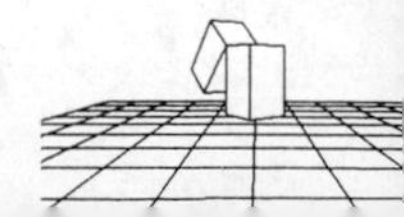

Table 8.4

t	hermite
0.0	0.000
0.1	0.043
0.2	0.218
0.3	0.590
0.4	1.229
0.5	2.200
0.6	3.571
0.7	5.410
0.8	7.782
0.9	10.757
1.0	14.400

where:

(x, y, z) is any vertex on the object
F is the current frame number within the allowed range

and

$$t = (F - F_{start})/10$$
$$h = hermite(0, 14.4, 0, 40, t)$$

Notice that the object's coordinates are continually modified for each frame, therefore the animation script will require to apply this procedure for the first ten frames, and then maintain the angular rotation constant at 14.4°/frame.

For another example, consider the problems of animating a simple articulated structure composed from two members A and B, such that A is free to rotate about the vertical y-axis, and B is hinged to A at an axis R to

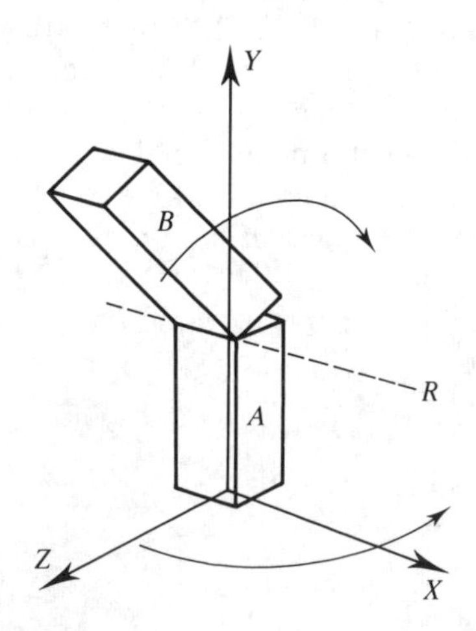

Figure 8.10
The objects A and B are hinged at an axis R such that the assembly is free to rotate about the y-axis.

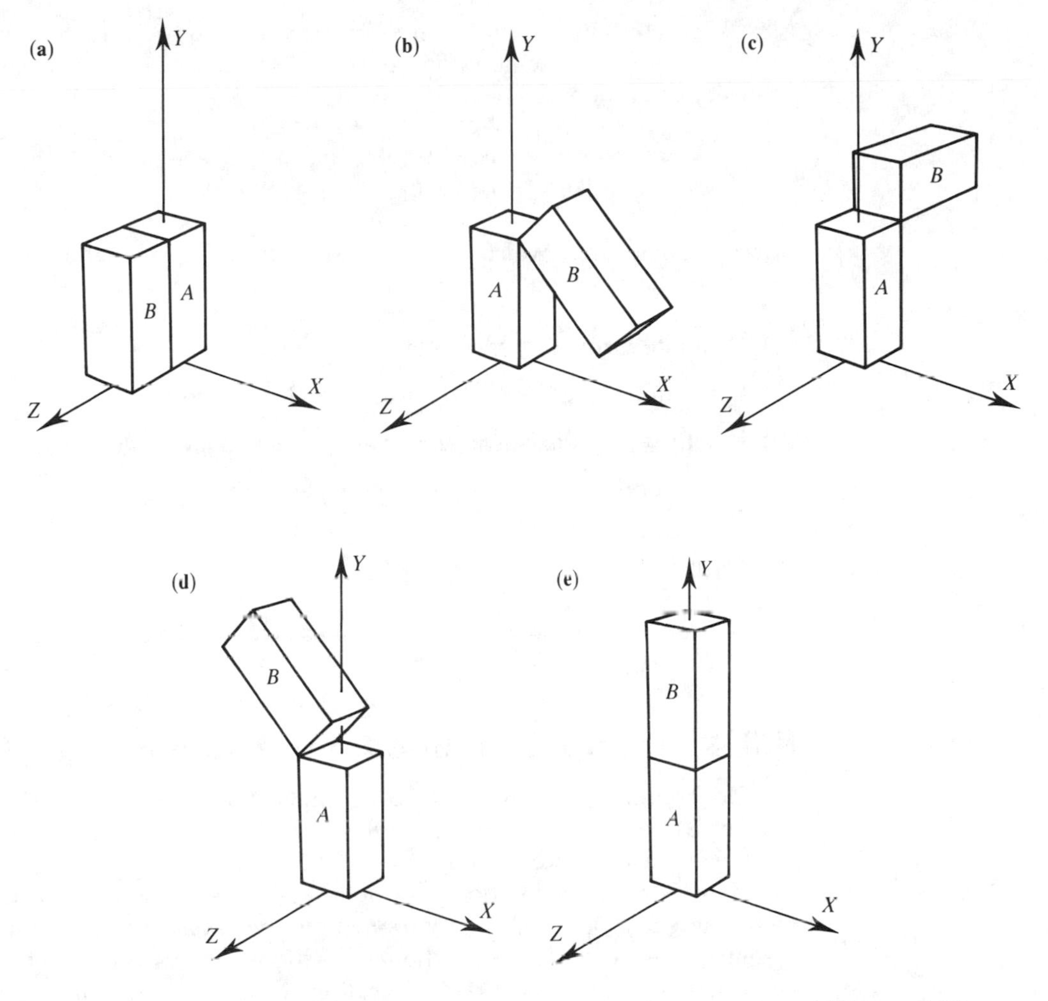

Figure 8.11
These five frames of animation show two objects *A* and *B* at (a) which are to be simultaneously rotated about the axis *R* and the vertical *y*-axis.

allow vertical elevational movements. This configuration is shown in Figure 8.10. The animation calls for block *B* to rotate from its starting position as shown in Figure 8.11a to a final position shown in Figure 8.11e. At the same time the combined assembly is rotating about the *y*-axis. A further requirement is that all rotational movements must be faired both at the start and end.

One approach assumes that objects *A* and *B* always remain in their initial position shown in Figure 8.11a, and we derive two other objects A' and B' which are used for animation purposes. As we do not know the number of frames over which the animation occurs, we will employ a parameter t to control this time span.

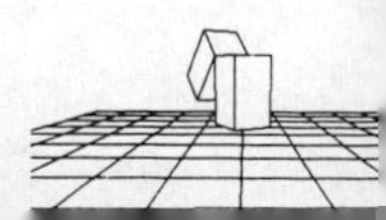

The Hermite function can once more be used to create the faired values to spin the assembly, and elevate B over A. These will have the following definitions:

$$\begin{aligned} spin &= 360\,hermite(0,1,0,0,t) \text{ \{spin 360°\}} \\ elevation &= 180\,hermite(0,1,0,0,t) \text{ \{elevate 180°\}} \end{aligned}$$

For any value of t, which varies between 0 and 1 over the animation sequence, the following steps are taken:

(1) Compute t from key frame data.

(2) Compute *spin* and *elevation* using the Hermite functions.

(3) Rotate B about axis R by *elevation* degrees to create B'.

(4) Rotate both A and B' *spin* degrees about the y-axis to create A' and B'.

(5) Display the assembly A' and B'.

This procedure will show the articulated structure animate as desired.

8.3.4 Interpolating roll, pitch and yaw angles

The orientation of an object, camera or light source can be specified with roll, pitch and yaw angles; these are the individual angles rotated about the x-, y- and z-axes to create some compound angular rotation. As shown in Figure 8.12, yaw is a rotation about the vertical y-axis; pitch is a rotation about the x-axis, and roll is a rotation about the z-axis. For a right-handed system of axes, the positive rotational directions follow the convention that when looking along the axis in question towards the origin, a positive rotation is anti-clockwise.

As mentioned earlier, rotations are not commutative, that is to say that if an object is subjected to three separate rotation matrices in the sequence A, B followed by C then, in general, this will not be equivalent to C, B followed by A. In order to develop a consistent approach to 3-D rotations we will adopt the convention of applying rotation matrices in the sequence roll, pitch followed by yaw. The matrices for these rotations are as follows:

$$\begin{bmatrix} \cos(roll) & -\sin(roll) & 0 & 0 \\ \sin(roll) & \cos(roll) & 0 & 0 \\ 0 & 0 & 1 & 0 \\ 0 & 0 & 0 & 1 \end{bmatrix}$$

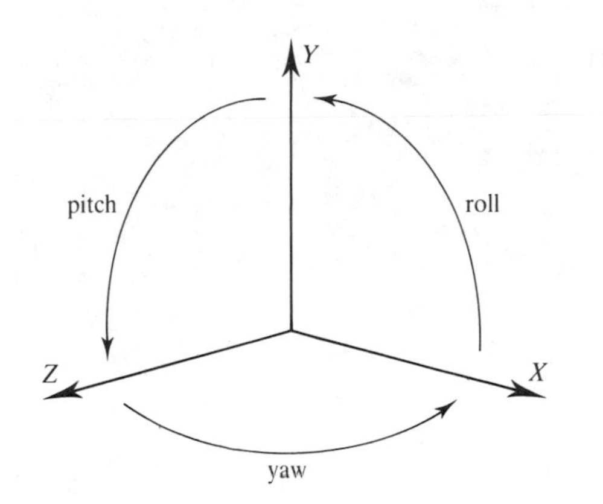

Figure 8.12

There are several conventions relating yaw, pitch and roll to axial rotations, but the illustrated convention has been used throughout this book.

$$\begin{bmatrix} 1 & 0 & 0 & 0 \\ 0 & \cos(pitch) & -\sin(pitch) & 0 \\ 0 & \sin(pitch) & \cos(pitch) & 0 \\ 0 & 0 & 0 & 1 \end{bmatrix}$$

$$\begin{bmatrix} \cos(yaw) & 0 & \sin(yaw) & 0 \\ 0 & 1 & 0 & 0 \\ -\sin(yaw) & 0 & \cos(yaw) & 0 \\ 0 & 0 & 0 & 1 \end{bmatrix}$$

and any point (x, y, z) can be rotated to another position (x', y', z') by applying the matrices as follows:

$$\begin{bmatrix} x' \\ y' \\ z' \\ 1 \end{bmatrix} = [\text{yaw}][\text{pitch}][\text{roll}] \begin{bmatrix} x \\ y \\ z \\ 1 \end{bmatrix}$$

In order to simplify the following examples only two matrix operations will be considered. As a first example, let us consider the rotations illustrated in Figure 8.13. In Figure 8.13a the point $P(0, 1, 1)$ is subjected to a roll of $-90°$ which moves it to $P'(1, 0, 1)$ as shown in Figure 8.11b. The point P' is further subjected to a yaw of $90°$ which moves it to $P''(1, 0, -1)$. Substituting these angles into the above matrices produces:

$$\begin{bmatrix} x'' \\ y'' \\ z'' \\ 1 \end{bmatrix} = \begin{bmatrix} 0 & 0 & 1 & 0 \\ 0 & 1 & 0 & 0 \\ -1 & 0 & 0 & 0 \\ 0 & 0 & 0 & 1 \end{bmatrix} \begin{bmatrix} 0 & 1 & 0 & 0 \\ -1 & 0 & 0 & 0 \\ 0 & 0 & 1 & 0 \\ 0 & 0 & 0 & 1 \end{bmatrix} \begin{bmatrix} x \\ y \\ z \\ 1 \end{bmatrix}$$

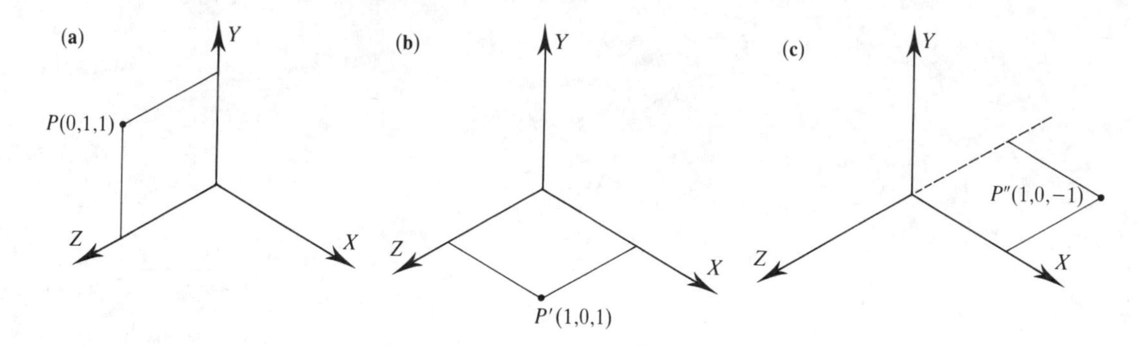

Figure 8.13

In these three illustrations we see a point $P(0, 1, 1)$ in (a) subjected to a roll of $-90°$ which moves it to $P'(1, 0, 1)$ in (b). After a yaw rotation of 90° it finishes up at $P''(1, 0, -1)$ in (c).

which concatenates to:

$$\begin{bmatrix} x'' \\ y'' \\ z'' \\ 1 \end{bmatrix} = \begin{bmatrix} 0 & 0 & 1 & 0 \\ -1 & 0 & 0 & 0 \\ 0 & -1 & 0 & 0 \\ 0 & 0 & 0 & 1 \end{bmatrix} \begin{bmatrix} x \\ y \\ z \\ 1 \end{bmatrix}$$

A test point $P(0, 1, 1)$ is transformed into $P''(1, 0, -1)$. However, what is difficult to imagine is how the point P moves to its resting position P'' if the yaw and roll operations are interpolated over time. To discover this trajectory in space we must develop the matrix operations so that the yaw and roll angles can be increased in steps. So returning to the original matrices and concatenating the roll and yaw matrices, we obtain:

$$\begin{bmatrix} \cos(roll)\cos(yaw) & -\cos(yaw)\sin(roll) & \sin(yaw) & 0 \\ \sin(roll) & \cos(roll) & 0 & 0 \\ -\sin(yaw)\cos(roll) & \sin(yaw)\sin(roll) & \cos(yaw) & 0 \\ 0 & 0 & 0 & 1 \end{bmatrix}$$

and if the angles *roll* and *yaw* are defined as:

$$roll = -90t$$
$$yaw = 90t$$

where t varies between 0 and 1, then the matrix will provide the interpolated rotations. In fact, Table 8.5 lists the coordinates of P as it moves from $(0, 1, 1)$ to $(1, 0, -1)$.

The table also includes a column marked 'dist' – this measures the linear distance moved from the previous point. Note that this is not linear, but shows a gradual reduction which would manifest as a gradual decrease in speed when animated.

Hopefully, this example illustrates the problems introduced by interpolating angles. To begin with, developing a rotation from three separate

Table 8.5

t	dist	x	y	z
0.0	–	0.000	1.000	1.000
0.1	0.313	0.311	0.988	0.963
0.2	0.313	0.603	0.951	0.856
0.3	0.313	0.858	0.891	0.685
0.4	0.313	1.063	0.809	0.464
0.5	0.311	1.207	0.707	0.207
0.6	0.309	1.285	0.588	−0.067
0.7	0.304	1.296	0.454	−0.340
0.8	0.298	1.245	0.309	−0.595
0.9	0.290	1.142	0.156	−0.819
1.0	0.278	1.000	0.000	−1.000

rotations about the origin is not very easy, and the interpolated path is difficult to predict and generally produces non-linear movements. Another phenomenon is that of 'gimbal lock', where one degree of rotational freedom is lost under certain rotations. To illustrate this, consider a gimbal mechanism used for supporting a compass or gyroscope; generally, three concentric rings or frames are used as shown in Figure 8.14a to control yaw, pitch and roll movements. If a roll of 90° is performed about the z-axis, the gimbal support adjusts to the orientation shown in Figure 8.14b. If now a pitch of 90° is made about the x-axis, the gimbal support moves to that shown in Figure 8.14c. This final orientation shows the gimbal locked, as it is unable to provide any roll action about the z-axis – in fact, the roll gimbal performs the same action as the yaw gimbal and one degree of freedom has been lost. This very same phenomenon can arise within computer animation systems, especially where an animator is interactively adjusting the orientation of an object using roll, pitch and yaw angles. Perhaps three controls are being used to adjust the three angles, and under certain conditions (as described above), it is impossible to roll the object about the z-axis, as it becomes transformed into a yaw rotation by the matrix operations.

An alternative approach to interpolating angles is through the use of quaternions, which is the subject of the next section.

8.3.5 Interpolating quaternions

In the early 19th century, Sir William Rowan Hamilton began his search to discover a way of representing the ratio of two 3-D vectors as a third vector: if such a technique existed it would provide a mechanism for rotating a vector by multiplying it by another. For 15 years he searched for such a system, and in 1843 an inspirational leap of the imagination identified an approach that was four-dimensional, to which he gave the name

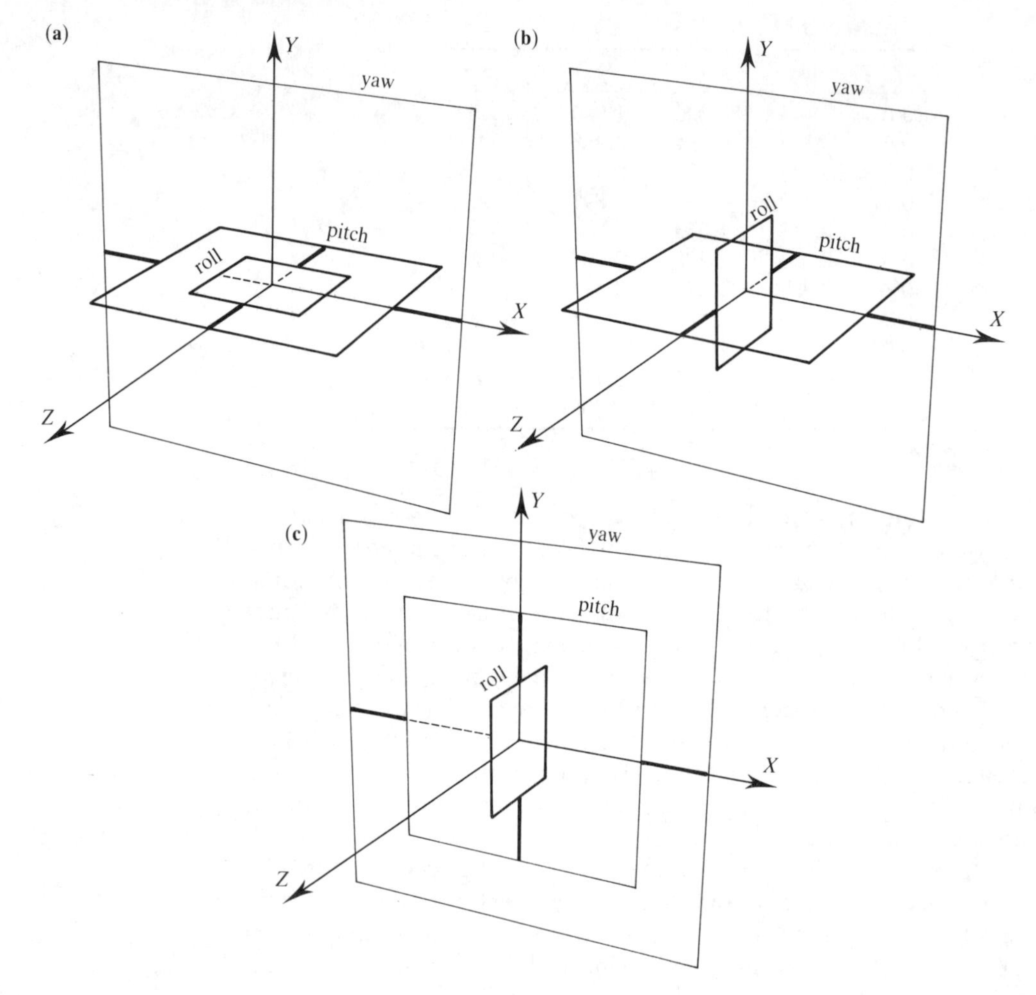

Figure 8.14

Diagram (a) shows a 3-ring gimball support capable of reacting to yaw, pitch and roll movements; (b) shows the status after a roll of 90°; (c) shows its position after a pitch of 90°. In this final position a gimball-lock condition has arisen where one degree of freedom has been lost, as any further roll is identical to a yaw rotation.

'quaternions'. Mathematicians now know that such systems only work with two, four or eight components – a 3-D equivalent is impossible.

We already know that a 3-D vector has three scalars representing the three spatial Cartesian components; however, a quaternion combines a 3-D vector with an extra scalar quantity. This can be used to describe a 4-tuple, which you may have difficulty in grasping, yet whether one is able to imagine this foreign space, or not, should not prevent us from using quaternions and exploiting some of their useful properties.

In animation the orientation of an object or camera is often described using roll, pitch and yaw angles which have some disadvantages, as we saw in the previous section. The quaternion approach provides a simple mechanism for rotating objects and cameras about an axis;

furthermore, we will discover that, given a sequence of quaternions, it is possible to interpolate them to create controlled complex rotations. Although the following is not intended to be a tutorial on quaternions, it does, however, show how they can be used to rotate points in 3-D space and interpolate angles of orientation.

In general, a quaternion **q** is defined by a scalar and a 3-D vector where **v** has three components:

$$\mathbf{q} = [s, \mathbf{v}]$$

Given two quaternions $\mathbf{q}_1$ and $\mathbf{q}_2$:

$$\mathbf{q}_1 = [s_1, \mathbf{v}_1]$$
$$\mathbf{q}_2 = [s_2, \mathbf{v}_2]$$

then they are added and multiplied together as follows:

$$\mathbf{q}_1 + \mathbf{q}_2 = [s_1 + s_2, \mathbf{v}_1 + \mathbf{v}_2]$$
$$\mathbf{q}_1\mathbf{q}_2 = [(s_1 s_2 - \mathbf{v}_1 \bullet \mathbf{v}_2), [s_1\mathbf{v}_2 + s_2\mathbf{v}_1 + \mathbf{v}_1 \times \mathbf{v}_2]]$$

where $\mathbf{v}_1 \bullet \mathbf{v}_2$ is the dot product of $\mathbf{v}_1$ and $\mathbf{v}_2$, and $\mathbf{v}_1 \times \mathbf{v}_2$ is the cross product. Note that in both cases the result is still a quaternion.

The magnitude of a quaternion **q** is defined as:

$$|\mathbf{q}| = \sqrt{x^2 + y^2 + z^2 + s^2}$$

where s is the scalar term, and x, y and z are the vector's components. The inverse quaternion is defined as:

$$\mathbf{q}^{-1} = \frac{[s, -\mathbf{v}]}{|\mathbf{q}|^2}$$

and it can also be shown that:

$$\mathbf{q}\mathbf{q}^{-1} - [1, [0, 0, 0]]$$

If one accepts this algebra, then it can be shown that a vector **v** can be rotated about an axis by the operation:

$$\mathbf{v}' = \mathbf{q}\mathbf{v}\mathbf{q}^{-1}$$

However, we wish to rotate points about an axis, which is not a problem as the coordinates of a point can also be interpreted as representing the components of a vector passing through the origin. Such a vector is called a position vector. Therefore, if the point to be rotated is specified as a position vector **A** which is represented in quaternion form as $[0, \mathbf{A}]$, then the following operation:

$$\mathbf{q}[0, \mathbf{A}]\mathbf{q}^{-1}$$

rotates **A** by an angle and about an axis that are encoded within **q**. When unit quaternions are used i.e. $|\mathbf{q}| = 1$, the quaternion **q** is equal to:

$$\mathbf{q} = [s, \sin(\theta/2)\mathbf{u}]$$

and has the following conditions:

$$s = \cos(\theta/2)$$
$$\mathbf{u} = \text{is a unit vector}$$

where θ is the angle of rotation, and **u** is the direction of the rotation axis passing through the origin.

For example, a yaw rotation about the y-axis is specified as:

$$\mathbf{q} = [\cos(\theta/2), \sin(\theta/2)[0, 1, 0]]$$

while a pitch rotation about the x-axis is specified as:

$$\mathbf{q} = [\cos(\theta/2), \sin(\theta/2)[1, 0, 0]]$$

and a roll rotation about the z-axis is specified as:

$$\mathbf{q} = [\cos(\theta/2), \sin(\theta/2)[0, 0, 1]]$$

where θ is the angle of rotation. Notice that the magnitude of **q** is always unity as:

$$\sin^2(\theta) + \cos^2(\theta) = 1$$

As a simple worked example, consider the point $(0, 1, 1)$ which has to be rotated 90° about the vertical y-axis. We can predict without the aid of quaternions that the answer will be $(1, 1, 0)$; nevertheless, it will be worth confirming this by the quaternion approach.

First, we transform the point to be rotated into a quaternion as $\mathbf{P}[0, [0, 1, 1]]$ with a zero scalar component. Second, the quaternion **q** which encodes the axis and angle of rotation is:

$$\mathbf{q} = [\cos(90/2), [0, \sin(90/2), 0]]$$

therefore the inverse quaternion is:

$$\mathbf{q}^{-1} = \frac{[\cos(90/2), [0, -\sin(90/2), 0]]}{|\mathbf{q}|^2}$$

As unit quaternions are being used i.e. $|\mathbf{q}| = 1$, the denominator in the inverse quaternion can be ignored, as it equals 1.

The calculation of the rotated quaternion $\mathbf{P}'$ is expressed by:

$$\mathbf{P}' = \mathbf{q}\mathbf{P}\mathbf{q}^{-1}$$

where the vector component of the quaternion $\mathbf{P}'$ will hold the rotated point. The evaluation proceeds in two stages which can be performed by a small program.

Stage 1

$$\begin{aligned}\mathbf{qP} &= [\cos(90/2), [0, \sin(90/2), 0]] \times [0, [0, 1, 1]] \\ &= [-\sin(45), [\sin(45), \cos(45), \cos(45)]]\end{aligned}$$

Stage 2

$$\begin{aligned}\mathbf{qPq}^{-1} &= [-\sin(45), [\sin(45), \cos(45), \cos(45)]] \times \\ &\quad [\cos(45), [0, -\sin(45), 0]]\end{aligned}$$

$$\mathbf{P}' = [0, [\sin(90), 1, \cos(90)]]$$
$$\mathbf{P}' = [0, [1, 1, 0]]$$

The vector component of $\mathbf{P}'$ confirms that the point $\mathbf{P}(0,1,1)$ is indeed rotated to $(1,1,0)$.

The above vector calculations may at first sight seem rather complicated, though when they are implemented in a computer program they provide a very useful geometric tool. Furthermore, specifying the axis of rotation as a vector is also very convenient, as it is easy to imagine and directly available from the edges of polygons used to construct objects. When it is required to rotate an object about an axis that does not pass through the origin, then the object is first translated such that the axis passes through the origin; it is then rotated about the axis, and then translated back to compensate for the original move.

Quaternions also relate to roll, pitch and yaw angles, which we already know specify a rotation in terms of three separate angles about the principal axes. However, in this relationship one must be extremely careful how the actions of yaw, pitch and roll are related to the 3-D axial system. For consistency, yaw will be interpreted as a rotation about the vertical y-axis; pitch will be a rotation about the horizontal x-axis, and roll will be a rotation about the remaining z-axis. Furthermore, the 3-D space will be right-handed so that positive angular rotations appear as anti-clockwise when looking along the axis towards the origin.

If the yaw, pitch and roll rotations are represented as quaternions as follows:

$$\begin{aligned}\mathbf{q}_{\text{yaw}} &= [\cos(\text{yaw}/2), \sin(\text{yaw}/2)\ [0,1,0]] \\ \mathbf{q}_{\text{pitch}} &= [\cos(\text{pitch}/2), \sin(\text{pitch}/2)\ [1,0,0]] \\ \mathbf{q}_{\text{roll}} &= [\cos(\text{roll}/2), \sin(\text{roll}/2)\ [0,0,1]]\end{aligned}$$

these can be multiplied together to create a single quaternion $\mathbf{q}$:

$$\mathbf{q} = \mathbf{q}_{\text{yaw}}\mathbf{q}_{\text{pitch}}\mathbf{q}_{\text{roll}}$$

We have already discovered that a quaternion performs a rotation by encoding the axis and angle of rotation within its four components, and if these components are modified then the degree and axis of rotation can be controlled. Now a quaternion that rotates by zero degrees is the identity quaternion $[1,(0,0,0)]$, and if these components are interpolated with

Table 8.6

t	**dist**	x	y	z
0.0	–	0.000	1.000	1.000
0.1	0.145	0.145	1.000	0.989
0.2	0.153	0.294	1.000	0.956
0.3	0.159	0.441	1.000	0.897
0.4	0.163	0.581	1.000	0.814
0.5	0.165	0.707	1.000	0.707
0.6	0.165	0.814	1.000	0.581
0.7	0.163	0.897	1.000	0.441
0.8	0.159	0.956	1.000	0.294
0.9	0.153	0.989	1.000	0.145
1.0	0.145	1.000	1.000	0.000

a second quaternion, then the intermediate quaternion can be used to rotate a point.

To illustrate this technique let us take the yaw quaternion as the second quaternion and interpolate its components with the identity quaternion $[1, [0, 0, 0]]$ as follows:

$$\mathbf{q}'[s, [x, y, z]] = (1 - t)[1, [0, 0, 0]] + t[\cos(\text{yaw}/2), \sin(\text{yaw}/2)[0, 1, 0]]$$

where:

$$\begin{aligned} s &= (1 - t)1 + t\cos(\text{yaw}/2) \\ x &= (1 - t)0 + t0 \\ y &= (1 - t)0 + t\sin(\text{yaw}/2) \\ z &= (1 - t)0 + t0 \end{aligned}$$

and t is the familiar linear interpolation parameter, and s, x, y, and z are the four components of the interpolated quaternion. These simplify to:

$$\begin{aligned} s &= (1 - t) + t\cos(\text{yaw}/2) \\ x &= 0 \\ y &= t\sin(\text{yaw}/2) \\ z &= 0 \end{aligned}$$

which is not a unit quaternion. Nevertheless, if this is used to rotate the point $\mathbf{P}(0, 1, 1)$, then the coordinates shown in Table 8.6 are obtained.

As the parameter t changes from 0 to 1 in steps of 0.1, the x-, y- and z-coordinates move from $(0, 1, 1)$ to $(1, 1, 0)$, and as the column labelled *dist* shows, the distance between two neighbouring points is not constant, but increases from 0.145 to 0.165, and back again. In animation terms, this would have resulted in a motion having an acceleration followed by a deceleration, which is caused by our arbitrary interpolation of a structure that has an inherent 4-D spherical geometry.

Table 8.7

t	dist	x	y	z
0.0	–	0.000	1.000	1.000
0.1	0.157	0.156	1.000	0.988
0.2	0.157	0.309	1.000	0.951
0.3	0.157	0.454	1.000	0.891
0.4	0.157	0.588	1.000	0.809
0.5	0.157	0.707	1.000	0.707
0.6	0.157	0.809	1.000	0.588
0.7	0.157	0.891	1.000	0.454
0.8	0.157	0.951	1.000	0.309
0.9	0.157	0.988	1.000	0.157
1.0	0.157	1.000	1.000	0.000

If this spherical geometry is respected then the following interpolant should be used:

$$\mathbf{q}' = \left[\frac{\sin((1-t)\theta)}{\sin(\theta)}\right]\mathbf{q}_1 + \left[\frac{\sin(t\theta)}{\sin(\theta)}\right]\mathbf{q}_2$$

where:

$\mathbf{q}'$ is the interpolated quaternion
$\mathbf{q}_1$ and $\mathbf{q}_2$ are the two quaternions being interpolated
$0 \leqslant t \leqslant 1$
$\cos(\theta) = \mathbf{q}_1 \bullet \mathbf{q}_2$ (the 4-D dot product), and when unit quaternions are being used, θ equals half the angle of rotation.

If this interpolant is used, Table 8.7 shows how the coordinates change for different values of t. This time, notice that the distance column remains fixed at 0.157, which in animation terms results in a constant velocity, while the x-, y- and z-coordinates adjust accordingly to provide for this constant motion. So, now we have a mechanism for interpolating between two arbitrary orientations in space.

Before we continue to develop this idea and investigate how the interpolation process can be controlled, it will be worth describing how the yaw, pitch and roll quaternions can be represented by a single quaternion, and how a quaternion can be converted into an equivalent matrix. First, if the above quaternions for **q**(yaw), **q**(pitch) and **q**(roll) are multiplied together in this sequence, they produce a single quaternion $\mathbf{q}[\mathrm{s}, [\mathrm{x}, \mathrm{y}, \mathrm{z}]]$, where:

$$s = \cos(\text{yaw}/2)\cos(\text{pitch}/2)\cos(\text{roll}/2) + \sin(\text{yaw}/2)\sin(\text{pitch}/2)\sin(\text{roll}/2)$$
$$x = \cos(\text{yaw}/2)\sin(\text{pitch}/2)\cos(\text{roll}/2) + \sin(\text{yaw}/2)\cos(\text{pitch}/2)\sin(\text{roll}/2)$$
$$y = \sin(\text{yaw}/2)\cos(\text{pitch}/2)\cos(\text{roll}/2) - \cos(\text{yaw}/2)\sin(\text{pitch}/2)\sin(\text{roll}/2)$$
$$z = \cos(\text{yaw}/2)\cos(\text{pitch}/2)\sin(\text{roll}/2) - \sin(\text{yaw}/2)\sin(\text{pitch}/2)\cos(\text{roll}/2)$$

which are interpolated with the components of the identity quaternion. The quaternion resulting from this operation is then used to operate directly upon a family of coordinates.

An alternative to quaternion multiplication is to convert the quaternion into an equivalent matrix:

$$\begin{bmatrix} M_{11} & M_{12} & M_{13} \\ M_{21} & M_{22} & M_{23} \\ M_{31} & M_{32} & M_{33} \end{bmatrix}$$

where:

$$\begin{aligned}
M_{11} &= 1 - 2y^2 - 2z^2 \\
M_{12} &= 2xy - 2sz \\
M_{13} &= 2xz + 2sy \\
M_{21} &= 2xy + 2sz \\
M_{22} &= 1 - 2x^2 - 2z^2 \\
M_{23} &= 2yz - 2sx \\
M_{31} &= 2xz - 2sy \\
M_{32} &= 2yz + 2sx \\
M_{33} &= 1 - 2x^2 - 2y^2
\end{aligned}$$

and the position of an interpolated point can be obtained from:

$$\begin{bmatrix} x' \\ y' \\ z' \\ 1 \end{bmatrix} = \begin{bmatrix} M_{11} & M_{12} & M_{13} & 0 \\ M_{21} & M_{22} & M_{23} & 0 \\ M_{31} & M_{32} & M_{33} & 0 \\ 0 & 0 & 0 & 1 \end{bmatrix} \begin{bmatrix} x \\ y \\ z \\ 1 \end{bmatrix}$$

So now we have discovered three methods of using quaternions: either in their original form using quaternion multiplication; or a single quaternion representing roll, pitch and yaw rotations, or a matrix equivalent.

Returning to the problem of controlling the interpolation process, there is nothing to prevent one from enhancing the linear interpolation mechanism with an additional non-linear function such as our Hermite function *hermite*. This could be incorporated as follows:

$$\mathbf{q}' = \left[\frac{\sin((1-h)\theta)}{\sin(\theta)}\right]\mathbf{q}_1 + \left[\frac{\sin(h\theta)}{\sin(\theta)}\right]\mathbf{q}_2$$

where:

$\mathbf{q}'$ is the interpolated quaternion
$\mathbf{q}_1$ and $\mathbf{q}_2$ are the two quaternions being interpolated
$h = hermite(0, 1, start, end, t)$ (as described in Section 8.2.2)
start is the starting slope
end is the ending slope
$0 \leqslant t \leqslant 1$
$\cos(\theta) = \mathbf{q}_1 \bullet \mathbf{q}_2$ (the 4-D dot product)

Table 8.8

t	dist	x	y	z
0.0	–	0.000	1.000	1.000
0.1	0.083	0.068	1.032	0.964
0.2	0.225	0.250	1.101	0.852
0.3	0.331	0.505	1.152	0.647
0.4	0.401	0.776	1.128	0.352
0.5	0.437	1.000	1.000	0.000
0.6	0.437	1.128	0.776	−0.352
0.7	0.401	1.152	0.505	−0.647
0.8	0.331	1.101	0.250	−0.852
0.9	0.225	1.032	0.068	−0.964
1.0	0.083	1.000	0.000	−1.000

To illustrate this technique let us interpolate a movement that incorporates a roll of $-90°$ with a yaw of $90°$. Table 8.8 lists the trajectory of the point $(0, 1, 1)$ as it moves to its rotated position of $(1, 0, -1)$ with the Hermite function having starting and terminal slope values of zero to create a cushioned start and end movement. Inspection of the values in the *dist* column in Table 8.8 confirm that the distance moved at each stage of the interpolation increases gradually, reaches a maximum half-way through the animation, and reverses the process during the second half of the movement.

This technique can be used to inbetween two camera orientations and provide the essential control that is needed in computer animation.

8.4 Animating the illumination environment

In Chapter 4 we examined the different types of light sources employed in computer graphics – these include point, spot and directional, together with an ambient component which simulates a pseudo-background illumination level. All of these sources of illumination are specified by a collection of parameters such as intensity, colour, position, direction, solid-angle and attenuation coefficient, which are all candidates for modification. Chapter 7 reviewed some of the blending techniques for changing one numeric value into another, while the current chapter addresses how such methods are applied within the animation environment.

We have also discovered that an object's position and orientation can be controlled by matrix operations, and intermediate animation frames can be computed by interpolating between two key frames using parametric techniques, roll, pitch and yaw angles and quaternions. Now even though light sources need no physical modelling in the form of polygons or patches, they can be interpreted as virtual objects and manipulated using the same techniques. For instance, the position of a light source can be inbetweened from one place to another by interpolating its key coordinate values; similarly its intensity, colour, direction, etc. can also be modified using the same techniques. As these spatial parameters are changed, they are reflected in animated illumination levels in the rendered scenes. However, one must be aware of the dangers of modifying too many of these parameters at once, as considerable time will be needed to balance light levels and maintain the desired continuity of illumination throughout an animation sequence.

Although there is no natural upper limit to the number of light sources employed in computer animation, one must be aware that rendering time will increase for every extra one used. Furthermore, one must be prepared to spend extra time rendering sequences over and over again to achieve a certain visual effect, which makes last-minute modifications to animation procedures a problem, as they could completely disturb previously computed illumination levels. In fact, in complex scenes, a good practice is to delay the animation of the illumination environment for as long as is possible, and perform the line testing using a lighting configuration that minimizes rendering time.

In the real world it is impossible for two objects to share the same space, yet in the virtual world of computer graphics almost anything is possible which, unfortunately, can cause problems in software, especially when they have not been anticipated by the programmer. For instance, point, directional and spot lights have no physical size, and therefore can be positioned anywhere within the WCS, which in practice means that they can be even located on or inside an object. One can easily appreciate the problems this causes, by considering a light source located at a vertex of an object being Phong-shaded by this light source. In calculating the Phong specular highlights, a vector is required linking the light source to the illuminated surface, but as these points are coincident at the light source, the vector cannot be defined, and could cause the rendering software to collapse.

Although a scene may be illuminated by several light sources, there is no requirement that every object must receive the illumination from every light, as this can lead to problems of saturation which can be difficult to resolve. A convenient technique which eases the problem of balancing illumination levels is to associate each object with one or more specific light sources. When a spot or directional light source is required to follow an object as it moves about in space, the animator can associate the relevant parameter controlling direction for the light source with some vertex of the object then, as the object is animated, the light source automatically follows its movements and guarantees that it remains illuminated.

Another point to appreciate is that a light source is only a point or direction in space from where light rays are assumed to emanate – there is no bright point of illumination. Consequently, when the camera is directed towards the source it will not register any luminous presence. If such a glow is needed, then it must be modelled as required.

To illustrate this idea, consider the case in which a bright glowing light is needed to create a sunrise. Rather than physically model a glowing sphere, it can be simulated by directly writing into the image buffer colour intensities that create a glow effect. This can be achieved by storing the glow intensities as a matrix of values, which are used to overwrite the image buffer at a selected position. The glow intensities can be represented as a central zone of pure white, and are then feathered into another radiant hue at the perimeter. If the image buffer already holds a background sky colour, the direct replacement of the glow intensities will not appear natural and therefore these initial values must become part of the glow. One solution is to read from the image buffer the required area of pixels that could be affected by the glow, modify them by the glow algorithm, and then write them back to their original position.

The animation sequence might then proceed as follows:

(1) Flood the image buffer with some gradated sky colour.
(2) Compute the initial centre pixel of the rising sun.
(3) Read the required area of pixels from the image buffer.
(4) Modify these pixels with a glow function.
(5) Write these modified pixels back to the image buffer.
(6) Render other elements of the scene.
(7) Record the image.
(8) Modify slightly the sky colour.
(9) Move the position of the sun.
(10) Return to the start of the sequence the required number of frames.

Exercises and projects

8.1 Why is it that no explicit system of units is associated with the WCS?

8.2 Explain why polar coordinates are preferred to Cartesian coordinates in directing the virtual camera.

8.3 Implement the Hermite algorithm explained in Section 8.2.2 and use it to blend the pan and tilt angles of a camera over two key frames.

8.4 Design a procedure to control a camera's orientation from data derived from interpolated values of focal point, focal distance, horizontal angle and elevation angle. Such a technique is described in Section 8.2.2 using Hermite blending.

8.5 Write a program which will extract two points from a cubic Bézier space curve and use them for the location and focal point of a camera. Explore the effect of moving the camera beyond the limits of the controlling parameter.

8.6 Design a procedure for inbetweening two 2-D contours having different vertex counts, using perimeter length as the controlling parameter. Develop the algorithm for 3-D contours.

8.7 Write a program which inbetweens the control points of two cubic Bézier curves and outputs the curve associated with a specific inbetween value. The input parameters for the procedure will be two sets of 2-D control values, and a parameter varying between 0 and 1 to control the degree of inbetween. The output of the program will be a list of x- and y-coordinates.

8.8 Write a program which will accept three lists of x-, y- and z-coordinates, three angles of rotation, and will generate coordinate data in a similar format, rotated by these angles.

8.9 Using the rotation procedure from Exercise 8.8 above, introduce the Hermite function to control the rate of rotation as explained in Section 8.3.3.

8.10 Write a procedure which can be used for interpolating roll, pitch and yaw angles. Design the program to accept a single 3-D vertex, roll, pitch and yaw angles, and a controlling parameter varying between 0 and 1. The procedure should return the interpolated rotated point. Confirm the results obtained in Section 8.3.4 in Table 8.5.

8.11 Use the procedure from Exercise 8.10 above to show that the distances moved by the rotated point are, in general, non-linear.

8.12 Write a program to multiply two quaternions together. This will require two extra procedures for the dot and vector product operations.

8.13 Write a program which will rotate a 3-D point using the quaternion operation described in Section 8.3.5. Confirm that a point $(0, 1, 1)$ is moved to $(1, 1, 0)$ when it is rotated 90° about the vertical y-axis.

8.14 For the ambitious reader, design a program to implement quaternion interpolation explained in Section 8.3.5 using the *sine* function interpolant. Test your algorithm against the exercise in this section.

8.15 If you have access to an animation system, explore the effects of animating light positions with a Bézier space curve.

Further reading

The 3-D animation environment This chapter basically applies the techniques of Chapter 7 to an animation environment, and the only new concept that is introduced is quaternions. These are also covered in Burger (1989), pp. 431–434, Shoemake (1987) and for those who demand the original author there is always Hamilton (1969)!

KEY POINTS

The WCS is the stage upon which an animation sequence is performed, and the animator's task is to direct the movement of objects, lights and cameras using any technique that solves the problem. The ease with which this is achieved is very dependent upon which of the available techniques – listed below – is chosen.

- The WCS tends to be a right-handed system: so too is the CCS, but the image space (IS) where the perspective image is captured is left-handed.
- Objects are effectively modelled in their own local object coordinate system (OCS) and established in the WCS with the aid of a matrix operation which may encode a scaling, translation, shearing or rotation operation.
- All operations are relative to the origin or some specified point. This results in basic scaling operations introducing a translation component.
- Defining the position of a camera requires several techniques including: Cartesian coordinates, polar coordinates for rotational movements, space curves together with non-linear blending for creating faired movements.
- Objects can be animated by inbetweening between values specified at key frames.
- Roll, pitch and yaw angles can be interpolated to animate rotational movements; however, this introduces non-linear angular velocities.
- Quaternions provide a coherent framework for undertaking rotational movements, and when their components are interpolated using a spherical interpolant, linear angular velocities result, which can be further modulated with non-linear blending operations.
- Light sources can be manipulated as though they were a physical object, where their position, intensity, colour and any other attribute can be changed dynamically.

Modelling and Animating

This chapter addresses the problems associated with constructing models that can be animated as required by a storyboard. This involves the construction of objects from a library of graphic primitives, the input of data from 3-D digitizers, capturing geometry from photographs and sliced models, or using a scanning laser digitizer. Even when the data is captured it may have to be processed to transform it into another format that makes it easier to animate.

The animation system must provide facilities to animate single objects and collections of objects, which means that hierarchies must be created by the animator. Such ordering is vital when it comes to the modelling and animation of linked structures, and the chapter examines the design of procedures that are used to resolve these problems.

Simulation is already playing an important role in the modelling and animation of some objects, and the modelling of cloth is examined in some detail to demonstrate the use of mathematical modelling.

The human form has been a major subject of research for many years, and the problems of modelling the head and the body are discussed, showing how different approaches have been used to resolve this fascinating subject. Finally, the chapter concludes by examining the role of particle systems in modelling, and in particular, their animation.

Introduction

The modelling of objects and their eventual animation are very closely coupled subjects, and in most cases it is impossible for the modelling process to proceed until it is known precisely how an object is to be animated. As an illustration, consider the modelling of a human head: this can be modelled by actually constructing a physical model out of plaster, which can then be cut into horizontal slices. These can then be digitized and input to an animation system where they can be connected into a triangular skin and rendered. Even though this is an acceptable method of modelling, it will not be easy to animate it as though it were talking.

If it is known that the intention is to manipulate the surface coordinates to mimic talking, one would, possibly, choose a polygon mesh which corresponded to muscle patterns, so that the cheeks, eyebrows and lips can be moved independently of one another. The storyboard can even call for two animation effects which cause a conflict to the modeller. For example, say it is required to show a talking head (which suggests a polygon modelling approach), but while the head is talking, the storyboard calls for the skin of the head to peel off, in the same way an apple would be peeled in one continuous spiral strip. The polygonal nature of the surface would not lend itself to the peeling process, and would be a headache for any animation/modelling system, and probably demand some special code to create the effect.

So, this is the theme of this chapter, and we will now investigate some of the various problems that face the computer animator in terms of which modelling process can be used to allow certain animation effects.

9.1 Physical models

Constructing a physical model from clay or plaster can provide an attractive method for designing an object for input to a computer. Today, laser-scanning digitizers and 3-D electromagnetic probes provide a very convenient method of capturing surface geometry. In the case of a 3-D digitizer, one particular model is capable of probing a hemispherical space of about 60 in (2.36 m) radius to a resolution of 0.016 in (0.063 mm). The digitizing process begins by drawing a useful mesh of triangles or polygons upon a surface, and then probing the common vertices where the x-, y- and z-coordinates are input to a host computer. Once within an animation environment, this data can be processed to cater for the needs of the animator.

When such useful technology is not available, the model geometry can be input by photographic methods as described later in Section 9.3, or by cutting the model into thin slices. The thickness would depend upon the

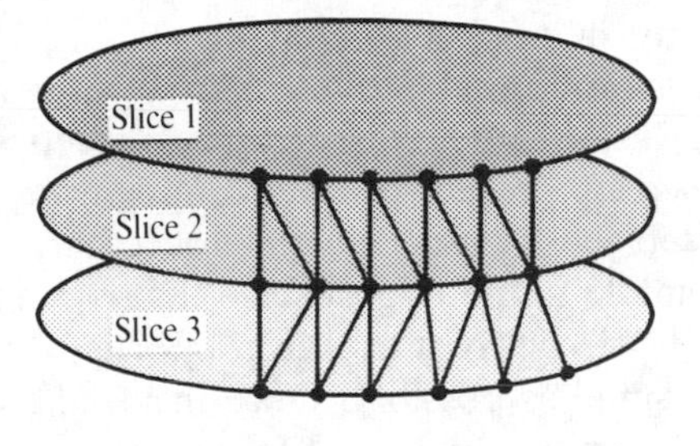

Figure 9.1
If these three contours are parts of three-dimensional slices through an object then they can be used to construct a 3-D triangular mesh by joining the vertices as illustrated.

level of detail required along the cutting axis, and upon the number of facets needed in the final surface. Before slicing begins there must be some method of aligning the cross-sections once they have been cut; this might be achieved by placing inside the model some form of extrusion to act as a reference origin. Another method is to enclose the model inside some convenient-sized box, which is then filled with a second substance, perhaps having a different colour to the model; the corners of the slices can then become reference marks.

When the slices have been cut, their shapes can be traced onto paper, together with the positions of the reference marks. As these slices will eventually have to be connected to one another as a surface mesh, the position of the points to be digitized on each slice is quite important. One method of fixing these points is to choose them at specific angular positions around the contour, perhaps every 5° to 10°; this ensures that neighbouring slices will have the same number of points, and enables them to be easily connected. Figure 9.1 shows how a triangular mesh can be created between any two slices by joining the points as illustrated. Obviously this slicing technique cannot cope with objects possessing fine concave features as found in the human ear. If the material is not too delicate, the slices can be directly digitized onto a tablet thus avoiding the tracing process.

Inside the computer the digitized slices will have only two coordinate values, say the x- and z-coordinates. To reconstitute the model the slices must be translated to their correct y-position – allowing for the slice thickness and material lost in the cutting process – and then linked up to form the 3-D skin.

9.2 Manual digitizing

A conventional digitizer or tablet is a standard piece of equipment in any computer animation facility and can be used in a variety of ways for inputting shapes that form the final 3-D model. We have already seen the modelling techniques for extruded and swept surfaces, and manual digitizing provides a convenient method of supplying the guide shapes to these tools.

The size of any shape that is manually digitized is quite important, because a digitizer is only capable of working to a certain resolution, say 0.005 in (0.02 mm); this, together with errors produced at the drawing stage and those introduced by the person digitizing can become visible in the final model. To keep these errors to some acceptable level, the original artwork should be made to the largest scale that is practical – this ensures that operator and digitizer errors are, in proportion to the dimensions of the coordinates, as small as possible. Once inside the modelling environment, these coordinates can be scaled to any convenient size to comply with the assumed physical dimensions associated with the WCS.

CAD-like digitizing systems can also be used for designing 3-D models where front-, plan- and end-elevations are drawn for an object and input using the specific commands of the software. Such systems permit the input surface geometry of objects where all three coordinate values are captured at the digitizer interface. This is achieved by the user selecting a particular elevation which allows the software to identify whether the view is described in x- and y-coordinates, y- and z-coordinates or x- and z-coordinates, and by identifying the same point in any two elevations, the three coordinates of the point can be extracted by the software and used to build a coherent 3-D model.

9.3 Orthogonal photographs

In the introducion to this section we touched upon the problems of inputting a 3-D human head, and suggested that it could be achieved by constructing a model out of plaster or clay, covered in a useful mesh of triangles, and perhaps digitized using a 3-D digitizer. Unfortunately, not everyone has access to these devices, and an alternative approach which involves the minimum of technology is through the use of orthogonal photographs. This technique can be used with a real or model human head, and starts by tracing a clear triangular mesh over the surface, anticipating the animation requirements, and altering the size of the triangles to match the curvature of the surface.

The second stage is to photograph the subject from the front and side, ideally with a long focal length lens as this minimizes the degree of perspective foreshortening in the image. Only one side is necessary as one can assume that the head is symmetric, and the second half can be constructed by forming a reflection of the one side modelled. The photographs can then be enlarged to some convenient format, perhaps twice life-size, and the triangles traced onto tracing paper, where they are annotated with a set of unique numbers associated with the vertices in each of the two views.

The third stage requires them to be mounted upon a digitizer and aligned as though they represent the true front- and side-elevations of the subject. The software which constructs the triangular mesh will allow the operator to probe the same vertex in both views, which provides the three coordinate values, and by traversing the views in triangle sequence, the 3-D surface can be captured.

A fourth stage develops the second half of the head by reflecting the original triangles about the central vertical plane of the head, but this reflection process will also reverse the vertex sequence of these triangles and, as this could be important to the renderer, these new triangles will have to be manipulated to correct this effect.

Figure 9.2 shows a front and side view of a head, which were used by Keith Waters in his research into facial expression. As each vertex exists in both views, its 3-D coordinates are easily obtained.

9.4 Laser scanning

A variety of laser-scanning digitizers are now available, through which certain models can be placed upon a slowly rotating turntable and, while rotating, the object is digitized in vertical lines by a scanning laser and the point of optical contact is measured by a camera to reveal its 3-D position in space. This is possible as the position of the laser source is known in relation to the detector and this geometry enables the observed illuminated point to be transformed back into the object space. These points can be input to a computer where they can be used to reconstruct a replica of the original model. Such devices are capable of generating large coordinate files, which are often used to drive a milling machine to form an excellent copy.

9.5 Flying logos

Most logos are generally company names, programme titles or a graphic symbol associated with an organization, and one of the first applications of computer animation was to make these fly though a virtual space and provide the audience with an exciting visual experience. Unfortunately, most audiences became quickly bored with extruded letters tumbling in through their televisions, and storyboard designers are now faced with the dilemma of how to introduce a name or title without using the cliché tumbles of yesterday. However, even though this causes some real anguish for professional designers, for the beginner coming to grips with computer animation for the first time, it is still useful to explore some of the ideas behind their modelling and animation.

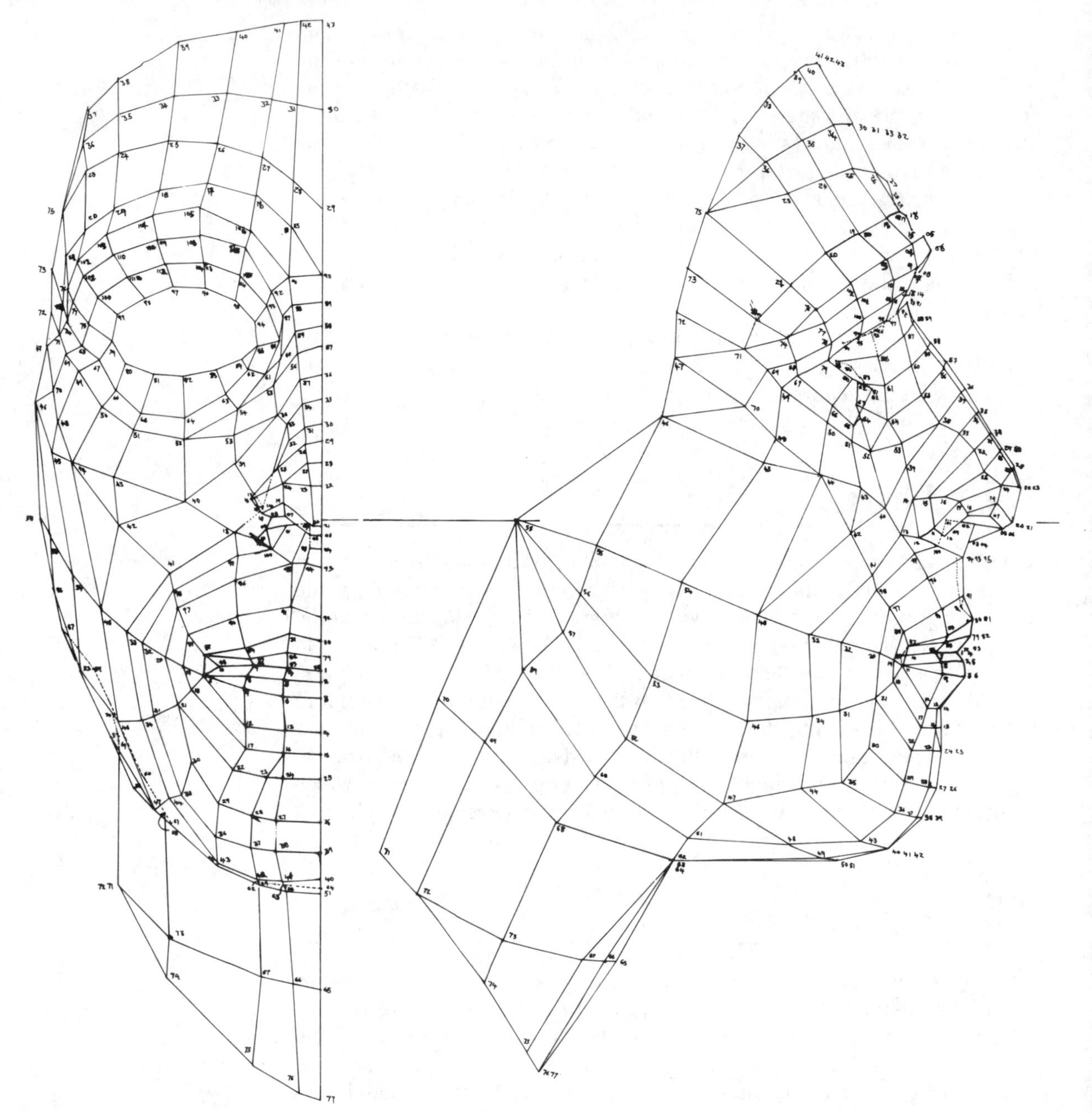

Figure 9.2

These two drawings were prepared by Keith Waters using two photographs of a subject covered with polygons. They were then digitized to form a 3-D polygonal mesh and then animated.

It is highly unlikely that one modelling technique will suffice to construct a logo, yet it is probable that extrusions and swept surfaces will play an important role in their design. Given a storyboard that requires various elements to move into a centre field position from some unseen positions, this alone is a signal that these elements must be modelled such that their final spatial relationships are preserved, and that their individual identity is also available to the animator in order that they can be manipulated independently from one another.

This simple sequence will require that the logo can be manipulated as a whole and also through its individual elements. It will also require that the positions of the axes about which the individual elements rotate are known, as well as the entire logo. These will either be defined explicitly by the animator or determined by a procedure which perhaps computes a pseudo-centre of gravity from bisecting the spatial volumes containing the elements.

Tumble sequences must now be specified such that as the elements enter the field of view they do not collide with one another; however, if the objects are supposed to collide with others, what technique will be used to detect a collision, and how will they bounce off? And, even more worrying, how can the animator keep these objects on course? Answering these questions raises all sorts of problems concerning physical realism, artistic licence and the time available to complete the sequence, though at some stage they will have to be resolved either by the use of cunning, cheating, physical dynamics, or some successful combination of all three.

Tumbling logos became uninteresting because of the predictability of the animation; nevertheless, in general, they were produced on a small budget and turned around in a few days. Both budgets and time scales can virtually fly out of the window, just as easily as logos fly in, when the storyboard calls for something out of the ordinary, for it may be that new software has to be designed and tested and interfaced with other systems, which often takes much longer than expected.

9.6 Linked structures

A linked structure consists of two or more elements that are connected in some way, normally through a joint mechanism that permits various degrees of freedom. A simple example is employed in a box where the lid is allowed to rotate about an axis aligned with one of the box edges. A more complex example is found in the mechanisms associated with reciprocating pistons in an internal combustion engine. The human body is also a linked structure and even though it has a mechanical basis for its bone structure, its animation demands special techniques to make its motion look life-like and spontaneous.

An important characteristic of linked structures is the hierarchy that binds them together, plus the constraints associated with their degrees of freedom, and somehow this connectivity must be built into the system. In the case of a box with a hinged lid, no matter how the box is animated the lid must be a coherent part of any movement. Yet the lid still possesses its own degree of freedom in that it can pivot about an axis associated with the box's frame of reference. In the case of the human frame, the arms, legs, shoulders, hands, fingers and spine can all move independently of one another, within certain limits; however, they must all hang together when the body is subjected to some global action such as walking, running or falling.

Without the aid of some professional animation system, this hierarchy of links must find its way into the animation environment either in the data structures that support the model geometry, or as part of the animation procedures. If they are embedded within the data structures, then the animator must be allowed to issue commands that manipulate any part of the hierarchy, knowing that the system will automatically apply the same process to elements lower in the structure. This can be appreciated in the case of animating a hand about the wrist joint: when the hand is rotated, the fingers – which are in turn assembled from smaller elements – must all be rotated by the same amount. However, when the first finger is animated with a tapping movement, the system must ensure that only this finger moves. Furthermore, it must be possible to set the finger tapping while the hand is rotating about the wrist joint.

This type of connectivity can be achieved by procedures that are designed from the outset with this hierarchy, and are easily implemented within an object-oriented programming language. A structure such as *HAND* can be designed to reference six elements: a palm, thumb and four fingers. *HAND* 'knows' its axis of rotation, and holds the pivot points for its own elements. When the animator issues a command to rotate the hand, *HAND* is activated in a rotate mode, which guarantees that the subservient palm, thumb and fingers are rotated accordingly. This rotation may be reflected directly as new coordinate values for these elements, or translated into new matrices that will be used to rotate the elements when they are eventually displayed. *HAND* could also be referenced in another mode where it is instructed to render its elements; this exploits the same connectivity used for its animation.

To illustrate this, let us consider a small problem of a linked mechanism formed from a rotating disk and the motion of a connecting rod. We require an animation sequence which will rotate the disk at any speed, and show the correct position of the linked rod that is constrained at one end to a sliding action along the x-axis. The disk and rod are modelled such that their initial positions are as shown in Figure 9.3. Although this example is two-dimensional, the same technique can easily be applied to a three-dimensional case.

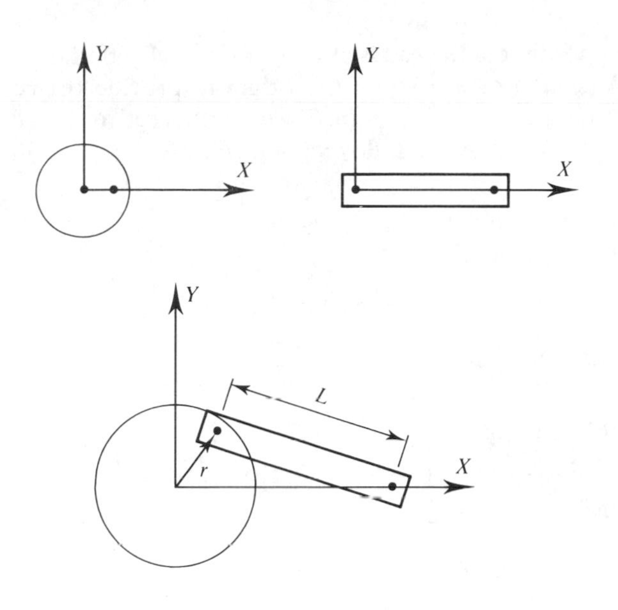

Figure 9.3
This linked structure shows a rod connected to a rotating disk, where the objective of an animation sequence is to show the rod in the correct position as the disk rotates. The two smaller diagrams show the initial positions of the two elements.

The animation can be achieved by a procedural approach which, given an angular rotation of the disk θ, will rotate the disk to its correct position, and orient the rod correctly. To solve the problem we need to understand the geometry in terms of the disk rotation θ, the radius r of the connection on the disk, and the length L of the rod's fixing points. Figure 9.4 shows that for certain values of r, θ and L it will be possible to compute an angle α which will enable the rod to be automatically positioned by an animation procedure.

The x- and y-coordinates of the point P are $(r\cos(\theta), r\sin(\theta))$, and:

$$\sin(\alpha) = r\sin(\theta)/L$$

and:

$$\cos(\alpha) = \sqrt{1 - \frac{r^2\sin^2(\theta)}{L^2}}$$

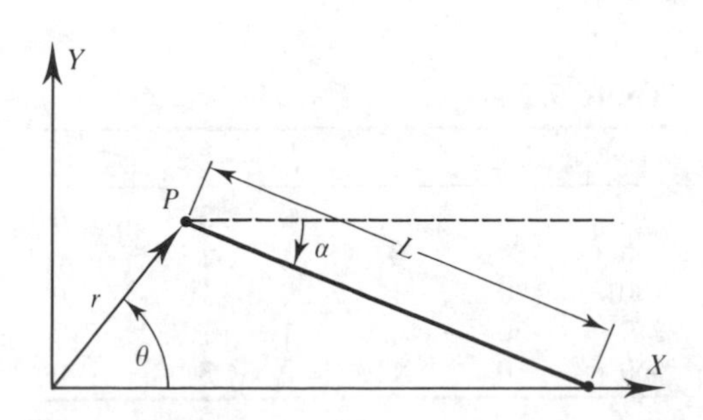

Figure 9.4
This diagram illustrates the constraints imposed upon the disk and rod, where, for any r, θ and L it is possible to compute α which enables the rod to be automatically positioned by an animation procedure.

If the initial position of the rod is always horizontal with the x-axis, this can be copied and rotated $-\alpha$ about the origin to provide the correct angle, and then translated $(r\cos(\theta), r\sin(\theta))$ to connect it to the rod. The first operation is achieved by the following matrix:

$$\begin{bmatrix} \cos(-\alpha) & -\sin(-\alpha) & 0 \\ \sin(-\alpha) & \cos(-\alpha) & 0 \\ 0 & 0 & 1 \end{bmatrix}$$

which simplifies to:

$$\begin{bmatrix} \cos(\alpha) & \sin(\alpha) & 0 \\ -\sin(\alpha) & \cos(\alpha) & 0 \\ 0 & 0 & 1 \end{bmatrix}$$

and the translation is achieved by:

$$\begin{bmatrix} 1 & 0 & r\cos(\theta) \\ 0 & 1 & r\sin(\theta) \\ 0 & 0 & 1 \end{bmatrix}$$

Concatenating these two matrices produces:

$$\begin{bmatrix} \cos(\alpha) & \sin(\alpha) & r\cos(\theta) \\ -\sin(\alpha) & \cos(\alpha) & r\sin(\theta) \\ 0 & 0 & 1 \end{bmatrix}$$

This final matrix can be used to rotate and translate a copy of the linking rod for any angular rotation θ of the disk. If we assume that $r = 1$, $L = 2$, and the coordinates of the left- and right-hand ends of the rod are (x_L, y_L) and (x_R, y_R) respectively, then Table 9.1 summarizes some of these coordinate values. These values of (x_L, y_L) and (x_R, y_R) confirm that the rod is

Table 9.1

θ	α	x_L	y_L	x_R	y_R
0	0	1	0	3	0
90	30	0	1	1.732	0
180	0	−1	0	1	0
270	−30	0	−1	1.732	0
360	0	1	0	3	0

indeed rotated and translated as the disk rotates – in fact, the procedure must not forget to also rotate the disk by θ.

The exciting aspect about this procedural approach is that it can be extended by other linkages to form very complex assemblies, which are left to the reader to explore.

9.7 Fabrics

One of the important developments in computer animation has been the ability to model and animate flexible objects such as flags, carpets and table cloths. The modelling can be achieved through the use of triangular meshes whose size prevents individual triangles becoming noticeable when rendered, and their animation exploits various techniques that depend upon the required level of physical realism.

In the case of a flag it can be animated by disturbing the vertices of a triangular mesh using sine waves, and Figure 9.5 shows such a flag fixed to the y-axis with its vertices offset in the positive and negative z-directions. The offset would be achieved by the following function:

$$z\_\text{offset} = amp \sin(2\pi x/w)$$

where:

amp is the amplitude of the offset
x is the position along the x-axis
w is the wavelength of the undulations

This function could put the flag into one undulated position, but it could easily be animated by adding a time parameter to force a cycle in so many frames. This can be achieved by the function:

$$z\_\text{offset} = amp \sin(2\pi(x/w + n/f))$$

where:

n is the frame number
f is the number of frames in one complete cycle

This introduces a problem concerning the flag's fixing at the y-axis. A completely rigid fixing will prevent the flag from moving at this point, and the above z_offset function will force the triangular mesh to move. This conflict could be resolved by either modifying the function to increase in value depending upon its x-coordinate, such as:

$$z\_\text{offset} = x\, amp \sin(2\pi(x/w + n/f))/con$$

where con is some suitable constant, or by introducing some procedural step where this condition is detected and the z_offset controlled.

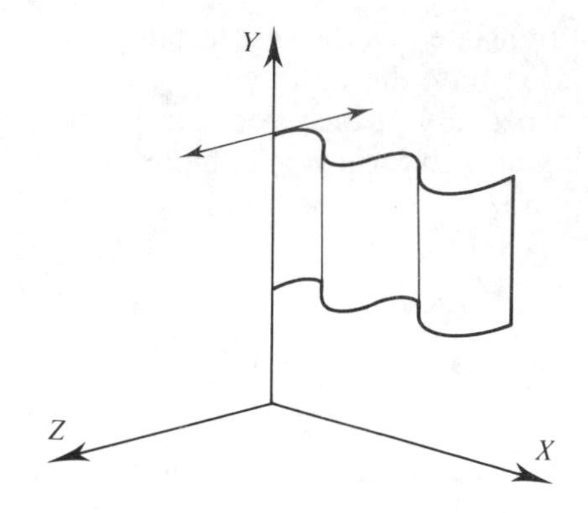

Figure 9.5
This flag has been modulated by a sine-wave function, which, when modified by a phase parameter, causes the flag to move. However, this will cause the flag to also move at its fixing point, which must be anticipated within the animating procedure.

In spite of this analysis the animation will not look realistic – it will appear that a plastic sheet is being mechanically distorted using perfect sine waves. So how can the physical realism be improved? For a start, the undulations could be made sensitive to the height of the flag pole, so that the waves could progress obliquely, though this will not have a dramatic effect. However, if we disturbed the triangular mesh with several functions that simulated the action of waves with different amplitudes, frequencies and phases, the movement would be much more realistic. Even then, the critical observer would notice that the flag always appears to hang in space as though it had some form of invisible support, and we know from experience that a flag will tend to succumb to the force of gravity when it is not being blown by some lifting breeze, therefore this downward force will have to be simulated, which is where physics comes to the rescue.

If the animation is to look realistic then we must resort to a solution based upon physical laws – in fact, the solution can only approximate the way real fabric behaves; still, if the movement is acceptable, then any errors introduced by the mathematical modelling could be tolerated.

One technique for modelling fabric is to represent it as a matrix of mass points connected together in a triangular mesh, where each mass is connected to its neighbours using springs as shown in Figure 9.6. The forces acting through these springs (which incidentally, have no mass) can be related to the masses they act upon using Newton's second law of motion, which states that the rate of change of momentum is directly proportional to the applied force. Although the 3-D solution to this problem is too lengthy to address here, the first stages of a 2-D solution are interesting to pursue.

Take, for example, a single 2-D thread fixed at its ends. This can be represented approximately by a sequence of mass points m connected to their neighbours with springs. Now imagine that the middle of the thread has been raised and allowed to fall under the action of gravity. If the springs have a length L in a relaxed condition, then Hooke's law states that

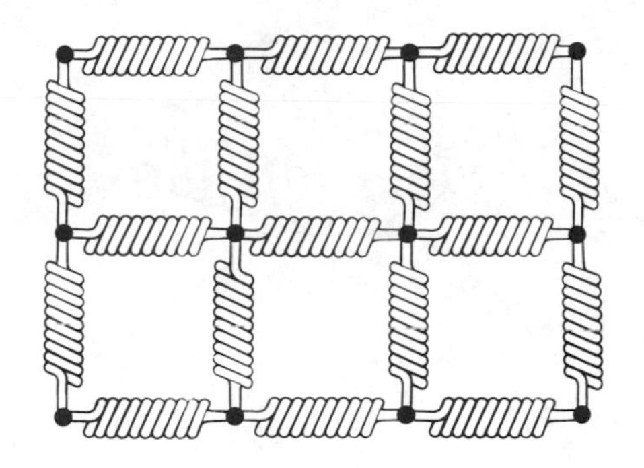

Figure 9.6
Fabric can be represented as a mesh of mass points connected to one another via stiff springs. The forces acting through these springs can be computed and used to move the mass point positions to simulate the behaviour of material under the forces of gravity.

their extension is proportional to the applied force. It is these forces that need to be calculated, but first the spring extension has to be computed.

Figure 9.7 shows the positions of the three mass points whose positions are specified by:

$$(x_{i-1}, y_{i-1}),\ (x_i, y_i) \text{ and } (x_{i+1}, y_{i+1})$$

then the left- and right-hand lengths L_L and L_R will be:

$$L_L = \sqrt{(x_{i-1} - x_i)^2 + (y_{i-1} - y_i)^2}$$
$$L_R = \sqrt{(x_{i+1} - x_i)^2 + (y_{i+1} - y_i)^2}$$

and the left- and right-hand spring extensions E_L and E_R will be:

$$E_L = L_L - L \quad \text{and} \quad E_R = L_R - L$$

With the spring extensions known, we now need to identify the horizontal and vertical components of the forces, which requires a knowledge of the spring's angles. These are:

$$\cos(\theta) = (x_i - x_{i-1})/L_L \qquad \sin(\theta) = (y_i - y_{i-1})/L_L$$

and

$$\cos(\phi) = (x_{i+1} - x_i)/L_R \qquad \sin(\phi) = (y_{i+1} - y_i)/L_R$$

Now, as the force exerted by a spring is proportional to its extension and stiffness S, then the horizontal forces acting on the ith mass using Newton's second law where force equals mass times acceleration (i.e. $F = ma$), are:

$$\text{ma}_\text{h} = \text{S}(E_R \cos(\phi) - E_L \cos(\theta))$$

therefore:

$$a_h = S/m((L_R - L)(x_{i+1} - x_i)/L_R - (L_L - L)(x_i - x_{i-1})/L_L) \qquad \textbf{(1)}$$

and a similar expression can be derived for the vertical acceleration:

$$a_v = S/m((L_R - L)(y_{i+1} - y_i)/L_R - (L_L - L)(y_i - y_{i-1})/L_L) - g/m \qquad \textbf{(2)}$$

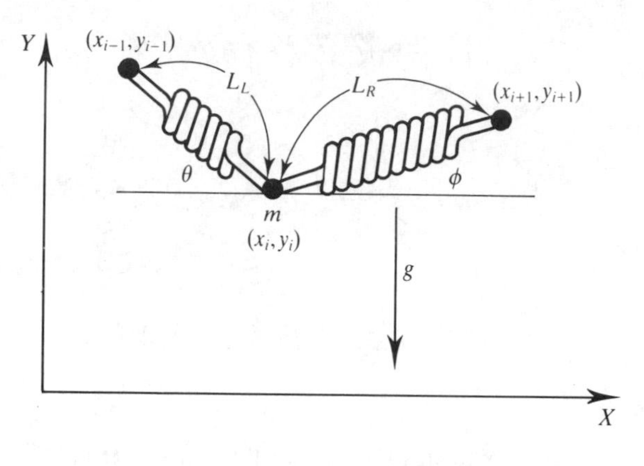

Figure 9.7
Given three mass points falling under the action of gravity (g), their changing positions in space can be determined by resolving the horizontal and vertical force components.

These two equations describe the horizontal and vertical accelerations of the central mass point, and we now require to determine values of the x- and y-coordinates that satisfy them. One approximate method which lends itself to animation is based upon Euler's method for numerical integration, which enables us to evaluate the mass point displacements by assuming that they move in small discrete amounts in small time intervals. Although this becomes more and more accurate as the time interval becomes infinitesimally small, for the purposes of computer animation we will be able to accept the small errors introduced by a finite time interval.

Now acceleration is a measure of the rate of change of velocity, which in turn is a measure of the rate of change of displacement with time. On an incremental basis, the horizontal acceleration can be defined in terms of the horizontal velocity as follows:

$$a_h = \frac{v_h(t + \Delta t) - v_h(t)}{\Delta t}$$

where t is any point in time, and Δt is a small increment. The velocity at time $t + \Delta t$ is therefore:

$$v_h(t + \Delta t) = v_h(t) + \Delta t a_h \tag{3}$$

but the velocity can also be defined as:

$$v_h(t) = \frac{x(t + \Delta t) - x(t)}{\Delta t}$$

therefore the new horizontal position for the mass point (which is what we require) is given by:

$$x(t + \Delta t) = x(t) + \Delta t v_h(t) \tag{4}$$

At t_0 when $t = 0$, the horizontal velocity and acceleration are zero:

$$v_h(t_0) = 0 \qquad \text{and} \qquad a_h(t_0) = 0$$

Therefore, we evaluate the original equation (1) relating horizontal forces with acceleration to discover the initial acceleration. This is substituted into equation (3) with some convenient small time interval Δt and an initial velocity of zero, to compute the new velocity, which in turn is substituted into equation (4) to determine the new position of the mid mass point. The same process is applied to equation (2) to derive the vertical displacement. When both the x- and y-displacements are known, the position of the mid mass point is updated, and the cycle repeated. Values of the stiffness S, the gravitational force g and the mass m will have to be invented by the animator to create the desired movement.

When this procedure is programmed and animated, one discovers that the central mass point falls very realistically and bounces about randomly – in fact, it behaves as though it were connected by two pieces of elastic. Furthermore, as we have modelled a mechanically perfect system, the initial energy of the system does not have to perform any work against friction or resistance, and as no heat is produced the animation will continue indefinitely. A simple ploy for absorbing some energy is to associate a damping factor on the mass point velocities; this guarantees to eventually bring the system to a halt.

This algorithm can be further enhanced by replacing the single spring by a Voigt element, which consists of a spring in parallel with a dash pot. The dash pot attenuates any oscillations as its reactive force is proportional to the velocity of its plunger, whereas the spring's reactive force is proportional to its extension.

Long threads can be modelled using the same technique, and entire triangular meshes can be animated creating very high levels of realism. Even though cotton thread does not behave as an elastic material, it does have some elastic properties, and this technique provides an excellent tool for modelling and animating fabrics, even though it is only an approximation.

The above technique is based upon Bill Scanlon's paper 'Animating the drape of cloth' (Scanlon, 1990), and the reader will discover alternative approaches, some much more mathematical, in the recommended references.

9.8 The human form

We are all aware that the human form is a very complex object comprising a skeletal frame upon which flesh, fat and muscle tissue are supported, all clothed in a skin which can slide, stretch and fold over this volume. It also moves in very subtle ways, as it is always attempting to achieve a state of balance within a gravitational field that continuously attracts every element towards the ground. The torso, head, arms and legs are all relatively large masses controlled by muscles that allow this articulated structure to move from one controlled position to another, whether this be an activity such as walking, dancing, running or sitting down in a chair. Attempting to model and animate such a structure seems to be an insurmountable task, which is why stylistic approaches are still being taken so that problems such as facial expression, walking, running, breathing and talking can be understood.

As this is such a complex area it will be impossible to address and analyse all of these topics, but some of the approaches taken by previous researchers will be briefly examined.

9.8.1 The human head

The general approach to modelling the human head is through polygons and/or patches, which are either derived by digitizing a physical model or from photographs employing the techniques outlined in Section 9.3. The model can then be animated using inbetweening, displacement animation, free-form deformation or by simulating muscle control. The technique of inbetweening has already been discussed in other situations, and to be effective in this application one really requires a fast interactive environment where vertices can be positioned at their key positions and then automatically inbetweened. The technique of displacement animation is covered in Section 10.5, and although free-form deformation, which is explained in Section 10.3, is a bending/squeezing operation, it does have some uses in facial animation.

Modelling the human face has always presented a challenge to computer animators and Fred Parke's PhD thesis (Parke, 1974) 'A parametric model for human faces' was a milestone in this area. His work at the University of Utah centered around the development of a face constructed from a polygonal mesh which was manipulated by interpolating facial features using translation, rotation and scaling. Parke suggested that fewer than ten parameters were required to produce reasonable facial speech synchronization and facial animation (Parke, 1982).

An alternative approach was investigated by Platt and Badler (Platt, 1981) for the simulation of human facial movements. Where Parke relied upon procedures to move vertices in a pre-defined way, Platt and Badler implemented a model that simulated the skin surface as a boundary of interconnected arcs. Further work into the scripting of facial animation was undertaken by Pat Hanrahan (Hanrahan, 1985), who used a real-time calligraphic display for evaluating the parameters controlling facial attributes.

More recently, Keith Waters (Waters, 1986) created a system of muscles which pulled at specific vertices of a polygonal mesh to mould it into various expressions. This is worth examining in closer detail as it could have applications in other areas. In Figure 9.8 we see a portion of a 3-D

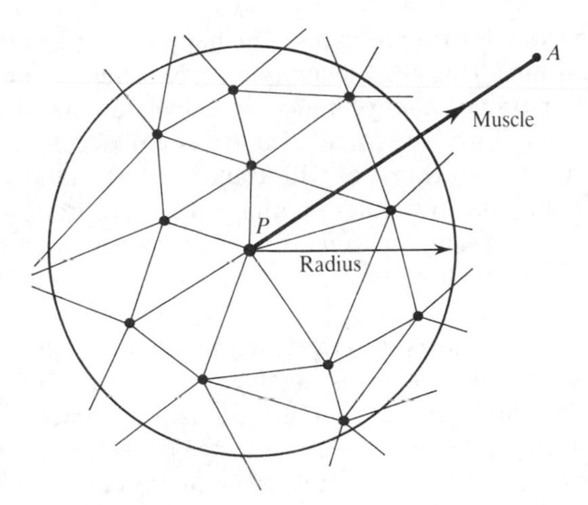

Figure 9.8
Keith Waters' approach to facial expression employs a polygonal mesh which can be distorted by moving vertices within a given radius towards a point A. Vertex P is subjected to the greatest movement, while others are attenuated by a cosine law which is effective over the radius.

polygonal mesh which is to be distorted by pulling vertex P towards a fixed point A. If the movement along the direction of the illustrated muscle is one unit, then the new position of P can easily be computed, though the movement of a single point will not have any real impact upon the overall expression. However, if surrounding vertices are also pulled towards the point A the effect will be much more obvious; but then a radius of influence needs to be defined to constrain the distortion to a finite zone of the face.

This is achieved by using a cosine function to attenuate the amount of pull over the radius of influence, and ensures that the vertex fixed to the muscle is subjected to the maximum pull, while others move smaller movements depending upon their distance from this point. The muscle action can also be enhanced by arranging that vertices trapped between points P and A are further attenuated to simulate the muscle and flesh tissue compressing beneath the skin. Plates 8 and 9 illustrate three wire-frame views of a head, together with three rendered images of the face animated showing an expression of surprise.

The face can now be animated with considerable effectiveness by inbetweening muscle parameters at key frames. However, a more powerful procedure can be used by storing muscle configurations associated with moods such as surprise, anger, happy, unhappy or relaxed, and these are inbetweened to create some very startling expressions. Once more, a fast interactive graphics workstation is vital to preview and explore the animated expressions.

9.8.2 The human body

When modelling the human form, one must know exactly what type of animation is required, for unless it is constructed with the correct joints and provided with a surface skin that accommodates the movements, the project will be frought with problems. The human body has been modelled and animated using a variety of techniques, from simple 'match-stick' men animated by key-frame inbetweening, to articulated structures animated by procedures that introduce forces, velocities and accelerations to create life-like movements. However, as with traditional animation, human locomotion is very difficult to mimic – perhaps it is because the human body and its motion are so familiar to us, that some synthetic attempts remain unconvincing. Nevertheless, some very interesting approaches have been made which we will now explore.

Traditional animators frequently employ rotoscoping as a method of making their images life-like: this involves tracing drawings from film or video to capture walk cycles or complex human movements encountered, for instance, in sport, gymnastics or dancing. However, these images are two-dimensional, whereas the computer animation environment is three-dimensional, and although conventional rotoscoping can be used for animating cartoon images associated with paint systems, 3-D rotoscoping is needed to drive a 3-D model. This involves obtaining the 3-D coordinates of the important joints while the subject is in motion. Two standard methods of deriving these coordinates are stereo photography and 3-D tracking. The first technique involves fixing registration marks to the subject's joints and recording the movement with two cameras located at known positions. The geometry of the recording environment enables the 3-D coordinates of the stereo images to be derived, albeit manually, which can then be used to fix the positions of the computer model's joints at every frame. While the computer model, perhaps in the form of a matchstick man, is being driven by these joint coordinates, the camera can be further animated to obtain perspective views of the motion.

One recent development which is influencing computer animation is virtual reality: this encompasses interface techniques that enable the user to physically interact with the virtual 3-D worlds created by computer graphics. The user may employ interactive gloves and suits fitted with transducers to track their position and physical status, and the data output by these devices is used to directly control the position and orientation of computer models. Various 3-D location trackers and low-cost gloves are already available and will increasingly influence the way we interact with our computer animation environment.

Our matchstick man could even be animated by placing it in various positions and inbetweening the joint angles, though by whatever process the model is animated, eventually it will have to be 'dressed' with some form of solid body. One very stylized approach is to replace the 'stick' elements by a sequence of rings representing the cross-section slices through the different body members; however, these slices still leave the mannequin transparent and not very realistic. Nevertheless, the slices do provide a framework for developing a continuous skin developed from polygons joining two slices together.

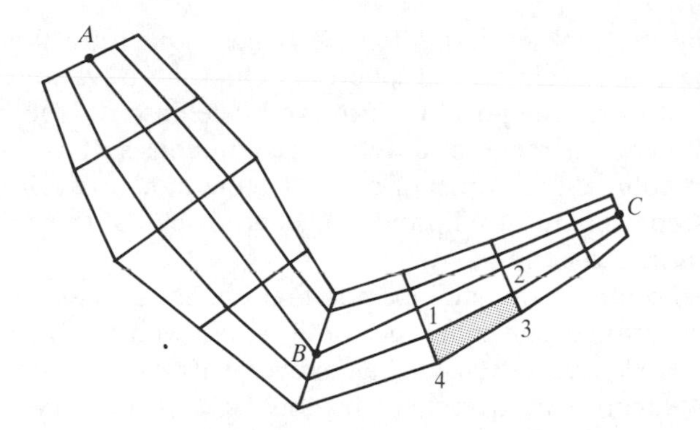

Figure 9.9
This side view of an elbow joint shows the two 'stick' elements *AB* and *BC* joined at the elbow *B*. Orthogonal slices can be used to develop the outer skin which adjusts dynamically as the joint moves. However, if the lower-arm is brought too close to the upper-arm, problems will arise through surfaces penetrating one another.

Figure 9.9 shows two stick elements AB and BC representing an arm with an elbow joint at B. The cross-sectional ring elements can be used to derive a polygonal mesh, which, when smooth-shaded, could produce an acceptable skin effect. In this illustration a shaded polygon has been created from two neighbouring slices forming the four vertices 1, 2, 3 and 4. When the lower-arm stick element is animated, the slices associated with it must also be moved, and as the surface skin is created from the slices, the skin will also be similarly animated. However, the elbow joint presents a problem, as the cross-sectional slice associated with the joint belongs to both the upper- and lower-arm elements.

A simple solution is to orientate the slice such that it bisects the 3-D angle at this joint. In this way, as the joint angle is interpolated, the polygonal skin is developed for each frame of animation without introducing any holes. Obviously it will be far from perfect, as human joints are very complex structures; still, it is one step away from the match-stick representation.

Clothing this skin with shirts, blouses, trousers or skirts is another problem, and if the model is always wearing them, then the cross-sectional slices should represent the clothes rather than the body. Perhaps where the neck and wrists show, these can be modelled separately, but their relative movement in the collar and sleeves will remain fixed unless some extra technique is developed to cause this movement. One landmark in computer animation that uses the above technique was produced by P. Bergeron (Bergeron, 1985) in a sequence called 'Tony de Peltrie'. More recently, Nadia and Daniel Thalmann (Magnenat-Thalmann, 1991a) have been leading research into synthetic actors using Marilyn Monroe as their database. Various projects have addressed the problems of realistic walking, facial animation, hair, automatic terrain following and sophisticated modelling schemes for her clothes.

A totally different approach, which is frequently used for modelling and animating skeletons, is to construct a 3-D system of contours representing the stick elements for the bones, which are then used as a basis for locating closely packed spheres or ellipsoids of various radii. Each bone element stores the position of the sphere/ellipsoid, together with the correct radii, and the renderer develops a continuous surface from the self-intersecting volumes. In terms of polygons, the model requires very little storage, as one sphere or ellipsoid is instanced several thousand times to build the entire structure.

When complex animation is not vital, the model can be constructed from a conventional polygonal mesh developed with the assistance of an interactive modelling system; subtle movements such as smiling can be created by inbetweening vertex positions. Other movements, such as breathing, can be achieved with free-form deformation or displacement animation, which are covered in Chapter 10.

Recently, commercial products have become available that provide the user with a 3-D mannequin database and which store a variety of choices such as male, female or child, selected from different age groups. Such androids can then be incorporated within mechanical systems for evaluating ergonomic problems. As each element of the mannequin can be assigned inertial properties, inverse kinematics (described in Chapter 10) can be used to translate user-defined motions into the joint torques required to cause that motion, and ultimately animate the android realistically.

Another approach to modelling the human form, which is efficient in terms of the amount of data required, is through the use of surface patches. We have previously discovered that Bézier and B-spline surface patches only require a matrix of control points to completely describe a portion of a free-form surface and, given the assistance of an interactive workstation and suitable software, it would be possible to construct parts or a whole mannequin. By moving various control points, parts of the surface geometry can be animated; however, one should not underestimate the complexity of the task in developing a system for modelling elements such as a hand, and its animation.

9.9 Natural phenomena

In the early days of computer graphics the polygon was the only building block from which 3-D objects were constructed, and the complexity of such models was further restricted by slow and small memory computers. Furthermore, prior to the development of the frame store, images had to be realized upon graph plotters or line printers, and perhaps no one even dared consider modelling things such as clouds, spray, fire, trees and rain. However, with modern software and ultra-fast multi-processor computers equipped with large memories, such tasks have been tackled with some success, and the subject of natural phenomena modelling has evolved rapidly.

Natural phenomena modelling, as one would imagine, is concerned with things and effects that occur naturally in our world, and has required the development of new modelling techniques like particle systems, together with mathematical procedural approaches for simulating atmospheric absorption effects, mirages, rainbows, sunsets and caustic light patterns in water. Fortunately there are many excellent research papers describing these projects, and the reader is forewarned that some of them are necessarily of a mathematical nature. To describe how sea waves break upon a sandy beach realistically, requires the support of wave theory and the mechanics of how a travelling surface wave interacts with a sloping beach.

Similarly, modelling and animating plants requires a close study of the growth mechanisms involved: how they are influenced by light and gravity, the importance of form and proportion, and how various levels of detail might be necessary to represent single, clusters and forests of these elements. Because of the scope and complexity of this subject area, only two topics will be described: particle systems and the procedural modelling of trees.

9.9.1 Particle systems

Particle systems were first used by Lucasfilm Ltd in 1982 for the film 'Star Trek II: The Wrath of Khan'. In the Genesis sequence, particles were used to model a wall of flame that engulfs a planet, and they have since been used to model grass, trees, water spray and firework effects. As the name suggests, a collection of particles is used to simulate the visual effects created by various natural phenomena. In the case of a distant tree, it is not necessary to model every branch, twig and leaf: as the eye is incapable of distinguishing this level of detail – all that has to be created is the visual effect of randomly placed colours that self-shadow one another and also reflect light according to stochastic (random) laws.

An individual particle can be assigned various attributes such as 3-D position, colour, size, velocity, acceleration, age and lifetime, which can be controlled and modified by programming procedures. In the case of a tree, rules are defined to control its height and width based upon mean values and a random modification. William Reeves (Reeves, 1985) used the following rules to create a tree shape for the animation sequence 'The Adventures of Andre and Wally B':

$$\text{height} = mean\_height + rand(\,)\,delta\_height$$
$$\text{width} = height(mean\_width + rand(\,)\,delta\_width)$$

where *mean_height* and *mean_width* are typical values for height and width associated with a tree type, and *delta_height* and *delta_width* represent the maximum deviation from the mean values. The function *rand*( ) returns a pseudo-random number uniformly distributed between -1.0 and 1.0. For example, for deciduous trees, Reeves used *mean_height* = 60, and *delta_height* = 12; whereas the *mean_width* = 0.6 and the *delta_width* was 0.05. Evergreens could also be created simply by declaring other values for these parameters.

Although the tree trunk and associated branches were modelled using conventional polygonal forms, the leaf decoration was produced by applying the above rules to generate about a million particles randomly about the central trunk axis. Even the colour of each particle was selected on the basis of other rules that decided on the chance of the particle being in shadow or illuminated by the sun.

Rendering particle systems requires special rendering techniques as individual particles may be much smaller than a pixel, and it is highly likely that many particles will impact upon one pixel which must reflect the collective colour of this cluster. If a particle is always assumed to be the size of a pixel and the particles and perhaps the camera are in motion, the images could be subject to annoying flickering aliasing artefacts.

Let us examine the use of particles to represent a 3-D fountain of water. This can be modelled by considering a 2-D jet of water particles which can be rotated by a random angle about a vertical axis to create a volume of spray. To begin with, a source is required which could be positioned on the ground as shown in Figure 9.10. Particles will be ejected from this point at some random angle to create the natural spread found with real fountains. As particles can be assumed to have slightly different masses, their exit velocities will also vary with a similar distribution, and during their upward path this initial velocity will reduce due to the attractive force of gravity, which implies that at some point gravitational forces will eventually bring the particle to a halt and then pull it down to the ground with increasing speed. When the particle hits the fountain's water surface, it could cause a splash where one or more particles journey upwards to eventually cause similar splashes. Just how many splashes will be allowed to be generated by the original particle is really up to the animator and the realism of the final images, but this can be controlled by the lifetime associated with the particle.

In order to control the particles, a table of entries is required in the software to record the various attributes, and let us assume that this table is capable of recording the status of 1000 such particles. Every particle is given an entry, and in order to prevent all the particles leaving the jet at once, their exit times will be spread over a finite period of time.

The animation proceeds by examining the table for a particle whose time has arrived to leave the jet. When one is found, it is assigned some

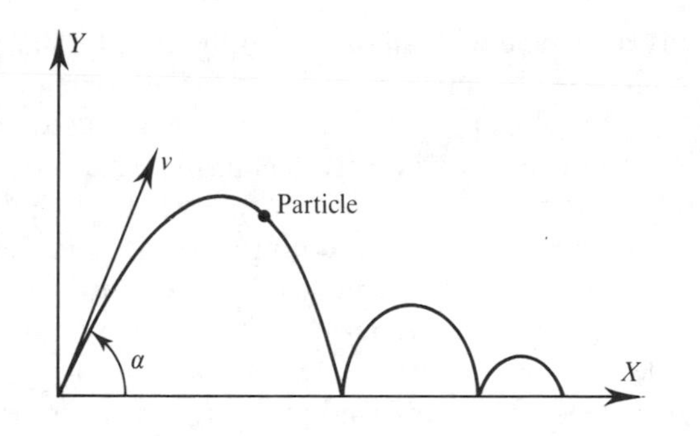

Figure 9.10

If a particle having mass and an initial velocity is projected away from the ground, it will describe a parabolic path due to the influence of gravity. An animation procedure can simulate this effect and can even arrange that when the particle returns to the ground, further particles can be generated which in turn will describe similar trajectories.

random velocity and angle perhaps based upon a similar rule used for locating leaves in the tree described above, such as:

$$v = mean\_velocity + rand(\,)delta\_velocity$$
$$\alpha = mean\_angle + rand(\,)delta\_angle$$

where v is the velocity of the particle and α is the angle it makes with the ground. This particle velocity and angle are the result of the energy imparted to the particle from the imaginary water pressure of the fountain, but as soon as the particle is created, gravity pulls it with an opposite force.

The velocity can be broken into two components: the vertical and the horizontal. The vertical component, which is subject to the influence of gravity, is $v\sin(\alpha)$, whereas the horizontal component, which remains constant unless air friction is taken into account, is represented by $v\cos(\alpha)$. Consequently, the height of the particle at time t is computed by:

$$y = v\sin(\alpha)t - \tfrac{1}{2}gt^2$$

where the negative term represents the height fallen by the particle under the influence of gravity. Similarly, the horizontal distance travelled by the particle is computed by:

$$x = v\cos(\alpha)t$$

If one plots the trajectories described by these formulae using different values of v and α, and rotates them about the vertical y-axis, a family of parabolas is created, giving the familiar curves associated with fountains.

Ignoring, for the moment, the splashes caused by the falling particles, the animation proceeds by storing in the particle table the time at which each particle begins its life and calculating where it should be at the current point in time. The table also holds the exit velocity v and angle α for each particle. Therefore, as time proceeds on a frame-by-frame basis, the spray of particles leaves the jet, rises to various heights until the particles fall randomly under the action of gravity. One could even arrange for the particles' colour to change slightly to add another touch of realism.

Eventually a particle will fall back into the fountain and give rise to a splash which could be the birth point of another particle or cluster of particles, and therefore this point in time must be detected and acted upon by the animation procedure. Its detection is simple as it is discovered when the y-coordinate of the particle is zero or negative, though its rebirth must be specified by the animator. To keep things very simple, let us just allow one single secondary particle to be projected back into the air with some fraction of the initial velocity, and perhaps at some new random exit angle. The particle table is updated to register the fact the original particle has been extinguished, and is now replaced by a new one at some known offset distance, which would have been the last 2-D x-coordinate of the original particle. This new particle will now rise and fall parabolically to create a secondary spray of water. When this eventually falls, the particle can either be extinguished and recycled, or allowed to continue creating further splashes.

Similar techniques can be used to mimic firework explosions where a cluster of particles are ejected from an exploding rocket. In this case the final position of the rocket is recorded and the particles ejected with a velocity that is damped by a fractional value; this captures the familiar rapid explosion which is quickly attenuated by the effect of air resistance. The drag of gravity can also be incorporated to simulate the particles' drift towards the ground, and before they reach the ground their random lifetime parameter ensures that they are extinguished individually.

Particle systems provide an exciting tool for modelling a wide range of effects from fire to aerosol sprays, and the reader is urged to implement some of the above ideas to discover the magic they can bring to computer animation sequences.

9.9.2 Growth models

In Section 3.4 the topic of fractals was investigated to see the role they played in modelling self-similar contours and 3-D surfaces, and one of the important features of this technique was the use of a procedure to develop a model. Continuing this idea, we can now examine another procedural approach to modelling which provides some interesting animation effects.

Consider the problem of growing a tree with a solid trunk, and a system of branches decorated with leaf texture. As we have already seen above, particle systems can be useful in simulating the foliage, but their major drawback is that millions of particles are required which leads to long rendering times. So let us examine an alternative approach where a procedure is used to generate the system of branches and a textured tiling technique with transparency provides the foliage.

One technique which lends itself to the automatic modelling and animation of a system of branches is with the use of Bézier curves. Once

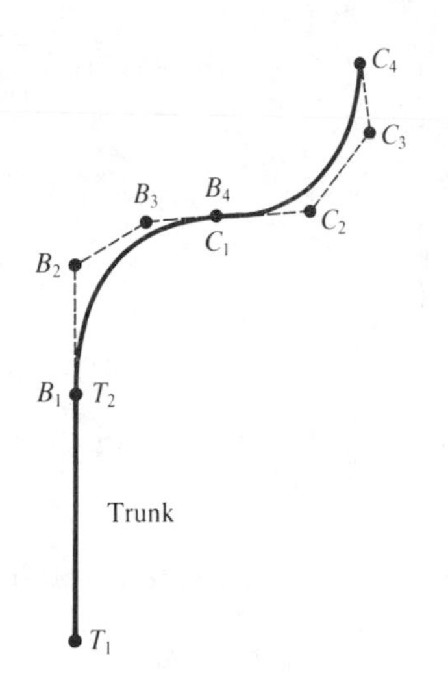

Figure 9.11
The first branch growing from the trunk continues growing in the same direction because the slope of the line connecting B_1 to B_2 is equal to the slope of the line connecting T_1 to T_2. The cubic Bézier curve defined by the four control points can then be grown and animated as required. Similarly, the branch defined by the control points C_1, C_2, C_3 and C_4 have slope continuity with the previous branch.

more, the idea is best explained through a two-dimensional example, which can easily be translated to three dimensions.

Figure 9.11 shows a trunk delimited by the points T_1 and T_2, from which a number of branches will be allowed to grow. To ensure that any branch leaves the trunk with some degree of slope continuity, four control points forming a cubic Bézier curve are used to aid this process; these are labelled B_1, B_2, B_3 and B_4. Notice that the slope of the line connecting B_1 to B_2 is identical to the trunk's slope. The control points will be selected using a procedure which ensures this slope continuity but applies some stochastic behaviour to the other points, together with the length of the branch, which will probably be proportional to the generation of the branch to ensure that initial large branches transform into smaller twigs.

Any reasonable number of similar branches can be allowed to grow from the trunk to create this first generation of branches, from which further growth will occur. In the same figure, four further control points C_1, C_2, C_3 and C_4 guide this next generation of growth, and the slope of the line connecting C_1 to C_2 matches the slope of the line connecting B_3 to B_4. This bifurcation process can be continued to any depth to achieve the required level of detail.

As mentioned above, not only is the modelling achieved automatically, but the tree can be animated to show it growing in time, and also reacting to forces created by wind and gravity. The modelling is not completely finished as the tree is only represented by thin lines; however, these can be the basis of solid polygonal extrusions when the procedure is implemented in three dimensions. The success of this modelling technique will be determined by whether the final tree is recognizable as a natural tree, which in turn will be governed by the stochastic rules used in the

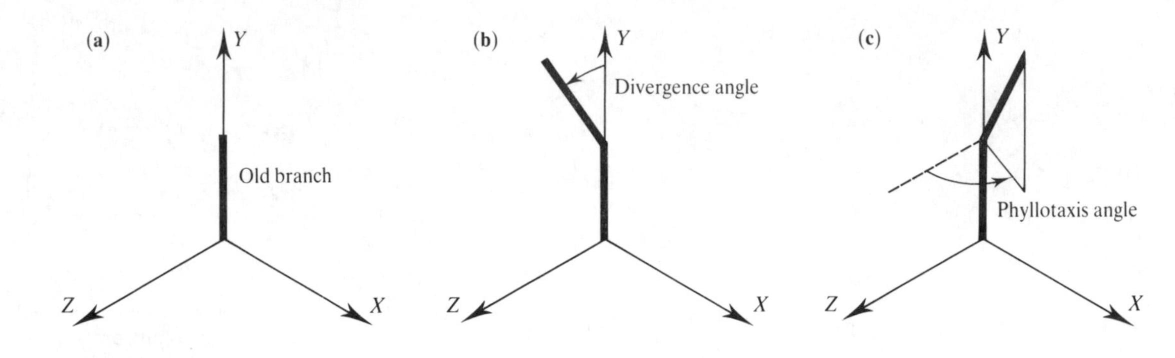

Figure 9.12

In (a) the axial system is aligned with the old branch and a new branch is grown by choosing a divergence angle (b) and a rotational phyllotaxis angle (c). This model is repeated until sufficient branches have been created.

procedure together with the parameters controlling branch length and branch angles.

An alternative technique proposed by Gordon Selley (Selley, 1990) develops the branch growth as shown in Figure 9.12, where an old branch gives rise to new growth by the selection of divergence and phyllotaxis angles; these are selected using a stochastic procedure controlled by minimum and maximum values to grow different tree types. This underlying wire frame geometry is then used to support a 3-D polygonal form to give the tree its natural solidity.

An interesting texture algorithm is also proposed by Selley (Selley, 1991) where a texture function is used to punch holes in any polygon influenced by this procedure. The original solid texturing technique described by D. Peachey (Peachey, 1985) defines a texture cube associated with an object or scene. The texture cube, which can take the form of a table of random numbers, is then used to influence surface detail during rendering. However, Selley uses a similar stochastic procedure to describe holes that will exist in any texture tile associated with his trees. These holes are real, and allow other parts of the model to be seen through them; furthermore, they will also influence the texturing of shadows derived from the shadow map algorithm covered in Section 5.4.

Plate 2 illustrates the effectiveness of this technique: in the foreground, trees modelled with a system of branches and texture tiles reveal the detail associated with natural trees, while in the background, the texturing is only applied to a swept surface. The scene is also subjected to a haze model which increases the sense of spatial depth.

Exercises and projects

9.1 Design a digitizing system which will allow a user to input two related projections of a 3-D object (perhaps a human head) and enable a 3-D data structure to be created. Allow the user to position the drawings anywhere on the digitizer, and force the user to develop the 3-D data by selecting sequentially the same point in the two views.

9.2 Write an animation sequence that enables the individual letters of a word to tumble in from behind the camera and finish in centre screen. Control the animation of the individual letters by some form of space curve so that collision avoidance is effected by manipulating the control points.

9.3 Animate a bouncing ball using its equations of motion, and introduce a damping factor to enable it to realistically come to rest.

9.4 Implement the example of a rod linked to a rotating disk as explained in Section 9.6.

9.5 Implement the algorithm for a simple 2-D thread explained in Section 9.7. Try it out initially with three mass points, and then develop it for any arbitrary sequence. Refer to Scanlon (1990) for further information.

9.6 Describe the degrees of freedom associated with the various elements belonging to a human arm and hand.

9.7 Design an algorithm which will convert a chain of 3-D line segments into a polygonal skin with different cross-sections at the joins. The technique for coping with the angle joints is described in Section 9.8.2.

9.8 Implement the particle algorithm to model a fountain described in Section 9.9.1, and animate the model.

9.9 Design a 2-D version of the tree growth model described in Section 9.9.2 and test it with various procedures for controlling the positions of control points. Implement a technique for controlling branch lengths at successive generations of growth.

9.10 Convert the algorithm from Exercise 9.9 above to work in three dimensions.

9.11 Introduce the force of gravity to control the vertical pull applied to the thinner branches; these will normally be the last branches to have grown.

9.12 Design an animation procedure to show the model developed for Exercise 9.9 above growing in time. Each branch point could be allocated a time value or frame count which must be reached during the tree's growth.

9.13 Perform the animation procedure of Exercise 9.12 above with a 3-D model.

Further reading

Modelling and animation It would be difficult to specify one or two references that cover this entire subject, for as the index to the references shows, a wide range of papers and articles are available that cover the entire spectrum. The reader is advised to refer to the index and examine the individual references.

KEY POINTS

Modelling and animation are inextricably linked together, and it is futile to attempt to plan one without knowing what is required by the other. This has resulted in a wide variety of techniques being developed to satisfy these conflicting requirements and they are summarized below.

- Existing physical models can be digitized by scanning 3-D laser digitizers; these capture fine surface geometry which has to be filtered for creating a boundary representation in the form of a polygonal mesh.
- Manual digitizing is a simple process for capturing 3-D geometry from drawn elevations.
- Orthogonal photographs provide a simple technique for the modelling of the human head.
- Linked mechanisms can be animated by studying the geometry of key points in the structure and developing a procedure or concatenated matrix which encodes the movement.
- Fabrics have been successfully modelled and animated by representing the surface by a system of mass points connected to their neighbours by stiff springs.
- Modelling and animating the human body is a non-trivial problem especially where high levels of realism, both visual and animated, are required. Many techniques are available from match-stick skeletons clothed in polygons, to complex surface patch descriptions.
- Natural phenomena has developed into a large subject area and particle systems have been successful in meeting the modelling and animation requirements of fire, spray, smoke, fireworks, gas and liquids.
- Growth models provide a framework for supporting the modelling and animation of plants and trees. Such systems allow for the implementation of strategies controlling branch height, branch angle, effects of gravity and light-seeking behaviour.

10 Special Animation Techniques

One of the major difficulties in this chapter is describing techniques that should really be explained with the aid of a graphics workstation, or with the visual support of animated sequences. Unfortunately, as both are unavailable, the techniques are explained descriptively and, where possible, are supported with relevant mathematics.

The chapter opens with key-frame animation which has already played an important part in previous chapters. It then considers the use of procedures to create animated movement, and takes the example of a clock to develop the rules for animating its hands.

As an introduction to free-form deformation, the mathematics of the one-dimensional case is developed and translated into two dimensions supported with practical examples. Its implementation in three dimensions then becomes a logical extension of this model.

The simple, yet useful technique of displacement animation is examined, supported by an example undertaken on a Symbolics animation system. The chapter then reviews some of the strategies used in behavioural animation where collections of objects are animated by a system of rules and force fields, which create very realistic animations. Finally, dynamic simulation techniques are examined to show how they are used to resolve the motion parameters of linked structures.

Introduction

In traditional animation every line drawn carries a message encoding shape, weight and speed. The storyboard is translated from a sequence of static sketches into an imaginary world brought to life by the animator's skills, which are the result of an innate drawing ability, supported by personal observations of everyday occurrences and an abundance of tricks acquired through practical experience. They enable an animator to contort cartoon characters into bizarre shapes and positions; rules of perspective are flexible, objects appear out of nowhere, and the natural physical laws can be suspended at a moment's notice. All of this is achievable simply by making marks upon sheets of paper.

3-D computer animation does not possess this degree of flexibility – the virtual reality it provides has to be constructed from polygons and patches that are animated by matrices and quaternions, and finally realized by renderers needing precise geometric forms upon which they perform their calculations. Because the drawing tools in computer graphics consists of keyboards, joysticks, mice and digitizers, a totally new set of skills must be perfected by the computer animator to animate this virtual world. Moreover, strange procedures and mathematical manipulations must be devised to mimic the effects the traditional animator enjoys; such devices are the subject of this chapter.

Many of the topics covered are of a mathematical nature and where possible, they will be explained; however, some are too complex to be covered with any rigour, and the reader will have to pursue them through the available technical research papers. Nevertheless, hopefully this chapter will reveal the level of investigation that is currently in progress, and the success that is being achieved.

10.1 Key-frame animation

Key-frame animation is a familiar technique in traditional animation where an animation sequence is derived by inbetweening two drawings depicting the start and end frames. These frames must have a reasonable level of image coherence, otherwise the inbetweener will have insufficient information to create the new images. In computer animation, everything apart from the names of objects is stored numerically, which enables a pair or sequence of values to be interpolated using any of the techniques described in Sections 7.4.1 and 3.2.7. Key-frame animation is therefore widely used in computer animation, and all professional systems provide facilities whereby an animator can specify those parameters to be interpolated.

Although we have already discovered situations where this inbetweening of key-frame parameters can be employed, one must also bear in mind that the parameters used in the techniques to be discussed in this chapter can also be inbetweened, which emphasizes the importance of the technique.

10.2 Procedural animation

In Section 9.6 on linked structures we examined the way in which, given certain physical mechanisms, these structures could be automatically animated by altering various parameters such as the angular rotation of a wheel. This type of animation comes under the heading of 'procedural animation', which encompasses any system that can be driven by rules contained within a programmed procedure.

Other examples of procedural animation are found in the control of particle systems, plant growth, waterscapes, dynamic simulation of physical systems and behavioural animation, some of which are major subjects in their own right. Rather than group them all under this heading, some general ideas of procedural techniques will be developed, and others left for individual attention later in this chapter.

Simple procedural techniques can be used for swinging pendulums, bouncing balls, driving snooker balls, accelerating rockets, vibrating objects and virtually anything that obeys simple mechanical laws, so let us examine an interesting example concerning the hands of a clock to be positioned according to any specified time.

To begin with, we must decide how the time is to be specified, and we will use the standard 24-hour system employing hours, minutes and seconds, where the hours cycle from 0 to 23, and the minutes and seconds cycle from 0 to 59. We will assume that 24 hrs 00 min 00 sec is equivalent to 00 hrs 00 min 00 sec. This time triplet will be translated into three angles for rotating the second, minute and hour hands of the clock.

The translation from time units [hrs, min, sec] to angles in units of degrees $[\theta_{hrs}, \theta_{min}, \theta_{sec}]$ can be achieved as follows:

$$\begin{aligned}\theta_{sec} &= 6\,\mathrm{sec}\\ \theta_{min} &= 6(\mathrm{min} + \mathrm{sec}/60)\\ \theta_{hrs} &= 30(\mathrm{hrs} + \mathrm{min}/60 + \mathrm{sec}/3600)\end{aligned}$$

This can be tested for correctness by substituting an example time [2 hrs, 45 min, 30 sec] which produces the angles [82.75°, 273.0°, 180.0°]. The second hand will be rotated 180°, which corresponds to 30 seconds; the minute hand is rotated 273°, which is made up from 270° representing 45 minutes, plus an extra 3° equivalent to the 30 seconds swept by the second hand, and the hour hand is rotated 82.75°, which similarly comprises the effects of the seconds and minutes added to the hours. These angles can now be used to rotate the elements representing the clock's hands, assuming that their initial position is in the vertical 12 o'clock position. However, one must remember that positive angular rotation is in an anti-clockwise sense, which means that the matrices rotating the hands must reverse the signs of the angles.

Now a mechanism is needed to drive the hands from the current frame number, and perhaps the clock has to start at a particular time. Let us assume that at frame 1 the start time is 4 hrs 0 min 0 sec, then for each subsequent frame the *sec* parameter must be increased by some amount which depends upon the speed of the animation. If this rate is taken to be 25 frames/sec, then each frame is equivalent to 0.04 seconds. Therefore, at frame N, $0.04N$ seconds will have elapsed, which must now be converted into seconds, minutes and hours. It is now possible to create a procedure which, given the time at a specified frame, together with the current frame, can automatically position the hands to represent the real elapsed time. If the procedure call was *the_time*, then for our example the call would be:

the_time$(1, 4, 0, 0, N)$

which informs the procedure that at frame 1 the time was 4 hrs 0 min 0 sec, and the clock's hands must now be postioned for the Nth frame.

The above example, although simple, sets out the level of analysis needed to design procedures; frequently they require considerable development as there are many opportunities for things to go wrong. In the case of the clock, the hands could have gone backwards if the sign of the angles had not been reversed; one hand could have become fixed at certain times, or they could have simply refused to move. These are the realities of programming and software development.

10.3 Free-form deformation

Computer graphics is still relatively young and computer animation has hardly begun, which is why researchers are still developing important techniques that have a major influence upon the state of the art. Free-form deformation is one such technique.

PICASO (Vince, 1976) included a command WARP3D which subjected 3-D objects to different laws acting on the x, y- and z-coordinates. For example, the x-coordinates might have been processed by a linear function which left them unchanged, while the y-coordinates were stretched, and z-coordinates compressed. This command enabled any object to be deformed simply by adjusting parameters in the warping functions. Unfortunately, there was little application for this technique as computer animation was in its infancy, and interactive computer graphics was a luxury for most research centres.

Scott Parry's PhD dissertation 'Free-form deformations in a constructive solid geometry modelling system' (Parry, 1986) shows how CSG models can be manipulated using deforming functions, and it has also appeared at SIGGRAPH 1986 (Sederberg, 1986). Within a very short period of time it has found its way into various animation sequences, in particular 'Locomotion' by Pacific Data Images, which is shown in Plate 11, and has since become an important animation tool.

The effects of free-form deformation (FFDs) are not, however, totally new; Albrecht Durer in his 'Treatise on Proportion' used rectangular grids to illustrate how the human face can be distorted by the grid to generate families of related silhouettes. D'Arcy Thompson (Thompson, 1961) in his celebrated book *On Growth and Form* employed the theory of transformations to compare related natural shapes such as leaves, metacarpal bones in oxen, sheep and giraffes, crustacea, hydroids, fish and mammal skulls. Figure 10.1 shows examples of this concept. However, the central idea behind FFDs is to enclose an object within a lattice of control points, which are capable of influencing the object's geometry, and as the control points are moved the enclosed object is deformed.

In order to appreciate exactly what is happening, it is worth examining the technique in a one-dimensional example, and then develop the technique in two- and three-dimensions. So let us consider how a sequence of points can be deformed by the positions of three control points. Some of the mathematical ideas will appear very familiar, as they were employed in fairing camera and object movements, and also in Bézier curves and surface patches in Chapter 7.

Figure 10.2 shows a single x-axis with a line drawn between the values 2 and 4. One could imagine the line consisting of an infinite number of points between these two limits which we require to reposition. To achieve this, three control points P_1, P_2 and P_3 are positioned in the middle and at the two ends as illustrated. Any point x along the line can now be expressed as a fraction t as follows:

$$t = \frac{(x - x_{min})}{(x_{max} - x_{min})}$$

where $x_{min} = 2$, and $x_{max} = 4$.

The position of any deformed point can now be defined as:

$$x' = P_1(1 - t)^2 + P_2(1 - t)2t + P_3t^2$$

If we substitute various values of x to obtain equivalent values of t, we discover that $x' = x$, therefore there is zero distortion. However, if the centre control point is adjusted to 3.5 instead of 3.0, all the points between the two end points will move. Table 10.1 shows the changes that occur.

We can see from these values that every point, apart from the end points, has been increased by different amounts, and if the central control

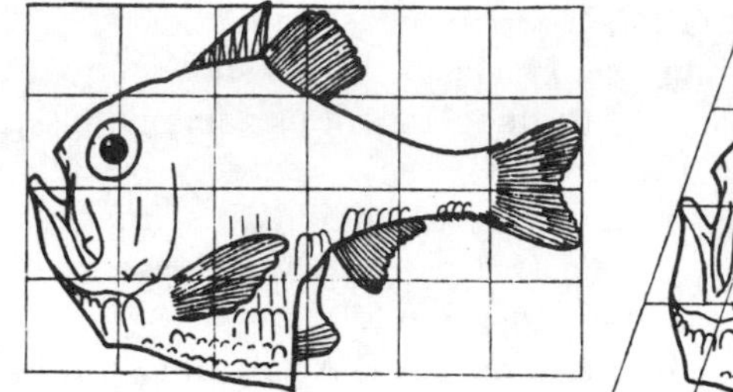

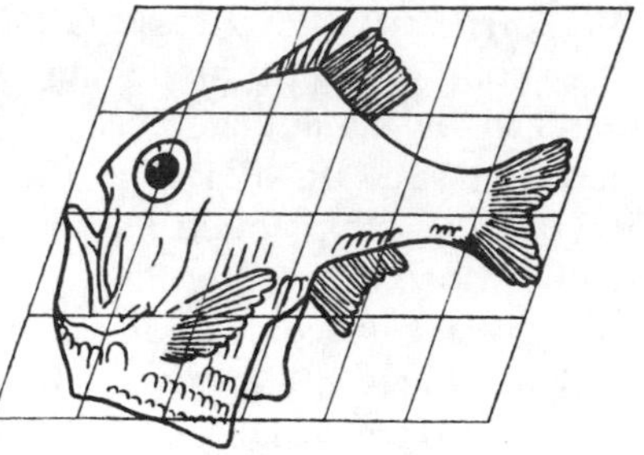

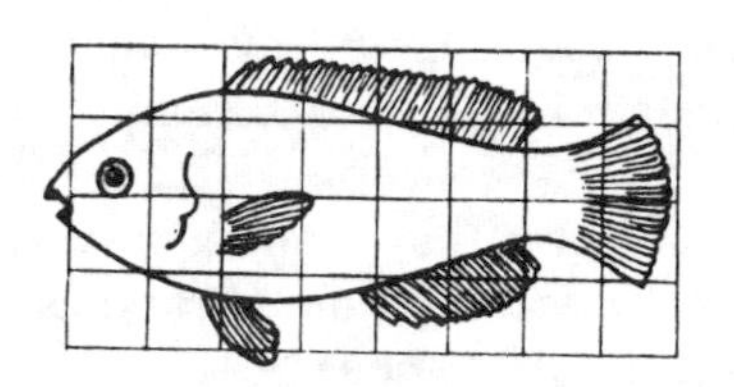

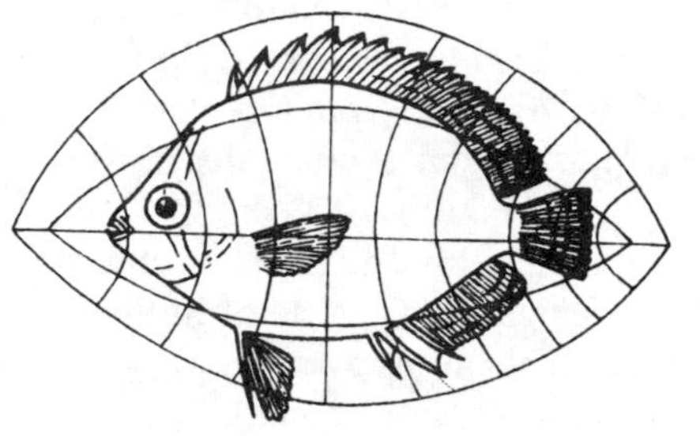

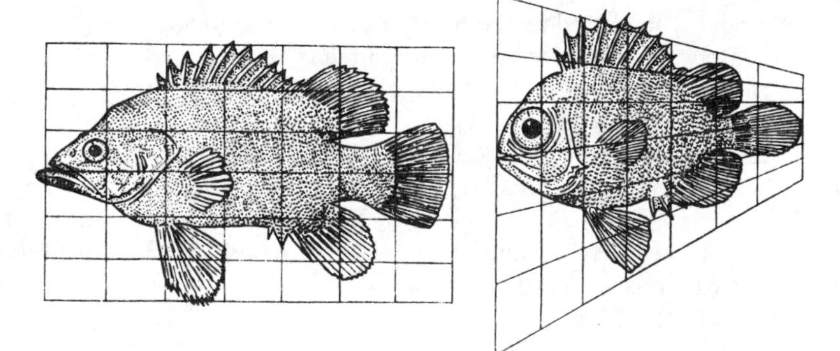

Figure 10.1

These illustrations from D'Arcy Thompson's book *On Growth and Form* demonstrate the idea behind the theory of transformations, which is central to the concept of free-form deformations. (Reproduced with kind permission by Cambridge University Press, from *On Growth and Form*, abridged edition, by D'Arcy Thompson).

point had been set at 2.5, then the points would have decreased and moved to the left. Though what would happen if one or both of the end points is moved? Well let us keep $P_1 = 2$, $P_2 = 3$ and set $P_3 = 5$. This produces the values shown in Table 10.2; from these we see that the entire line of points has been stretched and pulled along with the control point P_3.

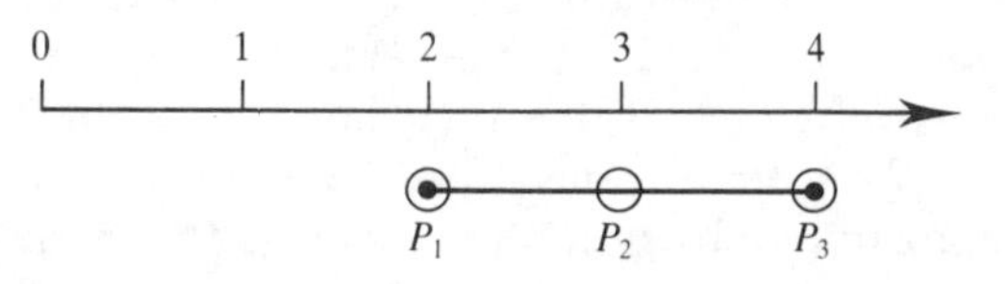

Figure 10.2

If a line exists between values 2 and 4, three control points P_1, P_2 and P_3 can be used to deform the distribution of the values between these limits.

Table 10.1

x	t	x'
2.0	0.0	2.00
2.2	0.1	2.29
2.4	0.2	2.56
2.6	0.3	2.81
2.8	0.4	3.04
3.0	0.5	3.25
3.2	0.6	3.44
3.4	0.7	3.61
3.6	0.8	3.76
3.8	0.9	3.89
4.0	1.0	4.00

From these examples it can be seen that the points comprising the original line can be compressed and stretched depending upon how the control points are positioned. Furthermore, the three control points could be increased to four and allow cubic terms in t to be used. In this case, for zero deformation the two central points must be positioned at 1/3 and 2/3 respectively. This is, perhaps, a convenient point to introduce the correct name describing the polynomial terms in the parameters – they are called the 'Bernstein polynomial terms'.

In two dimensions a matrix of control points is employed in precisely the same way that a Bézier surface patch is defined. For a quadratic interpolation, a 3 × 3 matrix is used, and for a cubic a 4 × 4 matrix, and in order to keep the formulae simple, the following example employs a quadratic form.

Table 10.2

x	t	x'
2.0	0.0	2.00
2.2	0.1	2.21
2.4	0.2	2.44
2.6	0.3	2.69
2.8	0.4	2.96
3.0	0.5	3.25
3.2	0.6	3.56
3.4	0.7	3.89
3.6	0.8	4.24
3.8	0.9	4.61
4.0	1.0	5.00

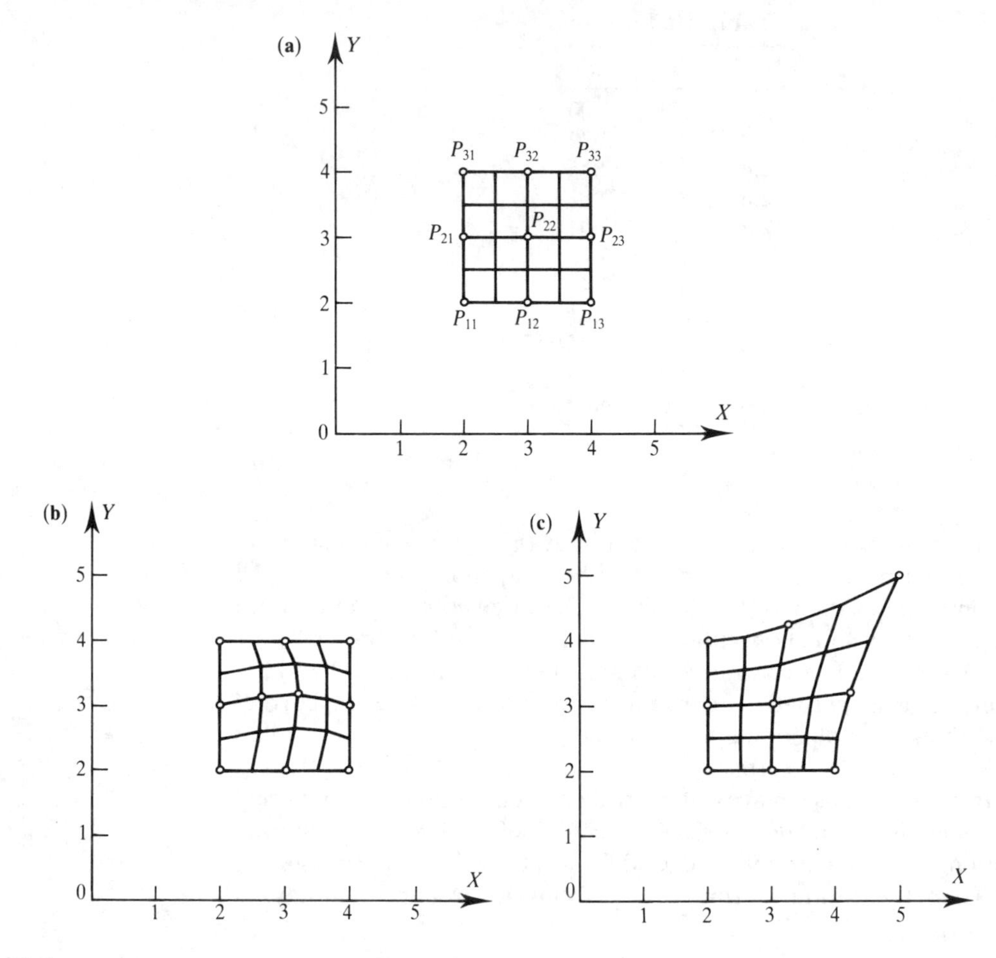

Figure 10.3
The mesh of nine control points shown in (a) can be used to deform the spatial distribution of any enclosed points. In (b), the central control point P_{22} has been moved from its position of (3.0, 3.0) to (3.75, 3.75), while in (c) P_{33} has been moved from (4.0, 4.0) to (5.0, 5.0). The coordinates of the deformed mesh points are shown in Tables 10.3 and 10.4 respectively.

Two parameters u and v are now needed to control the 2-D space where any point $P'(x', y')$ is defined as:

$$P'(x',y') = [(1-u)^2 \; 2u(1-u) \; u^2] \begin{bmatrix} P_{11} & P_{12} & P_{13} \\ P_{21} & P_{22} & P_{23} \\ P_{31} & P_{32} & P_{33} \end{bmatrix} \begin{bmatrix} (1-v)^2 \\ 2v(1-v) \\ v^2 \end{bmatrix}$$

where:

$$u = \frac{(x - x_{\min})}{(x_{\max} - x_{\min})} \quad \text{and} \quad v = \frac{(y - y_{\min})}{(y_{\max} - y_{\min})}$$

Figure 10.3a shows a 3 × 3 matrix of control points superimposed upon a grid representing the shape to be deformed. With the control points as shown, the grid is undistorted, but if the central control point P_{22} is

Table 10.3 Centre control point moved from [3.0, 3.0] to [3.75, 3.75].

x	y	x	y	x	y	x	y	x	y
2.00	2.00	2.50	2.00	3.00	2.00	3.50	2.00	4.00	2.0
2.00	2.50	2.61	2.61	3.14	2.64	3.61	2.61	4.00	2.5
2.00	3.00	2.64	3.14	3.19	3.19	3.64	3.14	4.00	3.0
2.00	3.50	2.61	3.61	3.14	3.64	3.61	3.61	4.00	3.5
2.00	4.00	2.50	4.00	3.00	4.00	3.50	4.00	4.00	4.0

moved from (3.0, 3.0) to (3.75, 3.75) the deformation shown in Figure 10.3b occurs. If the control point P_{33} is moved from (4.0, 4.0) to (5.0, 5.0) the distortion shown in Figure 10.3c occurs.

This clearly demonstrates how any 2-D shape can be deformed by disturbing one or more control points, and to obtain greater control, a cubic interpolation scheme could be used requiring nine control points. By inbetweening different sets of control points a continuous animation sequence can be obtained.

The extension into three dimensions is now quite obvious: three parameters are required, u, v and w, to control the x-, y- and z-directions and a 3-D lattice of control points. If quadratic interpolation is required in all three directions, 27 control points are needed as shown in Figure 10.4 – any point (x', y', z') within this volume can now be deformed by summing the Bernstein polynomial terms that multiply the control point values.

Although the above examples used a quadratic basis for the deformations, there is no reason why one should not mix these functions. For example, it might be needed to preserve the linearity of an object in the x-direction, while the y- and z directions are subjected to quadratic and cubic deformations respectively; this would reduce the number of control points needed.

Another consideration concerning the control points is the need to have a hierarchy of systems to permit an object to be subjected to some global deformation, while certain portions of the object are further deformed by other control points subservient to the master system.

Table 10.4 Control point [4.0, 4.0] moved to [5.0, 5.0].

x	y	x	y	x	y	x	y	x	y
2.00	2.00	2.50	2.00	3.00	2.00	3.50	2.00	4.00	2.0
2.00	2.50	2.50	2.50	3.02	2.52	3.54	2.54	4.06	2.5
2.00	3.00	2.52	3.02	3.06	3.06	3.64	3.14	4.25	3.2
2.00	3.50	2.54	3.54	3.14	3.64	3.82	3.82	4.56	4.0
2.00	4.00	2.56	4.06	3.25	4.25	4.06	4.56	5.00	5.0

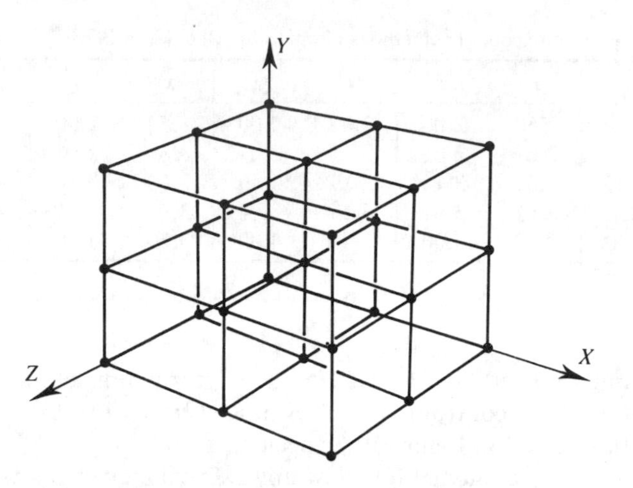

Figure 10.4
This diagram illustrates how a lattice of 27 control points is required to deform a volume of space using quadratic FFDs.

There is no doubt that free-form deformation will become an essential tool for the computer animator, and as graphics workstations are already able to display these deformations in real-time, this is bound to lead to more exciting and adventurous animation.

10.4 Displacement animation

Displacement animation provides a simple, yet useful, method of developing animated sequences by associating vectors with the vertices covering the surface of an object. The vector defines the path along which the vertex will travel depending upon some user-defined parameter, and can be created manually, or more probably from two intermediate positions of the surface. The vector may even be the resultant vector created from two or more displacements. Once more the effect is best approached through a 2-D example.

Consider, then, the line shown in Figure 10.5a containing the vertices A, B, C, D and E, where each vertex has an associated vector to control its path. Notice that the end vertices do not appear to have one; in fact they do exist but have zero magnitude. The displacement assigned to each vertex x_disp and y_disp can now be controlled by a parameter t which varies between 0 and 1, as follows:

$$x\_\text{disp} = t x\_\text{comp}$$
$$y\_\text{disp} = t y\_\text{comp}$$

where x_comp and y_comp are the vector's x- and y-components. When $t = 0.5$, each vertex is displaced halfway along its vector to produce the

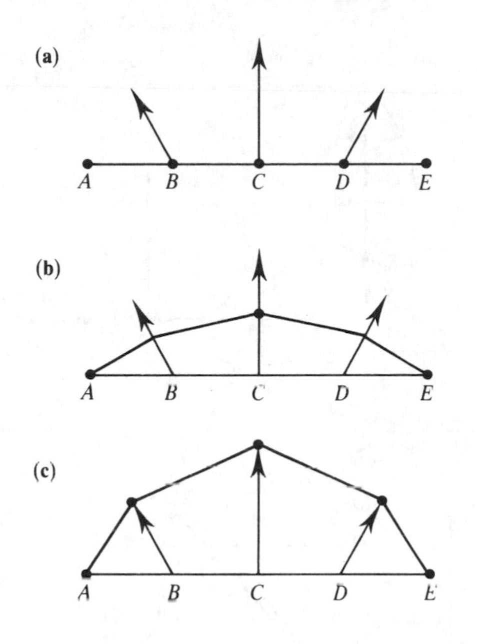

Figure 10.5
If the top line shown in (a) is assigned vectors at each vertex, it can be animated using a parameter which moves each vertex along its vector a proportional amount as shown in (b) and (c). The end vertices remain fixed as their vectors have zero magnitude. Values of t are (a) 0, (b) 0.5 and (c) 1.0.

shape shown in Figure 10.5b, and when $t = 1.0$, each vertex moves to the ends of their respective vectors as shown in Figure 10.5c. However, there is nothing to prevent the parameter t from exceeding 1, or even becoming negative, and as long as the resultant geometry is meaningful these effects can be exploited. By controlling the parameter t in some specified manner, the original shape can be animated according to these constraints.

As a practical example, say it was required to show a square being inbetweened into a circle, and the animation had to include an initial few frames where the square's movement included a slight inward implosion anticipating the transform, followed by an extra few end frames of overshoot before it settles down into the final circle. This can be achieved through displacements under the control of a suitable parameter. Figure 10.6a shows the two shapes with some of the vectors linking the corresponding sets of vertices. If the vertices of an intermediate shape are expressed as:

$$x = x\_\text{square} + t x\_\text{comp}$$
$$y = y\_\text{square} + t y\_\text{comp}$$

where x_square and y_square are the coordinates of a vertex on the square, and t is the familiar driving parameter – then the animation is specified by the nature in which t changes. The requirement is for a slight implosion, followed by a transform into the circle, followed with a slight overshoot until returning back to the circle. The general shape of the graph relating t with the frame count can be described by a cubic Bézier curve as shown in Figure 10.6b. If a polynomial is created in terms of t and a

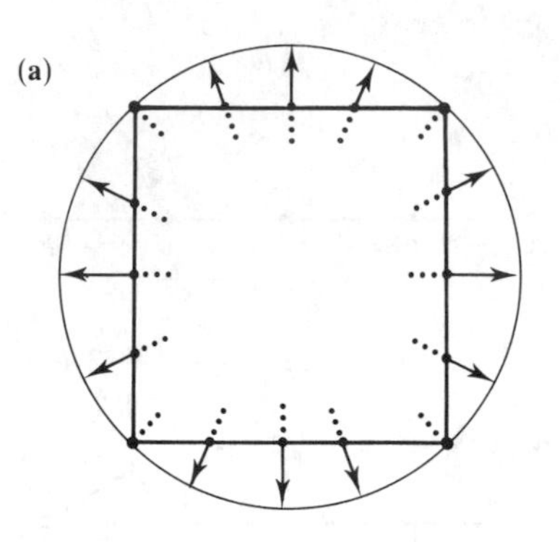

Figure 10.6
Displacement animation can be used to animate the square into the circle by moving the indicated vertices along their associated vectors, (a). If the controlling parameter is adjusted, (b), the transformation is anticipated by an initial contraction, and with an overshoot before finishing as a circle. Translated in 3-D means that very sophisticated movements can be achieved with a relatively simple procedure.

corresponding frame number, there will be no explicit description of t for any particular frame number – their distribution will indeed be cubic, though associated with non-integer frame numbers. To obtain precise values of t at particular frame numbers a virtual frame number F is defined as a cubic polynomial using the guide frames F_0, F_1, F_2 and F_3 as follows:

$$F = (1 - s)^3 F_0 + 3s(1 - s)^2 F_1 + 3s^2(1 - s) F_2 + s^3 F_3$$

where s is a parameter that varies from 0 to 1 over the animation range. This value of F will now move from F_0 to F_3 non-linearly as s moves from 0 to 1, and can be substituted in the following expression to derive another parameter f which provides the required value of t.

$$f = \frac{F - F_0}{F_3 - F_0}$$

$$t = (1 - f)^3 t_0 + 3f(1 - f)^2 t_1 + 3f^2(1 - f) t_2 + f^3 t_3$$

When f is substituted into the polynomial, a value of t is created, which, with suitable values of t_1 and t_2, will first go negative, increase and overshoot unity, and finally settle back to a value of 1.

If the above seems too mathematical, then it can be described at a higher level by hiding the polynomials within a function such as *bezier3* which returns an interpolated value from four numbers depending upon some separate parameter. For example, the above solution can be expressed as:

$$f = \frac{bezier3(F_0, F_1, F_2, F_3, s) - F_0}{F_3 - F_0}$$

$$t = bezier3(t_0, t_1, t_2, t_3, f)$$

$$x = x\_\mathrm{square} + tx\_\mathrm{comp}$$

$$y = y\_\mathrm{square} + ty\_\mathrm{comp}$$

where $0 \leq s \leq 1$ which requires a trivial level of programming.

As displacement animation involves vectors, the rules of vector addition and subtraction can be exploited by creating a resultant displacement from the individual displacements. If the magnitudes of these displacements are obtained through the action of separate parameters, very complex movements can be described.

The extension of the techniques into three dimensions is obvious as it only involves an extra z-component in the vector and, when the tool is implemented at a very high level, as found in Symbolics' animation system, the user can interactively manipulate the displacement vectors and graphically control the value of the parameters without recourse to the mathematics shown above. Figure 10.7 shows a sequence of faces animated using Symbolics' displacement animation tools.

10.5 Behavioural animation

Behavioural animation addresses the simulation of behaviour patterns exhibited by certain species of animals. It has been investigated by Susan Amkraut and Michael Girard (Amkraut, 1985), in their classic computer animation sequence 'Eurythmy' where force fields were employed to influence the behaviour of a flock of birds flying above a courtyard. During their flight, the birds' wings moved in a life-like fashion, while simultaneously avoiding contact with one another. Similar behaviour has also been investigated by Craig Reynolds (Reynolds, 1987), whose work at the Symbolics Graphics Division provided the software for the animation sequence 'Stanley and Stella: Breaking the Ice', which employed flocks of birds and fish shoals animated by behavioural flocking algorithms.

Animating large groups of objects that are oblivious of one another is not a problem. In the case of particle systems which may contain hundreds or thousands of discrete elements, each particle lives in its own little world and is not aware of the existence of any other particle.

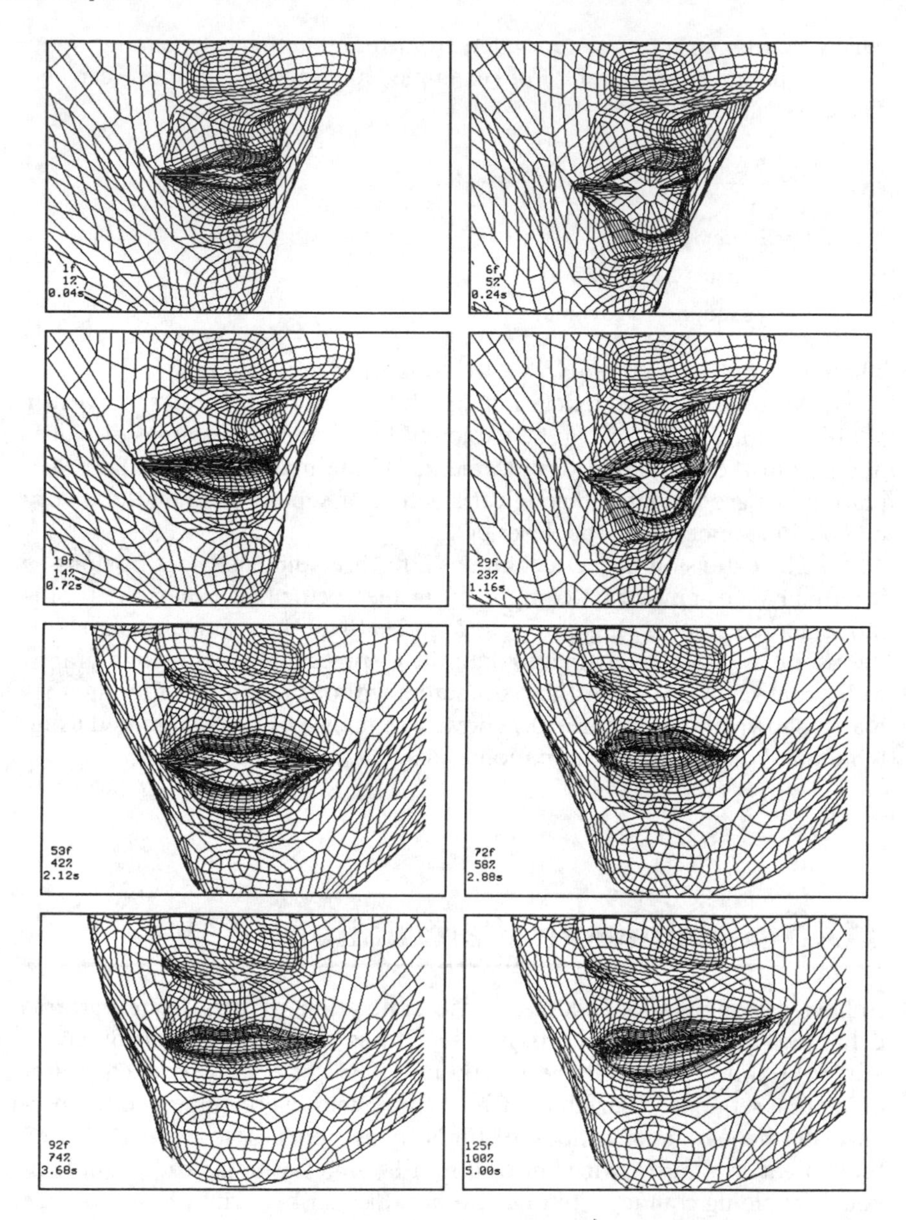

Figure 10.7
This sequence of illustrations are examples of displacement animation created by Symbolics' S-Animation system. Courtesy of Symbolics Ltd.

However, the stochastic nature of the births, ageing and deaths of the particles, together with some realistic physical simulation laws, can result in some interesting animation sequences. If the particles are now replaced by recognizable objects such as a bird, which is flapping its wings as though in flight, the bird's movement should be influenced by its immediate surroundings, and by any other rules that control its behaviour.

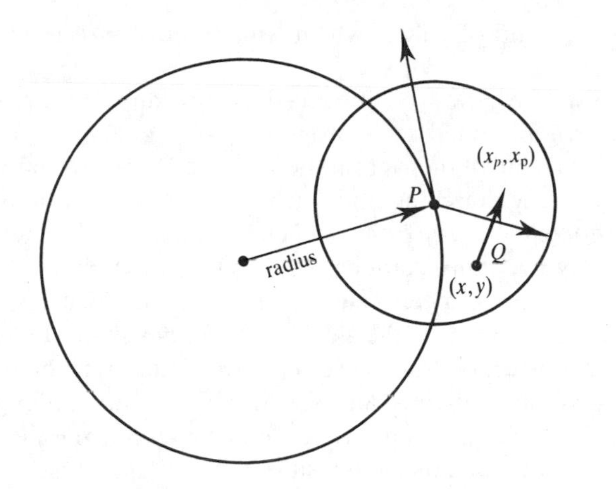

Figure 10.8
In this diagram the point $P(x_p, y_p)$ is constrained to rotate about a fixed point by a fixed radius, and at any point in time has a velocity orthogonal to this radius. A second point $Q(x, y)$, with some initial arbitrary velocity, has to be programmed such that it stays within a given radius of P. The procedures used to maintain this relationship are the basis of behavioural animation.

Such group or flocking behaviour is very dramatic in large flocks of starlings flying overhead – and although there is no apparent leader, the flock moves as a whole with signals rapidly transmitted across the flock's diameter communicating that a change of direction has occurred. Somehow the flock remains together even when it undergoes rapid complex manoeuvres, and it is this behaviour that is simulated in the flocking behaviour model.

Some of the principles behind flocking algorithms can be understood by considering the 2-D scenario illustrated in Figure 10.8. Here we see a point P rotating with a constant radius about a fixed point, and to its right another point Q which must attempt to keep up with P as it rotates. However, as there is no physical connection between P and Q, a set of rules is needed to support this mode of behaviour.

As part of these rules we may wish to introduce useful parameters such as the previous and current positions of both points. Their velocities will also be needed but perhaps the most interesting inclusion will be a rule that describes how near Q may approach P, and by how far it may wander. The rules could be applied as follows:

> *If* Q *continues moving with its current velocity, will it move too near or too far from* P?

In either case some action has to be taken, though if the radius rule is satisfied, P is allowed to move to its new rotated position and the new spatial condition between P and Q examined. If Q is moving too near or too far away from P, the action must resolve the situation by either modifying Q's heading or speed. The amounts by which the behaviour of Q are modified will be quite critical: too much, and the system could oscillate wildly; too little, and the dynamics might collapse completely; however, there will be a band of values which will support an interesting range of behaviour.

The system can now be enhanced by introducing more points whose attributes are maintained in a program table, and extra rules must be incorporated to control their group behaviour. Reynolds employs collision avoidance, velocity matching and flock centring. Collision avoidance creates the urge to steer away from a potential impact with a neighbour or an object; velocity matching complements collision avoidance by forcing the individual to match the speed of its neighbours, and flock centring provides the desire to move towards the flock's centre, which could be interpreted as a form of self-preservation. These characteristics must be translated into changes in position, heading and speed which need ranking in order of importance. For example, a point of the periphery of the flock could have three reasons to move to its next position: imminent collision, high relative speed and the possibility of predator attack, and it could be that the flock-centring instinct overrides everything.

The magnitude of any modification in behaviour can be controlled by functions which effectively measure the potential of a force field. In the case of electromagnetic radiation, we know that the intensity of light decreases with the inverse-square of the distance. Similar relationships can be introduced to apply a non-linear scale for measuring the importance of various conditions. Reynolds employs an inverse exponential field centred at the bird's local coordinate system to influence the sensitivity to collision. Such force fields can also be influenced by the speed of the object and also be more pronounced in the direction of flight. Although an explicit model of perception is not implemented within the behavioural model, the various techniques employed create an implicit awareness of the external world.

Moving a system of points about does not demand detailed programming; however, when each point is replaced by an animated bird, one must now ensure that its flying behaviour complements changes in speed, position and heading. Such changes are achieved through subtle modifications in wing-beat amplitude and frequency, banking angle, periods of glide and body attitude, though implementing all of these could be a problem.

If one flying object 'knows' how to avoid another, there is no reason why extra rules cannot be introduced to describe behaviour when encountering external objects, which raises the problem of collision detection between the dynamic flock and a static environment. Testing intersection between so many surfaces could require considerable processing, which is why force fields are effective in creating a force of repulsion associated with the objects. As each flying bird interacts with the force field, the leading birds will detect a greater force than trailing birds and take evasive action; this action will permeate throughout the flock and could even become the primary signal for other birds to anticipate similar evasive behaviour.

There is no doubt that behavioural animation promises to become a very important feature of computer animation and, hopefully, one day software tools will become available that will permit the easy implementation of rule-based animation and force fields within any animation environment. However, until that day arrives, one must expect to implement these systems from first principles.

10.6 Dynamic simulation

In cartoon animation the imaginary worlds created by animators are generally so outlandish that the question as to whether physical laws are being broken is really immaterial. One of the problems animators do have is convincing an audience that something is for real, such as an anvil falling upon some unsuspecting cartoon character. If the motion cannot be correctly specified, then the attribute it possesses – in this case mass – is normally translated into an exaggerated size. Unfortunately, the fact that something is big does not necessarily imply that it is heavy. A parachute, for example, is much larger than an anvil and falls under gravity in a totally different manner. So even a large anvil, if given the wrong motion, can create an impression that it is weightless, and possibly harmless, and totally destroy the illusion intended by the animator.

Motion specification, as we have seen, is not too difficult and there are many mathematical tools available to translate and rotate an object from one position to another. However, are these motions realistic? Do they convince an audience that objects move like this in the real world? The answer to both questions is probably no, especially if the audience has acquired a substantial knowledge of physical behaviour. They will realize instinctively that B-splines, Bézier curves and other mathematical shapes are not the stuff of the world. Objects move the way they do because of the way they interact with other objects; their shape, mass, centre of gravity and any connecting linkages all influence this behaviour.

A coin falling onto a table may first twist and tumble as it accelerates towards the surface. When it strikes the table its future behaviour depends upon its terminal velocity, rotational energy, its moment of inertia and many other parameters. Eventually it ends its journey by spinning about a point, getting lower and lower and increasing its rotational frequency before losing all of its potential and kinetic energy through friction, heat and sound. But is this degree of realism vital in animation? Perhaps not in the case of a coin falling, but when it comes to making an articulated character mimic human movement, attention to detail is vital.

This struggle for realism has its rewards in the satisfaction it gives in bringing something synthetic to life, and it also highlights the difficulty of simulating every nuance of some animated behaviour. In the case of human locomotion, unless the arms swing naturally, the body sways with its changing centre of gravity, the head rises and falls with leg action, and the feet push firmly against the floor as a driving force, it remains unconvincing. Nevertheless, how can this level of animated behaviour be simulated? Simple key-frame inbetweening would be far too time-consuming, and forcing limbs to slide along perfect mathematical curves would not only leave obvious visual artefacts but, like inbetweening, would require considerable animator involvement for each sequence.

An alternative to these techniques is to simulate the dynamics associated with a system of linked elements. This allows the attributes, properties and physical laws already mentioned such as mass, inertia, stiffness and gravity to be encapsulated within a computer procedure, which can then direct the frame-by-frame motion of a synthetic mannequin. This sounds promising – and it does work – but it has its drawbacks in the form of the method used to express the animation.

The language, as one might have suspected, is mathematics, and if the reader refers to current technical papers addressing these issues, a world will be discovered where Jacobians, tensors, Lagrangian dynamics, differential calculus and six-dimensional space provide a vehicle for expressing such ideas. Unfortunately, such notation is beyond the scope of this text; nevertheless, there are some important concepts associated with these techniques that can be addressed and understood without resorting to higher mathematics. Eventually, computer animation tools will evolve that incorporate this degree of mathematical support, but the animator will not be aware of their existence as they will be activated through a conventional computer graphics interface.

The concepts we need to explore in dynamic simulation are degrees-of-freedom, constraints, kinematics, and dynamics. The term 'degree-of-freedom' (DOF) is associated with abstract points, objects, joints and linked systems. When something is described as having three DOF it means that three independent parameters are needed to control its spatial freedom.

For example, a single point requires three coordinates to fix its position in space. As the point is an abstract concept, it has no size and therefore no orientation, consequently three numbers are sufficient to describe its spatial freedom and it is said to possess three DOF. Another example concerns a circular ring that can slide along a shaft: this has two DOF as two parameters are needed to control its position along the shaft and its angular rotation about the shaft's axis. Finally, any flying object has six DOF, as three coordinates are needed to position it in space and three further angles are required to fix its orientation.

Like a robot, our mannequin can be constructed from a system of links representing the arms, legs, feet, hands, body and head connected together with joints. In reality a knee, elbow, hip, wrist or ankle are complex joints possessing more than one DOF, and the joint's mobility is generally restricted by its own shape, associated tendons and muscles, and sometimes by the level of pain we wish to withstand. These physical constraints must become part of our computer model to ensure that the mannequin is not contorted into a physically impossible shape.

Constraints also influence the animation of a walking sequence where a mannequin's foot comes into contact with the ground. During the period when the heel strikes the ground, to the point when the sole of the foot rolls out of the stride, the system of links will be influenced by this ground constraint and affect the animated gait. In a computer animation environment the animator may wish to specify kinematic constraints to joints, to guarantee that they do not exceed set linear and angular velocities.

When so many joints are involved there will be many ways of satisfying a goal such as looking over one's shoulder, or stretching out to reach for a falling object. In the first case the head tends to rotate about the neck, which in turn seems to trigger off a shoulder twist, and possibly causes a lower-waist rotation. If this hierarchy of rotations does not achieve its objective, the feet could move and displace the entire body. Some of this motion can be simulated by introducing joint stiffness and masses to the linkages which can be used to make low-weight links and flexible joints the first to move.

When we talk about the kinematics of a system, we are basically referring to its motion and, in the case of a linked structure, the animator has a difficult task in specifying the velocity and acceleration of each link over a period of time. Take, for example, the problem of animating human locomotion. One simple, though not effective, way of creating the motion is to define the status of the legs at their extreme positions, and interpolate the positioning parameters to derive the inbetween positions. The problem with this approach is that there is no guarantee that the feet will touch the ground, and if they do, that they will not slide along or even go through the ground!

If a leg is considered as a system of links whose position is determined by parameters such as the link's length and twist, and the distances and angles between the links, then the position of the last link (the foot) can be determined by applying the given parameters. This is called 'forward kinematics'. However, this is not much use to an animator as there is no explicit control over the foot as its final position is determined by the other links. If, however, the position and the motion of the end link can be specified by the animator, the procedures of 'inverse kinematics' can be used to derive the motion of the interior links. These procedures may not take into account the masses of the links and their centres of gravity, which is why the term 'kinematics' is employed rather than 'dynamics'.

The PODA system, developed by Michael Girard and A.A. Maciejewski (Girard, 1985), provides an interactive environment in which the animator can specify the trajectories and footholds of end links (e.g. the

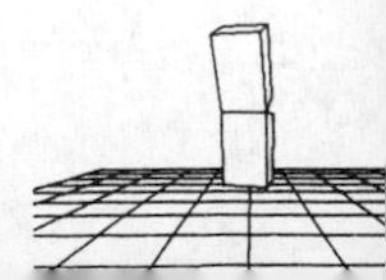

feet), and in which PODA computes the motion of the interior links using inverse kinematics. The main stumbling block in applying such techniques is the non-linear equations that result from analytic solutions. PODA overcomes this by assuming that the status of the links at two different points in time are linearly related if the time interval is small. Thus, the incremental changes in position can be related to the incremental changes in orientations using a matrix called a Jacobian. This matrix changes at each time interval, and as PODA employs inverse kinematics (i.e. incremental changes in orientation need to be derived by known increments in position), the Jacobian has to be inverted at each time interval.

Unfortunately, the nature of the matrix does not permit a true inverse to be calculated, and an approximate 'pseudo-inverse' has to be derived, which is mathematically stable, and provides the desired animation. PODA also provides the animator with direct control over gait patterns such as running and walking, gait cycles, footholds and body trajectory. PODA was used to produce the unforgettable animation in 'Eurythmy'. Plate 10 shows a frame from this animation.

As we have discovered previously, Newton's second law of motion can be summarized as 'force equals mass times acceleration', where any one of these parameters can be computed with a knowledge of the other two. However, as the masses remain constant, it is either a question of knowing the forces or the accelerations associated with a system of linkages. When the forces are known the accelerations can be computed using 'forward dynamics', and when the accelerations are known, the forces are computed using 'inverse dynamics'. The DYNAMO system developed by Paul Isaacs and Michael Cohen (Isaacs, 1987) employs the techniques of forward and inverse dynamics, which allows the animator to associate mass to the links of a linked structure, together with kinematic constraints and gravitational force fields. Such structures can then be animated with a mixture of key-framing and dynamic simulation.

Whether forward dynamics, inverse dynamics, or inverse kinematics is used, one is faced with solving sets of equations that are of no direct interest to the animator. This research is still in its infancy and very little has found its way into professional animation systems, but when this happens, computer animation will move into some very exciting directions.

Exercises and projects

10.1 Implement the procedure for animating the hands of a clock as explained in Section 10.2.

10.2 Design a procedure to alter the distribution of points between two given values using the technique explained in Section 10.3. Confirm the results obtained in Table 10.1.

10.3 Design a procedure for altering the distribution of points contained within a 2-D grid of control points, as explained in Section 10.3, and confirm the results illustrated in Figure 10.3. Use the program to bend the shape of some test image.

10.4 Design a free-form deformation procedure based upon a 3-D grid of quadratic control points. Test the correctness of the algorithm with some simple manipulations before exploring the effect on more complex objects.

10.5 What errors could free-form deformation introduce when processing many-sided polygons?

10.6 Take any useful 3-D object and derive the average unit surface normals for its vertices. Develop a procedure which will then animate the object by moving the vertices along these vectors.

10.7 Implement the procedure explained in Section 10.4 where displacement animation is used to animate a square into a circle.

10.8 Investigate the problem described in Section 10.5 where a point Q has to be given rules that will enable it to follow the path of a rotating point P. Once this works, associate some other trajectory to P and discover whether the point Q still exhibits its original behaviour.

10.9 Design a 2-D procedure by which, given the position of some reference point, the positions of 10 other randomly positioned points are adjusted such that they never approach one another (including the reference point) by a given amount. When they are moved, they travel in a direction away from the effective centre of the group. Test the procedure by moving the reference point along some path, and observe the behaviour of the other points.

Further reading

Special animation techniques For further information of FFDs the reader is referred to Parry (1986) and Sederberg (1986). For behavioural animation the papers by Reynolds are very informative (Reynolds, 1987a; 1987b). The references on dynamic simulation are shown in the index.

KEY POINTS

Apart from the animation techniques covered in previous chapters, this chapter addresses another group that have specific applications in well-defined areas of animation.

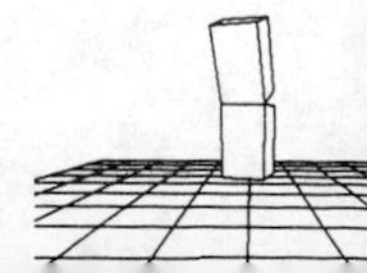

- Key-frame animation develops a continuous animated sequence by interpolating attributes at specific key frames. Such attributes could be anything related to an object, light source or camera.
- Procedural animation introduces algorithmic procedures to control the attributes of an object, light source or camera.
- Free-form deformation utilizes a 3-D lattice of control points to enclose a volume of space. When these points are moved, any contained object is deformed by an amount depending upon its relationship to the lattice points.
- Displacement animation takes two or more states of an object, from which an inbetween object is obtained to become part of an animated sequence.
- Behavioural animation is a powerful technique for animating collections of objects that have to exhibit group behaviour, such as that observed in birds and fish.
- Dynamic simulation is particularly useful in animating linked structures connected in some hierarchy. Forward and inverse kinematics are used for identifying the motion of links based upon specified motion attributes, while forward and inverse dynamics identify the motion of links using forces and accelerations.

11 Animation Systems

Over the past twenty years, researchers have developed a variety of software systems that undertook specific graphics tasks. Many systems originated within an academic environment and benefited from a continuous stream of researchers who left behind extra software when their project was completed. Maintaining these systems was a nightmare, as very little documentation was available, and eventually it was not worth the effort to support such incoherent software.

However, from these embryonic projects grew the commercial systems we have today, which are now so sophisticated that they require the dedicated support of a large programming team. Although these commercial systems offer an integrated animation environment, they are not identical. Each has its own characteristics and strengths that are strongly defended by different animators. Such strengths are in the user interface, modelling tools, animation features and rendering capabilities, and this chapter investigates five systems that are used within the animation industry. They are: Alias, Explore, SoftImage, Symbolics and Wavefront.

Introduction

During the past twenty-five years various researchers have identified ingenious solutions to fundamental problems associated with computer graphics; these have ranged from Bresenham's work on the efficient display of straight lines, to Mandlebrot's discovery of fractals. Parallel with this research has been a variety of projects whose objective has been to design systems that present a user with a unified environment in which computer graphics can be exploited as an aid to the design and visualization of 3-D objects. Today, it is possible to purchase a wide range of software packages and turnkey systems which can be used in desk-top publishing, printed circuit board design, television graphic design, architecture, computer-aided design and a host of other subjects, including animation.

The software supporting these activities has been designed to work with a variety of computers, from the humble microcomputer to the awesome supercomputer; and as one would expect, with this wide range of hardware there are bound to be differences in cost, speed, efficiency, effectiveness and ease of use. Software is also expensive to develop and maintain, and in the case of animation requires to be updated quite frequently as new techniques are invented, which is why some computer animation companies have preferred to develop their own in-house software rather than depend upon off-the-shelf products. Today, the trend is towards the use of workstations in combination with an off-the-shelf software package, which provides facilities for modelling, animation, dynamics and rendering. These systems generally allow the user to add extra programs to implement special effects that are not part of the standard specification.

In the previous chapters we have examined some of the geometric and mathematical techniques used in modelling, rendering, animation, camera control, illumination and special effects. We have seen that matrices, polynomials, parametric equations, vectors, quaternions and Jacobians perform operations upon coordinates to supply the final animation. Although such techniques are fundamental to any animation system, they are not the concepts an animator should have to wrestle with. Ideally, terms like 'rotate', 'twist', 'bend', 'slide', 'spin', 'slow-in', etc. must find their way into the user interface, and graphical techniques must aid the animator in the interpretation of space curves, illumination levels, colour, velocity, acceleration and model dynamics. Fortunately most animation systems employ these ideas and the animator does not need to know anything about the underlying mathematics; however, not everyone has free access to these systems and they must rely upon their own programming skills. So in this chapter the historical developments of computer animation systems will be reviewed, and then some of the major commercial animation systems currently available will be outlined.

11.1 Historical background

In the early 1960s, computer animators did not have acccess to the range of hardware and software techniques available today. Colour rendering had not evolved, which meant that images were nothing more than line drawings; these were either photographed from paper, cel or a storage tube, or captured directly by a film recorder. Interactive computing, as we know it, did not exist and programs were submitted to the computer using holes punched into paper tape and 80-column cards. The programs would be written in assembler language or FORTRAN, though other languages such as Algol and Pascal were used when they became available, and today, C and C++ seem to be the popular languages used for developing new computer graphics systems.

When writing in a high-level language such as FORTRAN, the programmer was responsible for defining every aspect of the animation which would have included defining the image size, clipping lines to the viewing window, computing the perspective projection, storing the coordinates, removing hidden-lines, and applying the matrix operations required to scale, translate and rotate objects. As these activities are part of any animation program, it is sensible to develop a library of sub-programs which, once written and debugged, can be used over and over again. This was, and still is, the strategy behind developing large programs that require frequent access to the same commands.

As a library of commands develops, a result is that quite sophisticated animation programs can be written in a short period of time. However, this approach does have one major disadvantage that was more important when computers were very much slower than their current speeds, and concerns the method of updating the various parameters which we have seen control an animation sequence. Every time a parameter is modified, the FORTRAN program must be translated into the host-computer's machine language, which could take several minutes. Obviously, this was very frustrating and tedious work and prompted the development of languages that the animator could use to directly control the computer without these delays.

The basic idea behind animation scripting languages is to allow the animator to express various animation sequences using words like 'ROTATE', 'TRANSLATE' and 'DRAW', together with names, parameters or coordinate values that describe things within the sequence. Such a script is input to a program which interprets the actions into library commands available to the system but, as the translating program is always resident in the computer, any modifications to the script become apparent when it is executed without the delay of a FORTRAN translation.

One of the most important centres where computer animation flourished in the 1960s was the Bell Telephone Laboratories; here, Ken

Knowlton (Knowlton, 1964) developed his FORTRAN IV BEFLIX language on an IBM 7094. It was used for creating many films at the centre, and in 1970 he developed EXPLOR as an aid to artists for creating simple 2-D images composed of repeated patterns with various levels of randomness. Further work by Ronald Baecker (Baecker, 1969a) at MIT, with his GENESYS system, identified the importance of expressing animation commands graphically. In modern systems where dynamic behaviour is simulated, this method of description and machine communication is fundamental to user-friendly interface design.

Other systems that were developed include:

CAMP by J. Citron and J. Whitney, 1968
CAFE by J. Nolan and L. Yarbrough, 1968
ANIMATOR by P.A. Talbot *et al.*, 1971
ARTA by L. Mezie and A. Zivian, 1971
MSGEN by N. Burtnyk and M. Wein, 1971
SCANIMATE by F.J. Honey, 1971
CAESAR by F.J. Honey, 1971
MOP by E. Catmull, 1972
CAAS by E. Catmull, 1972
ANTICS by A. Kitching, 1973
ANIMA by C. Csuri, 1975
GRASS by T. De Fanti, 1976
PICASO by J. Vince, 1976
ANIMA II by R. Hackathorn, 1977
ANTTS by C. Csuri *et al.*, 1979
TWEEN by E. Catmull, 1979
SOFTCEL by G. Stern, 1979
CGAL by P. Comninos, 1980
SAS by D. Zeltzer, 1982
ZGRASS by T. De Fanti, 1983
BBOP by G. Stern, 1983

The above list is testimony to the importance given to the development of a computer animation language, and even after 25 years of research there is no universal standard or interactive interface used by the animiation community. This does not imply that there never will be one, but perhaps suggests that it is too soon to standardize a subject which is still developing so fast.

As was mentioned above, some computer animation houses have developed their own in-house software, and more and more are turning to using off-the-shelf software to run on high-performance graphics workstations; these are the subject of the following section.

11.2 Commercial animation systems

This section surveys five major animation systems currently used by professional animation houses: the systems are Alias, Explore, SoftImage, Symbolics and Wavefront. Other systems are available, with some even running on PCs; however, this section is not intended to be a market survey – it is just an opportunity to demonstrate how different approaches have been taken by five leading companies.

11.2.1 Alias

The Alias PowerAnimator system has been developed at Alias Research, Inc. in Toronto, Canada, and runs on a variety of Silicon Graphics workstations and IBM's RISC System/6000 computers.

Modelling

Alias Research is not just known for its computer animation systems, but for sophisticated CAD systems used in every area of industrial design from automotive design to the space industry. These industrial links have meant that modelling tools have had to follow the latest developments in surface description, which has required the implementation of NURBS. You may remember from Section 3.2.7 that NURBS are a method of describing surface geometry with B-spline patches, and their rational form (where the parametric equations are expressed as a ratio of two polynomials) enables surfaces such as spheres, cylinders and toroids to be modelled precisely. Moreover, the parameters relating to the control points can have a non-uniform distribution which creates for a very flexible system for surface patch design.

The PowerAnimator product benefits from these modelling tools, allowing the animator to construct models from polygons and NURBS which can be further shaped with trimming tools that remove portions of a patch. Apart from the free-form surface modelling capabilities offered by NURBS, PowerAnimator exploits them to develop extrusions and surfaces of revolution.

Animation

The animation environment is activated through a menu-driven system which gives direct control over objects, light sources and virtual cameras. Any parameter controlling this world can be displayed graphically relating a numerical value with frame count. These curves (which are also NURBS) are easily modified by the animator, who can see their influence by playing back sequences in near real-time, forwards or backwards, until a certain dynamic behaviour is achieved.

The NURBS approach to surface geometry brings an added bonus in the form of object deformation by modifying the position of control points. The Metamorphosis feature can inbetween two sets of control points to create a very effective method of transforming one 3-D object into another.

NURBS are also used to design the trajectories of objects and cameras, and with the features of control point insertion and modification, effects of acceleration and deceleration are easily implemented. However, there are occasions when parameters have to be modified according to rules or conditions arising from some dynamic simulation; in these circumstances the animator prepares a procedure using the Scene Description Language (SDL); within this environment, characteristics controlling surface properties, lighting effects, texture and bump maps can be modified.

Rendering

The rendering features of PowerAnimator have anticipated the animator's need to preview shaded sequences in real-time, albeit at a lower level of picture fidelity. QuickShade provides this facility and enables the animator to check for clearance between objects, surface smoothness, intersecting surfaces and surface highlights as they move in real-time.

Light sources include point, spot, area and direction lights with the attributes of colour, brightness and decay, all of which can be modified through the SDL, or via the parameter curves. Object attributes such as colour, shininess and texture are declared interactively using the surface shaders and, as these are parameters available to the animator throughout a sequence, they can be modified via the SDL tools.

Apart from PowerAnimator's high-quality renderer QuickRender, two further features, RayCasting and RayTracing are available: RayCasting renders scenes with specular highlights and shadows using reflection maps, and RayTracing is an implementation of the classical ray tracing algorithm for revealing accurate multiple reflections, refractions and shadows. The Paint Box facility allows the animator to create and retouch images with a variety of standard electronic painting effects including airbrush and cut-and-paste operations.

Finally, Natural Phenomena is a set of pre-defined procedures for realistically creating solid textures such as sky, clouds, mountains, atmosphere and 2-D procedural textures. With these tools, objects can be made in wood using mahogany to maple; from stone using marble to jade, and their parameters are open to modification while the object is being animated.

11.2.2 Explore

Thomson Digital Image's Explore system has its origins in the simulation company Thomson–CSF and the Institut National de l'Audiovisuel, and is now widely used throughout the world for creating 3-D animations for television, advertising, simulation, architecture and industrial design.

The current system, Explore V2.3, runs on the entire range of Silicon Graphics workstations, from the Personal Iris to the highest-performance Power Series, and provides users with features for polygonal and surface modelling, 3-D animation, rendering and photorealism. Available options include NURBS-based modelling, hidden-line output, a family of 2- and 3-D fonts, ray tracing, particle systems and a paint system.

The user interface offers the animator with features such as pop-up menus, user-defined windows, dial boxes, real-time viewing and a segmented display area.

Modelling

FACE is the polygonal modeller and is controlled via the mouse, digitizing pad, keyboard or dial box. It is used for constructing extrusions and swept surfaces, object smoothing through bevelling; translating, rotating and scaling with linear transformations, and non-linear transformations for bend, sphere, twist and skew. Further bending is achieved through free-form deformation boxes which are responsible for some of the interesting character animation typical of recent animation sequences. The NURBS-based modelling option implements all of the interactive features offered by these flexible B-splines including a curve editor, surface generation through skinning, lofting, extrusion and sweeping, surface patch trimming and surface patch continuity, which are all complemented by Boolean operations on solids.

Animation

ANIM is a hierarchical module for controlling objects, light sources and the virtual camera. Key frames can be developed interactively and used to create inbetween sequences, which are manipulated using 2-D graphs relating parameters with time. Other important features include the automatic tracking of objects by the camera, an animated visualization of the camera's field of view and focal point, and a high-level scripting language for procedural effects.

As we have previously discussed, articulated structures are very important for developing realistic movements, and the ARTIC tool provides the animator with a powerful environment in which inverse kinematics is used to drive skeletal structures. ARTIC provides special tools for building linked structures and incorporating kinematic constraints in the form of limits of movement and joint resistance. Once they have been previewed in real-time using automatic inbetweening, the models can be read into the ANIM module where they can be integrated with other objects.

Rendering

The RENDER module performs scene rendering using a scan-line algorithm with the traditional Gouraud and Phong shaders, and also incorporates other useful features such as solid texturing, anti-aliased shadows, reflection mapping, layered fog and an alpha channel for handling mattes. TEX3D is an interactive material editor that allows users to produce realistically textured objects of any shape using solid textures. Sixteen solid texturing modules are available in which parameters controlling colour, filter shape, normal perturbation (bump mapping) and colour perturbation can be controlled by the user. Thirty-five further library textures such as wood, stone, marble and water are also available, which can be fine-tuned to create other variants.

The optional RAY module incorporates all of RENDER's features and uses ray tracing to develop accurate shadows, reflections, transparency and refraction; while PARTICLE is another option for exploiting the benefits of particle systems to model the effects of rain, snow, gas, fire, waterfalls and explosions. These systems can be assigned the attributes of position, colour, speed, weight and animated using dynamics, constrained to flow within a volume, or even made to follow user-defined trajectories. The particles can be rendered either with RAY or RENDER.

11.2.3 SoftImage

SoftImage Inc. was founded in 1986 by Daniel Langlois who was a co-director of the computer-animated film 'Tony de Peltrie'. It is based in Montreal, Canada but has subsidiary sales and support offices throughout the world. The SoftImage 3D system supports a wide range of applications including broadcast and film animation, product and industrial design, architecture and scientific visualization. It is a totally integrated system in that all functions are available in one program. The user can model, animate, play back and render in one continuous activity.

The window interface uses both orthogonal and perspective windows with full zoom and pan functions. The mouse is the primary interface device and is used for accessing pop-up menus, which invoke dialogue boxes for specific parameters. It is also used to provide dynamic manipulation of functions such as scaling, rotation and translation.

Modelling

The Model Module contains all the tools required to generate splines, surfaces and objects, as well as the tools to assemble them into complex structures. These have a boundary representation in the form of polygons and patches, and can be manipulated by Boolean operations and deformation lattices. A parametric library provides the user with an extensive range of primitives from a circle to a dodecahedron.

3-D curves can be traced as objects and can be defined as linear, B-spline or with Cardinal interpolation. Tools are also available to insert, delete and move points, set tension, merge splines and adjust continuity levels at each point on Bézier splines.

Further features are available for extrusions, surfaces of revolution, bi-cubic patches, lofting, bevelling, rounding and cutting, and at any stage the user can interactively create or delete vertices, edges and polygons on existing models.

Animation

The Motion Module provides full key-frame motion controls for all scene components including any object or group's position, rotation, scale and shape; attributes such as reflection, transparency and refraction; and for all other entities in the scene including light attributes, camera attributes, atmospheric effects and depth of field.

When key-frame positions are saved, motion paths are made available to the animator who can edit them and incorporate them into another scene. Motion paths can also be defined as splines and used to control objects, lights and the camera. Further path-based tools are available for adjusting the duration and offset timings for a model, camera or light source along the motion path, assigning objects to paths, and actually displaying the paths for line-testing.

The Actor Module allows interactive animation based upon kinematic and dynamically controlled articulated chains. These can be combined to form skeletons inside flexible envelopes which can be interactively deformed. This makes possible the creation of complex animations by combining kinematic chains with dynamic chains whose behaviour depends on physical properties (density, friction, inertia) and on physical forces such as gravity or wind which are applied by icons that can themselves be animated by conventional methods. Reaction to the environment is also provided through collision detection and connection constraints. These powerful dynamic features of gravity and wind can influence any type of object being animated.

Rendering

The Matter Module provides tools for assigning material and surface properties for creating wood, glass and water effects. Colours can be specified using RGB, HLS or HSV colour spaces, and shading models include Gouraud, Phong, faceted flat shading and constant colour fills.

Texture maps are filtered automatically with bilinear interpolation, and can be assigned a wide range of surface components including ambient, diffuse, specular, bump, transparency and reflection. The maps can then be applied using planar, cylindrical, spherical and patch-based projections.

Transparency mapping can be applied to modulate the opacity of a surface, and allows the creation of complex surface effects. The luminance of the image controls the amount of transparency, and the transparent surfaces coloured using this technique cast accurate shadows.

An adaptive ray tracer is automatically activated for areas of the image that consist of shadows, reflection or refraction; at all other times, a fast scan-line algorithm is used. The renderer is resolution and aspect ratio independent, and also supports field rendering.

11.2.4 Symbolics

The Symbolics animation system is unique in that it consists of an integrated hardware and software environment, although a version has recently been launched which runs on Apple Macintosh computers. It also differs from its competitors in that LISP is used to implement its object-oriented software, which allows the user to stop the system at any time, enter an extra procedure and continue processing without incurring any translation overheads.

The system is driven by a monochrome workstation into which commands are entered through a powerful menu-driven interface using a mouse. A typical screen is shown in Figure 11.1 which shows windows supporting the animated image, menus, a user command space, and graphical representations of animation parameters. A second monitor displays full-coloured rendered images and is also used for electronic painting tasks.

The software consists of five basic products: S-Geometry, S-Dynamics, S-Render, S-Paint, and S-Utilities, and an optional module for supporting off-line rendering on an SGI workstation.

Modelling

A sculpting approach is taken in the modelling system S-Geometry, where the user begins by either selecting a library object, or by defining some starting primitive volume. This is then developed interactively by the user selecting vertices, edges or faces which are manipulated to mould the desired form. The real-time nature of the workstation allows the user to view the building process from any point of view, zoom in to particular areas of interest, add detail and then return to the original viewpoint. When a project requires some unusual feature which can be resolved with a procedure, this can be typed in directly at the animation window or input separately in an editor buffer. As some scenes will be visually complex, a hidden-line removal facility is available to clarify the scene.

The object-oriented software provides an ideal environment for supporting hierarchical models, which permits the animator to interactively collect groups of objects or object parts and perform specific operations upon them. Hierarchical motion can also be used to control on single skinned objects.

Animation

S-Dynamics provides all of the standard animation tools of key-frame inbetweening, camera control, scripting, displacement animation and real-time line testing, and all of these tools are activated through a common

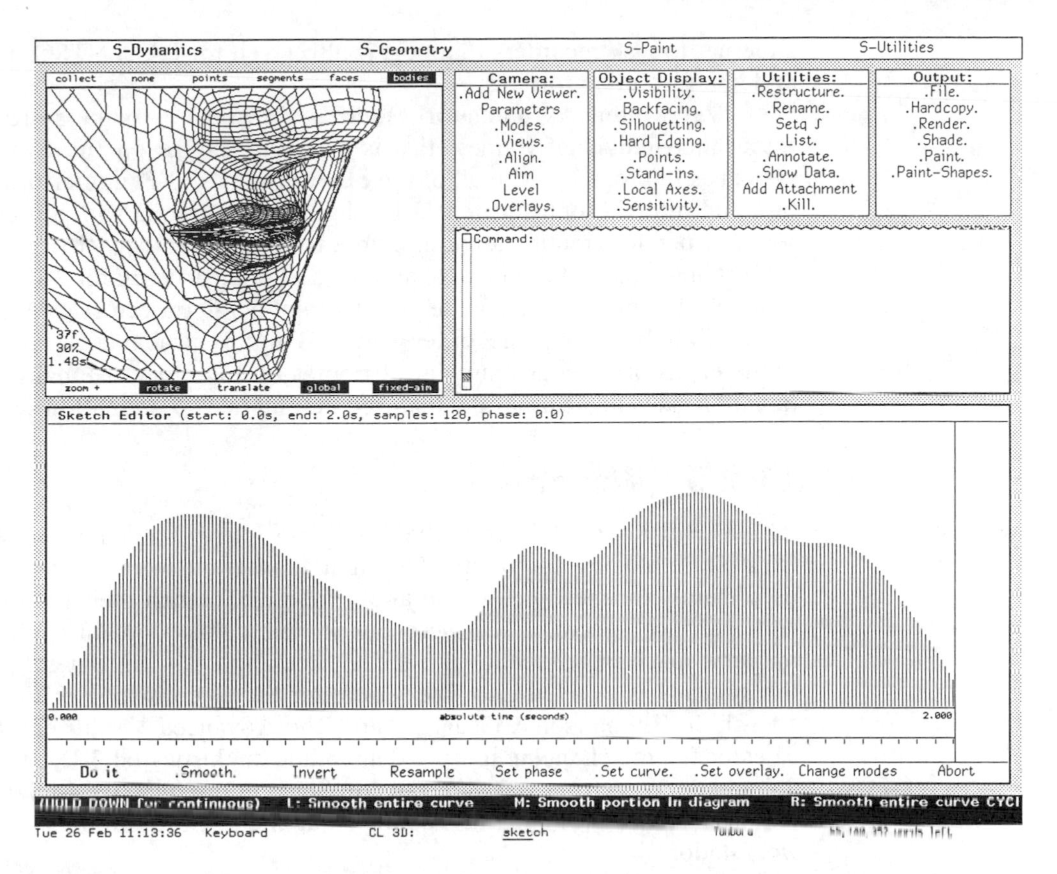

Figure 11.1
This screen dump from Symbolics' S-Animation system shows the windows supporting the animator's display area, interactive menus, the command space, and the graphical representation of an animation channel using tensioned splines.

interface in which dynamic attributes are displayed graphically. It is also possible to declare new dynamic operators which appear on these menus. Such curves are either developed using tensioned splines for the precise control of slow-in and slow-out movements, or through user-defined curves which could be hand-drawn from an external source, or even from an internal procedure. The same interface allows the animator to select specific sequences for playback at different speeds, backwards, forwards or in a continuous loop.

Rendering

The S-Render product undertakes all of the internal rendering tasks, whereas the Render Server uses a Silicon Graphics workstation when high-volume rendering is needed; this releases the Symbolics system to be used for other creative work. S-Render employs texture mapping, reflectance (environment) mapping, opacity mapping and bump mapping, which can be independently combined with opacity maps for controlling transparency effects. Images can be rendered directly to the monitor's screen, to a frame store for output to video tape or film, or digitially via CCIR 601 or

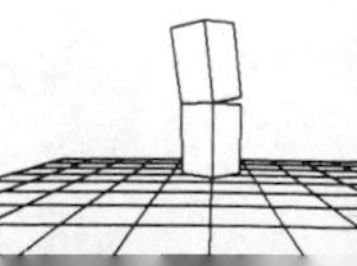

Ethernet to disk recorders. Support is also given for PAL, NTSC, HDTV and film resolution formats.

Very often an animator requires access to a paint system for retouching individual frames; this is a useful feature on the Symbolics system as it integrates with all of the other products. S-Paint performs this task and offers a sophisticated 32-bit digital paint system with a pressure-sensitive pen for creating texture, bump, reflectance and opacity maps, the retouching of any internal image and for designing artwork for 2-D animation. In addition, S-Paint can be used to paint a 3-D trajectory or encode a shape directly. Going the other way, S-Paint is available as a second renderer, as one can assign paint attributes to 3-D objects. Finally, Paintamation is available as a fully textured automatic 2-D animation system.

11.2.5 Wavefront

In 1984 Bill Kovacs left Bob Abel, and with Larry Barels formed Wavefront Technologies, Inc. Until 1987 their Wavefront software system was used mainly for media/television applications, but when their file formats and interface specifications were put in the public domain, industrial, military, space and educational users became important customers. Today, the system has evolved into The Visualizer Series consisting of the Data Visualizer, The Personal Visualizer and The Advanced Visualizer – this is to cater for the changing market demanding sophisticated 3-D computer animation. Wavefront software runs on Silicon Graphics, IBM RISC System 6000, Hewlett-Packard, Digital Equipment Corporation and SUN workstations.

Although the television industry has been the major user of computer-generated images, more and more scientific applications are requiring powerful visualization tools for transforming numeric data into animated 3-D pictures. The important observation appreciated by Wavefront is that the media and simulation applications share many common features for animating and rendering objects, with the latter needing extra facilities to interpret scalar and vector fields.

The Data Visualizer provides an interactive environment for visualizing technical data, possibly gathered from projects in computational fluid dynamics, oceanography, structural engineering and geology. To explore these data, which can be on regular, irregular or unstructured grids, the user has access to cutting planes for displaying cross-sectional views; isosurfaces for realizing 3-D surfaces of a specified scalar value; particle systems for highlighting vector fields; animation commands for key-frame inbetweening, and volume rendering.

The Personal Visualizer is directed at mechanical designers, architects, automotive engineers and product designers. It can import geometric descriptions from variety of CAD systems and then allows the user to edit these files and perhaps create exploded views of complex assemblies.

These can be illuminated by various light sources and rendered using conventional rendering tools, ray tracing, radiosity and a library of realistic textures.

The Advanced Visualizer provides users with modelling, animation and rendering facilities as well as accepting files from the Data Visualizer and the Personal Visualizer. It runs on all major UNIX platforms, and its open architecture makes it very flexible for interfacing to other systems.

Modelling

The current version supports polygons, Bézier and Cardinal surface patches, constructive solid geometry, NURBS and trimmed surfaces. The user can interactively sculpt objects with shape deforming commands such as skew, bend, twist, flare and taper, plus the benefits of free-form deformation. Objects can also be imported from CAD systems via an open ASCII file format, IGES or through direct translators for many systems including Intergraph, DXF, GDS, CADDS/4X, IDEAS, ANVIL, MOVIE.BYU and VDA-FS.

Animation

The animation module is called PreView and provides the animator with standard features such as key-frame interpolation, spline motion paths, object metamorphosis, and squash and stretch volume deformations. It also supports the animation of hierarchical structures and provides a scripting language for defining procedural animation sequences. A selected range of frames can be played in real-time forwards, backwards or in a continuous loop, displayed in wire frame, hidden-line, smooth shaded or completely rendered. Perhaps one of the important features of PreView is that almost 100 channels are available to drive any attribute of an animation sequence. This data might have an internal source, or an external source in ASCII or binary format. This allows an animation to be created using numeric data derived from a dynamic simulation process for creating life-like movements. Dynamic analysis software such as ADAMS from MDI can drive PreView directly.

There are many attractive features for character animation including position and velocity graphing, various cushioning commands and the ability to see hardware shaded deformations run in real-time by continuous adjustment of the model data displayed.

Rendering

The rendering module Image supports Gouraud and Phong shading, ray tracing, reflection mapping, fog effects, shadows, transparency, refraction and anti-aliasing. Objects can be assigned attributes such as shininess, transparency, refractive index, colour, texture and surface height features using bump maps; while lights can be controlled over intensity, scope, colour, and attenuation, together with the atmospheric effects of fog and ambient lighting. The renderer mixes scan-line and ray tracing techniques in one pass and deals very efficiently with large databases.

Finally, the system offers a range of compositing functions for creating complex scenes from independent images, these make possible effects such as variable transparency, gamma adjustment, frame size changes and animated backgrounds.

Further reading

Animation systems If one examines the reference index one will see the large number of papers and articles covering this subject, and it would serve no purpose to select one or two papers to represent animation systems. The reader should be prepared to search through this list to identify relevant papers to their subject area.

KEY POINTS

A variety of animation systems are available today from PC-based systems to turnkey systems that offer an integrated environment for modelling, animating and rendering. Professional computer animators claim that there is no 'perfect system', they each have their strengths and weaknesses.

- An animation system should provide the animator with tools for modelling, animating and rendering objects.
- Modelling will involve the user in an interactive activity in which objects are constructed with the aid of graphics primitives, extruding and sweeping tools, surface patches, trimming curves, Boolean operators and sculpting operations.
- To animate the objects, an interface must permit the animator to develop a script for describing the behaviour of the objects, light sources and the camera. This interface will probably introduce the use of channels for controlling individual attributes over frame ranges, and show this information graphically.
- Individual frames need to be rendered to adjust an object's colour and other features such as texture maps, opacity maps, environment maps and bump maps. Light sources require positioning and their intensities adjusted. Sequences are then rendered to disk or videotape and played back to review the result. This process is repeated until an optimum effect is achieved.

12 Computer Animation Hardware

This chapter is relatively brief compared to the other chapters as computer hardware has a habit of dramatically changing overnight. Techniques that appear highly relevant today can quickly become outmoded and published information simply becomes an historic record of the past. Nevertheless, as we approach the second millenium it is obvious that computer performance will surpass everything we take for granted today. Multi-processor systems, intelligent frame stores, hybrid designs will make available computer graphics systems that could never have been predicted 20 years ago. Therefore, the topics covered in this chapter must be seen against the backdrop of a computer animation industry moving through the last decade of the 20th century.

Introduction

It is only during the last few years that computer animation has provided a cost-effective alternative to creating animated images; this has been caused by technological developments in low-cost and faster computers, and complimentary advances in software. User interfaces now incorporate windows, icons and menus, keyboard activity has been substantially reduced by the introduction of the mouse, and at last we are beginning to see the arrival of true user-friendly systems.

12.1 Computers

A successful computer animation system requires, above all, a computer with adequate memory, high-speed processing performance, vast amounts of disk space and various input/output graphics peripherals. Five years ago, rendering times of 15 to 30 min/frame were common and meant that a 30 second animation sequence required between 200 and 400 hours to render the final sequence. Nowadays, with high-speed multi-processor workstations, it is still common to find frame rendering times in the order of several minutes. The increased hardware performance has virtually been compensated for by the complex and sophisticated images being demanded by clients, therefore one should never underestimate the processing performance required by computer animation.

Although some PCs are adequate for many computer graphics applications, they still cannot be considered as a valid alternative to the latest workstations incorporating integral frame stores, z-buffers and hardware matrix operations. Obviously much depends upon the nature of the application, and as computer animation projects exploit the benefits of dynamic simulation, behavioural animation, radiosity, ray tracing, texture mapping and anti-aliasing, there will be an ever-increasing demand for faster hardware.

12.2 Disk storage

As rendering times can be considerable, there is a tendency to store the images on disk so that they can be recalled at will within one or two seconds. Furthermore, there is a natural instinct to hoard images 'just in case they are needed in the future' – though one soon discovers that disk space, whether it is measured in tens, hundreds or thousands of megabytes, rapidly disappears if these policies are pursued. One does not need a computer to prove that 10 seconds of animation, at 25 frames/sec, to a screen resolution of 1 million pixels in full-colour requires 750 Mbytes of disk storage!

12.3 Image capture

Although some animation houses do store rendered images on disk, they eventually have to be stored on some other medium such as film or video. Whereas video is the ideal medium for television, commercial, corporate and educational applications, film is still used for handling the special effects sequences in movies. There is nothing to prevent a graphics screen from being filmed with a single frame cine camera, though the quality of the images will be degraded by screen curvature, spurious reflections, intensity changes over time and possibly image drift.

Special-purpose film recorders are available which will automatically take digital picture data and display this upon a high-resolution flat CRT; each additive primary colour component of an image is projected individually and photographed through a primary colour filter before the film is advanced for the next frame. These recorders can be left to run automatically under the control of the host computer, and can work in 16 mm, 35 mm film, and even record various single picture formats.

Advances in video technology have enabled single video frames to be recorded onto video tape. Even VHS format tapes have been used, however there is a tendency for some frames to be dropped, which may be acceptable during the development of an animation sequence but could not be tolerated under any other circumstances. Professional video recorders employing tapes formatted with timecodes can pre-roll the tape to a desired position and record the desired image. A disadvantage with this approach is that as the recorded sequence develops, the pre-roll operation becomes longer and the recording heads are subjected to extra wear. A much more satisfactory approach is employed on 1 in video recorders where digital controllers remove the need to pre-roll the tape; these are expensive, however.

A more recent development is in the use of replaceable optical disks which can be written to once and played back any number of times. They are ideal for developing full-colour animation sequences, and have a capacity for approximately 30 minutes of animation – they also become a convenient format for archiving projects.

12.4 Post-production

Very rarely is a piece of computer animation produced without it being subjected to some form of post-production; this might only consist of some simple editing, and could involve individual frames being modified in a paint system and digitally composited with other images. So sophisticated are these techniques that it is virtually impossible to distinguish between natural and synthetic elements in many of today's television graphics.

Perhaps Quantel's Harry editing system has had more influence upon the state of this art than any other piece of hardware. The digital nature of its image-processing functions means that any number of images can be composited without any deterioration in the final image quality. This has transformed the way computer animation sequences are prepared, making it possible to incorporate video, photographs, electronically painted backgrounds with elements of computer animation.

The style of computer animation in television and advertising has consequently been greatly influenced by these post-production processes. Graphic designers using Harry can now design storyboards that incorporate live action, and model shoots that can be composited seamlessly. Computer animated teapots, dancing milk bottles, breakfast cereal packets, boxes of washing powder can be rendered so effectively, that when they are composited with live action, it is impossible to distinguish between the real and synthetic elements.

Furthermore, computer-controlled cameras can be programmed to fly a prepared flight path over some scale model. At the end of the shoot, the coordinate data of the 3-D space curve can be input to a computer animation system which subjects its virtual camera to the same flight path. When the computer-animated images are composited with those from the model shoot, a common perspective guarantees that the composite is faultless.

KEY POINTS

Computer hardware is changing rapidly and, in spite of the dramatic developments in the past decade, rendering time is still measured in minutes. Processor performance is being almost matched by the increased image fidelity that is being required, not to mention the overhead of supporting the sophisticated interface through which the user operates.

- Computer animation is undertaken upon a wide range of computers from PCs to super computers – each having their own strengths in processing performance and cost effectiveness.

- Disk storage is vital to any computer animation system as images are often stored on disk in a rendered form. From there they can be enhanced using image processing techniques, composited with other images, retouched using a paint program before they are recorded onto film or videotape.
- Post-production techniques play an important role in modern computer animation. Digital edit suites provide a perfect environment for merging, cutting, fading, compositing and retouching images.

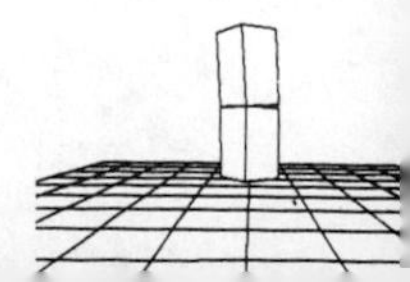

13 Applications for Computer Animation

In this chapter we investigate the practical uses of computer animation, which range from the modelling of a teapot to the simulation of a spiral galaxy. In television, computer animation is used for virtually anything from a company ident to an animated graphic depicting voting behaviour in an election. Industrial applications for computer animation take on a serious note where computer graphics techniques are used in the design and manufacturing processes of engineering components. Flight simulation reveals how computer animation is being used for creating virtual environments that enable a pilot to take off from London Heathrow, and land at Hong Kong ten minutes later. Architects, who are not new to computer graphics, are now discovering that 3-D computer animation provides them with a valuable insight into their projects long before the foundations are made. The world of advertising, where every image contains a message, are already sophisticated users of computer animation, and have stimulated the subject with their outlandish story-boards. The special effects industry have pushed computer animation to the limits, and have shown that we can no longer depend upon our eyes to say what is real, and what is fantasy. The cartoon industry seem to indicate that they would like to use computer animation, so long as they did not lose their valuable graphic identity. And lastly, the domain of scientific visualization finally demonstrates that a picture is worth a million numbers.

Introduction

In comparison to traditional animation, computer animation is still relatively young, and in the short period of its development has already demonstrated an unlimited potential in a wide number of applications. Moreover, it should not just be seen as another way of creating humorous cartoons; it is a revolutionary approach to simulating and visualizing an animated 3-D world. The ability to construct imaginary worlds within a computer's memory seems so fantastic as to be unbelievable, and as we have discovered in the previous chapters, creating and interacting with these virtual environments is based upon some relatively simple concepts.

One of the reasons for computer animation's success in different problem areas is that virtually the same hardware and software can be used with little modification. Company logos, car engines, molecules, furniture and buildings can all be represented by the basic modelling tools of polygons, surface patches and constructive solid geometry, which in turn can be animated and rendered by the various techniques with which we are now familiar. To demonstrate this incredible flexibility, we will now review how computer animation is being applied in various disciplines.

13.1 Television

One of the roles of a television graphic designer is to create animated graphics for programme titles, news programmes, seasonal promotions, current affairs and incidental animations. Traditionally, live action, scale models, character generators, cel animation and pieces of card would have been used to produce these sequences, however nowadays computer paint systems, digital compositing systems, motion control and 3-D computer animation are now familiar design tools.

Digital technology has revolutionized television production: the discrete nature of video images enables them to be stored within a computer which can then manipulate them as though they were a physical surface. These can then be rolled up, peeled back, exploded, seen in perspective, illuminated and incorporated with other synthetic 3-D objects. This integration of computer-generated images with digital video effects has provided designers with a potent creative medium which appears to have no apparent limitations.

News programmes have particularly benefited from computer animation by employing pseudo 3-D animations created on electronic paint systems such as Quantel's Paintbox. A late news item can quickly exploit a database of maps which can be composited with other generic symbols and images to create sophisticated animations for broadcast within minutes of receiving the original news. Although this makes exciting and informative television graphics, graphic designers are rapidly moving towards a near real-time mode of operation, which could be argued is not an ideal environment for creative design. Plates 12 and 13 are part of an animation sequence used for BBC Breakfast News opening titles.

Computer animation is a very flexible medium for creating title sequences for programmes, as it in no way restricts the graphic designer in the media he or she can use. The sequence could be prepared entirely with a computer, or a foreground sequence could be composited upon a live-action background. Even live action can be input to an animation sequence in the form of texture maps which can be mapped onto moving surfaces.

As mentioned in the previous chapter, motion control camera systems can provide 3-D flight paths which can be input to an animation system, then, with the use of a digital edit suite, the two image sequences can be composited to provide a seamless join. Very often, only the original designer knows how a sequence was prepared – the final image very rarely betrays its origins.

Computer-animated sequences also play an important part in incidental programme graphics for illustrating a complex 3-D process, a mathematical relationship, the components of an assembly, or even for visualizing statistical data. Prior to the availability of computer animation, such sequences would have either been hand-animated, or created using models. And in spite of all the advantages that computer animation may bring to the graphic designer's studio, one must never lose sight of the fact that it still must compete in terms of cost and efficiency with traditional techniques.

13.2 Industrial

Computer-aided design has always been identified as a major application for computer graphics, and with the advent of cost-effective animation, designers are now able to animate their virtual models and discover features that would not have been known until after the manufacturing process. For example, a component such as a sliding window within a car door can be animated to see whether it physically interferes with other elements. A car seat can be positioned within a car's interior to discover whether a range of drivers are able to reach the pedal controls and the steering wheel. Vehicles can be modelled and simulated to discover their suspension characteristics; centres of gravity calculations can be exploited to investigate stability under different loading conditions.

In reality, given any 3-D model of an assembly, individual components can be animated to discover their physical relationship with others.

However, this does not mean that any CAD system is able to undertake this work. Conventional CAD systems provide the necessary design tools to develop and visualize virtual objects, but if they are to be animated – rather than be viewed from different directions – facilities must be available to specify axes of rotation, surfaces of contact, linkages and sliding mechanisms. Furthermore, do not imagine that given a CAD database of a car engine, cutaway views of its interior revealing reciprocating pistons, sliding con-rods, exploding petrol vapour appear simply by initiating a menu command. Such sequences, which are a familiar feature of advertisements, may exploit the original database geometry but require extensive development to specify the animation.

Industrial applications for computer animation are varied. For instance, stop-frame animation is often used for preparing video disks; an example would be in showing workers the emergency exit routes on an offshore oil platform. This involves a camera team going to the platform and painstakingly photographing each position along every route. Unfortunately, the entire process may take two or three days, over which time the lighting levels change, not to mention the weather conditions. An alternative approach is to take the CAD database for the platform and remove the unwanted detail. The exit routes can now be selected and an animation sequence prepared by 'flying' the virtual camera along the different exit paths. In fact, the digital nature of the images simplifies the whole process of preparing the final video disk.

13.3 Flight simulation

Computer animation plays a key role in flight simulators where real-time image generators are used to provide realistic textured images of airports and the surrounding terrain. The pilot's cockpit, which is a working replica of some specific craft (perhaps a Boeing 767) effectively becomes the computer's virtual camera. The pilot's flying controls feed digital signals direct to a program simulating the flying characteristics of the plane. This in turn, predicts where the plane will be in a few milliseconds' time, and specifies a position in space with yaw, pitch and roll angles. Incremental quaternions also play a part in this process to ensure that no spurious directional errors creep in. From this data the image generator renders a texture-mapped scene in approximately 0.02 seconds. In reality, three images are created to provide a 180° field of view.

As the pilot 'flies' the simulator, a real-time 3-D view of the virtual environment is automatically generated. The images contain many of the features and characteristics discussed in earlier chapters. For example, other planes may be taking off or landing, which is achieved by dynamically moving the craft along pre-computed space curves. Buses and airport vehicles may be driving along taxi-ways; people are moving behind windows of the terminal building, and in dusk and night scenes, the lights of cars are animated along the highways.

Weather conditions are simulated using a variety of techniques. For example, fog, which is extrememly important in pilot training, can be set for any range. Similarly, when flying in cloud, the back-scattering of the flashing wing lights can be simulated. Snow is modelled by selecting a different set of texture maps and, by sliding a suitably painted map over the ground polygon, a realistic swirling snow effect is created. Falling snow can be simulated by particle systems that are displayed using the calligraphic feature of the display projectors; and as the pilot drives into the snow, one experiences the same effect when driving into real snow.

Cloud level can be set at any height, and when the plane moves through this layer, ground detail is faded away until a new texture map reveals a scenario where one is flying over the cloud layer. In storm conditions, lightning strikes are flashed on using strings of light points with a simultaneous momentary increase in image brightness.

Landing lights illuminate the runway using the spot light source characteristics, but as an airport contains many thousands of light sources it is impossible to compute their illumination effects in real-time. Consequently, they are simulated with luminous polygons which appear to be glowing, and luminous texture maps shaped by a transparent footprint.

The database for an airport generally requires six man-months to complete, as the airport may be located near a large city whose major landmarks such as tall buildings, bridges, rivers and coastline have to be accurately modelled. Because the range over which these models are viewed extends to several miles, they may be modelled three or four times to different levels of detail. Thus as the pilot approaches a scene, the image generator automatically fades the low detail model out and fades in the high-detail model. This form of model management ensures that the scene does not contain superfluous polygons, which ultimately dictates the rendering time.

13.4 Architecture

Architects have used 2-D computer graphics as an aid to the layout of floor plans and the organization of service networks such as gas, electricity, water, air and drainage systems for some time. Today, 3-D systems are playing an increasing role in the visualization of interiors and exterior views.

Although architecture seems to be an obvious application for computer animation, it must be appreciated that the database representing a large building could store several hundred thousand elements, each of which might have detailed geometry such as a window frame. It is not practical to render this level of detail and animate it as though it were a logo. Furthermore, Gouraud or Phong shading are not realistic shading models for visualizing the interiors illuminated by diffuse panel lights and daylight, and exteriors where the time of the day, weather conditions, reflections and shadows are important to the client.

However, ray tracing provides an excellent method for identifying shadows, reflections and specular highlights in buildings incorporating walls of glass, and radiosity has proved to be an effective method of revealing the complex lighting levels created by multiple diffuse reflections. Unfortunately, both techniques are relatively expensive in processing time, and it is not unusual for a ray traced scene to need ten hours of processing time to create just one image when using a realistic database.

Radiosity depends upon large numbers of form-factors which relate the diffuse light interaction between small portions of two surfaces, though once these have been computed, realistic images are quickly created. In fact, some systems are able to generate them in real-time. If the cost of these developments can be kept low, they will have a real impact upon architecture and enable animated walk-throughs of interiors to be experienced while the design is still on the digital drawing board. Plate 5 illustrates the level of realism that is possible using today's modelling and rendering tools.

However, in spite of these problems, computer animation is being used for visualizing large architectural and construction projects, in which it is difficult to imagine how new buildings and roads will impact upon the existing environment. Aerial sequences can provide a dramatic insight into the scale of these projects, and clarify areas of confusion created by looking at plan elevations on a drawing. But as the virtual camera can be placed anywhere within the database, there is nothing to prevent the camera from taking a car's view of the database as it is driven along proposed new roads.

Many large-scale projects have already employed these techniques, and with the trend towards fast and low-cost computers, computer animation will become an everyday feature of the architectural design process.

13.5 Advertising

Advertising is a popular application for computer animation because the projects often provide animators with the opportunity to explore and develop new techniques which they would not normally investigate. Storyboards can call for the modelling of entire kitchens, saxophones, pianos, boxes of detergent, sweets, biscuits, bathrooms, teapots, spoons, tubs of yoghurt and spinning galaxies. These elements are then animated with

FFDs, inbetweened, moved along B-spline curves, composited with live action and video until the client is convinced that the desired message will be communicated to the viewing public. Although the final sequence may only last a few seconds, arriving at this stage may need several weeks of intensive work.

Modelling is still a time-consuming activity especially when objects such as cars, engines, frogs and landscapes have to be built – it is not just the model's complexity that causes the problems, but identifying useful sources of data. Models have to be constructed with a knowledge of how they are to be animated, and last-minute changes in the storyboard can have dramatic repercussions on their construction.

Line testing the animation, balancing colours, selecting texture and adjusting illumination levels all require fine tuning, often requiring the sequence to be rendered over and over again, until deadlines are reached – at which point, the final rendered video or film is made.

Like television graphics, advertising also calls for a variety of media to be integrated – in particular, computer animation is often incorporated with images derived from live action. Balancing scale and perspective between the two systems is then very important; however, as computer models are dimensionless they can be interpreted at any level of scale by adjusting certain parameters in the viewing and perspective transforms.

The level of realism achieved in these sequences is very high, and sometimes the public are not aware that computers have been used at all! Perhaps all that they are aware of is that they find it difficult to understand how the effect was produced. Plate 15 demonstrates the extraordinary level of creative design that goes into making a modern commercial.

13.6 Film special effects

Films such as 'Tron', 'The Abyss', 'Flight of the Intruder', 'Terminator 2', 'Lawnmower Man' and 'Total Recall' have all demonstrated that there is a real place for computer animation in creating special effects. Although scale models and motion control systems have proved to be a cost-effective approach in simulating large alien scenes, computer animation has been very successful in modelling fire, smoke, explosions, space craft, humanoids and human heads made from water.

Matching scale and perspective between synthetic and live images is vital if the effect is to be convincing, and special effects teams go to great lengths to ensure that the final optical or digital composition does not betray the different origins of the images.

Even when a film only contains five minutes of computer animation, those few minutes are normally action-packed and include effects that could not have been created using a process costing less; otherwise, there would be no point in employing computer graphics. Five minutes at 25 frames/sec requires 7500 images, and if these take, on average, 15 minutes to render, a total of 1875 hours of rendering time is needed! But this is only for one rendering of the animation; it is highly likely to be rendered several times before a director is satisfied with the piece. Consequently, a large team of people is required to undertake such projects, with a complementary array of workstations.

The software supporting this industry often includes two or three proprietary animation systems, as they all possess various features that might resolve a particular problem. This software is further enhanced by in-house programs used on previous projects, and a team of dedicated programmers is on-hand to solve problems on the fly as they occur.

Modelling plays an important role in this work as storyboards never call for anything as simple as a tumbling logo or a teapot. It is more likely to be a humanoid walking through a wall of flames who, imperceptibly, dissolves into a live human over a matter of two seconds. Such a sequence requires the humanoid to be accurately modelled to the finest surface detail. It must be animated to walk with a gait identical to the actor's, and then with the aid of mattes, it can be digitally composited with the live action to create a seamless join. The lighting of the original model is vital if the two sources of imagery are to appear as one, so too will any reflections appearing on any polished surfaces. Animators are prepared to go to great lengths to ensure that reflection maps are accurate, and often model a copy of the studio set to create this level of realism.

13.7 3-D cartoons

3-D cartoons have been a convenient vehicle to demonstrate just how flexible computer animation can be. John Lasseter's 'Luxo Junior' (1986) is a landmark in the evolution of computer animation, and his subsequent titles 'Red's Dream' (1987), 'Tin Toy' (1988) and 'Knickknack' (1989) have all influenced the development of the computer animation industry. However, the potential of computer animation in 3-D cartoons was appreciated very early in the development of the subject – projects such as 'The Works' (1980) from the NYIT and 'Tony de Peltrie' (1985), were clear pointers to the way computer animation was evolving. With the continuous advances in hardware and software, more complex scenarios could be explored; rendering was improved, new animation techniques were discovered and computer animators found that story-telling was vital to the success of any animation sequence.

In recent years, other projects such as PDI's 'Locomotion' (1990), Gavin Miller's 'Eric, the Dynamic Worm' (1989), Videosystem's 'Don

Quixote' (1990) and 'Eurythmy' (1989) by Susan Amkraut and Michael Girard, have taken computer animation to new levels of realism, particularly in the area of motion. Unfortunately, these sequences are short and are the result of considerable research and dedication to solving complex problems. However, as they are resolved, we move closer to the day when a full-length 3-D cartoon is produced using nothing but computer animation.

In recent months, tremendous advances have been made into all sorts of areas, from the modelling and motion of elephants, to the modelling of galaxies and black holes. Today, it seems that virtually anything is possible given a budget and sufficient time.

Although it is inevitable that computer animation will establish a niche for a variety of graphic styles that have already begun to appear, the traditional cartoon industry will not abandon a lifetime's work in perfecting a style that is so appealing. This is not to say that the two production approaches will never merge; already, computer-animated sequences have been incorporated within cartoons prepared on back-painted cels. Such collaborative projects demonstrate that it must be possible to develop software that will enable animators to continue creating their cartoons, and also benefit from the advantages associated with digital technology.

13.8 Scientific visualization

Twenty-five years ago the humble 12in drum plotter was a desirable computer graphics peripheral, normally driven online by a mainframe computer boasting 24Kbytes of memory. It was normally used for displaying graphs relating quantities associated with experimental data sets, which though simple, represented the foundations of scientific visualization.

In the intervening years, we have witnessed the birth of the PC, the graphics workstation, minicomputers, massive mainframe systems and the super-computer. People are still drawing graphs, though advances in hardware and software now permit the rapid display of coloured three-dimensional surfaces using isometric and perspective projections. These techniques are used to interpret the vast data sets accumulating from scientific endeavours in geology, astronomy, oceanography, high-energy atomic physics and simulation. Although some of these data sets can be represented by static isosurfaces (surfaces representing a scalar value), many are not only three-dimensional in the spatial sense, but include attributes of pressure, temperature, velocity, direction, stress, compression, density, and material composition. Thus the fundamental problem facing modern scientific visualization is the graphical interpretation of multi-dimensional data.

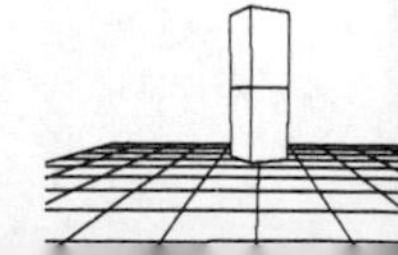

Squeezing several dimensions into the two physical dimensions of a display screen is not that difficult – in fact it is used every day on television networks in weather forecasting where a 2-D map shows the spatial distribution of the weather. Colour can be used to indicate local temperatures; arrows can be used to show wind direction and strength, and transparent diagrammatic clouds can reflect level of cloud cover.

In scientific visualization similar techniques are used to translate multi-dimensional data into visual models where physical attributes are translated into colour, position, shading, transparency and glow effects, together with the geometric aids of isosurfaces, vectors, particle systems, mesh structures, and polygonal objects. However, the extra dimension of time has now brought 3-D computer animation into the arena.

Computer animation systems are now being used by the scientific community to provide animated visualizations of time-dependent data sets. For example, in finite element analysis (FEA), where objects are represented within a computer as a linked spatial mesh of several tens-of-thousands of nodes, the internal representation can be processed mathematically to compute the stresses, strains and deflections resulting from imaginary forces and torques. When such data is visualized, the simulated structure can be seen to flex, and perhaps even vibrate, and the technique of pseudo-colouring used to reveal the points under most stress. Computer animation enables the model to be examined from any point of view or trajectory, and rendered with surface detail and shadows, incorporated with other models, and even composited with real-world images.

Another aspect of simulation is that of computational fluid dynamics (CFD), which is used for computing effects of wind flow or fluid flow over the surface of an object. This is of particular importance to the automotive, aeronautical and space industries. Wind tunnels are the conventional environment for discovering air flow and drag factors for an object, although with the advent of powerful computers, such simulations can be undertaken using a computer model. This means that a 3-D design can be input via a graphics workstation, evaluated for structural strength, examined for ergonomic suitability, simulated for aerodynamic performance and assessed aesthetically long before the final object is manufactured by numerically controlled machines driven by the synthetic database.

One last application for computer animation in scientific visualization is in the interpretation of dynamic simulation processes. We have already examined in Section 10.6 how dynamic simulation is being used to increase the realism of articulated structures; in industry, such techniques are important everyday design activities. Stability in robots, cars, lorries and earth-moving vehicles is vital to their safe use under various dynamic operating conditions. Once more these physical systems of linkages, springs, dampers, masses, centres of gravity and moments of inertia can be represented mathematically within a computer. These can then be subjected to forces and torques and, with the tools of forward and inverse dynamics, their motion can be accurately predicted. The numerical values representing these movements can easily be imported into an animation system, where the simulated behaviour is translated into realistic animations which, hopefully, will reveal any undesirable motion traits.

KEY POINTS

Computer animation is still developing and as the technology provides an increasing range of cost-effective opportunities for animating images, new applications are discovered. Nowadays, the major applications cover the areas listed below.

- Television employs computer animation for programme titles, animating news information, explanatory graphics, weather maps and station logos. Synthetic images mean that no traditional graphic design materials are needed in the design process, and dramatically reduces the time required to produce them.
- Many industrial processes already involve computers and CAD systems, therefore it is a natural development to introduce computer animation techniques for visualizing and simulation experiments while data is still in a digital form.
- Flight simulators employ real-time image generators for displaying 3-D scenes of airports and the surrounding terrain for training pilots.
- Architects also use CAD systems for developing and maintaining drawings, and computer animation provides valuable visualization tools for evaluating projects using external aerial views, and internal walk throughs.
- The advertising industry has exploited all the advantages offered by computer animation; the virtual 3-D world provides a perfect environment for performing visual tricks that would be impossible using physical counterparts.
- Special effects in films push computer animation to its limits, but such projects often create features that find their way into commercial animation systems very quickly. Special effects sequences normally involve the use of commercial animation systems, and the final images are rendered to a high-resolution 70 mm format.
- 3-D cartoons are also a vehicle for introducing new animation effects, and researchers have realized the importance of a storyline, even when revealing a new modelling, animation or rendering process. To date, the cartoon industry has not yet produced a full-length animation using only computers, although short sequences have been incorporated within cartoons made using traditional methods.

- Scientific visualization has become a perfect application for computer animation as it is difficult to imagine how some of their problems could have been resolved using any other method. The modelling, animation and rendering tools that are so effective for realizing images of familiar objects, are equally effective in translating the abstract multi-dimensional data sets derived from experiments and computer simulations, into informative animated sequences.

14 The Future

What does the future hold for computer animation? My personal belief is that we are moving towards an era when it will become impossible to distinguish between reality and virtual reality. This may still be some time away – however, there is no fundamental technological reason why it should not happen. Already today we have real-time rendering systems capable of generating realistic images in a few thousandths of a second. Display technology has progressed to the extent where head-mounted stereo display systems are available and used to substitute computer-generated images as the user's head is tracked in space. Virtual reality systems will allow us to interact with our animation environment in totally new ways. Models could be positioned with the aid of interactive gloves, and a mannequin could be animated by driving it with data taken from interactive suits.

Imagine how the developments in neural networks, knowledge-based systems and learning systems will influence computer animation. Why shouldn't collections of polygons (or whatever future models are built from) be given some level of intelligence, so that instead of being directed by the animator at each frame, they learn through rehearsing a sequence until the animator is satisfied with the movement? Why shouldn't we also be able to direct our future models through speech? Language is a natural way of communicating with other human beings, so it seems an obvious way to communicate with our synthetic counterparts.

As we move towards this technology, new modelling tools will have to be developed, which may involve the automatic digitizing of real-world scenes into digital form. Why construct surface terrain from maps when the 3-D geometry can be extracted from a stereo-pair of satellite images? Nature has a head-start in this area and could save us considerable work. Perhaps future systems will not require every surface to be explicitly described; maybe they can be sculptured in real-time by a designer who can not only see the evolving object, but feel its surfaces.

Now the above predictions are not really predictions – most of them already exist in one way or another. The real future of computer animation will be even more fantastic – exactly what form it takes might even be decided by you. If you have been stimulated by some of the ideas outlined in this book, you might be tempted to become involved in this exciting subject and undertake a project which advances the subject another step forward.

There is a temptation to accept that what exists today will remain for the next few decades and that there is very little remaining to be discovered. But this is not the attitude to take. We should not allow today's technology and system limitations to constrain our thinking. Just imagine how outlandish ray tracing must have seemed when it was first proposed to produce a picture by executing a program one million times! Today, ray tracing is regularly used, and some systems can even produce low-resolution images in near real-time.

There is no doubt that we are moving towards low-cost real-time systems, which will undertake in hardware the majority of the rendering currently performed in software. This will effectively remove the current bottleneck associated with the manipulation and display of pixel data, and push it forward towards the animator. In fact, it is highly likely that whereas today the animator is frequently waiting for the computer to render images, very soon a project's length will be determined by the skill of the animator, which means more effort must be directed towards more effective modelling tools, and new techniques for combining creative user-defined animation with those offered by dynamic simulation.

Research has already begun in these areas, so the future looks exciting, and maybe one day we will recall the early days of computer animation and ask, did we really build models from polygons? And how did we manage to produce any animation at all when it took ten minutes a frame? And why did we employ all of that mathematics? For the moment, though, the future has still not arrived, and the reason why we use polygons, and are prepared to wait several minutes for an image, and use mathematics is that we have no choice – and besides, we enjoy the subject, and that makes it all bearable!

Appendix

Supplementary Mathematics for Computer Graphics

Topics such as matrices, polynomials and quaternions are introduced at relevant chapters in the book, and no further description is offered here. However, the two subjects that require special treatment are trigonometric functions and vectors.

Trigonometric functions

Trigonometry is concerned with angles, their measurement and their relationships with one another. In computer animation we frequently need to derive angles between a pair of lines, or a line and a surface, or the angle between two planes. The two trigonometric functions that appear over and over again are sine (sin) and cosine (cos). Both of these functions can be understood with reference to Figure A.1(a) which shows a point P rotating anti-clockwise about a fixed point O. The angle θ is related to the measurements b, h and r as follows:

$$\sin(\theta) = \frac{h}{r}$$

$$\cos(\theta) = \frac{b}{r}$$

$$\tan(\theta) = \frac{h}{b}$$

These three functions are closely related in the following way:

$$\tan(\theta) = \frac{\sin(\theta)}{\cos(\theta)}$$

If we trace out the values of the sin and cos ratios for different angles they create the familiar wave pattern shown in Figure A.1(b). The values of the functions vary between -1 and $+1$ and extend indefinitely in the right-hand direction for positive anti-clockwise angles, and in the left-hand direction for negative clockwise angles.

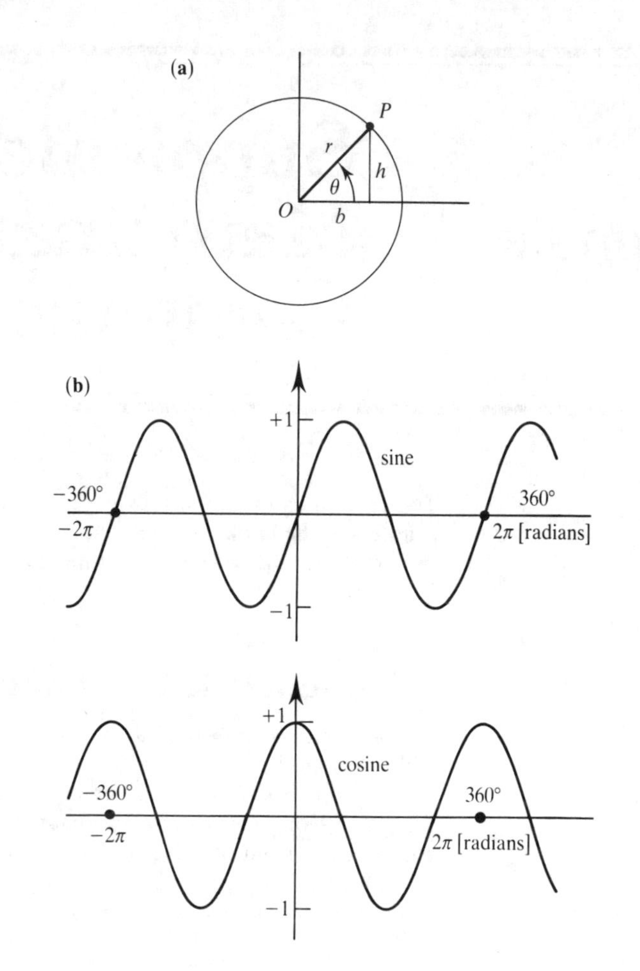

Figure A-1

When the point P rotates about O it creates a right-angle triangle which can be used to encode the rotated angle θ. When the height of the triangle h is plotted against the angle θ, the familiar sine waveform is produced.

Angles can be measured in units of degrees [°] or radians, where 2π [radians] are equivalent to 360°.

From the waveform shown in Figure A.1(b) the following observations can be made:

$$\cos(\theta) = \sin(\theta + \pi/2)$$
$$\cos(\theta) = \cos(-\theta)$$
$$\sin(\theta) = -\sin(\theta)$$

The theorem of Pythagoras states that:

$$r^2 = b^2 + h^2$$

which relates the sin and cos functions as follows:

$$\sin^2(\theta) + \cos^2(\theta) = 1$$

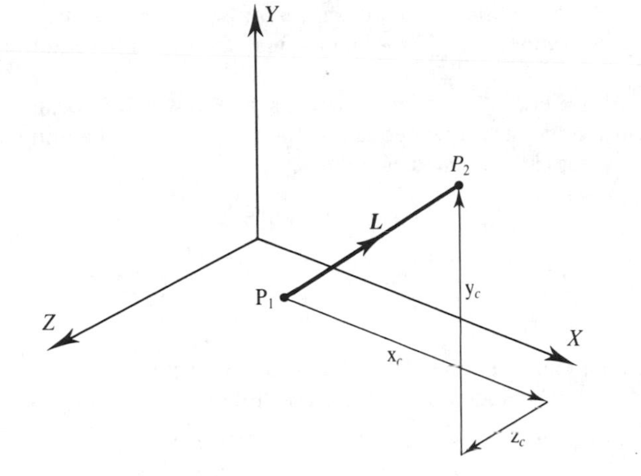

Figure A-2

The line segment $\{P_1, P_2\}$ can be represented by a vector **L** which has direction and magnitude. The direction is represented by the separate coordinate components $[x_c, y_c, z_c]$, and the magnitude is represented by $|\mathbf{V}| = \sqrt{x_c^2 + y_c^2 + z_c^2}$.

Other relationships that are given without proof are:

$$\sin(\theta + \alpha) = \sin(\theta)\cos(\alpha) + \cos(\theta)\sin(\alpha)$$
$$\cos(\theta + \alpha) = \cos(\theta)\cos(\alpha) - \sin(\theta)\sin(\alpha)$$
$$\sin(\theta - \alpha) = \sin(\theta)\cos(\alpha) - \cos(\theta)\sin(\alpha)$$
$$\cos(\theta - \alpha) = \cos(\theta)\cos(\alpha) + \sin(\theta)\sin(\alpha)$$

Vectors

Problems in computer graphics are often resolved using vectors, but it will only be necessary to revise those aspects that support their application in this book.

In geometry, a vector can be used to represent a line segment's direction and magnitude. For example, in the case of the 3-D line segment shown in Figure A.2, its direction can be specified in terms of the three axial components x_c, y_c and z_c. The line is shown to start at P_1 and end at P_2, but one can move from P_1 to P_2 by moving x_c units along the x-axis, z_c units along the z-axis and y_c units up the y-axis. Consequently, if x_c, y_c and z_c are made negative, the line's direction is reversed as P_2 to P_1. The magnitude of the line is given by Pythagoras' theorem:

$$\text{magnitude} = \sqrt{x_c^2 + y_c^2 + z_c^2}$$

Using vector terminology any line with end points $P_1(x_1, y_1, z_1)$ and $P_2(x_2, y_2, z_2)$ the values of x_c, y_c and z_c are given by:

$$x_c = x_2 - x_1$$
$$y_c = y_2 - y_1$$
$$z_c = z_2 - z_1$$

and the vector is defined as:

$$\mathbf{V} = \begin{bmatrix} x_c \\ y_c \\ z_c \end{bmatrix}$$

The bold face for **V** reminds us that it is a vector and consists of two or more values representing its components. Two-dimensional vectors only require two components.

The magnitude of a vector is written as $|\mathbf{V}|$ which is evaluated as shown above, and when the magnitude equals 1, the vector is called a unit vector.

Any vector can be scaled as follows:

$$\mathbf{V}' = s\begin{bmatrix} x_c \\ y_c \\ z_c \end{bmatrix} = \begin{bmatrix} sx_c \\ sy_c \\ sz_c \end{bmatrix}$$

where the individual components are scaled by the factor s.

Vectors can be added or subtracted as follows:

$$\mathbf{A} = \begin{bmatrix} x_a \\ y_a \\ z_a \end{bmatrix} \qquad \mathbf{B} = \begin{bmatrix} x_b \\ y_b \\ z_b \end{bmatrix}$$

$$\mathbf{C} = \mathbf{A} + \mathbf{B}$$

where:

$$\mathbf{C} = \begin{bmatrix} x_a + x_b \\ y_a + y_b \\ z_a + z_b \end{bmatrix}$$

Vectors cannot be multiplied together in the same way we multiply scalars, but there are two operations called the dot product and the cross product which involve multiplying together the components of two vectors.

The dot product

For two vectors **A** and **B**, the dot product is defined as:

$$\mathbf{A} \cdot \mathbf{B} = (x_a x_b + y_a y_b + z_a z_b)$$

which is a scalar, but also has the following meaning:

$$\mathbf{A} \cdot \mathbf{B} = |\mathbf{A}|\,|\mathbf{B}|\cos(\theta)$$

where θ is the angle between **A** and **B**.

Thus when the angle between two vectors is required, its cosine is found from:

$$\cos(\theta) = \frac{(x_a x_b + y_a y_b + z_a z_b)}{|\mathbf{A}|\,|\mathbf{B}|}$$

And when both vectors are unit vectors, this simplifies to:

$$\cos(\theta) = (x_a x_b + y_a y_b + z_a z_b)$$

The cross product

Given two vectors **A** and **B** the cross product is defined as:

$$\mathbf{A} \times \mathbf{B} = \mathbf{C}$$

where **C** is another vector. The length of **C**, i.e. $|\mathbf{C}|$ is given by:

$$|\mathbf{C}| = |\mathbf{A}|\,|\mathbf{B}|\sin(\theta)$$

where θ is the angle between **A** and **B**.

The components of **C** are evaluated as follows:

$$\mathbf{C} = \begin{bmatrix} y_a z_b - y_b z_a \\ z_a x_b - z_b x_a \\ x_a y_b - x_b y_a \end{bmatrix}$$

The vector **C** is perpendicular to the plane containing **A** and **B**. This can be visualized by taking one's right hand and arranging the thumb, first finger and middle finger as a set of 3-D axes. If the thumb is assumed to be **A**, the first finger **B**, then the middle finger is **C**.

Glossary

Absolute coordinate system The term absolute coordinate system is sometimes used in place of the world coordinate system.

A-buffer The A-buffer is a hidden-surface removal algorithm developed by Loren Carpenter at Lucasfilm Ltd as part of the Reyes renderer.

Achromatic light Achromatic light is light without colour.

Acute angle An acute angle is less than 90°.

Adaptive progressive refinement Adaptive progressive refinement is a technique used in radiosity which progressively refines the image.

Additive colour mixing Is the technique of creating colours by superimposing two or three light sources from the red, green and blue portions of the visible spectrum.

Additive primary colours The additive primary colours are red, green and blue.

Affine transformation An affine transformation preserves the concept of parallelism, with the implication that any lines parallel before an affine transformation will still be parallel after the operation.

Aim point The orientation of the observer in world coordinates can be effected by the eye point and the aim point; it is also called the focal point.

Algorithm An algorithm is a mathematical or logical procedure for solving a problem.

Aliasing (a) **Spatial**: In pixel-based display systems, visual artefacts such as jagged edges and moiré patterns caused by insufficient spatial sampling are referred to as spatial aliasing. (b) **Temporal**: Animation artefacts such as 'wagon wheels' apparently rotating backwards, caused by the insufficient temporal sampling of moving objects, is referred to as temporal aliasing.

Alpha channel The alpha channel is a video channel derived from a value called the alpha value associated with each pixel in a video frame store, and is used for storing mattes when compositing images.

Alpha value See **Alpha channel**.

Ambient light Ambient light is a constant term used to represent a background light level assumed to be caused by multiple diffuse reflections.

Ambient reflection coefficient The ambient reflection coefficient is a fractional value associated with a reflective surface that determines the level of ambient light it reflects.

Angle of incidence The angle of incidence is the acute angle formed by the surface normal and the incident ray illuminating the surface.

Angle of reflection The angle of reflection is the acute angle formed by the surface normal and the reflected ray away from the surface.

Angle of refraction The angle of refraction is the acute angle formed by the refracted ray and the reflected surface normal for a transmissive medium.

Angle of view The angle of view is the solid angle of incident light transmitted by the lens.

Animation Animation is the technique of creating continuously moving scenes by projecting a sequence of images in rapid succession.

Anti-aliasing Anti-aliasing encompasses strategies concerned with the removal or reduction of aliasing artefacts arising from the insufficient sampling of a pixel-based scene.

Anti-clockwise polygon An anticlockwise polygon is defined as one whose interior is to the left and whose exterior is to the right when its boundary is traversed in the direction of its edges.

Aperture Aperture is a measure of the physical area associated with a lens through which light can pass.

Approximating spline Approximating splines approach their control points without intersecting them.

Artefact Artefacts refer to unwanted visual features introduced by a type of technology or an inaccurate algorithm.

Aspect ratio The aspect ratio relates the vertical to the horizontal dimensions of an image or shape.

Attributes Attributes are properties associated with various entities within a computer graphics system.

Average normal An average normal is a single vector representing a collection of surface normals at a common vertex.

Axis An axis is (a) an arbitrary line in 2- or 3-D space about which operations such as reflection and rotation are performed; (b) a line used to construct a system of axes as in Cartesian notation.

Back clipping plane The back clipping plane in the viewing pyramid controls the distance up to which objects are visible.

Back face The back face of a planar polygon is invisible when its surface normal is facing away from the camera.

Back face culling See **Back face removal**.

Back face removal Back face removal, or back face culling, refers to the removal of all back-facing surfaces of a scene before it is rendered.

Bar sheets Bar sheets are used in animation projects as a reference document controlling dialogue, music and movements with frame numbers.

Behavioural animation Behaviour animation simulates effects such as flock centring, collision avoidance and velocity matching.

Bézier curve A Bézier curve is generated by computing the spatial coordinates of a point on the curve from control points weighted by terms from the Bernstein basis function.

Bézier surface patch Bézier surface patches employ a matrix of control points to define the geometry of a quadratic or cubic surface patch.

Bicubic patch A bicubic patch is a surface patch definition employing cubic equations of two parameters to generate the coordinates of any point on the patch.

Binary A binary number system employs a two-state code.

Bit A bit is an individual element of a binary-coded item.

Bit-Blit Bit-Blit or Bit-Blt operations are associated with Boolean operations performed upon rectangular areas of pixels.

Bit map A bit map is a digital image of bits.

Blending function A blending or interpolating function is used to blend together two or more numeric quantities.

Boundary representation (B-rep) B-rep schemes include methods of modelling objects through a surface representation, rather than the volumetric approach of constructive solid geometry.

Bounding box Like a bounding sphere, a bounding box is a minimum bounding volume in the form of a rectangular box associated with an object such that it completely encloses it.

Bounding sphere A bounding sphere is a minimum bounding volume in the form of a sphere.

B-rep See **Boundary representation**.

B-spline curve B-spline curves, especially their rational form as used in NURBS, are parametric curves whose shape is determined by a series of control points, whose influence is determined by basis functions.

B-spline surface patch A B-spline surface patch is a parametric surface patch controlled by a matrix of control points whose influence is determined by the product of two B-spline basis functions.

Bump map A bump map is a 2-D look-up table holding intensity levels used to modulate a surface normal while rendering.

Bump mapping Bump mapping perturbs a surface normal during rendering to create a bumpy surface.

Byte A byte is a group of eight bits which is capable of encoding 256 unique binary patterns.

C C is a computer programming language often used in computer graphics.

C++ C++ is an extended version of C, supporting object-oriented programming concepts.

Camera coordinate system (CCS) The CCS is a Cartesian axial system associated with the camera in a computer animation system.

Cartesian coordinates Cartesian coordinates enable a point in 2-D space to be represented by two measurements, and a point in 3-D space by three measurements, relative to some defined origin and system of orthogonal axes.

Catmull–Rom spline The Catmull–Rom spline belongs to the family of interpolating splines and is also known as the cardinal spline or the Overhauser spline.

CCS See **Camera coordinate system**.

Caustic When light reflects against a curved surface or is refracted through a curved object, caustic curves appear.

Cell animation Traditional animation employs thin sheets of clear acetate called cell or cel, which are hand-painted and overlaid to create multilayered scenes.

Centre of projection In a perspective projection, the centre of projection is the point through which all projection lines pass.

Character animation Character animation is a generic term for animating life-like characters.

Circle of confusion A lens is unable to focus every light ray onto a focal plane: some intersect before it, and others behind, but where they intersect the focal plane, small circles of light are formed called circles of confusion.

Clipping Clipping is the process of removing detail from a 2- or 3-D scene which is either invisible to the observer by way of projecting to a region of the viewplane not in the viewport, or not needed.

Clockwise polygon A clockwise polygon is a polygon whose interior is to the right and exterior to the left when its boundary is traversed in the direction of its edges.

Collision detection Collision detection refers to the mechanisms employed to identify those 3-D elements that have effectively touched or intersected one another.

Colour attributes Before an object can be rendered, it must be assigned colour attributes in the form of numerical values encoding some surface feature.

Colour model A colour model is a convenient system for organizing and specifying colours within an application-dependent colour gamut.

Colour monitor A colour CRT driven by unencoded colour signals is generally called a colour monitor.

Colour space A colour space is a 2- or 3-D method of organizing colour attributes.

Colour table A colour table is a look-up table whose entries store colour descriptions, perhaps in the form of levels of red, green and blue.

Compositing Compositing is the process of superimposing one image upon another to create a single 'composite' image.

Database A database is a structure employed to organize large quantities of data such that it can be interrogated efficiently without every item necessarily being investigated.

Data structure A data structure is a memory organization which maintains data in a format to ensure that individual items are easily accessed and processed.

Degree A degree is a unit of angular measurement and by definition there are 360 to one complete circular rotation. 360° is also equal to 2π radians.

Depth buffer See ***z*-buffer**.

Depth of field The depth of field of a lens defines the distance range in its object space over which an in-focus image is created; outside these limits, the image appears blurred.

Device coordinate system The device dependent coordinate system in which a specific hardware device is addressed is called the device coordinate system.

Diffuse reflection An illuminated perfect matte surface is a source of diffuse reflections, as any incident light is randomly reflected back into the illumination space.

Diffuse reflection coefficient The diffuse reflection coefficient is a fractional value used to control the amount of incident non-ambient light reflected from a matte surface.

Diffuse surface A diffuse surface is one which reflects light equally in all directions and obeys Lambert's cosine law.

Digitizer (a) **2-D**: A digitizer is used for translating artwork into a file of 2-D coordinate data; (b) **3-D**: A digitizer is used to capture 3-D coordinate data from a physical model using a probe whose position can be determined in space.

Digitizing Digitizing is the process of capturing real-world data using a digitizer, a scanner or frame grabber.

Directional light source A directional light source is assumed to be located at infinity and emits light in only one direction.

Displacement animation Displacement animation is a technique used by Symbolics to animate an object from one state to another.

Distributed light source A distributed light source radiates energy over a defined area, rather than from a single point light source.

Dodecahedron A dodecahedron is a platonic object constructed from 12 hexagons.

Dot product If vectors **p** and **q** are defined as follows:

$$\mathbf{p} = [a\mathbf{i} + b\mathbf{j} + c\mathbf{k}]$$
$$\mathbf{q} = [d\mathbf{i} + e\mathbf{j} + f\mathbf{k}]$$

then the dot product $\mathbf{p} \bullet \mathbf{q}$ is

$$\mathbf{p} \bullet \mathbf{q} = ad + be + cf$$

and

$$\mathbf{p} \bullet \mathbf{q} = |\mathbf{p}|\,|\mathbf{q}|\cos(\theta)$$

where θ = the angle between **p** and **q**.

Dynamic constraints The animation of physically constrained systems involving linkages, springs, gravitational fields etc., is governed by dynamic constraints.

Easing Easing is the technique of altering the speed of an animated object.

Edge An edge is either part of the border of a shape or a line formed where two surfaces meet.

Elastically deformable objects Elastically deformable objects include flags, faces, tyres, curtains and plastic materials.

Electrostatic plotter An electrostatic plotter prints in a raster format and, with the aid of nibs on a print head, charges selected areas of the paper which attract the visible toner.

Environment mapping Environment mapping is a rendering technique employing texture maps to create the impression of high-gloss surfaces such as mirrors and polished metal surfaces.

Euler angles Euler angles are the three angles for rotating an object about the *x*-, *y*- and *z*-axes.

Euler's rule Euler's rule states that, for a polyhedron without holes, the number of edges is always two less than the sum of the numbers of faces and vertices.

Explicit surface The geometry of an explicit surface is defined parametrically, e.g. a bicubic patch.

Extruding Extruding is a modelling technique where a 3-D volume can be created by specifying a 2-D cross-section contour and a path through which it is to be 'extruded'.

Facet A facet is a planar portion of some surface primitive.

Facet normal A facet normal is the normal vector associated with the facet.

Fairing See **Easing**.

Far plane See **Clipping**.

Field One television image frame consists of two interlaced fields which make up either all the odd or all the even scan-lines.

Flicker Flicker occurs when the frequency of a pulsating light source falls below the fusion frequency of the human visual system.

F-number The f-number of a lens is its focal length divided by its 'stopped' aperture.

Focal length The focal length of a lens is the distance of the focal plane to the lens when the incident light is from a distant source.

Focal plane A lens creates a real image in sharp focus on a surface positioned at its focal plane.

Form-factor In radiosity a form-factor represents the fractional radiant energy leaving one patch and arriving at another.

Forward dynamics Forward dynamics is concerned with the calculation of a body's acceleration when an applied force is known.

Forward kinematics Forward kinematics refers to the use of transformations in controlling the future position and motion of objects. Transformations such as rotation and translation can be employed by an animator to locate an object precisely between two extreme positions.

Fractal A fractal is a data set that exhibits similar properties and features at different scales.

Fractal curve A fractal curve is a curve exhibiting fractal properties as defined by one of a number of dimension rules.

Fractal dimension The fractal dimension D of a shape, fractal or otherwise, is given by:

$$D = \frac{\log(N)}{\log(1/S)}$$

where N is the number of equal subdivisions that could be made on a curve or surface and S is the scale factor associated with each subdivision.

Fractal surface A fractal surface is a surface exhibiting fractal properties.

Frame (a) **Animation**: A frame is a single image within an animation sequence. (b) **Video**: A frame is two interlaced fields forming a television picture.

Frame buffer See **Frame store**.

Frame grabber A frame grabber is a video device for capturing a video signal for input into a computer graphics/video system.

Frame store A frame store is a memory device used to hold a raster image where each pixel is mapped into a specific number of bits.

Free form deformation (FFD) Free form deformation is a computer animation technique for distorting 2-D and 3-D structures.

Free-form surfaces Free-form surfaces describe a class of surfaces that have no implicit geometric definition.

Front clipping plane The front, near or hither clipping plane, delineates the minimum distance where points are visible in the 3-D viewing frustum.

Front face The front face of a polygon is classified as visible when its surface normal is facing towards the camera in the camera's coordinate system.

Frustum A frustum is a truncated pyramid representing the camera's viewing volume.

Fusion frequency The fusion frequency is the minimum frequency for an alternating source of light to appear constant to the human visual system – this is approximately 50 Hz.

Gamma Gamma is the exponent term in the equation relating output light intensity with the input electron drive signal for a refresh CRT.

Global illumination model A global illumination model attempts to simulate the phenomena found within complex environments such as multiple reflections, shadow penumbrae, colour bleeding, as well as diffuse and specular reflections.

Gloss coefficient The gloss coefficient controls the degree of gloss exhibited by a surface, and is the specular exponent term in Phong shading calculations.

Goal-oriented animation Goal-oriented techniques are used for animating articulated structures subjected to various physical constraints, in which the structure can be given a goal in terms of a final position of one of its elements, and the orientation of the entire structure can then computed.

Gouraud shading Gouraud shading interpolates colour intensities to shade a surface.

Graphic primitive A graphic primitive is a shape or object which a graphic system uses as a building block for the construction of more complex scenes.

Graphics package A graphics package is a software system which undertakes a graphics task for a user, such as animation, modelling or painting.

Graphics tablet A graphics tablet is a small digitizer frequently associated with a workstation for the input of graphical data, or controlling the screen's cursor.

Grey levels The number of discrete intensity levels of a display is often expressed in terms of the number of grey levels.

Grey-scale image A grey-scale image has pixel values interpreted as different shades of grey.

Half space Two half spaces are created on either side of a planar surface.

Hermite curve The Hermite curve is a parametric cubic curve sensitive to the end point tangents.

Hermite interpolation Hermite interpolation uses parametric polynomials to interpolate between two points and their associated curve slopes.

Hermite patch A Hermite patch is a Cartesian product patch employing a Hermite interpolation between the corner points, corner slopes and corner twist vectors.

Hidden-line removal Hidden-line removal is a process for identifying edges that are invisible or partially occulted by surfaces and suppressing them before they are displayed.

Hidden-surface removal Hidden-surface removal is a hardware or software process for ensuring that the final rendered view of a 3-D scene has overlapping or penetrating surfaces correctly visualized.

Hierarchy A hierarchy is an organization of things connected in such a way that a unique path exists between any two.

Hither clipping plane See **Front clipping plane**.

Hold A hold is a single image frame repeated a specified number of times within an animation sequence.

Homogeneous coordinates Homogeneous coordinates extend Cartesian coordinates with an extra value such that if (x, y, z) are the existing Cartesian coordinates in 3-D, the homogeneous form is specified as (x', y', z', h) where $x = x'/h$, $y = y'/h$ and $z = z'/h$.

HSV colour model The HSV colour model uses the attributes hue, saturation and value to describe a colour.

Hue Hue is the attribute given to a colour to describe its relative position within the spectrum.

Hue circle A hue circle organizes colours in a circle so that any hue can be specified either by an angle between 0° and 360° or by a fractional number.

Icon An icon is a graphic design symbolizing an action or thing.

Icosahedron An icosahedron is a platonic object constructed from 20 equilateral triangles.

Illumination model An illumination model describes how light is emitted, reflected, transmitted and absorbed within a computer graphics environment.

Image plane The image plane is synonymous with picture plane.

Image space Image space is the image plane where a projection of a 3-D scene has been captured.

Implicit surface An algebraic surface is an implicit surface as it describes implicitly the relationship between three variables.

Inbetweening In the cartoon industry a skilled animator draws the key frames for a short sequence, and an 'inbetweener' develops the inbetween images.

Incident light Incident light is the light actually arriving at a surface and is the basis for computing the reflected light received by the camera.

Index of refraction See **Refractive index**.

Instance An instance of an object is a reference to the original geometry plus the matrix operations that position it in space.

Instance transform An instance transform is a matrix representing a scaling, rotation and translation operation to create an instance of an object.

Interactive computer graphics Interactive computer graphics is a generic term for computer systems providing users with real-time two-way graphical communication.

Interpenetrating objects Interpenetrating objects is the term given to the situation in which one object's data describes it as intersecting another's.

Interpolating spline Interpolating splines intersect their control points.

Interpolation Interpolation is the process of computing intermediate values between known values.

Inverse dynamics Inverse dynamics provides the numerical tools for determining the forces required to compute the movements of points on an articulated system of links.

Inverse perspective mapping Inverse perspective mapping is used to transform a point on the image plane back into the object space from whence it came.

Jaggies Jaggies is a popular name for the staircase stepping associated with pixel-based displays or graph plotters.

Key-frame animation Key-frame animation refers to the automatic process of generating images between selected key frames.

Knot A knot is the join between two curve segments forming a spline and is represented by a parameter value.

Knot vector A knot vector is a sequence of non-decreasing parameter values (knots) used in the generation of B-spline curves.

Lambert's cosine law Lambert's cosine law states that the light reflected from a dull matte surface is proportional to the incident light and the cosine of the angle between the incident light vector and the surface normal.

Left-handed axes A left-handed set of 3-D Cartesian axes is where one's left-hand thumb is aligned with the x-axis, the first finger with the y-axis and the middle finger with the z-axis.

Light source A light source is a virtual source of illumination upon which a renderer can make intensity calculations for surfaces.

Light source direction The light source direction for a directional, distributed or spot light source specifies the orientation of the radiant light in the form of a vector.

Linear A linear relationship is described by a polynomial of degree 1.

Linear interpolation Linear interpolation computes the values between two extreme values depending upon the status of some parameter such that linear changes in the parameter produce linear changes in the interpolated values.

Linear transformation Linear transformations such as shearing, scaling, rotation and reflection ensure that when they operate upon a linear combination of vectors this linearity is preserved.

Line test A line test is the testing of an animation sequence in real-time, normally while the images are still in line form.

Lofted surface A lofted surface or ruled surface is formed by linearly interpolating between several offset 3-D curves.

Look-up table (LUT) A LUT is a memory-based device used with frame stores, containing colour intensities substituted for the values held in the frame store.

Look-up table animation Look-up table animation creates an animated effect by altering the colour values stored in the LUT.

LUT See **Look-up table**.

Mach band Mach bands are created by the human visual system by emphasizing intensity changes occurring at a boundary.

Mapping A mapping is a transformation taking points or sets of points to other points or sets of points.

Material editing Material editing is a feature of an interactive system enabling a user to create and modify physical attributes assigned to objects such as texture, bumpiness or displacement.

Matrix A matrix is an n by m arrangement of numbers.

Matrix operation A matrix operation in computer graphics includes scaling, translation and rotation.

Matte Matte means (a) dull; or (b) an opaque shape (stencil) used to isolate a portion of an image. This is often found in paint systems and video animation techniques in which part of an image needs to be isolated.

Menu A menu is a choice of actions presented to a user in a tabular form within an interactive computer system.

Mid-point displacement Mid-point displacement is a fractal modelling technique where the midpoint of a 2-D line segment or a 3-D surface element is displaced by a Gaussian random offset.

Mip maps Mip maps are a hierarchical set of filtered texture maps developed to reduce the time spent in anti-aliasing during texture mapping operations.

Modelling Modelling is a variety of disparate techniques used for representing structures within a computer graphics system.

Model sheets In traditional animation, model sheets are used to illustrate a character from different angles and in a variety of poses.

Moiré patterns Moiré patterns are a moving wave-like effect often caused by interfering regular patterns such as repetitive texture displayed upon a raster device.

Monitor A monitor is a raster display device capable of accepting video signals direct from video equipment or a computer frame store, where the signals might be RGB or composite video.

Monochrome A monochrome image consists of a range of grey levels.

Motion blur Motion blur is based upon the observation that when moving objects are recorded upon film, they will leave a blurred image because of the finite exposure time.

Mouse A mouse is a pointing device used in interactive computer graphics systems to control the screen's cursor.

Natural phenomena modelling Natural phenomena modelling is the modelling of phenomena such as fire, water, mist, waves and trees.

Near plane See **Front clipping plane**.

Non-linear transformation A non-linear transformation such as bending, perspective, spherical, twisting or free form deformation does not preserve geometric properties such as area, length, angles and volume.

Normal The term normal is either used to imply an orthogonal relationship or is synonymous with surface normal.

Normalization Normalization refers to the process of adjusting a vector's magnitude to unity.

Normal vector A normal vector is orthogonal to a surface.

Normal vector interpolation See **Phong shading**.

NURBS NURBS is an acronym for non-uniform rational B-splines.

Object space Object space is the WCS.

Obtuse angle An obtuse angle is an angle between 90° and 180°.

Octahedron An octahedron is a platonic object constructed from eight equilateral triangles.

Octree An octree is a 3-D space partitioning strategy where a volume is recursively divided into a hierarchical organization of octants.

Opacity Opacity is an attribute associated with a surface describing its efficacy at absorbing light, and is the opposite of transparency.

Opacity map An opacity map is a table or matrix of numerical values representing the opacity levels to be applied to a surface during rendering.

Opacity mapping Opacity mapping is a rendering feature where an opacity map is used to modulate the opacity of a surface to reveal underlying detail.

Opaque surface An opaque surface will not transmit light.

Orthogonal Orthogonal means at right angles to some datum.

Painter's algorithm The painter's algorithm, which is also known as the depth sort algorithm, renders an image by rendering distant objects before close objects.

Paint system A paint system is an interactive computer graphics environment that allows a user to develop a coloured image upon a screen using actions and features of traditional painting.

PAL PAL is an acronym for phase alternation line and is the UK television standard.

Palette A palette is a collection of colours.

Panning Panning is the process of moving a camera or viewpoint horizontally or vertically across a scene.

Parallel Parallel lines and planes remain a constant distance apart.

Parameter A parameter is a variable used for controlling the value of a mathematical function.

Parameter space A parameter space refers to the spatial domain where parameters belonging to some parametric process can be organized and manipulated.

Parametric curve A parametric curve is defined by coordinates derived from functions sharing some common parameter.

Parametric surface patch A Bézier, B-spline, Coons and Ferguson are parametric surface patches.

Particle system A particle system consists of discrete particles controlled by numerical values representing their position, size, velocity, colour, lifetime, birth time, etc.

Patch A patch is a portion of a surface whose geometry is defined parametrically such that slope continuity is preserved at the boundaries.

Penumbra Penumbra is the blurred border of a shadow caused by multiple diffuse reflections or a distributed light source.

Perpendicular Perpendicular means at right angles to a line or surface.

Persistence Persistence is (a) a phosphor's ability to continue glowing after it is no longer being excited; or (b) the retina's ability to remain excited when it has been stimulated, creating an after-vision effect, and is also related to the eye's fusion frequency.

Perspective foreshortening Perspective foreshortening is the size reduction as an object recedes from an observer.

Perspective transformation A perspective transformation is used to create a perspective projection by projecting points in object space onto some picture plane.

Phong shading Phong shading employs average normal interpolation to compute the colour intensities across a surface.

Phosphor A phosphor is a substance which when excited by an electron beam radiates light of a certain colour.

Photorealism Photorealism is the quest of some researchers to create images that are indistinguishable from photographs of real-world scenes.

Picture plane The picture plane is the projection plane in projections such as parallel and perspective.

Piecewise curves Piecewise curves are curve segments that can be used to construct other complex curves.

Pinhole camera In a pinhole camera, a small hole on one side of a light-tight box allows light rays to impinge upon a photographic film on the opposite side of the box.

Pitch Pitch is a rotational movement about a horizontal x-axis orthogonal to the facing z-direction.

Pixel A pixel is the smallest picture element addressable upon a display screen.

Pixel footprint A pixel's footprint refers to its shape when it is projected back onto some surface in the object space.

Planar Planar is synonymous with flat.

Point light source A point light source radiates light equally in all directions.

Polar coordinates Polar coordinates are a system for locating a point in space using radial measurements and angles.

Polygon A polygon is a figure formed by a closed chain of straight line segments.

Polygonal mesh A polygonal mesh is a structure formed from a family of interlocking polygons.

Polyhedron A polyhedron is a multi-faceted solid object constructed from polygons.

Polynomial A monomial term in mathematics describes a quantity raised to any power. A polynomial may have many such terms.

Pop-up menu A pop-up menu literally 'pops up' on the screen when a specific task is requested and disappears after a menu item has been selected.

Post-production Post-production encompasses all the procedures needed to integrate the many individual sequences that go to make up the final piece of video graphics.

Primary colours A primary colour implies that it is pure in the sense that it is not the product of a mixing process.

Primitive A primitive is a graphical entity such as a line, circle, cube or sphere which can be used for constructing more complex structures.

Procedural animation Rule-based animation, or procedural animation, involves some algorithmic procedure to describe how an animation sequence proceeds.

Procedural texture Texture generated by functions rather than from texture maps is called procedural texture.

Program A program is an organized sequence of computer instructions.

Projection A projection is a mathematical technique for converting a system of n-dimensional points into an $(n-1)$-dimensional space.

Projection plane A projection plane is a planar surface, generally orthogonal to a principal 3-D axis, which enables points of intersection to be calculated where lines connect object vertices to a centre of projection.

Pseudo-colouring Pseudo-colouring or false-colouring refers to the substitution of levels stored in a frame store by colours held in a look-up table.

Quadratic A quadratic equation is a polynomial which has no terms with a power greater than two.

Quadratic surface patch A quadratic surface patch is a surface patch description which relies upon second-order equations to identify points upon the surface.

Quaternions Quaternions are an extension of the notion of complex numbers and are used in computer graphics to resolve the problems encountered when angles are used to control the rotation of objects and the observer.

Radian A radian is an angular measurement where, by definition, 2π radians is equivalent to 360°.

Radiosity Radiosity is a global illumination model used for computing surface light intensities resulting from multiple diffuse reflections.

Random Random implies without order.

Raster A raster refers to one line of pixels drawn upon a CRT.

Raster computer graphics Raster computer graphics encompasses those techniques associated with the display of images upon pixel-based devices.

Rational A rational number can be represented by a ratio of two whole numbers.

Rational polynomial Rational polynomials are expressed as the ratio of two polynomials.

Ray casting Ray casting is a hidden-surface detection strategy generally associated with rendering CSG objects.

Ray intersection point In ray tracing a ray intersection point identifies where a cast ray intersects with a surface in object space.

Ray intersection tree In ray tracing the ray intersection tree stores the hierarchy of rays transmitted and reflected for one sample point.

Ray tracing The ray tracing algorithm traces the origins of the single light ray which arrives through the centre of a pixel.

Real-time The term 'real-time' implies that a computer system is capable of reacting in the user's own time domain, so that there is no observable delay between a user command and a computer response.

Recursive algorithm A recursive algorithm references itself as part of its strategy in solving a problem.

Reflectance model A reflectance model is a basis upon which reflection calculations are made.

Reflection coefficient The reflection coefficient is a surface attribute controlling the quantity of light reflected back from some incident source.

Reflection vector A reflection vector identifies the direction of a reflected light ray away from a surface.

Refraction of light Refraction is the change of direction of light when it moves from one medium to another and undergoes a speed change.

Refresh rate The refresh rate is the frequency with which a raster display is refreshed.

Renderer A renderer is a program for creating a shaded synthetic image based upon 3-D geometric descriptions, surface attributes and an illumination model.

RenderMan Pixar's RenderMan product is a powerful interface specification between 3-D modelling and photorealistic rendering techniques.

Resolution Resolution is a measure of a system's ability to display fine detail accurately.

Reyes The Reyes rendering system is a software package whose name is derived from the claim that it 'Renders Everything You Ever Saw'.

RGB RGB is an acronym for red, green and blue.

RGB colour model The RGB colour model employs a colour space consisting of a 3-D set of Cartesian axes labelled red, green and blue.

Right-handed axes Cartesian axes can be formed with a left- or right-handed configuration: the latter would have one's right-hand thumb aligned with the x-axis, the first finger with the y-axis and the middle finger with the z-axis.

Rigid-body animation Rigid-body animation is concerned with the modelling and animation of rigid bodies physically interacting with one another over a period of time.

Rotation matrix A rotation matrix enables single vertices to be rotated about a point or axis by a specified angle.

Rule-based animation See **Procedural animation**.

Saturation Saturation relates to the purity of coloured light in terms of the white light component and the remaining colour component.

Scalar A scalar value is a quantity which has magnitude only.

Scaling matrix A scaling matrix performs a size change.

Scan-line A scan-line is a horizontal line of pixels forming one raster.

Scan-line algorithm A scan-line algorithm proceeds on a raster scan-line by scan-line in a certain order.

Scientific visualization Scientific visualization is concerned with the use of computer graphics to visualize multi-dimensional data associated with scientific projects as an aid to its understanding and interpretation.

Screen coordinates Screen coordinates is an addressing scheme for referencing pixels on a screen.

Set-theoretic modelling See **Constructive solid geometry**.

Shading Shading refers to the process of colouring the surfaces of an object.

Shading model A shading model defines the rules used to compute illumination levels in rendering.

Shadow volume A shadow volume is a volume of space associated with a light source and an object, and is constructed by developing projection lines from a light source to the silhouette edges of the object to define a projected volume behind the object in shadow.

Shear matrix A shear or skew matrix is an affine transformation which distorts a shape but preserves parallel lines.

Silhouette edge The boundary shape of an object, or its silhouette edge, is a projected view of a 3-D object.

Sine In the context of right-angled triangles, the sine of an angle is the ratio of the opposite edge over the hypotenuse.

Slow-in/slow-out In traditional animation slow-in/slow-out relates to the spacing of drawings in an animated sequence, and ultimately influences the degree of attack or hesitation incorporated into a movement.

Soft objects Soft objects describe a class of non-rigid structures that are modelled from surfaces of constant value from a scalar field.

Solid angle A solid angle measures a 3-D subtended angle formed by a surface to a point in units of steradians.

Solid modelling Solid modelling are modelling schemes for describing 3-D objects containing sufficient geometric detail that a numerically controlled machine can be used for their creation.

Solid texture Solid texture is generated by procedures capable of assigning texture modulations to a volume of space.

Space filling curves Space filling curves are theoretically capable of covering completely an area with an infinite length but finite area.

Spacers In animation spacers are blank frames used to set the location of other frames in compositing.

Spatial aliasing Spatial aliasing occurs in computer graphics when a geometric description of a shape is sampled at a spatial resolution incompatible with its highest detail.

Specular reflection A specular reflection is the reflection of a light source seen by an observer on a reflective surface.

Specular reflection coefficient The specular reflection coefficient is a fractional value used to modulate the intensity of the specular reflection.

Spline A spline is a polynomial curve that can be formed by a sequence of control points.

Spot light A spot light is a light source capable of illuminating a scene within a restricted angular cone.

Stochastic Stochastic is synonymous with random processes.

Storyboard A storyboard is a collection of drawings illustrating key images within an animation sequence.

Surface normal A surface normal is a normal vector at a particular point on a surface.

Surface of revolution See **Swept surface**.

Surface patch A complex surface can be constructed from a collection of surface patches which only have a simple geometric definition.

Swept surface A swept surface is a 3-D surface formed by rotating a 2-D contour about an axis.

Tablet A tablet is a small active surface used as a digitizer in conjunction with a stylus.

Temporal aliasing Temporal aliasing occurs when the sampling rate in the time domain is insufficient to detect spatial changes caused by moving objects.

Texel A texel is the smallest addressable element of a texture map.

Texture map A texture map is a 2-D pattern of pixel intensities derived synthetically, procedurally or input from an external image, for use as a surface decoration using a texture-mapping algorithm.

Texture mapping Texture mapping is the process of substituting detail stored within a reference source of texture (map) onto a surface having any arbitrary orientation.

Transformation In computer graphics, a transformation performs some mathematical operation upon one or more Cartesian coordinates.

Translation matrix A translation displaces a shape or object by specified distances.

Translucency Translucency describes a property associated with materials which, while transmitting light, destroy any coherence associated with the incident light.

Translucent surface A translucent surface transmits, refracts and reflects light without preserving any incident coherence.

Transparency Transparency is an attribute assigned to objects to mimic the transmissive qualities of substances such as glass.

Transparency coefficient A transparency coefficient is a fractional value associated to an object controlling the amount of incident light transmitted by the surface.

Transparent surface A transparent surface is a surface that will transmit any incident light, as determined by a transparency coefficient.

Transpose matrix A transpose matrix is formed by changing every element of a matrix $M_{\text{row, col}}$ into $M_{\text{col, row}}$.

Triangle A triangle is a three-sided polygon.

Triangulation Triangulation is the process of reducing a shape to a collection of triangles.

Twisted facet A twisted facet is not planar and has no single surface normal.

Twist vectors Twist vectors are associated with the definition of a Hermite surface patch where four twist vectors are used to control the degree of 'twist' applied to the corners.

Unit vector The magnitude of a unit vector is one.

Update rate The update rate defines the rate at which a display system is modified with new image detail.

***uv*-coordinates** In mapping operations, uv-coordinates are generally associated with a parameter space.

Value The Munsell colour system value is equivalent to the term lightness.

Vector A vector quantity has magnitude and direction.

Vector product Given two distinct vectors, the vector product operation creates a third vector orthogonal to the plane containing the original vectors.

Vertex A vertex defines the end of an edge.

Vertex colour A vertex colour is the colour assigned to a vertex for achieving a blended colour effect across a surface.

Vertex normal A vertex normal is an orthogonal unit vector associated with a vertex.

Video disk A video disk is a digital storage device holding raster images which can be retrieved at video rates with the aid of a laser-driven playback unit.

View vector A view vector establishes the orientation of the observer and can be defined by the position of the observer using the eye point and aim point.

Virtual reality (VR) VR technology permits the user to interact with the virtual worlds displayed by computer graphics systems.

Voxel A voxel is a volume of space and represents the 3-D equivalent of a pixel.

Walk-through The term walk-through is generally used in computer graphics systems employed for architectural applications, where the computer's 'eye' dynamically traces a path equivalent to a 'walk-through' in the modelled scene.

Wire frame The term wire frame is used to describe a view of a 3-D object, where all edges are drawn, producing a 'see-through' wire-like image.

Workstation A workstation is a configuration of a processor, screen, keyboard and local disk-storage, all of which are generally connected to a local area network (LAN).

World coordinate system (WCS) The world coordinate system is a reference space for constructing 3-D models, light sources, an observer and any trajectories employed for animation purposes.

Wrapping Wrapping is a mathematical operation for distorting an image to follow the surface contour of a reference object.

***x*-coordinate** The x-coordinate of a point is a linear measurement along the x-axis from the origin to the point.

Yaw Yaw is a rotational movement about a vertical *y*-axis and is normally used in conjunction with roll and pitch to orient an object or observer.

***y*-coordinate** The *y*-coordinate of a point is a linear measurement along the *y*-axis from the origin to the point.

Yon clipping plane See **Back clipping plane**.

z-buffer A z-buffer is a memory buffer normally built into graphics workstations, which stores for every pixel in an image *z*-depth values in eye coordinate space of the nearest surface.

z-buffer algorithm The z-buffer algorithm is a hidden-surface removal algorithm which uses a z-buffer.

***z*-coordinate** The *z*-coordinate of a point is a linear measurement along the *z*-axis from the origin to the point.

***z*-depth** The *z*-coordinates of objects represent the *z*-depths from the camera in the CCS.

Zoom Zoom is a facility to enlarge or decrease the size of part of an image.

zz-buffer The zz-buffer is a hidden-surface removal algorithm based upon the z-buffer algorithm but overcomes the latter's difficulties in handling transparent surfaces and anti-aliasing.

Subject References

To develop a thorough understanding of any subject it is often useful to read a number of books by different authors; this not only increases one's perspective of the subject but consolidates this knowledge through different examples, personal experiences and perhaps clearer descriptions. It is also necessary to read original research papers where an author has revealed an idea for the first time. Unfortunately, some researchers are not always able to present their discoveries to a level of detail often needed by their readers, while others can communicate this new knowledge with such clarity that they can be quickly implemented into one's own software.

In order that you can delve deeper into this fascinating subject, some useful books and technical papers are listed below. Some are in the form of Doctoral and Master's theses, which you may find difficult to obtain, but very often the author has also taken the trouble of presenting his or her results in an international technical journal. Many of the references refer to papers presented at computer graphic conferences, especially SIGGRAPH; these are very easy to obtain and are generally very informative. Others refer to books covering different aspects of computer graphics and computer animation and are still in circulation.

Not all of the sections and sub-sections in this book are identified, as the references are associated with the major subject relating to the topic. For example, references for *3.1 Wire frame* and *3.2 Boundary representation* are listed under *3 Introduction*. To simplify the list only the first author's name is given. Full details of the references can be found in the following chapter.

2 Review of Computer Graphics

Introduction

(Burger, 1989) (Earnshaw, 1985) (Foley, 1990) (Hayward, 1984) (Hearn, 1986) (Hunter, 1977) (Kunii, 1983) (Kunii, 1985b) (Levitan, 1977) (Lorig, 1986) (Magnenat-Thalmann, 1985b) (Magnenat-Thalmann, 1987) (Rogers, 1985) (Rogers, 1990) (Vince, 1985) (Vince, 1987) (Vince, 1989b) (Vince, 1990)

2.3 Clipping the camera's view

(Blinn, 1978a) (Blinn, 1991a) (Cyrus, 1978) (Liang, 1983) (Nicholl, 1987) (Sproull, 1968) (Sutherland, 1974)

2.4 Colour theory

(Boynton, 1979) (Foley, 1990) (Gregory, 1986) (Hunt, 1975) (Joblove, 1978) (Meyer, 1980) (Munsell, 1941) (Ostwald, 1931) (Robertson, 1988) (Smith, 1978) (Smith, 1979) (Watt, 1989)

2.5 Computer graphics hardware

(Shoup, 1979a)

3 Modelling Schemes

Introduction

(Barsky, 1984) (Bohm, 1984) (Burger, 1989) (Casale, 1985) (Devai, 1987) (Farin, 1988) (Foley, 1990) (Max, 1983) (Max, 1988) (Requicha, 1980) (Requicha, 1983) (Rogers, 1990) (Vince, 1990) (Woodwark, 1986)

3.2 Boundary representation

3.2.4 Free-form surfaces

(Barr, 1984) (Barsky, 1981) (Barsky, 1983) (Barsky, 1984) (Barsky, 1988) (Bedi, 1989) (Casale, 1987) (Chiyokura, 1987) (Coons, 1967) (Crocker, 1987) (Goldman, 1983) (Goodman, 1986) (Green, 1981) (Joe, 1987) (Miller, 1988b) (Rockwood, 1987) (Rockwood, 1989) (Sederberg, 1990a) (Sederberg, 1990b) (Shantz, 1987) (Steinberg, 1984)

3.2.7 Bézier surface patches

(Bézier, 1973) (Crow, 1987) (Farin, 1988)

3.2.9 B-spline surface patches

(Farin, 1988) (Forsey, 1988) (Loop, 1990) (Piegl, 1991) (Rogers, 1983) (Shantz, 1988) (Tiller, 1983)

3.3 Volumetric representation

3.3.1 Constructive solid geometry

(Arbab, 1990) (Dobkin, 1988) (Laidlaw, 1986) (Latham, 1989) (Latham, 1990) (Middleditch, 1985) (Wyvill, 1985)

3.3.2 Spatial subdivision

(Doctor, 1981) (Galyean, 1991) (Kunii, 1985a) (Yamaguchi, 1984)

3.4 Procedural modelling

3.4.1 Fractals

(Barnsley, 1988) (Brownrigg, 1987) (Carpenter, 1980) (Cheung, 1988) (Demko, 1985) (Foley, 1990) (Fournier, 1982) (Fournier, 1985) (Hart, 1991) (Mandelbrot, 1968) (Mandelbrot, 1975) (Mandelbrot, 1977) (Mandelbrot, 1982) (Marshall, 1980) (Peitgen, 1986) (Peitgen, 1988) (Voss, 1985)

3.4.2 Soft objects

(Blinn, 1982b) (Bloomenthal, 1987) (Bloomenthal, 1991) (McPheeters, 1990) (Muraki, 1991) (Nishimura, 1985) (Pasko, 1988) (Quarendon, 1987) (Wright, 1979) (Wyvill, 1986a) (Wyvill, 1986b) (Wyvill, 1986c) (Wyvill, 1987) (Wyvill, 1989) (Zyda, 1988)

3.5 Data structures

(Samet, 1988a) (Samet, 1988b) (Standish, 1980)

4 Rendering

Introduction

(Burger, 1989) (Foley, 1990) (McEwan, 1988) (Rogers, 1985) (Strauss, 1990) (Upstill, 1989) (Verbeck, 1984) (Watt, 1989)

4.2 Reflection models

(Blinn, 1977) (Blinn, 1982a) (Cook, 1982a) (Cook, 1982b) (Cook, 1984b) (Hall, 1986) (He, 1991) (Ikanage, 1986) (Kajiya, 1985) (Kajiya, 1986) (Poulin, 1990) (Tezenas du Montcel, 1985) (Torrance, 1967)

4.3 Shading techniques

(Gouraud, 1971) (Phong, 1973)

4.4 Hidden-surface techniques

(Burger, 1989) (Foley, 1990) (Rogers, 1985) (Watt, 1989)

4.4.5 A-buffer

(Carpenter, 1984) (Cook, 1987) (Haeberli, 1990) (Magnenat-Thalmann, 1986a)

4.4.6 ZZ-buffer

(Salesin, 1989) (Salesin, 1990)

4.5 Ray tracing

(Akimoto, 1991) (Burger, 1989) (Cook, 1984a) (Cook, 1986) (Dias, 1991) (Foley, 1990) (Glassner, 1984) (Glassner, 1989) (Hart, 1989) (Heckbert, 1984) (Kajiya, 1982) (Kajiya, 1983) (Kajiya, 1984) (Kay, 1979a) (Kay, 1979b) (Kay, 1986)

(Nishita, 1990) (Painter, 1989) (Roth, 1982) (Sequin, 1989) (Wallace, 1989) (Ward, 1988) (Watt, 1989) (Weghorst, 1984) (Whitted, 1980) (Wolff, 1990) (Youssef, 1986)

4.6 Radiosity

(Baum, 1989) (Baum, 1991) (Bergman, 1986) (Buckalew, 1989) (Campbell, 1990) (Chen, 1990a) (Chen, 1990b) (Cohen, 1985) (Cohen, 1986) (Cohen, 1988) (Foley, 1990) (George, 1990) (Goral, 1984) (Greenberg, 1989) (Hanrahan 1991) (Heckbert, 1990) (Immel, 1986) (Nishita, 1985) (Shao, 1988) (Sillion, 1989) (Wallace, 1987) (Watt, 1989)

5 Realism

Introduction

(Abram, 1990) (Amanatides, 1987a) (Amanatides, 1987b) (Carey, 1985) (Foley, 1990) (Greenberg, 1991) (Hanrahan, 1990) (Rogers, 1985) (Upstill, 1989) (Watt, 1989)

5.1 Anti-aliasing

(Barkans, 1991) (Blinn, 1989a) (Blinn, 1989b) (Blinn, 1989c) (Crow, 1981) (Crow, 1986) (Dippe, 1985) (Forrest, 1985) (Fujimoto, 1983) (Lee, 1990b) (Max, 1990b) (Mitchell, 1991)

5.2 Texture mapping

(Bennis, 1991) (Bier, 1986) (Blinn, 1976) (Blinn, 1990a) (Crow, 1984) (Fiume, 1987) (Gangnet, 1982) (Glassner, 1986) (Heckbert, 1986) (Hourcade, 1983) (Oka, 1987) (Samek, 1986) (Smith, 1987) (Turk, 1991) (Williams, 1983a) (Witkin, 1991)

5.3 Bump mapping

(Blinn, 1978b) (Cabral, 1987)

5.4 Shadows

(Bergeron, 1986) (Brotman, 1984) (Chin, 1989) (Crow, 1977) (Haines, 1986) (Hourcade, 1985) (Reeves, 1987) (Williams, 1978) (Woo, 1990)

5.5 Motion blur

(Glassner, 1988) (Goss, 1991) (Grant, 1985) (Haeberli, 1990) (Korein, 1983) (Max, 1985) (Potmesil, 1983)

5.6 Depth of field

(Chen, 1987) (Dippe, 1985) (Goss, 1991) (Haeberli, 1990) (Potmesil, 1981) (Potmesil, 1982)

5.7 Solid texture

(Lewis, 1989) (Monne, 1981) (Peachey, 1985) (Perlin, 1985) (Perlin, 1989) (Sims, 1991) (Wijk, 1991) (Wyvill, 1987)

5.10 RenderMan

(Apodaca, 1990) (Upstill, 1989)

6 Traditional Animation

Introduction

(Finch, 1973) (Laybourne, 1979) (Stern, 1979) (White, 1986)

6.1 History of animation

(Magnenat-Thalmann, 1985b) (Whitney, 1971)

7 Computer Animation Tools

Introduction

(Chuang, 1983) (Foley, 1990) (Fox, 1984) (Kallis, 1971) (Rogers, 1990) (Smith, 1985) (Upstill, 1989)

7.2 Animating numbers

(Fletcher, 1987) (Foley, 1990) (Rogers, 1990)

7.3 Parametric blending techniques

(Foley, 1990) (Kochanek, 1984) (Rogers, 1990)

7.4 Space curves

(Barry, 1988) (Barsky, 1985) (Barsky, 1990) (Bézier, 1973) (Burger, 1989) (Catmull, 1974) (Farin, 1988) (Fletcher, 1990) (Forrest, 1972) (Forsey, 1988) (Nielson, 1986) (Piegl, 1987b) (Rogers, 1990) (Smith, 1983a)

8 The 3-D Animation Environment

Introduction

(Foley, 1990) (Rogers, 1990) (Magnenat-Thalmann, 1986b)

8.3 Animating an object's attributes

8.3.1 Interpolating shape

(Reeves, 1980) (Reeves, 1981)

8.3.2 Interpolating position
(Badler, 1975) (Guenter, 1990)

8.3.3 Interpolating rotation
(Fillmore, 1984)

8.3.4 Interpolating roll, pitch and yaw angles
(Pletincks, 1988) (Shoemake, 1985)

8.3.5 Interpolating quaternions
(Funda, 1988) (Hamilton, 1969) (Heise, 1989) (Pletincks, 1988) (Rooney, 1977) (Shoemake, 1985) (Shoemake, 1987) (Taylor, 1986)

9 Modelling and Animating

Introduction
(Barr, 1984) (Carlbom, 1985) (Chaung, 1983) (Csuri, 1983) (Halas, 1974) (Hubschman, 1982) (Jansen, 1984) (Kessner, 1985) (Knowlton, 1981) (Siegel, 1987) (Vince, 1989a)

9.3 Orthogonal photographs
(Odgers, 1982) (Waters, 1986) (Waters, 1987a) (Waters, 1987b)

9.6 Linked structures
(Alt, 1988) (Armstrong, 1985) (Blinn, 1987) (Easterbrook, 1990) (Girard, 1987) (Phillips, 1991) (Raibert, 1991) (Sturman, 1984) (Wilhelms, 1985) (Wilhelms, 1987)

9.7 Fabrics
(Feynman, 1986) (Hinds, 1990) (Lloyd, 1980) (Lloyd, 1988) (Miller, 1984) (Scanlon, 1990) (Terzopoulos, 1987) (Terzopoulos, 1988a) (Terzopoulos, 1988b) (Weil, 1986)

9.8 The human form

9.8.1 The human head
(Parke, 1974) (Parke, 1975) (Parke, 1979) (Parke, 1982) (Platt, 1981) (Waters, 1986) (Waters, 1987a) (Waters, 1987b) (Waters, 1989) (Williams, 1990)

9.8.2 The human body
(Badler, 1979a) (Badler, 1979b) (Badler, 1980) (Badler, 1982a) (Badler, 1982b) (Badler, 1984) (Bergeron, 1985) (Gourret, 1989) (Herbison-Evans, 1983a) (Herbison-Evans, 1983b) (Magnenat-Thalmann, 1991a) (Monheit, 1991) (Murugaiyan, 1991) (O'Rourke, 1979) (Potter, 1975) (Rijpkema, 1991) (Weber, 1978) (Willmert, 1978)

9.9 Natural phenomena

(Barnsley, 1985) (Barr, 1987) (Berger, 1990) (Coquillart, 1984) (Day, 1988) (de Reffye, 1988) (Dungan, 1979) (Ebert, 1990) (Fournier, 1986) (Gardner, 1984) (Gardner, 1985) (Green, 1988) (Greene, 1989) (Guyett, 1989) (Halton, 1970) (Kajiya, 1989) (Kelley, 1988) (Lewis, 1989) (Marshall, 1980) (Mastin, 1987) (Max, 1986) (Max, 1990a) (Middleton, 1952) (Miller, 1986) (Miller, 1988a) (Miyata, 1990) (Musgrave, 1989) (Nakamae, 1990) (Nishita, 1986) (Nishita, 1987) (Oppenheimer, 1986) (Peachey, 1986) (Perlin, 1989) (Petrick, 1988) (Prusinkiewicz, 1988) (Rodwell, 1991) (Rushmeier, 1987) (Schachter, 1983) (Selley, 1990) (Smith, 1984) (Szeliski, 1989) (Viennot, 1989) (Watt, 1990) (Willis, 1987) (Yaeger, 1986)

9.9.1 Particle systems

(Allen, 1990) (Glazzard, 1987) (Goss, 1990) (Reeves, 1983) (Reeves, 1985) (Sims, 1990)

9.9.2 Growth models

(Selley, 1990) (Selley, 1991)

10 Special Animation Techniques

10.1 Key-frame animation

(Brotman, 1988) (Burtnyk, 1976) (Steketee, 1985) (Sturman, 1983)

10.3 Free-form deformation

(Comninos, 1989) (Coquillart, 1990) (Coquillart, 1991) (Parry, 1986) (Sederberg, 1986) (Thompson, 1961)

10.4 Displacement animation

(Schafer, 1989)

10.5 Behavioural animation

(Amkraut, 1985) (Bell, 1990) (Rainjonneau, 1990) (Reynolds, 1978) (Reynolds, 1985) (Reynolds, 1987a) (Reynolds, 1987b) (Wilhelms, 1990)

10.6 Dynamic simulation

(Alt, 1988) (Armstrong, 1985) (Badler, 1987) (Baraff, 1989) (Baraff, 1990) (Baraff, 1991) (Barzel, 1987) (Barzel, 1988) (Bruderlin, 1989) (Calvert, 1978) (Calvert, 1980) (Calvert, 1982a) (Calvert, 1982b) (Chadwick, 1989) (Dai, 1989) (Duff, 1976) (Fetter, 1982) (Girard, 1985) (Hahn, 1988) (Isaacs, 1987) (Kass, 1990) (Lee, 1990a) (Loizidou, 1990) (Maciejewski, 1990) (McKenna, 1990) (Miller, 1989) (Moore, 1988) (Niemoller, 1990) (Panne, 1990) (Paul, 1981) (Pentland, 1989) (Platt, 1988) (Sims, 1987) (Stern, 1983) (Vasilonikolidakis, 1989) (Vasilonikolidakis, 1990) (vonHerzen, 1990) (Wejchert, 1991) (Witkin, 1987) (Witkin, 1988) (Zeltzer, 1981) (Zeltzer, 1982a) (Zeltzer, 1982b) (Zeltzer, 1982c) (Zeltzer, 1983) (Zeltzer, 1985)

11 Animation Systems

Introduction

(Ackland, 1980) (Ashdown, 1988) (Balchin, 1983) (Booth, 1982) (Booth, 1983) (Brown, 1984) (Carlee, 1989) (Csuri, 1974a) (Csuri, 1974b) (Csuri, 1975) (DeFanti, 1976) (DeFanti, 1980) (DeFanti, 1983) (Dietrich, 1983) (Edwards, 1987) (Feiner, 1982) (Fortin, 1983) (Fuchs, 1983) (Fuchs, 1985) (Futrelle, 1974) (Geschwind, 1982) (Goldstein, 1971a) (Goldstein, 1971b) (Gomez, 1984) (Goss, 1983) (Hackathorn, 1977) (Hackathorn, 1981) (Herbison-Evans, 1978) (Herbison-Evans, 1982) (Inglish, 1988) (Kahn, 1976) (Kahn, 1979) (Knowlton, 1972) (Litwinowicz, 1991) (Magnenat-Thalmann, 1983a) (Magnenat-Thalmann, 1983b) (Magnenat-Thalmann, 1984) (Magnenat-Thalmann, 1985a) (Magnenat-Thalmann, 1985c) (Nicolas, 1989) (O'Donnel, 1981) (Potmesil, 1987) (Ressler, 1982) (Reynolds, 1982) (Steele, 1989) (Thalmann, 1984) (Thalmann, 1985) (Thornton, 1983) (Watt, 1992) (Williams, 1983b) (Wootton, 1990)

11.1 Historical background

(Baecker, 1969a) (Baecker, 1969b) (Baecker, 1970) (Baecker, 1971) (Baecker, 1976) (Borrell, 1981) (Burtnyk, 1971a) (Burtnyk, 1971b) (Burtnyk, 1974a) (Burtnyk, 1974b) (Carr, 1970) (Catmull, 1972) (Catmull, 1978) (Catmull, 1979) (Christopher, 1982) (Citron, 1968) (Crow, 1978) (Csuri, 1968) (Csuri, 1970) (Csuri, 1975) (Csuri, 1979) (Dietrich, 1983) (Dietrich, 1985) (Duff, 1976) (Fox, 1982) (Friesen, 1969) (Greenberg, 1983) (Haflinger, 1971) (Honey, 1971a) (Honey, 1971b) (Hopgood, 1969) (Kitching, 1973) (Knowlton, 1964) (Knowlton, 1965) (Knowlton, 1968) (Knowlton, 1970) (Levine, 1975) (Levoy, 1977) (Levoy, 1978) (Lieberman, 1971) (Lipscomb, 1981) (Mezei, 1971) (Mudur, 1985) (Negroponte, 1976) (Nolan, 1968) (Noll, 1965) (Noma, 1985) (Potel, 1977) (Potts, 1983) (Russet, 1976) (Shoup, 1979b) (Stern, 1978) (Talbot, 1971) (Thalmann, 1982) (Vince, 1976) (Vince, 1983) (Wallace, 1981) (Wein, 1976) (Weiner, 1968) (Whitney, 1971) (Zajac, 1966) (Zimmerlin, 1978)

12 Computer Animation Hardware

Introduction

(Staudhammer, 1991)

12.3 Image capture

(Blinn, 1990b) (Greenberg, 1987) (Odgers, 1983)

12.4 Post-production

(Duff, 1985) (Fishkin, 1984a) (Fishkin, 1984b) (Huitric, 1985) (Kaneda, 1989) (Lewis, 1984) (Nakamae, 1986) (Nakamae, 1989) (Porter, 1984a)

13 Applications for Computer Animation

Introduction

(Comninos, 1985) (Csuri, 1991) (Dungan, 1982) (Greenberg, 1985) (Huggins, 1969) (Hurn, 1981) (Spina, 1982)

13.6 Film special effects

(Duff, 1983) (Parke, 1980) (Patterson, 1982) (Porter, 1984b) (Smith, 1983b) (Sorensen, 1982) (Sorensen, 1983) (Taylor, 1983)

13.7 3-D cartoons

(Carlee, 1989) (Inglish, 1988) (Lasseter, 1987) (Nicolas, 1989) (Phillips, 1989)

13.8 Scientific visualization

(Helman, 1991) (Nielson, 1991) (Magnenat-Thalmann, 1991b) (Thalmann, 1990)

References

Abram G.D. and Whitted T. (1990). Building block shaders. In *Proc. SIGGRAPH 1990: Computer Graphics*, **24**(4), 283–288

Ackland B. and Weste N. (1980). Real-time animation playback on a frame store display system. In *Proc. SIGGRAPH 1980: Computer Graphics*, **14**(3), 182–188

Akimoto T., Mase K. and Suenaga Y. (1991). Pixel selected ray tracing. *IEEE, CG&A*, **11**(4), 14–22

Allen P. (1990). What goes up must come down. In *Proc. CG-90: Computer Animation*, London 161–172

Alt L. and Nicolas A. (1988). Animating articulated structures with multiple goals. In *Proc. CG-88: Computer Animation*, London 215–226

Amanatides J. (1987a). Realism in computer graphics: a survey. *IEEE, CG&A*, **7**(1), 44–56

Amanatides J. (1987b). Realism in computer graphics. In *Proc. CG-87: Computer Graphics*, London 1–25

Amkraut S., Girard M. and Karl G. (1985). Motion studies for a work in progress entitled 'Eurythmy'. In *SIGGRAPH Video Review*, 21, 2nd item, 3:58 7:35

Apodaca A.A. and Mantle M.W. (1990). RenderMan: pursuing the future of graphics. *IEEE CG&A*, **10**(4), 44–49

Arbab F. (1990). Set models and boolean operations for solids and assemblies. *IEEE CG&A*, **10**(6), 76–86

Armstrong W.W. and Green M.W. (1985). The dynamics of articulated rigid bodies for purposes of animation. In *Proc. Graphics Interface '85*, Toronto, Canada, 407–415

Ashdown P. and Banks I. (1988). Objects, symbols and computer graphics. In *Proc. CG-88: Computer Animation*, London 199–213

Badler N.I. (1975). Temporal scene analysis: conceptual descriptions of object movements. *PhD Thesis*, University of Toronto

Badler N.I., O'Rourke J. and Toltzis H. (1979a). A spherical representation of a human body for visualizing movement. In *Proc. IEEE*, **67**(10), 1397–1403

Badler N.I. and Smoliar S.W. (1979b). Digital representations of human movement. *Computing Surveys*, **11**(1), 19–38

Badler N.I., O'Rourke J. and Kaufman B. (1980). Special problems in human movement simulation. In *Proc. SIGGRAPH 1980: Computer Graphics*, **14**(3), 189–197

Badler N.I. (1982a). Human body models and animation. *IEEE CG&A*, **2**(9), 6–7

Badler N.I. and Morris M.A. (1982b). Modelling flexible articulated objects. In *Proc. CG-82: Computer Animation*, London 305–314

Badler N.I. (1984). What is required for effective human figure animation? In *Proc. Graphics Interface '84*, Ottawa, Ontario, 119–120

Badler N.I., Manoochehri K.H. and Walters G. (1987). Articulated figure positioning by multiple constraints. *IEEE CG&A*, **7**(6), 28–38

Baecker R.M. (1969a). Interactive computer-mediated animation. *PhD Thesis*, Dept. of Electrical Engineering, MIT, Cambridge MA

Baecker R.M. (1969b). Picture-driven animation. In *Proc. AFIPS*, 273–288

Baecker R.M. (1970). Current issues in interactive computer-mediated animation. In *Proc. Ninth UAIDE Annual Meeting*, Miami FL

Baecker R.M. (1971). From the animated student to the animated computer to the animated film to the animated student. In *Proc. Purdue 1971 Symp. Applied Computer Electrical Eng. Educ.*, Purdue University, Lafayette IN

Baecker R.M. (1976). A conversational extensible system for the animation of shaded images. In *Proc. SIGGRAPH 1976: Computer Graphics*, **10**(2), 32–39

Balchin N. (1983). Film animation by microcomputer. In *Proc. CG-83: Computer Animation*, London 197–204

Baraff D. (1989). Analytical methods for dynamic simulation of non-penetrating rigid bodies. In *Proc. SIGGRAPH 1989: Computer Graphics*, **23**(3), 223–232

Baraff D. (1990). Curved surfaces and coherence for non-penetrating rigid body simulation. In *Proc. SIGGRAPH 1990: Computer Graphics*, **24**(4), 19–28

Baraff D. (1991). Coping with friction for non-penetrating rigid body simulation. In *Proc. SIGGRAPH 1991: Computer Graphics*, **25**(4), 31–40

Barkans A.C. (1991). Hardware-assisted polygon antialiasing. *IEEE CG&A*, **11**(1), 80–88

Barnsley M.F., Ervin V., Hardin D. and Lancaster J. (1985). Solution of an inverse problem for fractals and other sets. In *Proc. National Academy of Science*

Barnsley M.F., Jacquin A., Malassenet F., Reuter L. and Sloan A.D. (1988). Harnessing chaos for image synthesis. In *Proc. SIGGRAPH 1988: Computer Graphics*, **22**(4), 131–140

Barr A.H. (1984). Global and local deformations of solid primitives. In *Proc. SIGGRAPH 1984: Computer Graphics*, **18**(3), 21–32

Barr A.H. *et al.* (1987). Topics in physically-based modelling. In *SIGGRAPH 1987 Course Notes*

Barry P. and Goldman R.N. (1988). A recursive evaluation algorithm for a class of Catmull-Rom splines. In *Proc. SIGGRAPH 1988: Computer Graphics*, **22**(4), 199–204

Barsky B.A. (1981). The beta-spline: a local representation based on shape parameters and fundamental geometric measures. *PhD Thesis*, Dept. of Computer Science, University of Utah

Barsky B.A. and Beatty J.C. (1983). Local control of bias and tension in beta-splines. *ACM Trans. Graphics*, **2**(2), 109–134

Barsky B.A. (1984). A description and evaluation of various 3-D models. *IEEE CG&A*, **4**(1), 38–52

Barsky B.A. and DeRose T.D. (1985). The beta2-spline: a special case of the beta-spline curve and surface representation. *IEEE CG&A*, **5**(9), 46–58

Barsky B.A. (1988). *Computer Graphics and Geometric Modelling using Beta-splines*. Berlin: Springer-Verlag

Barsky B.A. and DeRose T.D. (1990). Parametric curves tutorial: geometric continuity of parametric curves. *IEEE CG&A*, **10**(1), 60–68

Barzel R. and Barr A.H. (1987). Dynamic constraints, topics in physically based modelling. In *SIGGRAPH 1987 Course Notes*

Barzel R. and Barr A.H. (1988). A modelling system based on dynamic constraints. In *Proc. SIGGRAPH 1988: Computer Graphics*, **22**(4), 179–188

Baum D.R., Rushmeier H.E. and Winget J.M. (1989). Improving radiosity solutions through the use of analytically determined form-factors. In *Proc. SIGGRAPH 1989: Computer Graphics*, **23**(3), 325–334

Baum D.R., Mann S., Smith K. and Winget J.M. (1991). Making radiosity usable: automatic preprocessing and meshing techniques for the generation of accurate radiosity solutions. In *Proc. SIGGRAPH 1991: Computer Graphics*, **25**(4), 51–60

Bedi S. and Vickers G.W. (1989). Surface lofting and smoothing with skeletal-lines. *Computer Aided Geometric Design*, **6**(2), 87–96

Bell S. (1990). Pavlovian polygons. In *Proc. CG-90: Computer Animation*, London 253–262

Bennis C., Vezien J. and Iglesias G. (1991). Piecewise surface flattening for non-distorted texture mapping. In *Proc. SIGGRAPH 1991: Computer Graphics*, **25**(4), 237–246

Berger M. and Trout T. (1990). Ray tracing mirages. *IEEE CG&A*, **10**(3), 36–41

Bergeron P. (1985). Controlling facial expressions and body movement in the computer short Tony de Peltric. In *SIGGRAPH 1985 Course Notes*

Bergeron P. (1986). A general version of Crow's shadow volumes. *IEEE CG&A*, **6**(9), 17–28

Bergman L. *et al.* (1986). Image rendering by adaptive refinement. In *Proc. SIGGRAPH 1986: Computer Graphics*, **20**(4), 29–37

Bézier P. (1973). UNISURF system principles, programme, language. In *Proc. PROLAMAT '73*, Budapest, Hungary, 417–426

Bier E.A. and Sloan K.R. (1986). Two-part texture mappings. *IEEE CG&A*, **6**(9), 40–53

Blinn J.F. and Newell M.E. (1976). Texture and reflection in computer generated images. *Comm. ACM*, **19**, 542–547

Blinn J.F. (1977). Models of light reflection for computer synthesized pictures. In *Proc. SIGGRAPH 1977: Computer Graphics*, **11**(2), 192–198

Blinn J.F. and Newell M.E. (1978a). Clipping using homogeneous coordinates. In *Proc. SIGGRAPH 1978: Computer Graphics*, **12**(3), 245–251

Blinn J.F. (1978b). Simulation of wrinkled surfaces. In *Proc. SIGGRAPH 1978: Computer Graphics*, **12**(3), 286–292

Blinn J.F. (1982a). Light reflection functions for simulation of clouds and dusty surfaces. In *Proc. SIGGRAPH 1982: Computer Graphics*, **16**(3), 21–29

Blinn J.F. (1982b). A generalization of algebraic surface drawing. *ACM Trans. on Graphics*, **1**(3), 235–256

Blinn J.F. (1987). Nested transformations and Blobby Man. *IEEE CG&A*, **7**(10), 59–65

Blinn J.F. (1989a). Return of the Jaggy. *IEEE CG&A*, **9**(2), 82–89

Blinn J.F. (1989b). Dirty pixels. *IEEE CG&A*, **9**(4), 100–105

Blinn J.F. (1989c). What we need around here is more aliasing. *IEEE CG&A*, **9**(1), 75–79

Blinn J.F. (1990a). The truth about texture mapping. *IEEE CG&A*, **10**(2), 78–83

Blinn J.F. (1990b). Wonderful world of video. *IEEE CG&A*, **10**(3), 83–87

Blinn J.F. (1991a). A trip down the graphics pipeline: line clipping. *IEEE CG&A*, **11**(1), 98–105

Bloomenthal J. (1987). Boundary Representation of Implicit Surfaces. *Research Report CSL-87-2 Xerox PARC* (Draft)

Bloomenthal J. and Shoemake K. (1991). Convolution surfaces. In *Proc. SIGGRAPH 1991: Computer Graphics*, **25**(4), 251–256

Bohm W., Farin G. and Kahmann J. (1984). A survey of curve and surface methods in CAGD. *Computer Aided Geometric Design*, **1**, 1–60

Booth K.S. and MacKay S. (1982). Techniques for frame buffer animation. In *Proc. Graphics Interface '82*, 213–219

Booth K.S., Kochanek D.H. and Wein M. (1983). Computers animate films and video. *IEEE Spectrum*, **20**(2), 44–51

Borrell J. (1981). The magic of computer animation. *Computer Graphics World*, **4**(10), 25–33

Boynton R.M. (1979). *Human Colour Vision*. New York: Holt, Rinehart and Winston

Brotman L.S. and Badler N.I. (1984). Generating soft shadows with a depth buffer algorithm. *IEEE CG&A*, **4**(10), 5–12

Brotman L.S. and Netravali A.N. (1988). Motion interpolation by optimal control. In *Proc. SIGGRAPH 1988: Computer Graphics*, **22**(4), 309–315

Brown M.H. and Sedgwick R. (1984). A system for algorithm animation. In *Proc. SIGGRAPH 1984: Computer Graphics*, **18**(3), 187–194

Brownrigg D.R.K. and Angell I.O. (1987). Fractals for terrain maps and texturing. In *Proc. CG-87: Computer Animation*, London 203–215

Bruderlin A. and Calvert T.W. (1989). Goal-directed, dynamic animation of human walking. In *Proc. SIGGRAPH 1989: Computer Graphics*, **23**(3), 233–242

Buckalew C.D.F. (1989). Illumination networks: fast realistic rendering with general reflectance functions. In *Proc. SIGGRAPH 1989: Computer Graphics*, **23**(3), 89–98

Burger P. and Gillies D. (1989). *Interactive Computer Graphics*. Wokingham: Addison-Wesley

Burtnyk N. and Wein M. (1971a). A computer animation system for the animator. In *Proc. Tenth UAIDE Ann. Meeting*, Lafayette IN, 3:5–3:24

Burtnyk N. and Wein M. (1971b). Computer-generated key-frame animation. *J. SMPTE*, **80**(3), 149–153

Burtnyk N., Pulfer and J.K. and Wein M. (1974a). Computer graphics and film animation. *INFOR Journal*, **9**(1), 1–11

Burtnyk N. and Wein M. (1974b). Towards a computer animating production tool. In *Proc. Eurocomp Congres*, 174–185

Burtnyk N. and Wein M. (1976). Interactive skeleton techniques for enhancing motion dynamics in key frame animation. *Comm. ACM*, **19**(10), 564–569

Cabral B., Max N. and Springmeyer R. (1987). Bidirectional reflection functions from surface bump maps. In *Proc. SIGGRAPH 1987: Computer Graphics*, **21**(4), 273–281

Calvert T.W. and Chapman J. (1978). Notation of movement with computer assistance. In *Proc. ACM Annual Conf.*, **2**, 731–736

Calvert T.W., Chapman J. and Patla A. (1980). The integration of subjective and objective data in animation of human movement. In *Proc. SIGGRAPH 1980: Computer Graphics*, **14**(3), 198–203

Calvert T.W., Chapman J. and Patla A. (1982a). Aspects of the kinematic simulation of human movement. *IEEE CG&A*, **2**(9), 41–50

Calvert T.W., Chapman J. and Patla A. (1982b). The simulation of human movement. In *Proc. Graphics Interface '82*, Toronto, 227–234

Campbell III A.T. and Fussell D.S. (1990). Adaptive mesh generation for global diffuse illumination. In *Proc. SIGGRAPH 1990: Computer Graphics*, **24**(4), 155–164

Carey R.J. and Greenberg D.P. (1985). Textures for realistic image synthesis. *Computers and Graphics*, **9**(2), 125–138

Carlbom I., Chakravarty I. and Vanderschel D. (1985). A hierarchical data structure for representing the spatial decomposition of 3-D objects. *IEEE CG&A*, **5**(4), 24–31

Carlee J. (1989). Applying computer animation in a classical animation environment. In *Proc. CG-89: Computer Animation*, London 169–177

Carpenter L.C. (1980). Computer rendering of fractal curves and surfaces. In *Proc. SIGGRAPH 1980: Computer Graphics* (supplement), 1–8

Carpenter L.C. (1984). The A-buffer, an antialiased hidden surface method. In *Proc. SIGGRAPH 1984: Computer Graphics*, **18**(3), 103–108

Carr J.W. *et al.* (1970). Interactive movie making. In *Proc. Ninth UAIDE Annual Meeting*, Miami FL, 381–397

Casale M.S. and Stanton E.L. (1985). An overview of analytic solid modelling. *IEEE CG&A*, **5**(2), 45–56

Casale M.S. (1987). Free-form solid modelling with trimmed surface patches. *IEEE CG&A*, **7**(1), 33–43

Catmull E. (1972). A system for computer-generated movies. In *Proc. ACM Annual Conf.*, Boston, 422–431

Catmull E. and Rom R. (1974). A class of local interpolating splines. In Barnhill R. and Riesenfeld, eds., *Computer Aided Geometric Design*, San Francisco CA: Academic Press, 317–326

Catmull E. (1978). The problems of computer-assisted animation. In *Proc. SIGGRAPH 1978: Computer Graphics*, **12**(3), 348–353

Catmull E. (1979). New frontiers in computer animation. *American Cinematographer*, **60**(10), 1000–1003, 1049–1053

Chadwick J.E., Haumann D.R. and Parent R.E. (1989). Layered construction for deformable animated characters. In *Proc. SIGGRAPH 1989: Computer Graphics*, **23**(3), 243–252

Chaung R. (1983). 3D shaded computer animation step-by-step. *IEEE CG&A*, **3**, 18–25

Chen Y.C. (1987). Lens effect on synthetic image generation based on light particle theory. *Computer Graphics 1987*, (Kunii T.L., ed.), Tokyo: Springer-Verlag, 347–366

Chen H. and Wu E. (1990a). An efficient radiosity solution for bump texture generation. In *Proc. SIGGRAPH 1990: Computer Graphics*, **24**(4), 125–134

Chen S.E. (1990b). Incremental radiosity: an extension of progressive radiosity to an interactive image synthesis system. In *Proc. SIGGRAPH: Computer Graphics*, **24**(4), 135–144

Cheung S.L. (1988). Painting with fractals. In *Proc. CG-88: Computer Animation*, London 227–233

Chin N. and Feiner S. (1989). Near real-time shadow generation using BSP trees. In *Proc. SIGGRAPH 1989: Computer Graphics*, **23**(3), 99–106

Chiyokura H. (1987). An extended rounding operation for modeling solids with free-form surfaces. *IEEE CG&A*, **7**(12), 27–36

Christopher R. (1982). Digital animation does Dallas. *Videography*, **7**(2), 37–42

Chuang R. and Entis G. (1983). 3-D shaded computer animation – step by step. *IEEE CG&A*, **3**(9), 18–25

Citron J. and Whitney J. (1968). CAMP: Computer assisted movie production. In *Proc. AFIPS*, **33**, 1299–1305

Cohen M.F. and Greenberg D.P. (1985). The hemi-cube: a radiosity solution for complex environments. In *Proc. SIGGRAPH 1985: Computer Graphics*, **19**(3), 31–40

Cohen M.F. and Greenberg D.P. (1986). An efficient radiosity approach for realistic image synthesis. *IEEE CG&A*, **6**(3), 26–35

Cohen M.F., Chen S.E., Wallace J.R. and Greenberg D.P. (1988). A progressive refinement approach to fast radiosity image generation. In *Proc. SIGGRAPH 1988: Computer Graphics*, **22**(4), 75–84

Comninos P.P. (1985). Computer animation in interior design and industrial design. *Computer Graphics*, **9**(4), 449–453

Comninos P.P. (1989). Fast bends or fast free-form deformation of polyhedral data. In *Proc. CG-89: Computer Animation*, London 225–241

Cook R.L. (1982a). A reflection model for realistic image synthesis. *Master's Thesis*, Cornell University

Cook R.L. and Torrance K.E. (1982b). A reflectance model for computer graphics. *ACM Trans. on Graphics*, **1**, 7–24

Cook R.L., Porter T. and Carpenter L. (1984a). Distributed ray tracing. In *Proc. SIGGRAPH 1984: Computer Graphics*, **18**(3), 137–145

Cook R.L. (1984b). Shade trees. In *Proc. SIGGRAPH 1984: Computer Graphics*, **18**(3), 223–231

Cook R.L. (1986). Practical aspects of distributed ray tracing. In *SIGGRAPH 1986 Developments in Ray Tracing Seminar Notes*

Cook R.L., Carpenter L. and Catmull E. (1987). The Reyes image rendering architecture. In *Proc. SIGGRAPH 1987: Computer Graphics*, **21**(4), 95–102

Coons S.A. and Herzog B. (1967). Surfaces for computer-aided aircraft design. In *Proc. AIAA 4th Annual Meeting and Technical Display Conference*, Anaheim (Paper 67-895)

Coquillart S. and Gangnet M. (1984). Shaded display of digital maps. *IEEE CG&A*, **4**(7), 35–42

Coquillart S. (1990). Extended free-form deformation: a sculpturing tool for 3D geometric modelling. In *Proc. SIGGRAPH 1990: Computer Graphics*, **24**(4), 187–196

Coquillart S. (1991). Animated free-form deformation: an interactive animation technique. In *Proc. SIGGRAPH 1991: Computer Graphics*, **25**(4), 23–26

Crocker G.A. and Reinke W.F. (1987). Boundary evaluation of non-convex primitives to produce parametric trimmed surfaces. In *Proc. SIGGRAPH 1987: Computer Graphics*, **21**(4), 129–136

Crow F.C. (1977). Shadow algorithms for computer graphics. In *Proc. SIGGRAPH 1977: Computer Graphics*, **11**(3), 242–248

Crow F.C. (1978). Shaded computer graphics in the entertainment industry. *Computer*, **11**(3), 11–12

Crow F.C. (1981). A comparison of antialiasing techniques. *IEEE CG&A*, **1**, 40–47

Crow F.C. (1984). Summed-area tables for texture mapping. In *Proc. SIGGRAPH 1984: Computer Graphics*, **18**(3), 207–212

Crow F.C. (1986). Advanced image synthesis: anti-aliasing. In *Advances in Computer Graphics*, (Enderle I.G., Grave M. and Lillehagen F., eds.), Berlin: Springer-Verlag

Crow F.C. (1987). The origins of the teapot. *IEEE CG&A*, **7**(1), 8–19

Csuri C.A. and Shaffer J. (1968). Art, computers and mathematics. In *Proc. AFIPS*, **33**, 1293–1298

Csuri C.A. (1970). Real-time film animation. In *Proc. Ninth UAIDE Annual Meeting*, Miami FL, 289–305

Csuri C.A. (1974a). Real-time computer animation. In *Proc. IFIP*, **4**, 707–711

Csuri C.A. (1974b). Computer graphics and art. In *Proc. IEEE*, **62**(4), 503–515

Csuri C.A. (1975). Computer animation. In *Proc. SIGGRAPH 1975: Computer Graphics*, **9**, 92–101

Csuri C.A. *et al.* (1979). Towards an interactive high visual complexity animation system. In *Proc. SIGGRAPH 1979: Computer Graphics*, **13**(2), 289–299

Csuri C.A. (1983). Panel the simulation of natural phenomena. In *Proc. SIGGRAPH 1983: Computer Graphics*, **17**(3), 137–139

Csuri C.A. (1991). Art and animation. *IEEE CG&A*, **11**(1), 30–35

Cyrus M. and Beck J. (1978). Generalized two- and three-dimensional clipping. *Computers and Graphics*, **3**, 23–28

Dai F. (1989). Collision-free motion of an articulated kinematic chain in a dynamic environment. *IEEE CG&A*, **9**(4), 70–74

Day T., Muller J-P. and Richards S. (1988). SPOT the image: visualization of topographical data. In *Proc. CG-88: Computer Graphics*, London, 107–116

DeFanti T. (1976). The digital component of the circle graphics habitat. In *Proc. AFIPS*, **45**, 195–203

DeFanti T. (1980). Language control structures for easy electronic visualization. *Byte*, **5**(11), 90–106

DeFanti T. (1983). Extended memory use in the ZGRASS graphics system. *Computer Graphics Theory and Applications* (Kunii L., ed.), Tokyo: Springer-Verlag, 380–386

Demko S., Hodges L. and Naylor B. (1985). Construction of fractal objects with iterated function systems. In *Proc. SIGGRAPH 1985: Computer Graphics*, **19**(3), 271–278

de Reffye P., Edelin C., Francon J., Jaeger M. and Puech C. (1988). Plant models faithful to botanical structure and development. In *Proc. SIGGRAPH 1988: Computer Graphics*, **22**(4), 151–158

Devai F. (1987). An intersection-sensitive hidden-surface algorithm. In *Proc. Eurographics 87*, Amsterdam: North-Holland, 495–502

Dias M.L. (1991). Ray tracing interference color. *IEEE CG&A*, **11**(2), 54–60

Dietrich F. (1983). A microcomputer system for real-time animation. In *SIGGRAPH 1983 Tutorial Notes: The Artist Designer and Computer Graphics*, 43–47

Dietrich F. (1985). Visual intelligence: the first decade of computer art (1965–1975). *IEEE CG&A*, **5**(7), 33–45

Dippe M.A.Z. and Wold E.H. (1985). Antialiasing through stochastic sampling. In *Proc. SIGGRAPH 1985: Computer Graphics*, **19**(3), 69–78

Dobkin D., Guibas L., Hershberger J. and Snoeyink J. (1988). An efficient algorithm for finding the CSG representation of a simple polygon. In *Proc. SIGGRAPH 1988: Computer Graphics*, **22**(4), 31–40

Doctor L.J. and Torborg J.G. (1981). Display techniques for octree-encoded objects. *IEEE CG&A*, **1**(3), 29–38

Duff D.S. (1976). Simulation and animation. *Master's Thesis*, Dept. of Computer Science, University of Toronto

Duff T. (1983). Computer graphics in the biggest box office hit: return of the Jedi. In *Proc. CG-83: Computer Animation*, London, 283–289

Duff T. (1985). Compositing 3-D rendered images. In *Proc. SIGGRAPH 1985: Computer Graphics*, **19**(3), 41–44

Dungan W. (1979). A terrain and cloud computer image generation model. In *Proc. SIGGRAPH 1979: Computer Graphics*, **13**(2), 143–150

Dungan W. Jr. (1982). Computer animation at information international. In *SIGGRAPH 1982 Tutorial Notes: 3-D Computer Animation*

Earnshaw R.A., ed. (1985). *Fundamental Algorithms for Computer Graphics*, Berlin: Springer-Verlag

Easterbrook M. (1990). Animation of hierarchies and groups. In *Proc. CG-90: Computer Animation*, London, 297–305

Ebert D.S. and Parent R.E. (1990). Rendering and animation of gaseous phenomena by combining fast volume and scanline A-buffer techniques. In *Proc. SIGGRAPH 1990: Computer Graphics*, **24**(4), 357–366

Edwards G.J. (1987). SCRIPT: an interactive animation environment. In *Proc. CG-87: Computer Animation*, London, 173–192

Farin G. (1988). *Curves and Surfaces for Computer Aided Geometric Design*. London: Academic Press

Feiner S., Salesin D. and Banchoff T. (1982). Dial: a diagrammatic animation language. *IEEE CG&A*, **2**(7), 43–54

Fetter W.A. (1982). A progression of human figures simulated by computer graphics. *IEEE CG&A*, **2**(9), 9–13

Feynman C.R. (1986). Modelling the appearance of cloth. *Master's Thesis*, Dept. of Elect. Eng. and Computer Science, MIT, Cambridge MA

Fillmore J.P. (1984). A note on rotation matrices. *IEEE CG&A*, **4**(2), 30–39

Finch C. (1973). *The Art of Walt Disney*. New York: Harry N. Abrams

Fishkin K.P. and Barsky B.A. (1984a). A family of new algorithms for soft filling. In *Proc. SIGGRAPH 1984: Computer Graphics*, **18**(3), 235–244

Fishkin K.P. and Barsky B.A. (1984b). Algorithms for brush movement in paint systems. In *Proc. Graphics Interface '84*, Ottawa, Ontario, 9–16

Fiume E. *et al.* (1987). Conformal texture mapping. In *Proc. Eurographics 87*, Amsterdam: North-Holland, 53–64

Fletcher G.Y. and McAllister D.F. (1987). An analysis of tension methods for convexity-preserving interpolation. *IEEE CG&A*, **7**(8), 7–14

Fletcher G.Y. and McAllister D.F. (1990). Automatic tension adjustment for interpolatory splines. *IEEE CG&A*, **10**(1), 10–17

Foley J., Van Dam A., Feiner S. and Hughes J. (1990). *Computer Graphics: Principles and Practice* 2nd edn. Wokingham: Addison-Wesley

Forrest A.R. (1972). Interactive interpolation and approximation by Bézier polynomials. *Computer Journal*, **15**(1), 71–79

Forrest A.R. (1985). Antialiasing in practice. *Fundamental Algorithms for Computer Graphics* (Earnshaw R. A., ed.), Berlin: Springer-Verlag, 113–134

Forsey D.R. and Bartels R.H. (1988). Hierarchical B-spline refinement. In *Proc. SIGGRAPH 1988: Computer Graphics*, **22**(4), 205–212

Fortin D., Lamy J.F. and Thalman D. (1983). A multiple track animator system. In *Proc. SIGGRAPH/SIGART 1983 Interdisciplinary Workshop on Motion: Representation and Perception*, Toronto, 180–186

Fournier A., Fussell D. and Carpenter L. (1982). Computer rendering of stochastic models. *Comm. of the ACM*, **25**(6), 371–384

Fournier A. and Milligan T. (1985). Frame buffer algorithms for stochastic models. *IEEE CG&A*, **5**(10), 40–46

Fournier A. (1986). A simple model of ocean waves. In *Proc. SIGGRAPH 1986: Computer Graphics*, **20**(4), 75–84

Fox D. and Waite M. (1982). Computer animation with color registers. *Byte*, **7**(11)

Fox D. and Waite M. (1984). *Computer Animation Primer*. New York: McGraw-Hill

Friesen D.P. (1969). A professional animator looks at computer animation. In *Proc. Eighth UAIDE Annual Meeting*, 187–194

Fuchs H., Abram G.D. and Grant E.D. (1983). Near real-time shaded display of rigid objects. In *Proc. SIGGRAPH 1983: Computer Graphics*, **17**(3), 65–72

Fuchs H. *et al.* (1985). Fast spheres, shadows, textures, transparencies and image enhancements in pixel-planes. In *Proc. SIGGRAPH 1985: Computer Graphics*, **19**(3), 111–120

Fujimoto A. and Iwata K. (1983). Jag-free images on raster displays. *IEEE CG&A*, **3**(9), 26–34

Funda J. (1988). Quaternions and Homogeneous Transforms in Robotics. *Master's Thesis*, Dept. of Computer and Information Science, The University of Pennsylvania, Philadelphia

Futrelle R.P. (1974). GALATEA: Interactive graphics for the analysis of moving images. In *Proc. IFIP Congress '74*, Amsterdam: North-Holland, 712–715

Galyean T. (1991). Sculpting: an interactive volumetric modelling technique. In *Proc. SIGGRAPH 1991: Computer Graphics*, **25**(4), 267–274

Gangnet M., Perny D. and Coueignoux P. (1982). Perspective mapping of planar textures. In *Proc. of Eurographics '82*, Amsterdam: North-Holland, 115–123

Gardner G.Y. (1984). Simulation of natural scenes using textured quadratic surfaces. In *Proc. SIGGRAPH 1984: Computer Graphics*, **18**(3), 11–20

Gardner G.Y. (1985). Visual simulation of clouds. In *Proc. SIGGRAPH 1985: Computer Graphics*, **19**(3), 297–303

George D.W., Sillion F.X. and Greenberg D.P. (1990). Radiosity redistribution for dynamic environments. *IEEE CG&A*, **10**(4), 26–34

Geschwind D.M. (1982). The 'Nova' opening: a case study in digital animation. In *Proc. CG-82: Computer Animation*, London, 325–335

Girard M. and Maciejewski A.A. (1985). Computational modelling for the computer animation of legged figures. In *Proc. SIGGRAPH 1985: Computer Graphics*, **19**(3), 263–270

Girard M. (1987). Interactive design of 3D computer-animated legged animal motion. *IEEE CG&A*, **7**(6), 39–51

Glassner A.S. (1984). Space subdivision for fast ray tracing. *IEEE CG&A*, **4**(10), 15–22

Glassner A.S. (1986). Adaptive precision in texture mapping. In *Proc. SIGGRAPH 1986: Computer Graphics*, **20**(4), 297–306

Glassner A.S. (1988). Spacetime ray tracing for animation. *IEEE CG&A*, **8**(2), 60–70

Glassner A.S., ed. (1989). *An Introduction to Ray Tracing*. London: Academic Press

Glazzard N. (1987). Particle systems: methods, implementation techniques and experiences. In *Proc. CG-87: Computer Animation*, London, 135–147

Goldman R.N. (1983). An urnful of blending functions. *IEEE CG&A*, **3**(7), 49–54

Goldstein R.A. (1971a). A system for computer animation of 3-D objects. In *Proc. Tenth UAIDE Annual Meeting*, Lafayette, IN, 3:128–3:139

Goldstein R.A. and Nagel R. (1971b). 3-D visual simulation. *Simulation*, **16**(1), 25–31

Gomez J.E. (1984). Twixt: a 3-D animation system. In *Proc. Eurographics 84*, Amsterdam: North-Holland

Goodman T. and Unsworth K. (1986). Manipulating shape and producing geometric continuity in beta-spline curves. *IEEE CG&A*, **6**(2), 50–56

Goral C.M., Torrance K.E., Greenberg D.P. and Battaile B. (1984). Modeling the interaction of light between diffuse surfaces. In *Proc. SIGGRAPH 1984: Computer Graphics*, **18**(3), 213–222

Goss T. (1983). Animation and the new machine. *Print*, **37**(2), 57–65

Goss M.E. (1990). A real time particle system for display of ship wakes. *IEEE CG&A*, **10**(3), 30–35

Goss K.M. (1991). Multi-dimensional polygon-based rendering for motion blur and depth of field. *PhD. Thesis*, Dept. of Computer Science, Brunel University

Gouraud H. (1971). Computer display of curved surfaces. *PhD Thesis*, University of Utah

Gourret J., Magnenat-Thalmann N. and Thalmann D. (1989). Simulation of object and human skin deformations in a grasping task. In *Proc. SIGGRAPH 1989: Computer Graphics*, **23**(3), 21–30

Grant C.W. (1985). Integrated analytical spatial and temporal anti-aliasing for polyhedra in 4-space. In *Proc. SIGGRAPH 1985: Computer Graphics*, **19**(3), 79–84

Green M. (1981). A system for designing and animating objects with curved surfaces. In *Proc. Canadian Man-Computer Comm. Soc. Conf. '81*, Waterloo, Ontario, 377–384

Green M. and Sun H. (1988). A language and system for procedural modeling and motion. *IEEE CG&A*, **8**(6), 52–64

Greenberg J., Every I. and Franklin J. (1983). A computer to videotape interface for computer animation. In *Proc. CG-83: Computer Animation*, London, 205–217

Greenberg J.M. (1985). Computer animation in distance teaching. In *Proc. Graphics Interface '85*, Montreal, 419–424

Greenberg J. (1987). Computer animation: direct to video. In *Proc. CG-87: Computer Animation*, London, 39–49

Greenberg D., Cohen M., Hall R., Rushmeier H. and Wallace J. (1989). In *Proc. SIGGRAPH 1989 Course Notes: Radiosity*

Greenberg D.P. (1991). More accurate simulations at faster rates. *IEEE CG&A*, **11**(1), 23–29

Greene N. (1989). Voxel space automata: modelling with stochastic growth processes in voxel space. In *Proc. SIGGRAPH 1989: Computer Graphics*, **23**(3), 175–184

Gregory R.L. (1986). *Eye and Brain the Psychology of Seeing*. London: Weidenfeld and Nicolson

Guenter B. and Parent R. (1990). Computing the arc length of parametric curves. *IEEE CG&A*, **10**(3), 72–78

Guyett R. (1989). The logo flies away. In *Proc. CG-89: Computer Animation*, London, 131–141

Hackathorn R. (1977). ANIMA II: a 3-D color animation system. In *Proc. SIGGRAPH 1977: Computer Graphics*, **11**(2), 54–64

Hackathorn R., Parent R., Marshall B. and Howard M. (1981). An interactive microcomputer-based 3-D animation system. In *Proc. Canadian Man-Computer Comm. Soc. Conf. 1981*, Waterloo, Ontario, 181–191

Haeberli P. and Akeley K. (1990). The accumulation buffer: hardware support for high-quality rendering. In *Proc. SIGGRAPH 1990: Computer Graphics*, **24**(4), 309–318

Haflinger D.J. and Ressler P.C. (1971). Animation with IGS. In *Proc. Tenth UAIDE Ann. Meeting*, Lafayette IN, **10**, 3:227–3:234

Hahn J.K. (1988). Realistic animation of rigid bodies. In *Proc. SIGGRAPH 1988: Computer Graphics*, **22**(4), 299–308

Haines E.A. and Greenberg D.P. (1986). The light buffer: a shadow testing accelerator. *IEEE CG&A*, **6**(9), 6–16

Halas J., ed. (1974). *Computer Animation*. New York: Hastings House Publishers

Hall R. (1986). A characterization of illumination models and shading techniques. *The Visual Computer*, **2**(5), 268–277

Halton J.H. (1970). A retrospective and prospective survey of the Monte-Carlo method. *SIAM Review*, **12**(1)

Hamilton Sir W.R. (1969). *Elements of Quaternions* 3rd edn. New York: Chelsea Publishing

Hanrahan P. and Sturman D. (1985). Interactive animation of parametric models. *Visual Computer*, **1**, 260–266

Hanrahan P. and Lawson J. (1990). A language for shading and lighting calculations. In *Proc. SIGGRAPH 1990: Computer Graphics*, **24**(4), 289–298

Hanrahan P., Salzman D. and Aupperle L. (1991). A rapid hierarchical radiosity algorithm. In *Proc. SIGGRAPH 1991: Computer Graphics*, **25**(4), 197–206

Hart J.C., Sandin D.J. and Kauffman L.H. (1989). Ray tracing deterministic 3-D fractals. In *Proc. SIGGRAPH 1989: Computer Graphics*, **23**(3), 289–296

Hart J.C. and DeFanti T. (1991). Efficient antialiased rendering of 3-D linear fractals. In *Proc. SIGGRAPH 1991: Computer Graphics*, **25**(4), 91–100

Hayward S. (1984). *Computers for Animation*. Woburn MA: Focal Press

He X.D. (1991). A comprehensive physical model for light reflection. In *Proc. SIGGRAPH 1991: Computer Graphics*, **25**(4), 175–186

Hearn D. and Baker M.P. (1986). *Computer Graphics*. Prentice-Hall International Editions

Heckbert P.S. and Hanrahan P. (1984). Beam tracing polygonal objects. In *Proc. SIGGRAPH 1984: Computer Graphics*, **18**(3), 119–128

Heckbert P.S. (1986). Survey of texture mapping. *IEEE CG&A*, **6**(11), 56–67

Heckbert P.S. (1990). Adaptive radiosity textures for bidirectional ray tracing. In *Proc. SIGGRAPH 1990: Computer Graphics*, **24**(4), 145–154

Heise R. and MacDonald B.A. (1989). Quaternions and motion interpolation: a tutorial. In *Proc. of CG International 1989. New Advances in Computer Graphics* (Earnshaw and Wyvill, eds.), Tokyo: Springer-Verlag, 229–243

Helman J.J. and Hesselink L. (1991). Visualizing vector field topology in fluid flows. *IEEE CG&A*, **11**(3), 36–46

Herbison-Evans D. (1978). NUDES 2: a numeric utility displaying ellipsoid solids, Version 2. In *Proc. SIGGRAPH 1978: Computer Graphics*, **12**(3), 354–356

Herbison-Evans D. (1982). Real-time animation of human figure drawings with hidden lines omitted. *IEEE CG&A*, **2**(9), 27–33

Herbison-Evans D. (1983a). Manipulating ellipsoids in animation. *Computer Graphics World*, **6**(7), 78–82

Herbison-Evans D. (1983b). Hidden arcs of interpenetrating and obscuring ellipsoids. *The Australian Computer Journal*, **15**(2), 65–68

Hinds B.K. and McCartney J. (1990). Interactive garment design. *The Visual Computer*, **6**, 53–61

Honey F.J. (1971a). Artist-oriented computer animation. *Journal SMPTE*, **80**(3), 154

Honey F.J. (1971b). Computer animated episodes by single axis rotations. In *Proc. Tenth UAIDE Ann. Meeting*, Lafayette IN, **10**, 3:120–3:226

Hopgood F.R.A. (1969). GROATS: a graphic output system for Atlas using the 4020. In *Proc. Ninth UAIDE Ann. Meeting*, Miami FL, **9**, 401–410

Hourcade J.C. and Nicolas A. (1983). Inverse perspective mapping in scanline order onto non-planar quadrilaterals. In *Proc. of Eurographics 1983*, North-Holland, 309–319

Hourcade J.C. and Nicolas A. (1985). Algorithms for antialiased cast shadows. *Computers and Graphics*, **9**(3), 259–265

Hubschman H. and Zucker S.W. (1982). Frame-to-frame coherence and the hidden surface computation: constraints for a convex world. *ACM Trans. on Graphics*, **1**(2), 129–162

Huggins W.H. and Entwisle D.R. (1969). Computer animation for the academic community. In *Proc. AFIPS*, **34**, 623

Huitric H. and Nahas M. (1985). B-spline surfaces: a tool for computer painting. *IEEE CG&A*, **5**(3), 39–47

Hunt R.W.G. (1975). *The Reproduction of Colour in Photography, Printing and Television*. Fountain Press

Hunter G.M. (1977). Computer animation survey. *Computers and Graphics*, **2**(4), 225–229

Hurn B. (1981). Computer animation for industrial training. *Computer Graphics World*, **4**(10), 65–68

Ikanage M. (1986). Caustics and specular reflection models for spherical objects and lenses. *The Visual Computer*, **2**(6), 379–383

Immel D.S., Cohen M.F. and Greenberg D.P. (1986). A radiosity method for non-diffuse environments. In *Proc. SIGGRAPH 1986: Computer Graphics*, **20**(4), 133–142

Inglish D.S. (1988). Computer assisted animated images at Walt Disney. In *Proc. CG-88: Computer Animation*, London, 237–240

Isaacs P.M. and Cohen M.F. (1987). Controlling dynamic simulation with kinematic constraints, behaviour functions and inverse dynamics. In *Proc. SIGGRAPH 1987: Computer Graphics*, **21**(4), 215–224

Jansen F.W. (1984). Data structures for ray tracing. *Computer-Aided Design and Geometry*. Amsterdam: North-Holland, 57–73

Joblove G.H. and Greenberg D. (1978). Color spaces for computer graphics. In *Proc. SIGGRAPH 1978: Computer Graphics*, **12**(3), 20–25

Joe B. (1987). Discrete beta splines. In *Proc. SIGGRAPH 1987: Computer Graphics*, **21**(4), 137–144

Kahn K.M. (1976). An actor-based computer animation language. *MIT AI working paper No. 120*, MIT, Cambridge MA

Kahn K.M. (1979). *Creation of Computer Animation from Story Descriptions*. Technical Report 540, MIT Artificial Intelligence Laboratory (PhD Thesis)

Kajiya J.T. (1982). Ray tracing parametric patches. In *Proc. SIGGRAPH 1982: Computer Graphics*, **16**(3), 245–254

Kajiya J.T. (1983). New techniques for ray tracing procedurally defined objects. In *Proc. SIGGRAPH 1983: Computer Graphics*, **17**(3), 91–102

Kajiya J.T. (1984). Ray tracing volume densities. In *Proc. SIGGRAPH 1984: Computer Graphics*, **18**(3), 165–174

Kajiya J.T. (1985). Anisotropic reflection models. In *Proc. SIGGRAPH 1985: Computer Graphics*, **19**(3), 15–21

Kajiya J.T. (1986). The rendering equation. In *Proc. SIGGRAPH 1986: Computer Graphics*, **20**(4), 143–150

Kajiya J.T. and Kay T. (1989). Rendering fur with three dimensional textures. In *Proc. SIGGRAPH 1989: Computer Graphics*, **23**(3), 271–280

Kallis S.A. Jr. (1971). Computer animation techniques. *Journal SMPTE*, **80**(3), 145–148

Kaneda K., Kato F., Nakamae E., Nishita T. and Tanaka H. (1989). Three-dimensional terrain modelling and display for environmental assessment. In *Proc. SIGGRAPH 1989: Computer Graphics*, **23**(3), 207–214

Kass M. and Miller G. (1990). Rapid stable fluid dynamics for computer graphics. In *Proc. SIGGRAPH 1990: Computer Graphics*, **24**(4), 49–55

Kay D.S. (1979a). Transparency, refraction and ray tracing for computer synthesized images. *Masters Thesis*, Program of Computer Graphics, Cornell University

Kay D.S. and Greenberg D. (1979b). Transparency for computer synthesized images. In *Proc. SIGGRAPH 1979: Computer Graphics*, **13**(2), 158–164

Kay T.L. (1986). Ray tracing complex scenes. In *Proc. SIGGRAPH 1986: Computer Graphics*, **20**(4), 269–278

Kelley A.D., Malin M.C. and Nielson G.M. (1988). Terrain simulation using a model of stream erosion. In *Proc. SIGGRAPH 1988: Computer Graphics*, **22**(4), 263–268

Kessner L.R.A., Peters F.J. and van Lierop M.L.P., eds. (1985). Data structures for raster graphics. In *Proc. of Data Structure Workshop*, Steensel, Springer-Verlag

Kitching A. (1973). Computer animation – some new ANTICS. *British Kinematographical Sound & Television Society J.*, **55**(12), 372–386

Knowlton K.C. (1964). A computer technique for producing animated movies. In *Proc. AFIPS*, **25**, 67–87

Knowlton K.C. (1965). Computer-produced movies. *Science*, **150**(3700), 1116–1120

Knowlton K.C. (1968). *Computer-Animated Movies, Emerging Concepts in Computer Graphics*. (Secrest D. and Nievergelt I., eds.), New York-Amsterdam: Benjamin/Cummings Publishing Corp. 343–369

Knowlton K.C. (1970). EXPLOR – A generator of images from explicit patterns, local operations and randomness. In *Proc. Ninth UAIDE Ann. Meeting*, Miami FL, **9**, 543–583

Knowlton K.C. (1972). Collaborations with artists: a programmer's reflections. In *Proc. IFIP Working Conf. on Graphic Languages*, Amsterdam: North-Holland Publishing Co., 399–418

Knowlton K.C. (1981). Computer animation as an aid to comprehending the universe. In *Computers for Imagemaking* (Clark D.R., ed.), Oxford: Pergamon Press 131–139

Kochanek D. and Bartels R.H. (1984). Interpolating splines with local tension, continuity and bias control. In *Proc. SIGGRAPH 1984: Computer Graphics*, **18**(3), 33–42

Korein J. and Badler V.R. (1983). Temporal anti-aliasing in computer generated animation. In *Proc. SIGGRAPH 1983: Computer Graphics*, **17**(3), 377–388

Kunii T.L., ed. (1983). Computer graphics. In *Proc. InterGraphics '83*, Tokyo: Springer-Verlag

Kunii T.L., Satoh T. and Yamaguchi K. (1985a). Generation of topological boundary representations from octree encoding. *IEEE CG&A*, **5**(3), 29–38

Kunii T.L., ed. (1985b). Computer graphics. In *Proc. of InterGraphics '85*, Springer-Verlag

Laidlaw D.H., Trumbore B.W. and Hughes J.F. (1986). Constructive solid geometry for polyhedral objects. In *Proc. SIGGRAPH 1986: Computer Graphics*, **20**(4), 161–170

Lasseter J. (1987). Principles of traditional animation applied to 3D computer animation. In *Proc. SIGGRAPH 1987: Computer Graphics*, **21**(4), 35–44

Latham W. (1989). Form synth: the rule-based evolution of complex forms from geometric primitives. *Computers in Art, Design and Animation* (Earnshaw R. *et al.*, ed.), New York: Springer-Verlag

Latham W. and Todd S. (1990). Animating abstract forms. In *Proc. CG-90: Computer Graphics*, London, 275–288

Laybourne K. (1979). *The Animation Book*. New York: Crown Publishers

Lee P., Wei S., Zhao J. and Badler N.I. (1990a). Strength guided motion. In *Proc. SIGGRAPH 1990: Computer Graphics*, **24**(4), 253–262

Lee M.E. and Redner R.A. (1990b). A note on the use of nonlinear filtering in computer graphics. *IEEE CG&A*, **10**(3), 23–29

Levine S.R. (1975). Computer animation at Lawrence Livermore Laboratory. In *Proc. SIGGRAPH 1975: Computer Graphics*, **9**, 81–84

Levitan E.L. (1977). *Electronic Imaging Techniques*. New York: Van Nostrand Reinhold Co.

Levoy M. (1977). A color animation system based on the multiplane technique. In *Proc. SIGGRAPH 1977: Computer Graphics*, **11**(2), 65–71

Levoy M. (1978). Computer-assisted cartoon animation. *Master's Thesis*, Cornell University, Ithaca

Lewis J.P. (1984). Texture synthesis for digital painting. In *Proc. SIGGRAPH 1984: Computer Graphics*, **18**(3), 245–252

Lewis J.P. (1989). Algorithms for solid noise synthesis. In *Proc. SIGGRAPH 1989: Computer Graphics*, **23**(3), 263–270

Liang You-Dong and Barsky B. (1983). An analysis and algorithm for polygon clipping. *Comm ACM*, **26**, 868–877

Lieberman L.I. (1971). Compufilms: a computer animation process. *Simulation*, **16**(1), 33–36

Lipscomb J.S. (1981). Reversed apparent movement and erratic motion with many refreshes per update. In *Proc. SIGGRAPH 1981: Computer Graphics*, **14**(4), 113–118

Litwinowicz P. (1991). Inkwell: a 21/2-D animation system. In *Proc. SIGGRAPH 1991: Computer Graphics*, **25**(4), 113–122

Lloyd D.W. (1980). The analysis of complex fabric deformations in mechanics of flexible fibre assemblies. *NATO Advanced Study Institute Series E: Applied Sciences*, **38**, Sijthoff and Noordhoff, 311–342

Lloyd D.W., Norton A.H. and Postle R. (1988). Approaches to the modelling of the mechanical properties of fabrics and the physical representation of fabrics as flexible surfaces using differential geometry. In *Proc. Mathematics and Computation of Deforming Surfaces*, Cambridge

Loizidou S. and Clapworthy G.J. (1990). Automating the motion for figure animation. In *Proc. CG-90: Computer Graphics*, London, 205–217

Loop C. and DeRose T. (1990). Generalized B-spline surfaces of arbitrary topology. In *Proc. SIGGRAPH 1990: Computer Graphics*, **24**(4), 347–356

Lorig G. (1986). *Advanced Image Synthesis: Shading, Advances in Computer Graphics* (Enderle I.G., Grave M. and Lillehagen F., eds.), Berlin: Springer-Verlag, 441–456

MacBeath A.M. (1964). *Elementary Vector Algebra*. Oxford University Press

Maciejewski A.A. (1990). Dealing with the ill-conditioned equations of motion for articulated figures. *IEEE CG&A*, **10**(3), 63–71

Magnenat-Thalmann N. and Thalmann D. (1983a). The use of high-level 3-D graphical types in the Mira animation system. *IEEE CG&A*, **3**(9), 9–16

Magnenat-Thalmann N. and Thalmann D. (1983b). Actor and camera data types in computer animation. In *Proc. Graphics Interface 83*, Edmonton, 203–210

Magnenat-Thalmann N., Thalmann D. and Fortin M. (1984). MIRA-SHADING: a language for the synthesis and the animation of realistic images. In *Proc. Computer Graphics*, Tokyo, T2-2, 1–13

Magnenat-Thalmann N., Thalmann D. and Fortin M. (1985a). Miranim: an extensible director-oriented system for the animation of realistic images. *IEEE CG&A*, **5**(3), 61–73

Magnenat-Thalmann N. and Thalmann D. (1985b). *Computer Animation*. Tokyo: Springer-Verlag

Magnenat-Thalmann N. and Thalmann D. (1985c). Three-dimensional computer animation: more an evolution than a motion problem. *IEEE CG&A*, **5**(10), 47–57

Magnenat-Thalmann N., Thalmann D. and Bland S. (1986a). The integration of particle and polygon rendering using an A-buffer algorithm. In *Proc. Eurographics '86*, Amsterdam: North-Holland, 161–169

Magnenat-Thalmann N. and Thalmann D. (1986b). Special cinematographic effects with virtual movie cameras. *IEEE CG&A*, **6**(4), 43–50

Magnenat-Thalmann N. and Thalmann D. (1987). An indexed bibliography on image synthesis. *IEEE CG&A*, **7**(8), 27–38

Magnenat-Thalmann N. and Thalmann D. (1991a). Complex models for animating synthetic actors. *IEEE CG&A*, **11**(5), 32–44

Magnenat-Thalmann N. and Thalmann D. (1991b). *New Trends in Computer Animation and Visualization*. John Wiley & Sons

Mandelbrot B. and van Ness J. (1968). Fractional Brownian motions, fractional noises and applications. *SIAM Review*, **10**(4), 422–437

Mandelbrot B. (1975). Stochastic models of the earth's relief, the shape and fractal dimension of coastlines and the number area rule for islands. In *Proc. National Academy of Science*, USA, **72**(10), 2825–2828

Mandelbrot B. (1977). *Fractals Form, Chance and Dimension*. San Francisco: W.H. Freeman and Co.

Mandelbrot B. (1982). *The Fractal Geometry of Nature*. San Francisco: W.H. Freeman and Co.

Marshall R., Wilson R. and Carlson W. (1980). Procedural models for generating three-dimensional terrain. In *Proc. SIGGRAPH 1980: Computer Graphics*, **14**, 154–162

Mastin G.A., Watterberg P.A. and Mareda J.F. (1987). Fourier synthesis of ocean scenes. *IEEE CG&A*, **7**(3), 16–23

Max N.L. (1983). Computer representation of molecular surfaces. *IEEE CG&A*, **3**(5), 21–29

Max N.L. and Lerner D.M. (1985). A two-and-a-half-D motion-blur algorithm. In *Proc. SIGGRAPH 1985: Computer Graphics*, **19**(3), 85–93

Max N.L. (1986). Atmospheric illumination and shadows. In *Proc. SIGGRAPH 1986: Computer Graphics*, **20**(4), 117–124

Max N.L. and Getzoff E.D. (1988). Spherical harmonic molecular surfaces. *IEEE CG&A*, **8**(40), 42–50

Max N.L. (1990a). Cone spheres. In *Proc. SIGGRAPH 1990: Computer Graphics*, **24**(4), 59–66

Max N.L. (1990b). Antialiasing scan-line data. *IEEE CG&A*, **10**(1), 18–30

McEwan S. (1988). State-of-the-art in image synthesis. In *Proc. CG-88: Computer Graphics*, London, 173–182

McPheeters C.W. (1990). Isosurface modelling of soft objects in computer graphics. *PhD Thesis*, National Centre of Computer Animation, Bournemouth Polytechnic

McKenna M. and Zeltzer D. (1990). Dynamic simulation of autonomous legged locomotion. In *Proc. SIGGRAPH 1990: Computer Graphics*, **24**(4), 29–38

Meyer G.W. and Greenberg D. (1980). Perceptual color spaces for computer graphics. In *Proc. SIGGRAPH 1980: Computer Graphics*, **14**, 254–261

Mezei L. and Zivian A. (1971). ARTA: an interactive animation system. In *Proc. Information Processing '71*, North-Holland, 429–434

Middleditch A.E. (1985). Blend surfaces for set theoretic volume modelling systems. In *Proc. SIGGRAPH 1985: Computer Graphics*, **19**(3), 161–170

Middleton W.E.K. (1952). *Vision through the Atmosphere*. University of Toronto Press

Miller L. (1984). Computer graphics and the woven fabric designer. In *Proc. Computers in the World of Textiles*, Hong Kong, 634–644

Miller G.S.P. (1986). The definition and rendering of terrain maps. In *Proc. SIGGRAPH 1986: Computer Graphics*, **20**(4), 39–48

Miller G.S.P. (1988a). The motion dynamics of snakes and worms. In *Proc. SIGGRAPH 1988: Computer Graphics*, **22**(4), 169–178

Miller J.R. (1988b). Analysis of quadratic-surface based solid models. *IEEE CG&A*, **8**(1), 28–42

Miller G.S.P. (1989). Goal-directed snake motion over uneven terrain. In *Proc. CG-89: Computer Graphics*, London, 257–270

Mitchell D.P. (1991). Spectrally optimal sampling for distribution ray tracing. In *Proc. SIGGRAPH 1991: Computer Graphics*, **25**(4), 157–164

Miyata K. (1990). A method of generating stone wall patterns. In *Proc. SIGGRAPH 1990: Computer Graphics*, **24**(4), 387–394

Monheit G. and Badler N.I. (1991). A kinematic model of the human spine and torso. *IEEE CG&A*, **11**(2), 29–38

Monne J., Schmitt F. and Massaloux D. (1981). Bidimensional texture sythesis by Markov chains. *Computer Graphics and Image Processing*, **17**, 1–23

Moore M. and Wilhelms J. (1988). Collision detection and response for computer animation. In *Proc. SIGGRAPH 1988: Computer Graphics*, **22**(4), 289–298

Mudur S.P. and Syngh J.H. (1985). A notation for computer animation. *IEEE Trans. Systems, Man and Cybernetics*, **8**(4), 308–311

Munsell A.H. (1941). *A Color Notation* 9th edn. Baltimore: Munsell Color Company

Muraki S. (1991). Volumetric shape description of range data using 'Blobby Model'. In *Proc. SIGGRAPH 1991: Computer Graphics*, **25**(4), 227–235

Murugaiyan E. and Clapworthy G. (1991). Producing deformable figures using CISS's. In *Proc. CG-91: Computer Graphics*, London, 47–58

Musgrave F.K., Kolb C.E. and Mace R.S. (1989). The synthesis and rendering of eroded fractal terrains. In *Proc. SIGGRAPH 1989: Computer Graphics*, **23**(3), 41–50

Nakamae E., Harada K. and Ishizaki T. (1986). A montage method: The overlaying of the computer generated images onto a background photograph. In *Proc. SIGGRAPH 1986: Computer Graphics*, **20**(4), 207–214

Nakamae E., Ishizaki T., Nishita T. and Takita S. (1989). Compositing 3D images with antialiasing and various shading effects. *IEEE CG&A*, **9**(2), 21–29

Nakamae E., Kaneda K., Okamoto T. and Nishita T. (1990). A lighting model aiming at drive simulators. In *Proc. SIGGRAPH 1990: Computer Graphics*, **24**(4), 395–404

Negroponte N. and Pangaro P. (1976). Experiments with computer animation. In *Proc. SIGGRAPH 1976: Computer Graphics*, **10**(2), 40–44

Nicholl T.M., Lee D.T. and Nicholl R.A. (1987). An efficient new algorithm for 2-D line clipping: its development and analysis. In *Proc. SIGGRAPH 1987: Computer Graphics*, **21**(4), 253–262

Nicolas X. (1989). Revolutionary animation. In *Proc. CG-89: Computer Graphics*, London, 217–224

Nielson G.M. (1986). Rectangular v-splines. *IEEE CG&A*, **6**(2), 35–40

Nielson G.M., Foley T.A., Hamann B. and Lane D. (1991). Visualizing and modelling scattered multivariate data. *IEEE CG&A*, **11**(3), 47–55

Niemoller M. and Leiner U. (1990). Approximative dynamic simulation of objects in computer animation systems. In *Proc. CG-90: Computer Graphics*, London, 229–240

Nishimura H., Mirai M., Kawai T., Kawata T., Shirakawa I. and Omura K. (1985). Object modelling by distribution function and a method of image generation. *Trans. Institute of Electronics and Communication Engineers of Japan*, J68-D(4), 664–666

Nishita T. and Nakamae E. (1985). Continuous tone representation of three-dimensional objects taking account of shadows and interreflection. In *Proc. SIGGRAPH 1985: Computer Graphics*, **19**(3), 23–30

Nishita T. and Namkamae E. (1986). Continuous tone representation of three-dimensional objects illuminated by sky light. In *Proc. SIGGRAPH 1986: Computer Graphics*, **20**(4), 125–132

Nishita T., Miyawaki Y. and Nakamae E. (1987). A shading model for atmospheric scattering considering luminous intensity distribution of light sources. In *Proc. SIGGRAPH 1987: Computer Graphics*, **21**(4), 303–310

Nishita T., Sederberg T.W. and Kakimoto M. (1990). Ray tracing trimmed surface patches. In *Proc. SIGGRAPH 1990: Computer Graphics*, **24**(4), 337–345

Nolan J. and Yarbrough L. (1968). An on-line computer drawing and animation system. In *Proc. IFIP Congres 1968*, Amsterdam: North-Holland, 605

Noll A.M. (1965). Computer-generated three-dimensional movies. *Computers and Automation*, **14**(11), 20–23

Noma T. and Kunii T.L. (1985). A framework for generating 3-D engineering animation from 2-D. In *Proc. Graphics Interface '85*, Montreal, 83–90

Odgers C.R. (1982). Criteria for choosing a camera for use in a video digitizing system. In *SIGGRAPH 1982: Computer Animation (tutorial notes)*, 108–119

Odgers C.R. (1983). Fundamentals of video recording for computer animation. In *SIGGRAPH 1983: Computer Animation (tutorial notes)*, 175–186

O'Donnel T.J. and Arthur J.O. (1981). GRAMPS – a graphics language interpreter for real-time, interactive, three-dimensional picture editing and animation, computer graphics. In *Proc. SIGGRAPH 1981: Computer Graphics*, **15**(3)

Oka M., Tsutui K., Ohba A., Kurauchi Y. and Tago T. (1987). Real-time manipulation of texture-mapped surfaces. In *Proc. SIGGRAPH 1987: Computer Graphics*, **21**(4), 181–188

Oppenheimer P.E. (1986). Real time design and animation of fractal plants and trees. In *Proc. SIGGRAPH 1986: Computer Graphics*, **20**(4), 55–64

O'Rourke J. and Badler N.I. (1979). Decomposition of three-dimensional objects into spheres. *IEEE Trans. Pattern Analysis and Machine Intelligence*, PAMI-**1**(3), 295–306

Ostwald N. (1931). *Colour Science, Vol. I and II*. London: Winsor & Winsor

Painter J. and Sloan K. (1989). Antialiased ray tracing by adaptive progressive refinement. In *Proc. SIGGRAPH 1989: Computer Graphics*, **23**(3), 281–288

van de Panne M., Fiume E. and Vranesic Z. (1990). Reusable motion synthesis using state-space controllers. In *Proc. SIGGRAPH 1990: Computer Graphics*, **24**(4), 225–234

Parke F.I. (1974). A parametric model for human faces. *PhD Thesis*, University of Utah, Salt Lake City, Utah

Parke F.I. (1975). A model for human faces that allows speech synchronized animation. *Computers & Graphics*, Pergamon Press, **1**(1), 3–4

Parke F.I. (1979). Computer graphic models for the human face. In *Proc. Compsac '79 – IEEE Computer Soc. Third Int'l Computer Software and Applications Conf.*, IEEE Computer Society, Los Alamitos CA, 724–727

Parke F.I. (1980). Adaptation of scan and slit-scan techniques to computer animation. In *Proc. SIGGRAPH 1980: Computer Graphics*, **14**(3), 178–181

Parke F.I. (1982). Parameterized models for facial animation. *IEEE CG&A*, **2**(9), 61–68

Parry S. (1986). Free-form deformations in a constructive solid geometry modelling system. *PhD Thesis*, Dept. of Civil Engineering, Brigham Young University

Pasko A.A., Pilyugin V.V. and Pokrovskiy V.N. (1988). Geometric modelling in the analysis of trivariate functions. *Computers and Graphics*, **12**(3) 457–465

Patterson R. (1982). The making of Tron. *American Cinematographer*, **63**(8), 792–795, 813–819

Paul R.P. (1981). *Robot Manipulators: Mathematics, Programming and Control*. Cambridge: The MIT Press

Peachey D.R. (1985). Solid texturing of complex surfaces. In *Proc. SIGGRAPH 1985: Computer Graphics*, **19**(3), 279–286

Peachey D.R. (1986). Modeling waves and surf. In *Proc. SIGGRAPH 1986: Computer Graphics*, **20**(4), 65–74

Peitgen H. and Richter P.H. (1986). *The Beauty of Fractals*. New York: Springer-Verlag

Peitgen H. and Saupe D. (1988) (eds.). *The Science of Fractal Images*. New York: Springer-Verlag

Pentland A. and Williams J. (1989). Good vibrations: modal dynamics for graphics and animation. In *Proc. SIGGRAPH 1989: Computer Graphics*, **23**(3), 215–222

Perlin K. (1985). An image synthesizer. In *Proc. SIGGRAPH 1985: Computer Graphics*, **19**(3), 287–296

Perlin K. and Hoffert E.M. (1989). Hypertexture. In *Proc. SIGGRAPH 1989: Computer Graphics*, **23**(3), 253–262

Petric J. (1988). Terrain modelling using fractal interpolation functions. In *Proc. CG-88: Computer Graphics*, London, 95–105

Phillips G.B. and Badler N. (1991). Interactive behaviors for bipedal articulated figures. In *Proc. SIGGRAPH 1991: Computer Graphics*, **25**(4), 359–362

Philips F. (1989). The animation environment at Pixar. In *Proc. CG-89: Computer Graphics*, London, 243–255

Phong B. (1973). Illumination for computer generated images. *PhD Thesis*, University of Utah, also in *Comm. ACM*, **18**, 311–317

Piegl L. (1987). Interactive data interpolation by rational Bézier curves. *IEEE CG&A*, **7**(4), 45–61

Piegl L. (1991). On NURBS: a survey. *IEEE CG&A*, **11**(1), 55–71

Platt S.M. and Badler N. (1981). Animating facial expressions. In *Proc. SIGGRAPH 1981: Computer Graphics*, **15**(3), 245–252

Platt J.C. and Barr A.H. (1988). Constraint methods for flexible models. In Proc. *SIGGRAPH 1988: Computer Graphics*, **22**(4), 279–288

Pletincks D. (1988). Quaternion animation. In *Proc. CG-88: Computer Graphics*, London, 153–165

Porter T. and Duff T. (1984a). Compositing digital images. In *Proc. SIGGRAPH 1984: Computer Graphics*, **18**(3), 253–259

Porter T.K. (1984b). Computer graphics and major motion pictures. In *Proc. CAMP '84*, Berlin, 545–547

Potel M.J. (1977). Real-time playback in animation systems. In *Proc. SIGGRAPH 1977: Computer Graphics*, **11**(2), 72–77

Potmesil M. and Chakravarty I. (1981). A lens and aperture camera model for synthetic image generation. In *Proc. SIGGRAPH 1981: Computer Graphics*, **15**(3), 297–305

Potmesil M. and Chakravarty I. (1982). Synthetic image generation with a lens and aperture camera model. *Trans. on Graphics*, **1**, 85–108

Potmesil M. and Chakravarty I. (1983). Modelling motion blur in computer-generated images. In *Proc. SIGGRAPH 1983: Computer Graphics*, **17**(3), 389–399

Potmesil M. and Hoffert E.M. (1987). FRAMES: software tools for modelling, rendering and animation of 3D scenes. In *Proc. SIGGRAPH 1987: Computer Graphics*, **21**(4), 85–93

Potter T.E. and Willmert K.D. (1975). Three-dimensional human display model. *Computer Graphics*, **9**(1), 102–110

Potts J. (1983). Animating the indescribable. *Government Data Systems*, **12**, 10–13

Poulin P. and Fournier A. (1990). A model for anisotropic reflection. In *Proc. SIGGRAPH 1990: Computer Graphics*, **24**(4), 273–282

Prusinkiewicz P., Lindenmayer A. and Hanan J. (1988). Development models of herbaceous plants for computer imagery purposes. In *Proc. SIGGRAPH 1988: Computer Graphics*, **22**(4), 141–150

Quarendon P. (1987). *Winsom User's Guide*. IBM UKSC Report 123

Raibert M.H. and Hodgins J.K. (1991). Animation of dynamic legged locomotion. In *Proc. SIGGRAPH 1991: Computer Graphics*, **25**(4), 349–358

Rainjonneau S., Prouvost O., Duthen Y. and Caubet C. (1990). A behavioral simulation model for computer animation. In *Proc. CG-90: Computer Graphics*, London, 219–228

Reeves W.T. (1980). Quantative representations of complex dynamic shape for motion analysis. *PhD Thesis*, Dept. of Computer Science, University of Toronto

Reeves W.T. (1981). Inbetweening for computer animation using moving point constraints. In *Proc. SIGGRAPH 81: Computer Graphics*, **15**(3), 263–269

Reeves W.T. (1983). Particle systems – a technique for modelling a class of fuzzy objects. In *Proc. SIGGRAPH 1983: Computer Graphics*, **17**(3), 359–376

Reeves W.T. (1985). Approximate and probabilistic algorithms for shading and rendering structured particle systems. In *Proc. SIGGRAPH 1985: Computer Graphics*, **19**(3), 313–322

Reeves W.T., Salesin D.H. and Cook R.L. (1987). Rendering antialiased shadows with depth maps. In *Proc. SIGGRAPH 1987: Computer Graphics*, **21**(4), 283–291

Requicha A.A.G. (1980). Representations for rigid solids: theory, methods and systems. *ACM Computing Surveys*, **12**(4), 437–464

Requicha A.A.G. and Voelcker H.B. (1983). Solid modeling: current status and research directions. *IEEE CG&A*, **3**(7), 25–37

Ressler S.P. (1982). An object editor for a real-time animation processor. In *Proc. Graphics Interface '82*, 221–226

Reynolds C.W. (1978). Computer animation in the world of actors and scripts. *SM Thesis*, Architecture Machine Group, MIT

Reynolds C.W. (1982). Computer animation with scripts and actors. In *Proc. SIGGRAPH 1982: Computer Graphics*, **16**(3), 289–296

Reynolds C.W. (1985). Description and control of time and dynamics in computer animation. In *SIGGRAPH 1985: Course on Advanced Computer Animation*

Reynolds C.W. (1987a). Flocks, herds and schools: a distributed behavioural model. In *Proc. SIGGRAPH 1987: Computer Graphics*, **21**(4), 25–34

Reynolds C.W. (1987b). Flocks, herds and schools: a distributed behavioural model. In *Proc. CG-87: Computer Animation*, London, 71–87

Rijpkema H. and Girard M. (1991). Computer animation of knowledge-based human grasping. In *Proc. SIGGRAPH 1991: Computer Graphics*, **25**(4), 339–348

Robertson P.K. (1988). Visualizing color gamuts: a user interface for the effective use of perceptual color spaces in data displays. *IEEE CG&A*, **8**(5), 50–64

Rockwood A. (1987). A generalized scanning technique for display of parametrically defined surfaces. *IEEE CG&A*, **7**(8), 15–26

Rockwood A., Heaton K. and Davis T. (1989). Real-time rendering of trimmed surfaces. In *Proc. SIGGRAPH 1989: Computer Graphics*, **23**(3), 107–116

Rodwell N. (1991). Riding the waves. In *Proc. CG-91: Computer Graphics*, London, 33–45

Rogers D.F., Satterfield S.G. and Rodriguez F.A. (1983). Ship hulls, B-spline surfaces and CAD/CAM. *IEEE CG&A*, **3**(9), 37–45

Rogers D.F. (1985). *Procedural Elements for Computer Graphics*. Maidenhead: McGraw-Hill

Rogers D.F. and Adams J.A. (1990). *Mathematical Elements for Computer Graphics* 2nd edn. Maidenhead: McGraw-Hill

Rooney J. (1977). A survey of representation of spatial rotation about a fixed point. *Environment and Planning Board*, **4**, 185–210

Roth S.D. (1982). Ray casting for modelling solids. *Computer Graphics and Image Processing*, **18**, 109–144

Rushmeier H.E. and Torrance K.E. (1987). The zonal method for calculating light intensities in the presence of a participating medium. In *Proc. SIGGRAPH 1987: Computer Graphics*, **21**(4), 293–302

Russet R. and Starr C. (1976). *Experimental Animation*. New York: Van Nostrand Reinhold

Salesin D. and Stolfi J. (1989). The ZZ-Buffer: a simple and efficient rendering algorithm with reliable antialiasing. In *Proc. PIXIM 89*, Paris, 451–466

Salesin D. and Stolfi J. (1990). Rendering CSG models with a ZZ-buffer. In *Proc. SIGGRAPH 1990: Computer Graphics*, **24**(4), 67–76

Samek M., Slean C. and Weghorst H. (1986). Texture mapping and distortion in digital graphics. *The Visual Computer*, **2**(5), 313–321

Samet H. and Webber R.E. (1988a). Hierarchical data structures and algorithms for computer graphics. *IEEE CG&A*, **8**(3), 48–68

Samet H. and Webber R.E. (1988b). Hierarchical data structures and algorithms for computer graphics. *IEEE CG&A*, **8**(4), 59–75

Scanlon W. (1990). Animating the drape of cloth. In *Proc. CG-90: Computer Graphics*, London, 263–274

Schachter B.J. (1983). Generation of special effects. In *Computer Image Generation*, (Schachter B.J., ed.). New York: John Wiley, 155–172

Schafer M. (1989). Displacement animation. In *Proc. CG-89: Computer Graphics*, London, 197–216

Sederberg T.W. and Parry S.R. (1986). Free-form deformation of solid geometric models. In *Proc. SIGGRAPH 1986: Computer Graphics*, **20**(4), 151–160

Sederberg T.W. (1990a). Tutorial Part I: Techniques for cubic algebraic surfaces. *IEEE CG&A*, **10**(4), 14–25

Sederberg T.W. (1990b). Tutorial Part II: Techniques for cubic algebraic surfaces. *IEEE CG&A*, **10**(5), 12–21

Selley G. (1990). The texture of trees. In *Proc. CG-90: Computer Graphics*, London, 183–188

Selley G. (1991). TWIGS: trees and woods I.G. system. *PhD Thesis*, Coventry Polytechnic

Sequin C.H. and Eliot K.S. (1989). Parameterized ray tracing. In *Proc. SIGGRAPH 1989: Computer Graphics*, **23**(3), 307–314

Shantz M. and Lien S. (1987). Shading bicubic patches. In *Proc. SIGGRAPH 1987: Computer Graphics*, **21**(4), 189–196

Shantz M. and Chang S. (1988). Rendering trimmed NURBS with adaptive forward differencing. In *Proc. SIGGRAPH 1988: Computer Graphics*, **22**(4), 189–198

Shao M., Peng Q. and Liang Y. (1988). A new radiosity approach by procedural refinements for realistic image synthesis. In *Proc. SIGGRAPH 1988: Computer Graphics*, **22**(4), 93–101

Shoemake K. (1985). Animating rotation with quaternion curves. In *Proc. SIGGRAPH 1985: Computer Graphics*, **19**(3), 245–254

Shoemake K. (1987). Quaternion calculus and fast animation. In *SIGGRAPH 1987: Computer Animation Notes: 3D Motion Specification and Control*

Shoup R.G. (1979a). Color table animation. In *Proc. SIGGRAPH 1979: Computer Graphics*, **13**(2), 8–13

Shoup R.G. (1979b). SUPERPAINT ... the digital animator. *Datamation*, **25**(5), 150–156

Siegel H.B. (1987). An overview of computer animation and modelling. In *Proc. CG-87: Computer Animation*, London, 27–37

Sillion F. and Puech C. (1989). A general two-pass method integrating specular and diffuse reflection. In *Proc. SIGGRAPH 1989: Computer Graphics*, **23**(3), 335–344

Sims K. (1987). Locomotion of jointed figures over complex terrain. *SM Thesis*, MIT Media Laboratory

Sims K. (1990). Particle animation and rendering using data parallel computation. In *Proc. SIGGRAPH 1990: Computer Graphics*, **24**(4), 405–413

Sims K. (1991). Artificial evolution for computer graphics. In *Proc. SIGGRAPH 1991: Computer Graphics*, **25**(4), 319–328

Smith A.R. (1978). Color gamut transformation pairs. In *Proc. SIGGRAPH 1978: Computer Graphics*, No. **12**, 12–19

Smith A.R. (1979). Tint fill. In *Proc. SIGGRAPH 1979: Computer Graphics*, **13**(2), 276–283

Smith A.R. (1983a). *Spline Tutorial Notes*. Technical Memo No. 77, Computer Graphics Project, Lucasfilm

Smith A.R. (1983b). Digital film making. *Abacus*, **1**(1), 28–45, Berlin: Springer-Verlag

Smith A.R. (1984). Plants, fractals and formal languages. In *Proc. SIGGRAPH 1984: Computer Graphics*, **18**(3), 1–10

Smith A.R. (1985). Introduction to computer animation, In *SIGGRAPH 1985: Course Notes*

Smith A.R. (1987). Planar 2-pass texture mapping and warping. In *Proc. SIGGRAPH 1987: Computer Graphics*, **21**(4), 263–272

Sorensen P. (1982). Tronic magery. *Byte*, **7**(11), 49–74

Sorensen P. (1983). Movies, computers and the future. *American Cinematographer*, **64**(1), 69–78

Spina L. (1982). Paint-by-pixels: computer power comes to TV artists. *Millimeter*, **10**(2), 81–95

Sproull R.F. and Sutherland I.E. (1968). A clipping divider. *1968 Fall Joint Computer Conference*, Thompson Books, Washington, DC, 765–775

Standish T.A. (1980). *Data Structures Techniques*. Reading MA: Addison-Wesley

Staudhammer J. (1991). Computer graphics hardware. *IEEE CG&A*, **11**(1), 42–44

Steele B. (1989). OOP: gets the message across. In *Proc. CG-89: Computer Graphics, London*, 207–216

Steinberg H.A. (1984). A smooth surface based on biquadratic patches. *IEEE CG&A*, **4**(9), 20–23

Steketee S.N. and Badler N.I. (1985). Parametric keyframe interpolation incorporating kinetic adjustment and phrasing control. In *Proc. SIGGRAPH 1985: Computer Graphics*, **19**(3), 255–262

Stern G. (1978). Garland's animation system – a computer-aided system for animated motion pictures. *PhD Thesis*, University of Utah, Salt Lake City, UT

Stern G. (1979). SoftCel: an application of raster scan graphics to conventional cel animation. In *Proc. SIGGRAPH 1979: Computer Graphics*, **13**(2), 284–288

Stern G. (1983). BBOP: a system for 3-D key frame figure animation. In *SIGGRAPH 1983: Computer Animation Tutorial*, 240–243

Strauss P.S. (1990). A realistic lighting model for computer animators. *IEEE CG&A*, **10**(6), 56–64

Sturman D. (1983). Interactive key frame animation of 3-D articulated models. In *Proc. Graphics Interface 1983*, 35–40

Sturman D. (1984). Interactive key frame animation of 3-D articulated models. In *Proc. Graphics Interface 1984*, 35–40

Sutherland I.E. and Hodgman G.W. (1974). Reentrant polygon clipping. *Comm ACM*, **17**, 32–42

Szeliski R. and Terzopoulos D. (1989). From splines to fractals. *Computer Graphics*, **23**(3), 51–60

Talbot P.A. *et al.* (1971). Animator: an on-line two-dimensional film animation system. *Comm. ACM*, **14**(4), 251–259

Taylor R. (1983). Designing for the feature film. In *SIGGRAPH 1983: The Artist/Designer and Computer Graphics* (tutorial notes), 31

Taylor R.H. (1986). Planning and execution of straight-line manipulator trajectories. In *Robot Motion: Planning and Control*, (Brady R. *et al.*, eds.), Cambridge: The MIT Press, 265–286

Terzopoulos D., Platt J. and Fleischer K. (1987). Elastically deformable models. In *Proc. SIGGRAPH 1987: Computer Graphics*, **21**(4), 205–214

Terzopoulos D. and Fleischer K. (1988a). Modelling inelastic deformation: viscoelasticity, plasticity, fracture. In *Proc. SIGGRAPH 1988: Computer Graphics*, **22**(4), 269–278

Terzopoulos D. and Witkin A. (1988b). Physically based models with rigid and deformable components. *IEEE CG&A*, **8**(6), 41–51

Tezenas du Montcel B. and Nicolas A. (1985). An illumination model for ray-tracing. In *Proc. Eurographics 85*, Amsterdam: North-Holland, 63–75

Thalmann D., Magnenat-Thalmann N. and Bergeron P. (1982). Dream flight: a fictional film produced by 3-D computer animation. In *Proc. CG-82: Computer Graphics*, London, 353–368

Thalmann D. and Magnenat-Thalmann N. (1984). Towards an artist-oriented approach to 3-D computer animation. In *Proc. CAMP '84*, Berlin, 523–527

Thalmann D. and Magnenat-Thalmann N. (1985). A formal approach to 3-D computer animation. In *Proc. Graphics Interface '85*, Montreal, 91–96

Thalmann D., ed. (1990). *Scientific Visualisation and Graphics Simulation*. John Wiley

Thompson D'Arcy (1961). *On Growth and Form*. Abridged edn. (Bonner J.T., ed.), London: Cambridge University Press

Thornton R. (1983). Computer-assisted animation at NYIT. In *Proc. CG-83: Computer Graphics*, London, 277–282

Tiller W. (1983). Rational B-splines for curve and surface representation. *IEEE CG&A*, **3**(6), 61–69

Torrance K.E. and Sparrow E.M. (1967). Theory for off-specular reflection from roughened surfaces. *Journal of the Optical Society of America*, **57**, 1105–1114

Turk G. (1991). Generating textures on arbitary surfaces using reaction-diffusion. In *Proc. SIGGRAPH 1991: Computer Graphics*, **25**(4), 289–298

Upstill S. (1989). *The RenderMan Companion: A Programmer's Guide to Realistic Computer Graphics*. Wokingham: Addison-Wesley

Vasilonikolidakis N. and Clapworthy G.J. (1989). Animating articulated figures. In *Proc. CG-90: Computer Graphics*, London, 143–158

Vasilonikolidakis N. and Clapworthy G.J. (1990). Animating human walking using Lagrangian dynamics. In *Proc. CG-90: Computer Graphics*, London, 189–203

Verbeck C.P. and Greenberg D.P. (1984). A comprehensive light-source description for computer graphics. *IEEE CG&A*, **4**(7), 66–75

Viennot X.G., Eyrolles G., Janey N. and Arques D. (1989). Combinatorial analysis of ramified patterns and computer imagery of trees. In *Proc. SIGGRAPH 1989: Computer Graphics*, **23**(3), 31–40

Vince J.A. (1976). PICASO: a computer graphics system for art and design. *PhD Thesis*, Brunel University

Vince J.A. (1983). The development of computer graphics at Middlesex Polytechnic. In *Proc. CG-83: Computer Graphics*, London, 175–184

Vince J.A. (1985). *Computer Graphics for Graphic Designers*. London: Francis Pinter

Vince J.A. (1987). Fundamental concepts of computer graphics. In *Proc. CG-87: Computer Graphics*, 1–38

Vince J.A. (1989a). The art of simulation. *Computers in Art, Design and Animation* (Earnshaw R.A. *et al.*, eds.), Berlin: Springer-Verlag, 235–245

Vince J.A. (1989b). Computer graphics: its application and potential. In *Proc. CG-89: Computer Graphics*, London, 1–19

Vince J.A. (1990). *The Language of Computer Graphics*. London: ADT Press

Von Herzen B., Barr A.H. and Zatz H.R. (1990). Geometric collisions for time-dependent parametric surfaces. In *Proc. SIGGRAPH 1990: Computer Graphics*, **24**(4), 39–48

Voss R.F. (1985). Random fractal forgeries. *Fundamental Algorithms for Computer Graphics*, (Earnshaw R.A., ed.), Berlin: Springer-Verlag, 805–836

Wallace B.A. (1981). Merging and transformation of raster images for cartoon animation. In *Proc. SIGGRAPH 1981: Computer Graphics*, **15**(3), 253–262

Wallace J.R., Cohen M.F. and Greenberg D.P. (1987). A two-pass solution to the rendering equation: a synthesis of ray tracing and radiosity methods. In *Proc. SIGGRAPH 1987: Computer Graphics*, **21**(4), 311–320

Wallace J.R., Elmquist K.E. and Haines E.A. (1989). A ray tracing algorithm for progressive radiosity. In *Proc. SIGGRAPH 1989: Computer Graphics*, **23**(3), 315–324

Ward G.J., Rubinstein F.M. and Clear R.D. (1988). A ray tracing solution for diffuse interreflection. In *Proc. SIGGRAPH 1988: Computer Graphics*, **22**(4), 85–92

Waters K. (1986). Expressive three-dimensional faces. In *Proc. CG-86: Computer Graphics*, London

Waters K. (1987a). A muscle model for animating three-dimensional facial expression. In *Proc. SIGGRAPH 1987: Computer Graphics*, **21**(4), 17–24

Waters K. (1987b). Animating human heads. In *Proc. CG-87: Computer Graphics*, London, 89–97

Waters K. (1989). Towards autonomous control for three-dimensional facial animation. *Computers in Art, Design and Animation*, Berlin: Springer-Verlag, 253–263

Watt A. (1989). *Fundamentals of Three-Dimensional Computer Graphics*. Wokingham: Addison-Wesley

Watt M. (1990). Light-water interaction using backward beam tracing. In *Proc. SIGGRAPH 1990: Computer Graphics*, **24**(4), 377–385

Watt A. and Watt M. (1992). *Advanced Animation and Rendering Techniques*. Wokingham: Addison-Wesley

Weber L., Smoliar S.W. and Badler N.I. (1978). An architecture for the simulation of human movement. In *Proc. ACM Annual Conf.*, 737–745

Weghorst H., Hooper G. and Greenberg D. (1984). Improved computational methods for ray tracing. *ACM Trans. Graphics*, **3**(1), 52–69

Weil J. (1986). The synthesis of cloth objects. In *Proc. SIGGRAPH 1986: Computer Graphics*, **20**(4), 49–54

Wein M. and Burtnyk N. (1976). Computer animation. In *Encyclopaedia of Computer Science and Technology*, **5**, (Belzer J., ed.), New York: Marcel Dekker, 397–436

Weiner D.D. and Anderson S.E. (1968). A computer animation movie language for educational motion pictures. In *Proc. AFIPS Conf. 1968*, **33**, 1318

Wejchert J. and Haumann D. (1991). Animation aerodynamics. In *Proc. SIGGRAPH 1991: Computer Graphics*, **25**(4), 19–22

White T. (1986). *The Animator's Workbook*. Phaidon

Whitney J.H. (1971). Analog and digital computer graphic systems applied to a new motion-picture fine art. *J. SMPTE*, **80**(3), 196

Whitted T. (1980). An improved illumination model for shaded display. *Comm. ACM*, **23**(6), 343–349

Wijk J.J. (1991). Spot noise: texture synthesis for data visualization. In *Proc. SIGGRAPH 1991: Computer Graphics*, **25**(4), 309–318

Wilhelms J. and Barsky B. (1985). Using dynamic analysis to animate articulated bodies such as humans and robots. *Graphics Interface*

Wilhelms J. (1987). Using dynamic analysis for realistic animation of articulated bodies. *IEEE CG&A*, **7**(6), 12–27

Wilhelms J. and Skinner R. (1990). A 'notion' for interactive behavioural animation control. *IEEE CG&A*, **10**(3), 14–22

Williams L. (1978). Casting curved shadows on curved surfaces. In *Proc. SIGGRAPH 1978: Computer Graphics*, **12**, 270–274

Williams L. (1983a). Pyramidal parametrics. In *Proc. SIGGRAPH 1984: Computer Graphics*, **17**(3), 1–11

Williams L. (1983b). Overview of 3-D animation. In *SIGGRAPH 1983: Computer Animation* (tutorial notes), 212–219

Williams L. (1990). Performance-driven facial animation. In *Proc. SIGGRAPH 1990: Computer Graphics*, **24**(4), 235–242

Willis P.J. (1987). Visual simulation of atmospheric haze. In *Proc. SIGGRAPH 1987: Computer Graphics*, **6**(1), 35–41

Willmert K.D. (1978). Graphic display of human motion. In *Proc. ACM Annual Conf.*, 715–719

Witkin A., Fleischer K. and Barr A. (1987). Energy constraints on parameterized models. In *Proc. SIGGRAPH 1987: Computer Graphics*, **21**(4), 225–232

Witkin A. and Kass M. (1988). Spacetime constraints. In *Proc. SIGGRAPH 1988: Computer Graphics*, **22**(4), 159–168

Witkin A. and Kass M. (1991). Reaction-diffusion textures. In *Proc. SIGGRAPH 1991: Computer Graphics*, **25**(4), 299–308

Wolff L.B. and Kurlander D.J. (1990). Ray tracing with polarization parameters. *IEEE CG&A*, **10**(6), 44–55

Woo A., Poulin P. and Fournier A. (1990). A survey of shadow algorithms. *IEEE CG&A*, **10**(6), 13–32

Woodwark J. (1986). *Computing Shape*. London: Butterworths

Wootton C. (1990). Channelling the byte-stream. In *Proc. CG-90: Computer Graphics*, London, 125–145

Wright T. and Humbrecht J. (1979). ISOSRF – an algorithm for plotting iso-valued surfaces of a function of three variables. *Computer Graphics*, **13**(4), 182–189

Wyvill G. and Kunii T.L. (1985). A functional model for constructive solid geometry. *The Visual Computer*, **1**(1), 3–14

Wyvill G., McPheeters C. and Wyvill B. (1986a). Data structure for soft objects. *The Visual Computer*, **2**(4), 227–234

Wyvill B., Wyvill G. and McPheeters C. (1986b). Animating soft objects. *Visual Computer*, **2**(4), 235–242

Wyvill B., McPheeters C. and Garbutt R. (1986c). The University of Calgary 3D computer animation system. *J. SMPTE*, **95**(6), 629–636

Wyvill G., Wyvill B. and McPheeters C. (1987). Solid texturing of soft objects. *IEEE CG&A*, **7**(12), 20–26

Wyvill B. and Wyvill G. (1989). Using soft objects in computer-generated character animation. *Computers in Art, Design and Animation*, Berlin: Springer-Verlag, 283–297

Yaeger L., Upson C. and Myers R. (1986). Combining physical and visual simulation – creation of the planet Jupiter for the film 2010. In *Proc. SIGGRAPH 1986: Computer Graphics*, **20**(4), 85–93

Yamaguchi K., Kunii T.L. and Fujimura K. (1984). Octree-related data structures and algorithms. *IEEE CG&A*, **4**(1), 53–59

Youssef S. (1986). A new algorithm for object oriented ray tracing. *Computer Vision, Graphics and Image Processing*, **34**, 125–137

Zajac E.E. (1966). Film animation by computer. *New Scientist*, **29**, 346–349

Zeltzer D. and Csuri C. (1981). Goal-directed movement simulation. In *Proc. Canadian Man-Computer Communications Soc. Conf. '81*, Waterloo, Ontario, 271–280

Zeltzer D. (1982a). Representation of complex animated figures. In *Proc. Graphics Interface 1982*, 205–211

Zeltzer D. (1982b). Motor control techniques for figure animation. *IEEE CG&A*, **2**(9), 53–59

Zeltzer D. (1982c). Representation of complex animated figures. In *Proc. Graphics Interface '82*, Toronto, 205–211

Zeltzer D. (1983). Knowledge-based animation. In *Proc. SIGGRAPH/SIGART 1983: Interdisciplinary Workshop on Motion*, Toronto, 187–192

Zeltzer D. (1985). Towards an integrated view of 3-D computer character animation. In *Proc. Graphics Interface '85*, Montreal, 105–115

Zimmerlin T., Stanley J. and Stone W. (1978). A sensor simulation and animation system. In *Proc. SIGGRAPH 1978: Computer Graphics*, **12**(3), 105–110

Zyda M.J. and Walker R.A. (1988). Design notes on a single board multiprocessor for real-time contour surface display generation. *Computers and Graphics*, **12**(1), 91–97

Index